Theory and Perspectives in Social Work

Theory and Perspectives in Social Work

Samta P. Pandya

RAWAT PUBLICATIONS
Jaipur • New Delhi • Bangalore • Hyderabad • Guwahati • Kolkata

ISBN 978-81-316-0633-9

Reprinted, 2020

Published by
Prem Rawat for **Rawat Publications**
Satyam Apts, Sector 3, Jawahar Nagar, Jaipur 302 004 (India)
Phone: 0141 265 1748 / 7006 Fax: 0141 265 1748
E-mail: info@rawatbooks.com
Website: www.rawatbooks.com

New Delhi Office
4858/24, Ansari Road, Daryaganj, New Delhi 110 002
Phone: 011 2326 3290

Also at *Bangalore, Guwahati* and *Kolkata*

Typeset by Rawat Computers, Jaipur
Printed and bound in India

Contents

Foreword

Social work history has witnessed several ideological shifts in keeping with the larger paradigms and scientific revolutions in theory, positions of ideologues and movements. Social work epistemology has traditionally been governed by residual and incremental models of welfare. With changing polity and shifts in focus from structure to culture and emergence of subaltern positions and voices (of caste, class, gender, sexuality, ethnicity, age and ability) the curriculum and hence education has visualised landmark moves towards empowerment-developmental, radical-anti-oppressive and postmodern stances. Dominance and hegemonies and patronage and exploitation regimes have been perpetually under scrutiny – the curriculum lending way thus to comprehending micro-theory and micro-politics of power. Complexities are further intensified by governmentalities and dialectics in the establishment and structure. This postcolonial-poststructural turn has reversed several colonial legacies and unveiled the dynamics of a globalised era which social work needs to closely examine.

There is a thus need to have a work that brings together on one platform theories and perspectives that form a part of social work. Several discourses in the west have seriously looked at developing a theoretical base for social work and hence its perspectives. This book is one such attempt in India which can be a base for social work epistemology.

This work first covers domains in social theory from positivism to postmodernism and beyond. This is then followed by a critical discourse on positions offered and created by religion particularly in the public sphere. Social justice and human rights which need to be understood by social work students through their theoretical lenses and variations are discussed. The author then talks about postcolonial India and thoughts on social reform, Gandhi, nationalism and Dalit movements as offering first perspectives on social work in India. She then moves on to movements of identity and assertions. Eventually the focus is on looking at the conventional social work perspectives – charity, ecological, radical, feminist and anti-oppressive in the light of the larger theory deliberations. I propose that this work would be a useful guide for graduate students of social work, social work educators and practitioners. This could then be a move towards making practice more informed by perspectives and what is now popularly debated as virtue ethics.

The effort is then that social work education attunes itself to diversities and identifies the intersections between 'race', class and gender in order to develop a wider non-oppressive, anti-discriminatory form of social work theory and practice. Ethics of care and justice should be embedded in praxis with themes of: empathy, equality, addressing power micropolitics and self-disclosure. Informed perspective based practice should then bring out dialogic client-worker relationships where people are encouraged to locate themselves in their social context and envisage social transformation through personal change. This would require a commitment on the part of social workers to critical self-examination, plurality of opinions and diversity which a thorough grounding in perspectives can provide. Further this commitment to egalitarianism can transform social relations with an appreciation of 'relativism' as a new perspective which can play a valuable role in criticising dogmatic positions.

H. Beck
Professor and Dean, School of Social Work
Tata Institute of Social Sciences, Mumbai

Preface

The key to informed practice and intervention in social work lies in building and establishing a base that comprises deliberations on theory, positions and movements. They play a key role in taking 'studied positions' and 'cultivated interventions' that then reflect the epistemic maturity of the profession mirroring onto praxis. Paradigm shifts in social theorising can be simultaneously appreciated with practice positions in social work. Positions are in themselves continuously evolving through different ideologues and time periods and movements in turn build on those paradigm shifts and positions to assert in the praxis realm. The history of social work in itself contains 'epistemic shifts' in keeping with the larger paradigms and scientific revolutions in theory, positions of ideologues and movements.

This book attempts to bring together on one platform theories, positions and movements that influence the episteme of social work. The commencing point is the domain of social theorising from positivism to postmodernism. This is followed by positions offered by religion and faith and the deliberations in that realm. The third aspect is the 'modern' and 'postcolonial' realm falling within which are discussions on social reform, Gandhian thought and nationalism as also deliberations on social justice and human rights. Movements entail subaltern voices and praxis commencing with Dalit and tribal movements, transnational and indigenous discourses in the women's movement, queer theorisations and movements of alternative sexuality, discourses on ecology and disability.

Finally, the attempt is to link discussions on theory, positions, movements and social work perspectives ranging from charity to critical practice. This book proposes a comprehensive view of social theorisation, positions and movements that interface with social work and lend to a consolidation of perspectives. It is proposed that this would serve as reference material for graduate students in social work. This analysis would be useful for comprehending broader categorical imperatives of justice, equity and empowerment. Through these connections the 'social' aspect of social work can be looked at through the intertwining of moral and ethical reasoning, taking studied positions and rolling out of anchored interventions.

Acknowledgements

First and foremost, I would like to thank Almighty God for giving me the strength and understanding to pursue this book and to my parents, especially my mother, for all the support, care and continuous encouragement. To the libraries of the Asiatic Society, Bharatiya Vidya Bhavan and Tata Institute of Social Sciences, a sense of gratitude for housing the huge collections and providing ease of access for reference work. A big thank you to the students of social work and colleagues at Tata Institute of Social Sciences where I began teaching history of social work courses and who were earnest in their comments and feedback for suggesting improvisations in the curriculum. This book is a further development on the same. Finally, I thank all my friends and well-wishers for their support and belief in me.

Samta P. Pandya

1

Theory, Positions, Movements and Social Work

An Introduction

Social theorising is about developing abstract laws of social processes that are perpetually in transition. There is what is called 'double hermeneutics', that is, concepts and generalisations used by social scientists to understand social processes can be further employed by agents to alter these processes, thereby potentially obviating the generalisations of 'science' (Turner, 1987). This precisely becomes the core endeavour of social theorising – comprehending and analysing social processes, change and continuity with a conceptual view of agents and actors involved in these processes. With the inclusion of actors there are also elements of reflexivity which further bring the dimensions of 'critique' which is the second organ of social theory. Social theory's tasks are twofold – that of critique or social criticism and of developing 'sensitising concepts' that provide insights into society, its norms and forms with a propensity for change. In the sense that active social processes are comprehended through agents and actors that produce and reproduce social structures while at the same time being intrinsically a part of these structures.

Social theory quintessentially provides, in the Kuhnian parlance, paradigm dialogues – multitude shifts in ontologies, epistemologies and methodologies. In the conception of Giddens (1987) they provide a 'sensitising conceptual scheme' gradually moving from the naturalistic/positivistic stance of locating realities in given typologies of empirical events towards a reflexive stance of unearthing various combinations of epistemic categories to interpret events – the phenomenological consciousness. There is thus a communication of the duality of 'structure' – social structure is used by active agents and in using this very structure they transform or reproduce it. The epistemes are provided on the nature of the structure, agents who use this structure and ways that these are mutually implicated in each other to produce varying patterns of social praxis.

The approach to comprehend social theory is discerned through the building bricks through which social philosophy is constructed and deconstructed – that of ontology, epistemology and praxis (Durant, 1961). Ontology is concerned with the nature of being or reality – attributes, order, aspects of pluralism and dynamism (Steenberghen, 1952). Epistemology is concerned with what is knowledge and how is it possible to acquire knowledge (Stroll, 1967). The paradigm shifts are in terms of conceptions and nature of social reality, the nature of relationship between the knower and the knowable reality (that is the agents and processes that construct the knowledge of reality and who are in turn constructed by those very processes) and the way to comprehend the reality – objective, reflexive, subjective or deconstruction. These paradigm shifts capture movements which then reflect critical insights of the social fabric – conceived in structuralist, functionalist, interactionist, conflict and poststructuralist modes. The purport then is to provide sharper insights into social categorical imperatives (in the Kantian sense) of caste, class, gender and ethnicity – going beyond conventional stratification approaches backed by structural and conflict theorising towards approaches that reveal micropolitics of power. Social theory thus helps us to understand social stratification, power and social processes more critically. Functioning as critique, it brings in the importance of human agency and thereby understandings of power along with a dialectical interplay of agency and structure. In the journey there is a sense of critical import which implies that each theoretical premise has some determinate content that will rule out some other theoretical orientations.

Typically the sojourn of social theorising commences from positivism and realism towards the interpretative school comprising phenomenology, hermeneutics and social construction of reality. The discussion then moves towards Marxism and its Frankfurt School component of critical theorising. Linguistic structuralism precludes the deliberations on poststructuralism, postmodernism and postcolonialism as also the subaltern school. Feminism as a social theorising genre brings in the engendered lens. The sojourn of social theorising is thus an epistemological entourage into objectivity-subjectivity, realism-surrealism-critical realism, idealism-materialism, structuralism-poststructuralism and modernity-postmodernity. Renditions and discourses of structure, culture, hegemony, power and gender are quintessential to the repertoire. Further deliberations on 'being' (being in itself and being in relation to the significant other), the social base and the superstructure as sites of contesting meanings, antagonisms and contradictions form the core (Pandya, 2009).

Positions or ideological positions can be defined through a discussion that distinguishes them from philosophy and perspectives. Philosophy is understood as a subject of study that encompasses cosmology, metaphysics, ethics, logic and world view in its fold. Philosophies can thus be social, political and moral – expounding tenets that have relevance for the study of socio-political structure, culture and self. Perspectives on the other hand propound points of view, visions and 'ways of seeing'. The adherence is to multiple theoretical strands and philosophical angles, to develop a unique set of stances for the subject matter under study. Hence, for instance, perspectives or alternatively approaches in social work practice such as the clinical, feminist or radical would draw from multiple disciplines as well as philosophies of the liberal, Marxian and feminist schools.

The conceptual framework of ideological positions derives its basis from Marx and Engels' work 'The German Ideology' (1848) which has examined the existence of living human individuals, their physical organisation and consequent relation to the rest of nature. Society is viewed as a product of the reciprocal actions of humans, and individuals are believed to express their lives through modes of production and relations of production. Productive forces are thus looked at as the basis of all history and that consciousness expresses itself in the form of ideology/position. Marxian Louis Althusser has, in his structuralist version of Marxism, introduced the concept of 'ideological state apparatus' further endorsed by Maurice Godelier, Nicos Poulantzas and Pierre Bourdieu. They argue that different structures that constitute any given social formation all have certain autonomy, and while the economic structure has to be constituted as ultimately determinant, other structures may nevertheless be dominant in constituting and reproducing a particular form of society. It is the development of contradictions both within and between structures which lead to the breakdown of existing social formations and development of newer ones. The state and the 'ideological apparatus' (through which the dominant cultural outlook is reproduced) undergo a development and have a major influence on social formation. The Marxist notion of crisis has been interpreted in accordance with these views and Althusser has introduced the term 'overdetermination' to express the idea of a confluence of separate lines of development and a conjunction of crises occurring independently in different spheres of society which result in a revolutionary transformation (Bottomore, 1978). German sociologist Karl Mannheim's version of ideology emerges from traces of Marxian influence found in his sociology of knowledge and culture. Mannheim proposed the concept of collective consciousness – that is for every social unit there is a corresponding mentality and thus categories of thought vary with social groupings. Mannheim (1954) discusses this collective consciousness as ideology and distinguished it from utopia. Utopia according to him was a collection of thoughts which takes exception to reality and tries to change it through action. Ideology is a totalistic way of thinking about a given situation and varies from group to group. Ideological positions are not scientifically deterministic and hence they do not obey the criteria of truth or falsity. In that sense there is an element of reflexivity in them (based on social settings within which they are situated) and hence an epistemological relativism embedded therein (McLellan, 1986).

Movements translate these ideological positions into praxis. The combination of a vision of reality, the consciousness for change and praxis form an ideology or a position which then feeds into *movements* for assertion, negotiation and change. The distinguishing feature is thus a component of 'action' that is embedded into it – that defines change and ensures continuity. Hence, positions consist of certain interrelated theoretical convictions, evaluations and norms that justify actions, attitudes and movements. They contain comprehensive patterns of cognitive and moral beliefs about human beings, society, universe and universe in relation to human beings and society. For fulfilling a sociopolitical function, they propose transcendental elements in worldview and elements of subjectivity. This transcendence and subjectivity grants an 'emic' element to ideological positions – that emphasises on non-essentialism, indigenisation, culture and context specificity (Damle, 1993).

Social work is comprehended as an interdisciplinary field of inquiry and praxis that has several normative and ideational strands that have developed through historicity. Further the form of social work has also evolved and undergone changes. The key and interrelated constructs are – charity, welfare, altruism, philanthropy, volunteerism, voluntarism, development and rights. Through an understanding of these constructs and following the method of difference, the professional face of social work can be explicated. The fact is that these form an integral part of social work and are not distinctive. The key point is that social work in its historical journey has developed many norms and forms in the realm of episteme and praxis. With this historical gear, social work perspectives have evolved and are gradually being concretised. Social work epistemology can be broadly understood to compose of the following: some key dimensions of theoretical philosophy that involve logic, ethics and altering worldviews; theology in its pristine form and rational and postmodern theology as subsequent manifestations; the paradigm dialogues (term drawn from Guba, 2002) – theology-rationalism, idealism-materialism, structuralism-poststructuralism and modernism-postmodernism; theoretical perspectives that dominate social theory; linkage among preceding tenets as a conceptual schemata to understand philanthropy, organised and scientific charity, clinical, radical and feminist forms of social work practice and a simultaneous treatment of the core categories of social analysis – caste, class, gender and geographies (the hegemonic regimes and emergent answers in the form of cultures of dissent) (Pandya, 2008).

The key to informed practice and intervention in social work lies in building and establishing a base that comprises deliberations on theory, positions and movements. They play a key role in taking 'studied positions' and 'cultivated interventions' that then reflect the epistemic maturity of the profession mirroring onto praxis. That positions are in themselves continuously evolving is a postulate that possesses theoretical underpinnings – to which social theory provides the adequate grounding. Paradigm shifts in social theorising can be simultaneously appreciated with practice positions in social work. The basic premise of social theory thus is to deliberate on the nature of social reality, epistemology and social praxis. Multiple vantage points emerge through the sojourn, which provide insights into worldviews, hegemony and power and emancipatory discourses. This has significant relevance for social work epistemology in terms of endowing a theoretical base to praxis. The history of social work in itself contains 'epistemic shifts' in keeping with the larger paradigms and scientific revolution.

The core point of deliberation on theory, positions, movements and social work is an overview of shifts in practice positions (welfare-clinical-ecological-radical-feminist-critical). The understanding that emerges is that social theory 'anchors' the episteme of practice norms – harbouring in itself the hermeneutics for change. For each of the ideological position oriented discussions and movements, there are aligning theoretical ones that need to be sufficiently comprehended to make positions cogent and coherent. These in turn interface with shifts in social work perspectives. Conceptually thus *some preliminary connections and initial arguments* (Pandya, 2009) can be discussed as follows:

- Theological positions technically precede positivist-realist stances in terms of history/origins in Indic, Greek and medieval philosophers. Here one finds text references on the 'social'. Theological discourses however continue in the enlightenment era thereafter taking forms of syncretism and new faith movements. With 'modernisations' last whistle' as discussed by Arjun Appadurai, Veena Das and Saurabh Dube, faith has emerged out of the private realms alone to become crucial in public discourses. This is captured in discourse on religion, faith and social work traversing pre-enlightenment, enlightenment and 'post'-modern eras – highlighting textual tenets with social leanings, organisational/institutional manifestations and communal dimensions. To look at religion and faith as a continually evolving complex, social meta-category – comprising an amalgam of theory, ideological positions and movement orientations – is the contention. Hence, the discussion on religion-faith literal and critical positions is placed in this book after discussions on pure theory.
- The positivist-realist-rationalist paradigm shift can be can be visualised from the pre-enlightenment theological-orthodox orientation to one which has been informed by empiricism, rationalism, logic and Kantian transcendentalism. There is a certain allegiance towards the positivism discourse in domains of welfare and organised and scientific charity approaches – particularly positivism's penchant for scientism and logic.
- The next shift comprising the phenomenological assertions of intersubjectivity finds correspondence with the ecological approach to social work. The realist propositions of causality and non-essentialism (particularly the relative truth contentions),

phenomenological flavours of subjectivity and differential consciousness and the hermeneutics of social construction feed into an informed comprehension of the systems and ecological approaches of practice characterised by a fetish for interdependency and multi-causalities stemming from social consciousness.

- The Marxian and the critical theory veins with propositions of materialism, dialectics, critique, reason and justice feed into flavours of radical practice with inclinations for social action and the rights-based leanings. The radical-feminist-postmodernist approaches in social work are also evidently informed by poststructuralist-feminist- postmodernist theorisations, positions and movement orientations. The social categorical imperatives of class, culture and power which are characteristic constituencies of these approaches find alignment in ideological debates informed by Marxian leanings, Gramsci, Foucault. An adequate understanding of class-culture-power can be developed by comprehending the materialist conception of history as a departure from Hegelian idealism, historical and dialectical materialism and Gramscian historicism and culture (Choudhary, 2002). Appreciating Foucault through the lens of structuralist-poststructuralist shifts would lend credence to the dialogue.
- The postcolonial ventures and poststructuralist contentions enable the contextualising of social justice and human rights discourses and positions in the national and international contexts. The 'social reform enterprise' and nationalism with Gandhian and other significant tenets in the Indian context can then be located in this vein to comprehend the global political economy dynamics. Social reform may also be posited against the Frankfurt School theorists to understand the decolonisation process better. Further postcolonial and subaltern school positions enrich the understanding of Dalit movements in the indigenous context.
- Postmodernism allows for a criticality emerging from mirconarratives, celebration of difference and deconstruction that provides scope for re-conceptualisation and revisiting hegemonies beyond conventional analysis. This puts in perspective the logic of disintegration as propelled by new social movements and emancipatory projects.
- Poststructuralism and postmodernism, with propositions of deconstruction, micropolitics, power/knowledge/discourse

deliberations and a celebration of plurality, difference and multinarratives, provide testimonies to that flavour of radical praxis/approach in social work which has structuralist/poststructuralist overtones – viewing oppression, hierarchy, hegemony and anti-establishment stances as the core of interventions.

- The clear leanings towards indigenous voices and narratives from the below which is the locus classicus of social work interventions and people centred dialogues of emancipation and empowerment find its epistemic locale in postcolonial and subaltern renditions. Aspects of centre-periphery discourses, the repertoire of truth, order and reality, politics of identity and reconstructing historiographies by countering bourgeoisie nationalisms and signifying a paradigm shift from structure to culture as the fulcrum of the lever of interventions are the key arenas. These aspects signify the iconographies of critical practice/approach to practice also understood as anti-oppressive practice.
- The engendered view of reality lent by feminist ontologies and epistemologies, as also domains of gender, sexuality and alternate sexuality orientations, feed into discourses on feminist social work.

This book attempts to *bring together on one platform theories, positions and movements that influence the episteme of social work*. The commencing point is the domain of social theorising from positivism to postmodernism. This is followed by positions offered by religion and faith and the deliberations in that realm. The third aspect is the 'modern' and 'postcolonial' realm falling within which are discussions on social reform, Gandhian thought and nationalism as also deliberations on social justice and human rights. Movements entail subaltern voices and praxis commencing with Dalit and tribal movements, transnational and indigenous discourses in the women's movement, queer theorisations and movements of alternative sexuality, discourses on ecology and disability.

Finally, the attempt is to link discussions on theory, positions, movements and social work perspectives ranging from charity to critical practice. Building on the earlier works of Yelloly (1980), Howe (1987), Barker (1987), Fook (2002), Desai (2002) and Lavalette and Ferguson (2007), this book proposes a comprehensive view of social theorisation, positions and movements that interface with social work and lend to a consolidation of approaches.

The next chapter on theory and social epistemology commences with positivism which signifies a departure from theological orthodoxy towards scientistic and logical approach to social reality and the social world. Positivism demonstrates an affinity towards grand theorisations and transductive methods in comprehending the world. Realism carries forward the positivist argument with a focus on truth claims and related verification mechanisms. Phenomenology, as a move away from the straitjacketing of scientism, signifies an intersubjectivity, relativism and focus on differential consciousness. Social construction of reality as emergent through phenomenological propositions emphasises on the role of subjectivism and historicism in the construction of reality – not attributing primacy to pre-ordained structures and a reality 'out there', but a social world that, according to Kantian tenets, is a product of the combination of thought processes and objectivities. What is attempted here is a discussion of the core propositions of the theorists within each social theorisation genre of positivism, realism, phenomenology and social construction of reality and the cumulative understanding that emerges therefrom.

Chapter 3 discusses the core tenets of Marxism as a grand narrative and an ideational schemata and the Frankfurt School of critical theory as a post-Marxian theoretical development. Key propositions have been deliberated to encompass the range of understandings forwarded by Marx, along with Engels and Plekhanov as methodological collaborators to his enterprise. The basic conjunctions of critical theory through its main proponents Horkheimer, Adorno, Marcuse and Habermas have been presented.

Chapter 4 is an examination of the various domains within structuralism, poststructuralism, postmodernism and postcolonialism as social theorisations. Further, the school of subaltern studies with its varied nuances have also been discussed. Within structuralism, the positions of Saussure and Levi-Strauss along with certain aspects of Durkheimian and post-Durkheimian thinking predominate. The 'post' genres have references to threefold modes of thinking – poststructuralism, postmodernism and postcolonialism. Poststructuralism is characterised by the works of Jacques Derrida and Michel Foucault. The renditions of Jameson, Baudrillard and Lyotard characterise the postmodernist school of thought. Postcolonialism takes a position, drawing from radical legacies, of views beyond colonial temperaments and mentalities and the subaltern genre, and builds critical historiographies that emphasise on alternate visions of history and realities. Feminism as a social theorisation genre provides a way of looking at the world that sees women's issues and inequalities between men and women as central political issues. There are, however, variations in interpretations on the nature and causes of women's inequality, subordination or oppression and hence feminism contains several competing epistemic strands. Feminism can be understood in terms of feminist ontology, epistemology and praxis. Feminist ontology refers to an engendered view of reality, epistemology as an engendered construction of knowledge and methodology in terms of praxis. This chapter delves into a brief narrative history of feminism, discourses on the historiography of patriarchy and emergent genus of thought.

Chapter 5 is an attempt at simultaneously comprehending the nuances of religion and faith and connections to social work. Commencing with a conceptual comprehension on religion, theism, theology and faith, this chapter discusses the theoretical positions and forms of religion as a preamble. Focusing primarily on organised forms of religion and subsequent manifestations, global and Indic conceptualisations and positionalities of organised forms of religion in terms of genesis and textual traditions, medieval manifestations, institutional developments and postmodern/poststructuralist influences have been discussed. Further, global and indigenous facets of discourses on religion from an engendered lens have been deliberated. As the connections are sought with social work, within textual traditions and organisational dimensions, discussions have then been catapulted onto synthesising the 'social' in the global and indigenous discourses on religion.

The critical domains emerge with the politics of conversion, assimilation and adoption as visualised through pluralism and syncretism. In the macro sphere, the role of religion as a public institution, relegated to the private realm by Enlightenment rationality's penchant for pure reason, has been discerned through post-'modernity' discourses on religion and civil society. The culminating level of discussion is on comprehending communalism and the communal agenda as the critical realist manifestations of the social domains of religion – the postulates, facets, phases and faces. The emergent epistemes, epistemologies and vantage points have then been consolidated to build an understanding of religion for social work.

The main points that this chapter makes are as follows. Textual embeddedness provides testimonies to altruism and philanthropy as well as a moral and value orientedness. Engendered discourses, pluralism and syncretism blend 'positionalities, alterities and subalternities' – a differential voice and lens in understanding of religion – which can systematically be linked to positions in social work from a theistic lens. Spaces for heteronormativities and hypernormalities are also simultaneously provided through the concerned discussions. Communalism brings in structurally, psychoanalytically and sociologically the domains of the 'critical' and through the range of deliberations on 'othering' and 'otherness', a juxtaposition of the radical with the social.

Highlighting the modern and postcolonial turn in positions, Chapter 6 examines the interrelated domains of social reform, Gandhian thought and nationalism. Social reform, primarily understood as a nineteenth-century phenomenon in the Indian context, has two broad formations: transitional and acculturative. With reform agendas as visualising change universally, the geographical manifestations have unearthed differentials. The stances have been pro-establishment and colonial towards then developing an anti-colonial consciousness by celebrating indigenous sentimentalities. The discussion has examined reform endeavours in Maharashtra, Bengal, Punjab and the south with variations therein. The problematics associated with social reform in terms of its elite bias, acute emphasis on religion, androcentric bias (dealing with the women's questions primarily from a patriarchal lens) and ambiguity in terms of the role of missionaries and personal-public polarities have also been highlighted. In terms of Gandhi, the main philosophical tenets of truth and nonviolence have been placed in a discursive plane and deliberated. The transcultural and transnational implications of the nonviolence relationality along with critique arising from the subaltern groups have been presented. Nationalism as an overarching temporality (as an outcome of modernity and hence parallel to the legacies of reform and Gandhi) has been discussed in terms of its forms and norms in the global scenario, its alignments with modernity and intertwining with domains of power and culture. In the indigenous context, the anti-colonial consciousness precipitated through nationalism and versions of ethnic and religious nationalisms have been deliberated.

Chapter 7 discusses social justice and human rights as positions traversing modernities and postmodernities. Deliberations of social justice have unearthed early references to justice in Greek philosophy and seventeenth-century philosophers such as Locke, Rousseau, Hume and later thinkers such as Thomas Paine, Spencer and Kropotkin. The versions of political theorists of the twentieth century in the United States and Britain as well as key figures such as John Rawls, Freire and Martha Nussbaum have been deliberated. A similar journey through historicity has been undertaken in the realm of human rights – commencing with classical, modern and contemporary thinkers. Further, indigenous perspectives as also non-western strands have been mentioned. Justice seems to be a wider rubric subsuming within it the discourse of human rights – as would be evident in the overlapping epistemes through historicity.

Chapter 8 has looked at assertions in the realms of praxis that have revealed multiple standpoints – emerging from positions of ideologues in the process. The examination has been simultaneously indigenous and transnational – both the renditions woven intermittently. Commencing with Dalit movements and assertions, the chapter then examines the positionalities of tribal movements in the indigenous context. The manifestations of women's movement have been mapped in their transnational/global and Indian formats – the visions, versions and strategies. Prominent ecology and environment discourses that feed into the environmental movement trajectories have been looked at. Lastly, in the vein of contemporary social movements, queer theorisations and sexuality discourses that form the realpolitik of alternative sexuality orientations has been deliberated. Some dimensions of disability discourses have also been mentioned – the voices of disability providing differential assertions in the social domain. The lens to examine the praxis has been the positions of Dalits, women, tribes, ecology and sexual orientations.

Chapter 9 finally examines the positionalities in social work through historicity, the epistemic and praxis interlinkages with theory, positions and movements. Such an attempt has been previously undertaken by Howe (1987) in looking at social work theory. Using the paradigms of Burrell and Morgan (1979), Howe (1987) has developed four distinct paradigms that would help analyse social theory – radical humanism (consciousness raising), radical structuralism (revolution), interpretivism (meaning search) and functionalism (fixing). Within functionalism are located the systems theory, psychoanalysis and behavioural social work. Within interpretivism is client-centred and interactionist social work. Radical humanists as raisers of consciousness, tackle alienation of fourfold nature: reification of society (Georg Lukacs), notion of ideological hegemony (Antonio Gramsci), idea of the one dimensional man (Marcuse) and pathology of communication (Habermas). Consciousness raising is through radical practice and feminist social work. Based on a materialist view of the world, radical structuralists operate on norms of conflict and aim at redistribution of wealth and power through the method of socialist welfare work and Marxist practice.

This chapter looks at the various extant positions in social work: organised and scientific charity, clinical social work, ecological social work, radical social work, feminist social work and critical and anti-oppressive social work. For each of the perspectives, the linkages with social theory, positions and movements are sought – attempting thereby to strengthen the understanding of the stances through their epistemological roots. The trajectory that is followed is that each of the perspectives has been explained through history and current positions and subsequently the linkages are sought. The discussion is supplemented with diagrammatic representations and ensuing discussions.

The chapters in this book thus collectively emphasises that theory, positions and movements provide the base to social work epistemology and that positions need an epistemic base and cannot operate in a vacuum. Beginning with a discussion on key domains of social theorising from positivism to postmodernism, positions from religion-related discourses to social reform, Gandhi and nationalism and further, social justice and human rights have been presented. The movement genre, i.e., subaltern voices and praxis commencing with Dalit and tribal movements, transnational and indigenous discourses in the women's movement, queer theorisations and movements of alternative sexuality, discourses on ecology and disability have been deliberated in terms of normative and ideational stances. Eventually the epistemic link of social work to social theory, positions and movements has been established.

2

Theory and Social Epistemology–1

Positivism and Post-Positivism

This chapter endeavours to examine the social theorisations commencing from positivism and subsequently realism, phenomenology and social construction of reality. In terms of the commencing realms of social epistemology, positivism signifies a departure from theological orthodoxy towards scientistic and logical approach to social reality and the social world. There is an affinity to grand theorisations and transductive methods in comprehending the world. Realism carries forward the positivist argument with a focus on truth claims and related verification repertoire. Phenomenology is a move away from the straitjacketing of scientism and signifies an intersubjectivity and relativism and focuses on differential consciousness. Social construction of reality as emergent through phenomenological propositions emphasises on the role of subjectivism and historicism in construction of reality – not attributing primacy to preordained structures and a reality 'out there'; but a social world that, according to Kantian tenets, is a product of a combination of thought processes and objectivities. What is attempted here is a discussion of the core propositions of the theorists within each social theorisation genre of positivism, realism, phenomenology and social construction of reality and the cumulative understanding that emerges therefrom.

Positivism

The underlying tenets of positivism are that any event is an instance of well-supported regularity which can be scientifically explained and presented as a form of logical argument. Two most prevalent models of explanation are – deductive and inductive. Deductive model enables us to predict an event which has not yet occurred, and inductive model enables us to explain an event by showing that it belongs to an established generalised theory/notion. For positivists, theories consist of sets of highly general universal statements whose truth or falsity can be assessed by means of systematic observation and experiment. Either one can confirm established theories through field realities or falsify them. Other concepts linked to positivism are scientism, naturalism or phenomenalism, value fact dichotomy, empiricism instrumental knowledge and analytical realism. Scientism is the view that the meaning of knowledge is defined by naturalistic science alone. Naturalism purports that there is also a unity in the subject matter of science. Science is a study of reality that can be reduced to observable units or naturalistic phenomena. Positivistic naturalism generally entails reductionism or atomism (that everything can be reduced to atomic units); correspondence theory of truth (that there is a correspondence between truths of science and nature of reality) and phenomenalism or objectivism (an objectifying attitude in which nature is seen as something that can be neutrally observed). The value-fact dichotomy proposes that things and social phenomena do not have values in themselves; values are attributed to them by persons studying those facts/phenomena. Empiricism holds that all notions that cannot be derived from sensory experience are scientifically not relevant. Instrumental knowledge emphasises on the use value of knowledge and takes the form of political or unpolitical knowledge. Analytical realism posits the existence of an external knowable social world, congruent with the order of human logic. The complexities can be reduced through the unification of knowledge and codification – implying that generalisations derived from unconnected investigations into different areas are explained by some common factor that codifies them (Delanty, 1997).

Positivists believe that there is no 'logic of discovery' by which we can arrive at theories through observations. Without grand theories, observation in the field is not meaningful; theory and observation are distinct and observation feeds into theory through correspondence rules. Positivism operates on the logic of science and in that sense positivism is naturalism. Society as per the positivists' rule operates as per the laws of nature. Further, knowledge is rational and objective and it needs to be formulated in certain kinds of statements open to public scrutiny and discussion. There is a distinction/dualism between subject (observer) and object (social phenomena/facts). Further there is an element of distinction between the observable and the theoretical in positivism (Klee, 1999). Positivism proposes a definition of scientific theories – circumscribed pieces of a formal language expressed in what is called first-order logic. A scientific theory is identified with two general classes of statements expressed as formal first-order sentences: a set of fundamental laws of theory and a set of further statements to be described as correspondence rules. The vocabulary of a scientific theory is to be split into three classes of mutually exclusive terms: formal/mathematical terms, observational terms and theoretical terms. Terms of the first class are meaningful by definition alone; terms of the second class are meaningful through association with prior sensory experience and terms of the third class are relevant only if logically precise rules of use called correspondence rules can be provided (Klee, 1999).

The early origins of positivism may be traced to Aristotle who in his Posterior Analytics has provided the basis of modern inductive and deductive methodology. However, the main roots of positivism lie in the Renaissance. An early exponent of positivism was the thirteenth-century predecessor of the Renaissance, Roger Bacon, who stressed the importance of observable data as the basis of knowledge, and William of Ockham who argued that knowledge must proceed in a razor-like manner from an examination of empirical cases. The experimental methodology was epitomised by Francis Bacon who advanced an inductive methodology of observation. By mid-seventeenth century, rationalism had replaced Aristotelian scholasticism, Platonic legacy of metaphysics as well as the unitary Christian worldview of the middle ages. Modern rationalism was born in the decentring of consciousness from the divinely ordained laws of the universe to those that modern science is capable of uncovering. Rationalism reached its zenith in the Cartesian method of Rene Descartes who established the foundation of a rationalistic conception of science as the search for absolute truths based on first principles. The Cartesian method consists of the belief in the certainties of the clear and distinct perceptions of the solitary individual sceptically contemplating an external reality. This was also the beginning of empiricism; the two other classical scholars of the vein were Thomas Hobbes and John Locke.

The core proponent of positivism was Auguste Comte who proposed positivism as a method of scientific investigation and a stage in the development of the human mind; the evolutionary stages being – theological, metaphysical and positivist. There are logical structures and methods with which to explain society which are called social laws composing of social statics and social dynamics. Social statics reveal the manner in which social facts co-exist at any given time and social dynamics reveal how events succeed one another in time; statics explain social order and dynamics explain human progress. Comte owed many of his ideas most immediately to Saint Simon, who drew from Condorcet and Montesquieu, who both had tempered the enthusiasms of the Enlightenment with a rigidly applied version of the subservience of society to natural laws of development. The core aspects of Comte's thought are as follows: reconstruction of history as the realisation of the positive spirit and with the development of the 'scientific outlook' the prehistory of human species is completed; positive philosophy as the logical explanation of the canons of the scientific method; observation and empiricism in defining 'facts' and theories which in turn connect these facts to universal propositions or laws; scientific knowledge concerns explanation of the interdependence of the phenomena and the foreknowledge yielded by science makes possible technological control which is then linked to moral-material progress of humankind (akin to Francis Bacon's thoughts). Hence, the overall object of science is to discover the relations between phenomena (Giddens, 1978). In his work 'Course of Positive Philosophy', Comte proposed that positive science is a 'useful and certain knowledge' based on empirical methodology. This focus on methodological investigation proposed that there is a domain of objectively existing facts and science is the observation of those facts. Hence, Comte viewed positivism as a theory of history in which improvements in knowledge are both the motor of progress and the source of social stability; sound knowledge is grounded in the science of observation and all sciences can be integrated into a single natural system (Halfpenny, 1982).

In Britain, positivism was reflected in the writings of Victorian utilitarians such as Mill and Spencer. Mill in his work 'A System of Logic' (1843) defended empiricism as an inductive science of general causal laws. According to him, all explanations have the same logical structure and society can be explained by laws governing nature. Spencer, under the influence of Charles Darwin, developed a functionalist evolutionary social science, which had a considerable impact on the subsequent history of social sciences. The basic ideas of this approach are that social structures are explained in terms of the functions they perform and social change is the result of functional adaptation. His *Social Statics* (1850) has clearly shown the influence of Comte and a concern with social order typical of Victorian social thought. Spencer thus proposed that positivism is a theory of history in which the motor of progress that guarantees the emergence of superior forms of society is the contradiction between differentiated individuals.

The other French positivist theorist is Emile Durkheim who has forwarded that there are discoverable social laws comparable to those governing the rest of nature; social facts are also facts of nature. Durkheim's main contribution has been the elaborate analysis of social facts that are believed to be formed objectively: scientific observations and definitions as being necessary to explain social phenomena. Durkheim's conceptions of social sciences are laid down in his *Rules for Sociological Method* (1895) which has argued for a model of social sciences based on natural sciences, but has discarded the philosophy of history. He proposed that all of social reality can be broken down into facts and analysed in specific case studies. His approach was an anti-naturalist realism, since he stressed on the difference between social facts and natural facts. Facts are raw data and the aim of social science is to search for causal explanations. Theory is subsequent to observation which proceeds inductively from facts through hypotheses to general causal laws. These general laws are conceived in terms of their functions, and social phenomena are explained in terms of their social functions. Furthering the positivist vein, Max Weber has focussed on causal explanations and the comparative method, and recurring cause-effect relations in society. The logic of causal explanations of social facts is believed to be identical with those of natural events. Works of Merton and Parsons also inherited the positivist conceptions of social science as a value-free inquiry – establishing a close relationship between functionalism and positivism.

The Vienna Circle of scholars developed positivist thought of Comte combined with ideas of Wittgenstein to develop a school of thought called logical positivism. Logical positivism was inspired by new developments in physics such as Albert Einstein's theory of relativity and quantum mechanics and stood for the ideals of a unified science based on the certain knowledge of mathematical logic. A second influence was linguistics or as the British philosophers put it, linguistic analysis which involved an examination of extralinguistic data and concerned with the true meaning of propositions (Copleston, 1956). One of the key ideas was that there are only two kinds of knowledge: empirical knowledge and logical knowledge. Empirical knowledge is gained through sense experience and logical knowledge does not require deployment of senses and is generally of two kinds: analytic and synthetic (Joad, 1950). Mach offered one of the classic formulations of logical positivism as the methodological objectification of reality in the analysis of laws governing facts. Rudolf Carnap's 'The Logical Structure of the World' (1928) became one of the enduring treatises of logical positivism. The most famous statement of the school was Wittgenstein's correspondence theory of truth in his *Tractatus-Logico-Philosophicus* (1922), a work that Wittgenstein later refuted when he moved towards the relational theory of truth. Logical positivism radicalised this view by proposing that the only valid kind of knowledge is observable and verifiable knowledge. Neurath, himself a Marxist, applied logical positivism to sociology in his advocation of a 'physicalist' science of society. Hempel likewise applied logical positivism to history in the search for general historical laws that could be used for predictions: explanations must have the power of predictions. The other concept given by Hempel was 'operationalism'. This school was very influential in the Anglo-American conceptions of science, such as the realist and the analytical traditions associated with Bertrand Russell, A.J. Ayer, Ernest Nagel, Gilbert Ryle and William Quine (Halfpenny, 1982; Delanty, 1997).

An important principle of the theorists of the Vienna Circle was the Verification Principle. This principle proposes positivism as a theory of meaning combining phenomenalism and the logicistic method, and captured by the principle of verifiability according to which the meaning of a proposition consists in its method of verification. The method that was developed was the deductive-nomological method wherein explanation involves reference to two types of statements brought together – general laws and statements that specify particular circumstances in which those laws have applications. The statement referring to the event or phenomenon to be explained (the explanandum) is deduced as a necessity from the conjunction of these two. The objective testing of a scientific explanation hence involves empirical confirmation of the statement describing the initial or 'boundary' conditions; empirical confirmation of the laws in relation to which the explanandum is deduced and logical confirmation of the deduction made. There is believed to be a 'structural equality' between explanation and prediction (Giddens, 1978). Applied to social sciences, logical positivism proposes that generalisations are statistical uniformities rather than universal laws subject to verification and that functional analysis can capture the patterns and repetitive modes of social conduct examined in relation to states of the larger social system. Hence, it is a syntactic and semantic unification of the sciences – the strength of which lies in its empiricism. Hence, only those propositions have meaning that are empirically verifiable (Joad, 1950; Copleston, 1956).

One of the latter positivist thinkers who was a proponent of falsification is Karl Popper who proposed the hypothetico-deductive method. This basic method of Popper was called critical rationalism – demolishing the basic belief of classical positivism that science proceeds from observation of data by means of experiments, which when repeated are verified, allowing us to infer general laws about the nature of reality. Popper shows that the logic of science is determined not by the path to absolute verifiable knowledge, but by attempts to falsify the results of other theories and thus the theories science provides are the only ones that have withstood falsification. Science progresses by conjecturing hypotheses and attempting to refute them, so that false conjectures are eliminated and corroborated ones retained. Popper's epistemology is sceptical, involving rejection to any claim to certainty or authoritative knowledge, thereby lending credence to criticism. However, in Popper's scheme of things there is an attempt to provide a progressive view of science without justifying theories. Hence, Popper's epistemology is viewed as showing the operation of Darwinian biological process of trial-and-error elimination in the realm of conscious knowledge (O'Hear, 1980). In his work 'The Logic of Scientific Discovery', Popper (1959) has discussed that scientific knowledge is distinct from common sense knowledge and is concerned with the new way of ideas. Linguistic analysis may not provide the adequate base to explain scientific knowledge and hence conjectures and explanations become crucial. Some structural components of the scientific method according to Popper are causality, explanation, deduction of predictions, axiomatic systems and universality levels, falsifiability, degree of testability, logical probability and corroborablity. His understanding on conjectural knowledge was developed in his work *Objective Knowledge* (Popper, 1972), wherein scientific knowledge has been looked at not as integral to human subjectivity, but as exposed to objective criticism – scientific knowledge as growing through critical selection. The limitations of determinism and reductionism have been placed in favour of indeterminism and re-emergence that laid grounds for systems thinking.

In his work *Realism and the Aim of Science* (Popper, 1983) (as his Postscript to the Logic of Scientific Discovery), Popper has formulated the nonjustificationist theory of knowledge. Science aims as true explanatory theories and yet it cannot prove or finally establish any of its theories as true. So there is an emphasis laid on the continuous questioning and criticism of all theories, even those which happen to be true (thus laying the grounds for the falsification thesis). But some theorisations may be preferred over the other on grounds of corroborability, testability and correctness/explanation power. Hence, although Popper refuted the fact that theories possess a criterion of truth, he nevertheless looked at the criterion of progress for theories towards truth and theoretical explanations. He has replaced the utopian aim of theory justification by the realistic aim of submitting them to theoretical and empirical criticism. Through the lens of falsification, truth renditions emerge which lay grounds for Popperian tenets of humanism and rationality.

The critique of positivism emerges through arguments of context specificities and subjective experiences that are crucial to comprehend reality and that all reality cannot be subsumed under unifying tenets. One of the most important early breakdowns of positivism was the Duhem-Quine thesis of the underdetermination of scientific theories by evidence. Quine had established a relationist theory of truth and the indeterminacy of reference, which undermined the inductionalist and foundationalist basis of classical positivism. For Quine, truth is the function of the relationship between words, and not of the correspondence between words and reality – the idea of theory dependency in observation. The other departures from traditional positivism include Kuhnian theory

(Thomas Kuhn) of paradigmatic shifts as means of scientific progress, Imre Lakatos' sophisticated falsification (not singular theories are falsified but entire programmes), realism and constructivism. Realism, particularly critical realism of Roy Bhaskar, looks at both an explanatory and interpretative approach to science. The aim is to retain the claims of science to objectivity and truth without conceding anything to scientism and the absolute unity of the scientific method. Constructivism is the post-empiricist approach stressing on subjectivity and relativism (Delanty, 1997). There was also a tradition of philosophers and theorists who stood on the ground between positivism and post-positivism, one figure being the Austrian philosopher, Alexius von Meinong who struck a balance between phenomenological thought and a worldview strictly on scientific grounds. Language, experience and meaning have been integrated to account for both the scientific and intuitive aspects of consciousness and discourse (Lindenfeld, 1980).

Realism

Realism is about answering the 'why' of the social phenomena/reality, i.e., to discover the 'natural relations' that exist in the real world and establish relative truth claims to the same. It claims that knowledge is descriptive of the general and particular features of the universe (Feyerabend, 1981). Realism implies that in explaining phenomena it is imperative to not only make reference to the 'events' which initiate the process of change, but also give a description to the 'process' itself. In understanding all the mechanisms and structure of a phenomenon, the explanations are not subsumed under existing explanations developed under ideal conditions. Further, the answers to the 'why' of social phenomena requires the answers to the 'how and what' of social phenomena/reality for which the various entities of the social phenomena/process as well as their nature/essences are required. The core realist propositions can be enumerated thus: the cause/explanation of any social phenomena is a set of conditions or factors which when taken together are a sufficient condition for the same; no single explanation is a sufficient condition – each may be termed as 'a cause' or 'a causal condition' in contrast to the complete cause; and even within regular and predictable relations in social phenomena, it is necessary to delve more deeply into the various intervening and causal conditions. A social phenomenon is a logical conjunction of discrete conditions, and realist explanations are through analogies and models. But the main point is that analogies and models are only 'ideal' explanations – the intervening conditions of different phenomena are different and hence each phenomenon will have its own differential explanations. From a realist standpoint, descriptions and explanations of context-specific structures and mechanisms are more important than sweeping generalisations; hence, the belief that what actually exists then is far bigger than what is known to the human mind. According to realists, we can only test claims and provide descriptions to social situations and phenomena; the entire meaning can never be fully discerned. Hence, explanations in realist terms are always partial descriptions of the whole truth. There are 'correspondence rules' that explain social phenomena which draw from theory and modify the same to develop a suitable explanation to observable phenomena. The distinguishing feature of realist explanation is that it takes into account the unobservable entities, it is critical because it is not essentialist (Heim, 1998; Chattopadhyaya et al., 2000).

Although realism draws from positivism and logical positivism in particular, the lines of thought were more systematically developed by Bertrand Russell, G.E. Moore and Reat Perry. Hicks (1938) has discussed that realism is based on the principle of direct experience and that space, time, matter and natural objects have real natures of their own. Further realism favours epistemology in favour of metaphysics – and that only inductively and empirically it can be shown that what knowledge is possible, how it is possible and what are the limits to knowledge and truth claims. Perception or ipso facto an apprehension of reality is the way to understand reality and realism purports an inherent dichotomy between the subject (knower or reality) and the object (reality known).

Several versions of realism prevail: the first one, inspired by Copernicus, is about establishing the truth of theories; and the second version as per Kepler who discusses that realism is about searching for entities, properties and causal effects in reality that can be expressed through theory. The third version (with Maxwell and Einstein as its key proponents) proposed that realism is about discovering laws and phenomena in social reality and attributing theories to them. In this two different domains or layers prevail – on the one side there are phenomena, facts, things, qualities as well as concepts for the direct expression of their properties and relations; on the other hand there is an abstract language in which 'phantom pictures', i.e., scientific theories are formulated. These pictures are correlated to phenomena, facts, things and qualities of the first domain (Feyerabend, 1981). Giving credence to experience, realism proposes that general assumptions are convenient means for systematisation of the data of our experience. These general assumptions are interpretations which can be pragmatic or phenomenological – subject to explanation, reduction and empiricism. Neo-realists Saul Kripke and Hilary Putnam have argued for realist tenets in the wake of further interpretative and nonessentialist approaches. In that endeavour they have forwarded the causal theory of naming and necessity construed by analogy with procedures of discovery in the natural sciences. They believe in a aposteriori (empirical) 'necessity' to validate scientific knowledge and also to the way such 'names' are secured. By this they refer to just those kind of substances in virtue of the knowledge thus acquired which concerns their salient properties and features (like the definition of water as a substance with molecular composition H_2O).

Ontological realism as a social theorisation position thus pre-supposes thought experiment or speculative theory that would carry some measure of demonstrative or probative force. Hence, vis-a-vis theorisations on language and representation based on the arbitrary nature of the sign (as in structuralism discussed in further chapters), realism has a clear object domain and scientific referential bearing on which to base truth-claims, hypotheses and conjectures. Taking the argument further in the light of the developments of the postmodern genre (wherein there is an emphasis on performativity rather than truth claims and wherein science strives to maximise dissensus and produce a range of heterogeneous narratives, discourses and phrase-genres rather than rational consensus or truth), realism, as Norris (1997) discusses, re-affirms a truth-functional semantics, theory of belief content and a naturalised epistemology. Roy Bhaskar's critical realism combines the 'intransitive' (real world and causally efficacious) objects, processes and events from the 'transitive' realm (of humanly intelligible purposes, motives and intentions) employing a context transcendent criteria of truth and falsehood.

Truth claims are thus another arena of deliberation in realism. This includes logician Tarski's disquotational theory of truth (i.e., truth as circular equivalence). Truth is also viewed as a formalised relationship between first- order statements of empirical facts and a second- order (metalinguistic) discourse of generalised validity conditions. An important development is Roy Bhaskar's causal realist approach wherein truth claims get operationalised in cause-effect relations. There is also a naturalised non-reductionist version of truth wherein through language and interpretation, the substantive content of various true and false beliefs can be subject to a rational assessment on the basis of a shared understanding (Norris, 1997).

Some points of critique of the realist stance emerge from its negation of abstract laws to explain reality, and not giving enough importance to the discourse of difference.

Phenomenology

Phenomenology as a social theory recognises the fact that the social world comprises differential consciousness. There is a stress on an intuitive study of essences of a particular phenomenon and thus an emphasis on subjectivity (Emad and Maly, 1994). The social phenomenon is ordered in such a way that it is not according to established viewpoints but through the categories and understanding that emerge from reality itself. Positing a critique of pure stances in favour of field/reality inspired ones, the credence is bestowed on thought processes, belief systems, experience vis-a-vis extant models and theories. Phenomenology is thus a detailed thought on 'being' – existence, subjectivity and essence, with a motto of 'to the things themselves'. Comprehending the society through the phenomenological approach would imply doing away with pre-conceptions and engaging with the notion of 'first seeing'. There is an element of intuitive seeing and a certain reverence to the social world and its various manifestations and essences. The phenomenological method comprises the following steps: investigation of a particular phenomenon (implying to intuitively grasp, analytically examine and freshly describe a particular phenomenon); investigation of general essences (looking at some general explanations and then develop particular explanations/concepts from the same to then develop new generalisations); apprehending essential relationships among essences (meaning to discover some basic anchoring points for the particular explanations which are internally and externally consistent); watching modes of appearing (to see the way the social phenomena occurs and its various manifestations);

watching the constitution of phenomena in consciousness (i.e., how the understanding of social phenomena takes shape – what constitutes the explanations and how are these gradually processed by the individuals who wish to observe and intervene in the social world); and suspending beliefs in the pre-existence of explanations to a particular phenomenon (implying not being 'reductionist').

The origins of phenomenology are sought in the writings of Franz Brentano who proposed the following from the lens of psychology – the empirical source of knowledge, the importance of experience and intuition. He distinguished psychological phenomena from physical phenomena and developed the doctrine of intentionality as the decisive content of psychological phenomena – acts which depict states of consciousness and transitory processes. Psychological phenomenon was divided into three basic classes: representations, judgements and emotive acts. Overall Brentano's contribution to phenomenology included widening of traditional empiricism by admitting experiences and noninductive insights into the essential structures and relationships of empirical material; intentional reference and analogues of self-evidence in ethics. Carl Stumpf proposed an experimental phenomenology, main subject matters of phenomenology being primary and secondary phenomena, distinction between substance and attributes in understanding the social world (substance being the whole and attributes as manifestations to be experienced) and 'the discovery of structural laws among empirical materials not based upon induction – also called the phenomenological intuition of material essences.

The German phase of phenomenology was presided over by its pioneer Edmund Husserl (1859–1938) whose understanding of phenomenology underwent three distinct phases: 1) the pre-phenomenological phase begins with an attempt to interpret mathematics by a descriptive psychology of the acts of mathematical thinking (its partial failure took him to the formulation of an objectivist programme of a pure logic free from psychology); 2) the early phases of phenomenology involved an emphasis on both the subjective and objective aspects of experience in their essential correlation; and, 3) the last phase is that of pure phenomenology wherein the subjective is supposed to be the source of all objectivities and that this subjective is conceived of on a higher, 'transcendental' level above empirical psychology. In Husserl's analysis, the roots of the phenomena lay in the consciousness of the knowing subject to whom these phenomena appeared – something called transcendental subjectivity. The radicalism in his understanding appears from the aspiration to view phenomenology as a philosophy free from presuppositions. The method to corroborate this thought was that of phenomenological reduction which implied the reduction from particular facts to general essences (also called eidetic reduction or intuition of essences). Phenomenological reduction undergoes phases – cogitations (Husserl referred to noesis as the act of cogitating and noema to the object of cogitation – referents or intentional objects) to arrive at essences or pure consciousness (Farber, 1943; Pivcevic, 1970; Spiegelberg, 1982).

Developing on Husserl's thought, the subjectivity element was further emphasised by Alexander Pfander (1870–1941) and Adolf Reinach (1883–1917). Pfander focused on viewing the object under consideration from the perspective of the subject, laying simultaneous emphasis on acts of believing, modes of givenness and the modes of belief. Adolf Reinach emphasised on the first-hand intuiting of the essential core of the phenomena and the approach is composed of transposing ourselves into the intuited object or the phenomena. Besides the intuiting of phenomena and their essences, Reinach stressed another step of the study of essential connections among the phenomena and their laws. Such essential connections occurred, according to Reinach, not only among the formal structures of logic and general ontology, but also in the structures of concrete material phenomena. Three other figures in the phenomenological scene in Germany were Max Scheler, Nicolai Hartmann and Martin Heidegger. Max Scheler (1874–1928) emphasised on the following domains of phenomenology: intuitive experience, attention to the essential and the apriori in experiences. Nicolai Hartmann furthered the tenets of intuition of essences and essential connections between the subjective and the objective in social phenomena. The basic theme in Heidegger's phenomenology is the quest for being, truth and time, and he employed Husserl's method in finding the answers to the existentialist questions posed. Commencing with the thesis of 'being', Heidegger proposed that the meaning of being is through the understanding and comprehension of being or the fundamental state of existence. Heidegger's existentialist phenomenology proposes that there are different modes of existence and that the essence of a human being lies in its existence (Grossman, 1984).

The French phase of the phenomenological movement was influenced by the writings of Gabriel Marcel, Jean-Paul Sartre, Maurice Merleau Ponty, Paul Ricoeur and Emmanuel Levinas. For Marcel (1889–1974), phenomenology represented the analytic description of the contents of experience with reflection as a typical feature of the phenomenological approach. According to Marcel, however, one of the core purposes of phenomenology is to undertake an inquiry into the 'exigency of being'. Jean-Paul Sartre (1905–1980) combined the positions of Husserl and Heidegger in his phenomenological propositions – the central theme being the deliberation on freedom versus being (subjective freedom and objective being and the attempt at reconciliation between the two).

Maurice Merleau Ponty (1908–1961) recognised the importance of dialectics in phenomenology – particularly the 'mediations' between the subject and the object and the synthesis of history into phenomenological method. However, he maintained an allegiance to Husserl in terms of phenomenological description and reduction (Smith, 1962). Paul Ricoeur's existentialist propositions called for a reconciliation of man with himself and the world. This reconciliation or restoration would be through transcendence, and the comprehensive philosophy of the same could be sought in phenomenology. The procedure that Ricouer aligned to was 'going to the things themselves and respecting all the very complex aspects of consciousness'. For the purpose, three levels of investigation were posited: the level of descriptive analysis, transcendental constitution (determining the constitution of phenomena in consciousness) and the level of ontological phenomenology or of an ontology of consciousness (i.e., determining the status of consciousness in the total framework of being). Emmanuel Levinas moved from a critique of ontology towards metaphysics and ethics. His phenomenological philosophy moved with the following propositions: the subject as always in relation to the Being; the Being traditionally conceived of as a totality needs to be thought of as a radical exteriority so that transcendence is actually possible and for which the return to metaphysics is essential and ethics form the base of Being and the counterpart of Being which is 'being'. This then leads to pure existence and pure consciousness – which is the subject matter of phenomenology (Edie, 1965; Spiegelberg, 1982).

The application of phenomenological propositions to the social world has been undertaken by Alfred Schutz (1899–1959) who has drawn from Husserl and Weber. Schutz's framework develops particularly on the concept of the lifeworld – the major themes being the cognitive setting of the lifeworld, acting in the lifeworld, the world of social relationships and the realms of experience. In terms of the cognitive setting of the lifeworld, there is a discussion on the subjective experiences of daily life and the interpretation of the world which emerges from it and the analysis of the socially given means of orientation and interpretation at the disposal of the individuals. There is also an investigation of the factors which make for selective attention to aspects of the environment experienced, and the ensuing spheres and systems of relevance – including the process of typifications and the application of type concepts. Typification is considered by Schutz as the process of classification of the myriads of phenomena into types – language being one medium of typification. Within the lifeworld, action is governed by the motivational functions of reasons and goals and guided by anticipations. These combined with issues of volition, choice, freedom and determination in the context of human action comprises the subjective theory of human actions. The world of social relations is then considered to be an analysis of interactional relationships issuing from intersubjective processes. There are multiple realms of experience which are realised through the conceptions of multiple universes and realities through which varied provinces of meanings are created which build into the lifeworld. These meanings range from the realities of daily life to the provinces of scientific cognition (Schutz, 1970).

Later works in phenomenology have been concerned with two domains: one in terms of consolidation of the epistemological foundations and the second in terms of its linkages with existentialism. In terms of epistemological consolidation, the trends that are visualised are description of experience as the basis for a theoretical conclusion and a concern with the 'total construct' of experience in its multi-layered concreteness rather than with reductionist abstraction. Gurwitsch (1965) has moved beyond Husserl in his analysis of perceptual experience to understand the organisational aspects of perception. On the basis of the works of the psychologists Piaget and Gestalt, he criticises and rectifies Husserl's view of horizons and sedimentations of perceptual experience. He proposes a view which does not interpret the sedimentations of experience simply as layers of meaning superimposed upon a fundamental which would itself remain unchanged, but rather as a continual and substantial re-organisation of experience into new forms, each with its own autochthonous and irreducible meaning structure. Kaelin (1965) has combined the understanding of Merleau Ponty and Gestalt theory to explain the task of phenomenology in the area of aesthetic experience. It is to describe the manner in which various strata of meaning and relationships interact in our perceptions in order to determine the particular effect that they have in combination. There is a concrete description of the 'what' of experience, both in its noetic attitude and in its noematic correlate prior to and as the basis for the development of explanatory hypotheses. Wild (1965) has combined subjectivity aspects of phenomenology in existentialism proposing that the dialectical reconciliation of the subjective and objective elements in moral action determine authentic existence. Authenticity then becomes a new category of existential ethics rather than relativism. Edie (1965) and Olson (1965) have proposed that phenomenology is effectively a study of human expressivity. This is evident in concepts such as a pre-reflexive and apriori existence of implicit meanings of human action and language and the 'rheoscopic' studies on human behaviour (which focus on expression in thinking and its relation to language, volition and human emotions) as having a phenomenological base. Phenomenological deliberations have further led to the development of a new branch of inquiry called phenomenological psychology – transcendental and existential branches of phenomenology having impact on aspects of perception. The central assumption is that of intentionality which presents human beings as active interpreters of their experience of the world rather than passive reactors to both biophysical and environmental forces while at the same time acknowledging the role and impact of the world in shaping the means through which investigations are structured (Spinelli, 2005).

Phenomenology is also closely intertwined with the interpretative school and hermeneutics (interpretation) – which stands for the subordination of explanation and description to interpretation. Hermeneutics accompanies an anti-scientism (separation of facts from values), relativism and humanism. Society is viewed as linguistically and meaningfully constituted and intersubjectivity which brings in elements of cultural construction that can lead to self-understanding or world disclosure. The strand of hermeneutical tradition which draws from phenomenology is inspired by the tradition of philosophy of language stemming from Heidegger. For Heidegger, the understanding of social reality was constitutive of the lifeworld and not something that could be arrived at through pure understanding. With Heidegger, understanding became a part of 'being' itself: method and ontology collapsed into one another. He argued that understanding is the fundamental ontological characteristic of the lifeworld and is embodied in language. Interpretation that cannot transcend the lifeworld context for consciousness is not independent of language. Hence, science is constrained by the social context – laying the foundations of a subjective hermeneutics incorporating relativism and historicism (Langan, 1959). Further the next proponent of hermeneutics, Ludwig Wittgenstein in his *Philosophical Investigations* (1953), provided a theory of the 'linguistification of the social' – language games (reality mediated by language and it being a linguistic construction). Two other theorists in this genre were Hans-Georg Gadamer and Paul Winch. In his *Truth and Method* (1960), Gadamer proposed that in hermeneutics there is always a component of untranslated subjectivity and hence interpretation can never be complete. Paul Winch's approach focused on the method of social sciences, rejecting causal explanations in favour of interpretative approach. In the hermeneutical approach, reality is untouched and the understanding of alien cultures for interpretation is always culture specific (Delanty, 1997).

Social Construction of Reality

Drawing from phenomenology and hermeneutics (primarily the interpretative school), social construction of reality proposes that social reality is not 'out there' but carefully constructed in the minds of individuals. These constructions occur through the socialisation processes that people go through and hence it is essentially subjective. It includes interpretation which entails viewing the constructions in reality that are already meaningful. This interpretation of the construction is through the subjective self of the interpreter. Reality is socially constructed through subjective interpretations, pre-dispositions and the socialisation processes. When reality is socially constructed it entails: self-reproducing sets of sites of authority; subject (human agent) and object (society and social institutions) as both constituted through recurrent practices; social systems as regularised practices reproduced across time and space; structure as 'recursively organised rules and resources' and that structure is 'reconstituted in social interaction' (Berger and Luckmann, 1967).

From the lens of social construction, society and individuals are transcendental conditions – they are in theoretical terms 'noema' constituted in the process of 'noesis'. It is a figuration – changing patterns of constructions created by social actors through their minds and social interactions, which include interdependencies and unintended consequences. Interdependencies take cognisance of the fact that actors enter the field of interaction already connected with other actors through socially shared resources, which further institutionalises social constructions. The logic to social construction (also called figurational logic) proposes that the networks of dependencies are essential for a social framework, i.e., some constructions are inevitable to explain the social phenomena. To study social constructions, it is essential to describe and analyse unconscious motives of action; understand different versions of truth explanations of a particular social phenomena and shift the focus from the 'system' towards the 'actor'.

Berger and Luckmann (1967), in explaining social construction of reality, have looked at the objective and the subjective sides of society. That is, how components embedded within the understanding of society as objective reality and as subjective reality build into the theory of social construction. In describing the objective reality element, there are aspects of institutionalisation (occurs when there is a reciprocal typification of habitualised actions by types of actors also implying historicity and control), sedimentation and traditions. Legitimation is the other process which produces new meanings that serve to integrate the meanings already attached to disparate institutional processes. The function of legitimation is to make objectively available and subjectively plausible the first-order objectivations that have been institutionalised and hence it is called second-order objectivation of meaning. Objective reality purports the existence of symbolic universes and conceptual machineries of universe maintenance – mythology, theology, therapy and nihilation. The subjective reality aspect has to do with internalisation of norms and forms of society. This happens through ontogenetic processes of socialisation which are primary (childhood phase and membership related) and secondary (induction of an already socialised individual into new sectors of the objective world of society). These contribute to the subjective reality, the maintenance and transformation of which contribute to the continued process of dialectics.

Social construction as an epistemic category has certain problematic embedded in the same. First, since structures are the essence of social construction, there is an inherent hierarchy in social construction. Second, the idea of structure conveys the recognition of the fact that in a certain set of events, probabilities are not distributed at random. There is a risk of hypostatis – since we are then asking only 'how questions' and not 'why questions', there arises the whole thing of unquestioningly accepting the structure. Third, social construction limits the possibility of social action; the opposition between personality, culture and society, and the opposition between the 'actor' and the 'system' is ruled out.

In Summary

The commencing plane to comprehend positivism and realism is empiricism and rationalism. The social world is composed of experiences and truth propositions which are either perceived by the senses (empiricists) or emergent through the mind (rationalists). In the ideational frames of empiricists Locke, Berkeley and Hume, comprehensions of the world arise from sense perceptions derived through experience generating two kinds of meanings: analytic and synthetic. Hence, the creations of social meanings are through associations and imaginations to create a coherent whole. This construction of the social whole is through induction (Baconian (Francis Bacon) interpretations of going beyond the deductive methods of Aristotle's syllogism). The social 'whole' in Spinoza's terms is composed of substance, attributes and modes which develop from the first existential proposition – the 'being' in the Cartesian cogito. Rationalists proposed the knowledge of the external world as constituted by innate ideas which are mind originated and endowed by reason (Masih, 2002).

Kant has translated this theory of innate ideas into apriori truths and proposed 'transcendentalism' – at the juncture of rationalism and empiricism. Kantian transcendentalism proposes that in knowledge, sense experience is at once moulded and transformed by the apriori elements contributed by the mind. 'Knowledge of the social world is thus a joint product of sense and understanding' – material supplied by the sense are ordered and synthesised into cognitive statements by the apriori form of the mind. The connection depends on the subjective constitution of the human mind and yet it is valid for all as all social beings have the same constitution – the same knowledge of the phenomena.

Popper's positivist propositions draw from Kantian stances of transcendental reason. They forward a theory of reason and experiences and an understanding of the world through conjectures and refutations. Positivist epistemology proposes a rationality of scientific frames to explain social phenomena. The critical element arises in revisiting earlier propositions and re-stating new claims (Popper, 1963). In tune with Bertrand Russell's claims of the finiteness of knowledge governed by 'truth' which is in itself above human authority (Durant, 1961), positivist epistemological theses proposes to comprehend the social with a world focus on facts – reality out there. Reality is comprehended through assertions and consequences which are empirically verifiable; knowledge of the existential world is a modification of apriori truths – traditions and conjectures as developing the modus operandi. History and apriori truths as epistemological resources are beyond interrogation.

Realism focuses on discourses of 'truths' – objective truth values, independent of the means of knowing them. In realism the definition of truth is given in terms of correspondence and this correspondence can be said to be in correspondence with facts (the semantic concept of truth in deciphering the social world is explained in philosopher's Tarski's correspondence theory, where what exists as social reality is a fact and hence a truth). Hence, truth is subject to external reality (which in realist terms gives absolute and relative conceptions of truth), which leads to formations of epistemologies.

Epistemology in realist parlance is truth governed by external realities and is arrived at through propositional functions; that lead to the highest generality. Realist methodology is the move from the determinate to general. For determinateness to become generality it needs validity through propositional functions – the creation of which is the task of logic (Chattopadhyay et al., 2000). Latter philosophers Frege and Strawson highlight realisms disconnect with histories and time-space geographies. Logic with its methods of designation–nondesignation and conditionality-difference has developed binaries addressed by poststructuralists in their contentions.

Phenomenological assertions move beyond the positivist frame of reference in favour of 'inter-subjectivity'. The phenomenological stance attributes primacy to 'consciousness' in being – cosmos' relations, inquiring into structures formed by essences, notions of intersubjectivity and ontology of the life-world. The main thesis is thus a rejection of science's fetish for objectivity and reductionism and re-affirming subjectivity along Kantian lines as an attempt to return to the primordial ontological basis of man. Subjectivity thus goes beyond Popperian scientific determinism and encompasses phenomena whose very meaning science rejects and usually having a base in the transcendental or the psychic. This subjectivist epistemology and naturalistic methodology derives from Kant and Husserl, particularly Husserlian transcendental phenomenology embodying the critique of scientism. Kant and Husserl's conceptions are that actors (beings) are teleological and subjectivist in their account of the world. There is a certain alliance to critical realism (Roy Bhaskar, 1975), with a possibility of causal explanations, acceptance of the hermeneutic notion of social reality as being communicatively constructed and a critical dimension to understanding social reality, called epistemological relativism.

For social theory, Schutz's phenomenology assumes importance which proposes a subjectivist account of the world. Influenced by Husserl and Weber – albeit liberating it from purely transcendental arguments towards a social leaning, the focus is on a 'reciprocity of perspectives' and 'construction of reality and interactions' (Giddens, 1987). Schutz phenomenology proposes that social reality engulfs a creation and maintenance of an intersubjectivity – common subjective world among pluralities of interacting individuals. The propositions are that: reality is beings' stock knowledge and this existence of stock knowledge bestows a sense of reality on events in a given world. Stock knowledge is learnt/constructed and beings operate under a number of assumptions that allow them to create a reciprocity of perspectives (the Kantian stance). Beings use typifications gained from stock knowledge, assumptions and reciprocity of perspectives to understand/construct the social world/reality (Turner, 2004). Hence, there is a focus on critical realist ontology, subjectivist epistemology and grounded praxis.

Social construction of reality is emergent through phenomenological propositions and hermeneutic leanings –

accommodating the primal belief that reality is socially constructed and that the sociology of knowledge must analyse the process in which this occurs. This thought incorporates the twin Marxian concepts of substructure – superstructure, historicism and a relative natural worldview. The basis of this thought is Karl Mannheim's relationism involving a modification of Durkheimian theory of society by the introduction of a dialectical perspective derived from Marx and an emphasis on the constitution of social reality through subjective meanings derived from Weber (Berger and Luckmann, 1967). Social construction of reality's notion of symbolic universes (bodies of theoretical tradition that integrate different provinces of meaning and encompassing of the institutional order in a symbolic totality) led to the origination social dialectics – having contentions such as: the whole is a relation among parts; properties take their meanings from the whole; parts and wholes interpenetrate and change is primary.

3

Theory and Social Epistemology–2

Marxism and Critical Theory

This chapter discusses the core tenets of Marxism as a grand narrative and an ideational schemata and the Frankfurt School of critical theory as a post-Marxian theoretical development. Within the social theorisation repertoire, the discussion is around the ontology, epistemology and methodology of Marxian thought and the subsequent dissensions that arose in terms of critical theory. Key propositions have been deliberated to encompass the range of understandings forwarded by Marx and Engels and Plekhanov as methodological, collaborators to his enterprise. The basic conjunctions of critical theory through its main proponents Horkheimer, Adorno, Marcuse and Habermas have been presented. The overall endeavour in this chapter is to highlight some key domains of an often frequent arena of epistemological deliberations.

Marxism: Influences, Origins and Core Tenets

Marxism as an epistemological and theoretical enterprise can be discussed in terms of the Hegelian influences, the origins in terms of departures from Hegelian idealism, philosophical tenets, economic analysis and renditions on political economy, dialectical and historical materialism, the Hegelian version of Marxism as discussed by Kautsky and Gramsci and later theoretical developments.

The Influences

The chief influence of Marx has been the Hegelian philosophy which is essentially idealist in character. The origin of the dialectic can, however, be traced to the contingency of human existence as found in the soteriology of Plotinus and Plato – the contingency of man's being lying in the fact that his true essence is outside himself and a return to noncontingency lies in the return to the Absolute. Similar contentions on temporality are found in the writings of St. Augustine who has forwarded the Christian version of Platonism. Eriugena as a Christian theologist has further discussed that dialectics is embedded in the thought that non-Absolute realities are a necessary phase in the Absolute's growth towards self-realisation and this function of theirs justifies the course of world history. Other ideas that served as a precursor to dialectical thought are Eckhart's dialectic of deification, Nicholas of Cusa's contradictions of Absolute Being, Bohme's duality of being, and Kantian duality of being (nature-freedom, desire-duty, passive contingent existence-active noncontingent existence) and Fichte's immanent dialectic (dialectic that makes human subjectivity the absolute point of departure, subject and object being a duality which sought to find synthesis in infinite progress) (Kolakowski, 1978). The chief departure point was, however, Hegelian dialectics – the account of the historical process whereby consciousness overcomes its own contingency and finitude by constant self-differentiation. This overcoming of contingency is the same as freedom of spirit. Young Hegelianism singled out the principle of permanent negation as the dominant theme in Hegel's philosophy. Subsequently, they posited an opposition between facts of history and normative reason and the importance of revolution – which laid the foundations of Marxian thought (Kolakowski, 1978).

The Origins

The origins of Marxian thought thus lay in its departure from Hegelian idealism towards materialism with two core motifs of his thought being the thesis of alienation and scientific determinism. Marx's explanation of social change and development accorded privilege to the economic factors over all other factors with emphasis on forces of production and relations of production. Relations of production are exploitative as the proletariat are forced to work for subsistence pay and the bourgeoisie appropriate the surplus. Classes are defined in terms of ownership of means of production, and the expansion of productive forces determines society's relations of production. The relations of production are the base of society and on them are founded the legal and political structures to which correspond definite forms of social consciousness (Crossley, 2005). Hence, the general consciousness of society is shaped by the nature of production – social existence determining consciousness of beings. Further, Marx proposed that in the long run, the ways of producing will be changed to facilitate functioning and define newer relations of production thereby proposing a sense of continued change in societal norms and forms.

Marx has forwarded twin conceptions of ideology – one which refers to a false consciousness or a distortion of sorts and the other which refers to the totality of forms of social consciousness or to the political ideas of social classes. At the heart of Marxian analysis of ideologies is the contention on inversions and contradictions. There are three kinds of inversions – alienation (basic inversion of the subject and the object), the market and the process of circulation which inverts the former inversion and presents it as a natural process of objectification realising freedom and equality, and finally ideology which reproduces the level of appearances in the mind, thus inverting the inner twisted relations. The concept of contradiction is also related to the notion of inversion which needs to be understood in historical terms which can be concretely transcended (Larrain, 1983).

The dialectical movement with its three fundamental concepts of truth, going beyond and disalienation characterise every aspect of Marxian writings (Lefebvre, 1968). Marxian praxis implies a dialectical relationship between man and nature and consciousness and things. This praxis perpetuates certain forms which are fetishised and may lead to a reification of society. The schema of praxis operates at three levels: the base or foundation (productive forces, techniques, organisation of labour), structures (production and property relations) and superstructures (institutions, ideologies).

The base of Marxian thought, which is maintained throughout the works, can be outlined thus:

- Marx's point of departure is the eschatological question derived from Hegel. Marx, following Feuerbach, places at the centre of his picture the reality of Man as opposed to Hegelian Spirit.
- Marx, like Feuerbach, looks forward to man's final reconciliation with the world, himself and others. Further, he does not see this in terms of recognition of being as a product of self-knowledge, but in recognition of sources of alienation in man's terrestrial lot and in the overcoming of this state of affairs.

- Alienated labour is a consequence of the division of labour, which in its turn is due to technological progress and is thus an inevitable feature of history. Alienation means subjugation of man by his own works which have assumed the guise of independent things. The transcendence of alienation is through communism.

Philosophical Tenets

Core of Marxian philosophy is based on the critique of Hegelian idealism wherein there is an insistence to change social reality by using philosophical theory to move the masses into action. Marx was concerned with the nature of finite human existence and in that sense he was a philosophical humanist. With the contention that capitalism impedes people from achieving their development as individuals, his arguments are built in his Paris Manuscripts (1844) and in the German Ideology (1845). Callinicos (1983) has discussed the Hegelian and analytic flavour of Marxian philosophy. Marx according to Callinicos (1983) advocated a materialist humanism implying that man's alienation could only be abolished in a communist society. Further, the genesis of Marxian philosophy is attributed to the critique of Hegelian idealism – the point of contention being Hegel's conception of the dialectic as a 'contradiction of appearances as unity in essence, in the idea'. This transcendence of contradictions in Hegel's Absolute, in Marxian terms, serves to conceal the real contradictions constitutive of existing society – between civil society and the state. Further, Marx provided a critique of Hegel's logical principles. In his Philosophy of Right, Hegel's contention of what is real is rational and vice versa, reality is ideal only insofar as it is a finite, empirical moment of an infinite Idea. According to Marx, this implies that Hegel subordinates reality to thought and that he obtains an identity between the ideal and the real by reducing reality to an appearance, a predicate of the ideal. Marx, like Feuerbach, protests against this idealization saying that it deprives the real of its own subsistence. Reality and not the idea is primary according to Marx – ideal is a predicate of reality. Hence in the political sphere, the state would be the result, rather than the cause of social relations (Dupre, 1966).

Feuerbach conceptualized man as having a passive relationship to the world, whereas Marx defined 'being' by his essentially active relation to the environment. Hence, there is the conception of human nature as constituted by an active, redirective and transformative relationship to nature through the labour process. This is Marxian Prometheanism, the essentially Aristotelian belief that beings fulfil themselves through the exercise of their powers – thereby laying the foundation of a humanist aesthetic tradition. Hence, instead of looking at alienation as a mental phenomenon (as in Feuerbach), Marx located the source of alienation in the structure of society rather than the state of man's consciousness. The process of alienation according to Marx follows a dialectical procedure akin to Hegel: original unity, self-estrangement and transcendence to a higher unity.

At the core of the Paris Manuscripts is a teleological philosophy of history in which the development of social forms is explained by their role in bringing about the culmination of the historical process as communism. As the first treatise on the materialist conception of history, the German Ideology outlines concepts such as productive forces, the level of development of man's control over nature and the form of intercourse, the social framework within which this control is organised as primary (Callinicos, 1983). Parallels of Marxian materialism are viewed in terms of analytic philosophy, particularly the doctrine that the ideal is a material world reflected in the mind of man and translated into the forms of thought. Hence, truth claims are determined by the state of the world, thoughts reflect rather than constitute the world and instrumentalism is rejected, i.e., the unobservable entities posited to explain the observable behaviour of things exist independently of thought. Further in terms of the thesis on alienation, Marx along Hegelian lines proposes that man realises his essence in labour and he becomes himself through a process of alienation. However, the core to alienation lies in man's estrangement from nature in threefold ways: alienation from the product, from the act of producing and from his own social nature (Dupre, 1966).

Marx's Economic Analysis

Marx's economic analysis rests upon the labour theory of value which holds that the ratio of exchange between commodities is proportional to the hours of labour that went into producing them. Physical labour is the source of value; machines do not create value, but transfer to the product part of the value crystallised in them. Since capitalism is founded in the competitive search for profits, technological innovations is the only way to ensure profits. But since technology does not generate additional value, gradually the rate of profit on total investment declines. Depressed profits then lead to depressed wage levels which then lead to under-consumption, resulting thereby in the crisis of overproduction and the bane of the capitalist system of production. The eventuality would be the unity of the proletariat that would then destroy the capitalist system transgressing, thereby from the bourgeoisie towards the communist mode of production.

The vantage point for Marxian economic analysis was his critique of the ahistorical standpoint of the classical economists. As a materialist, Marx proposed that categories of economy were a product of historical development of the social relations of production. In his seminal work *Capital,* he has demonstrated as to how all the economic relations of bourgeoisie economy grow – and the growth is both logical and historical – out of the relations of simple commodity production. Thus, the aim was to demonstrate that the essence of all the contradictions of the bourgeoisie economy has a source within the commodity relation itself (Pilling, 1980). Labour in the Marxian scheme was a social category and thus in dealing with the relationship of labour to value, he referred to abstract labour. Under capitalism, the private labour of each individual is transformed into its opposite, social labour, only through the transformation of concrete labour into abstract labour.

Political Economy

The understanding of Marxian political economy developed through his 1857 work on Grundrisse, a part of which later became the famous work 'Capital'. The core contentions of political economy analysis are as follows: The economic structure with the relations of production is the real foundation of society and the basis of legal and political superstructure corresponding to definite forms of consciousness. Capital is a relation of social production that depends for its existence on the division of society into classes with respect to the means of production or private property. Marx's analysis presupposes a distinction between two types of value (understood as a social relationship between people) – use value and exchange value. Fetishism of the commodities derives from the social character of the labour by which they are produced – more specifically from their exchange value as opposed to the use value. When product of labour is a commodity and hence destined to be exchanged, the material relations between individuals in the process of production take the form of social relations between products themselves. Class analysis is another realm in political economy discourses. According to Marx, classes are a creation of history and class divisions are linked to the generation of surplus, are inherently conflictual and class struggle is the chief 'motor' of historical development.

In the context of political economy discourses, there are twofold realms of theorisations – the theories of capitalist development and the theories of capitalist breakdown. Theories of breakdown of capitalism were initiated during the Second International with dominant propositions that at some point capitalism will cease to exist as a dominant mode of production and that the end would be caused by a range of contradictions inherent and internal to the economy. The three identifiable traditions in the breakdown theories are as follows: the orthodox position primarily drawing from neo-Kantianism which adopt causal explanations and assume the primacy of economic forces in capitalist breakdown; structural position which assumes not only the primacy of economic forces but also lending credence to the superstructural factors and their role in engineering the breakdown; and the anti-orthodox position wherein the primacy of economic forces are rejected and the superstructural phenomena are given a predominant role (Hansen, 1985).

Further, the role of the state has been another arena of deliberation in Marxian political economy. Holloway and Piccotto (1978) have stressed on the need for an adequate understanding of the state in the process of capital accumulation and proposed a materialist theory of the capitalist state. The aim has been to derive the state from the category of the capital – separating thereby the political from the economic in the analysis of capital. Hence, there is an emphasis on the unifying totality of capitalist social relations and the historically conditioned fragmentation of those relations into fetishized forms. This approach takes as its starting point the antagonistic relation between capital and labour in the process of accumulation, thus providing the frame for a historical and materialist analysis of the state. There is further the emphasis on form analysis – understanding of the state based on the dialectic of the form and content of the class struggle.

Orthodox Marxism

The chief proponents of orthodox Marxism are Frederick Engels, Karl Kautsky and Georgi Plekhanov. Two key concepts in this vein are historical materialism (implying the economic dimension of history as prior to all other factors) and dialectical materialism (proposing that a dialectic or clash between forces of production and relations of production lead history from one stage to another). Orthodox strand of Marxism proposes that the economic structure of society, composed of relations of production corresponding to a stage in the development of forces of production, underlies the legal and political superstructure corresponding to definite forms of social consciousness. The aggregate of productive forces determine the conditions of society, and hence the history of humanity must always be studied in relation to the history of industry and exchange. There is a reciprocal action between mode of production and forms of consciousness, the two forming a totality in which the mode of production is the basis, with various elements of the superstructure exercising their influence upon the course of historical struggles. There is a need for a material transformation of the economic conditions of production which also implies a transformation of the ideal forms (Lakatos and Musgrave, 1970).

The term *historical materialism* has been introduced by Engels which is a view of history according to which the economic dimension is prior to all other factors. The first premise of all human history is the existence of all living human individuals which involves their physical organisation and consequent relations to the rest of nature. With productive forces as the basis of all history, certain mode of production involves a certain mode of cooperation. Consciousness is a social product and there are material roots of consciousness. Through differential stages in human history, differential division of labour arises; forms of property ownership emergent through different stages of development determine nature of division of labour. The bourgeoisie form of private property with advanced division of labour posits growth of two major social classes – the capitalist who has the means of production and the wage earning proletariat. The state is a product of division of labour representing conflicting interests albeit patronising the bourgeoisie. The material premise of a communist society is the development of social forces (combining productive forces, capital funds and social forms of intercourse). The history of all societies is considered to be the history of class struggle, and the material elements of a revolution are the existing productive forces and a revolutionary mass.

The terms *dialectical materialism* has been introduced by Georgi Plekhanov positing contradiction as the motive force in history. The main contradiction is presupposed in the economic sphere, between relatively conservative social relations of production and the relatively dynamic development of means of production (technology). At certain nodal points of human history, this conflict is resolved leading the society to a higher state of social development in which the relations and means of production are brought to a relative harmony. This process of conflicting forces and their dynamic resolution is reflected in ongoing class struggles and revolutions in human society. Dialectic is not only the affirmative recognition of the existing state of things but also the recognition of breaking up of that state. It considers every historically developed social form in 'fluid movement' and hence it is 'critical and revolutionary' (Craig, 1998).

Karl Kautsky followed the principle of strict determinism and the belief that human history is a continuation of natural history and can be explained by the same laws and thus he proposed a naturalistic interpretation of human consciousness. There was a belief in the objective necessity of socialist society and in that sense he aligned to scientific socialism. The proletariat struggle was not a result of poverty but that of class antagonism and the collapse of capitalism would be due to anarchy, crises of overproduction and mass unemployment. The other theorists who supported the core of orthodox Marxian doctrines were Rosa Luxemburg, Bernstein, Jean Jaures, Paul Lafargue, Georges Sorel, Antonio Labriola, Ludwik Krzywicki, Kazimierz Kelles-Krauz, Stanislaw Brzozowski and Austro Marxists. Rosa Luxemburg re-instated the belief in revolution to overthrow capitalism in her principal theoretical work 'The Accumulation of Capital'. She developed the Marxist thesis of compound reproduction as it exists in capitalism and the contention that its internal contradictions would bring an end to capitalism. Bernstein's philosophy was that of revisionism. He critiqued the belief in total revolution and the creative role of political violence and the theory of value. Class polarisations according to Bernstein are not bipolar but increasingly complex as technology and the organisation of society produced a middle class. He rejected traditionalist claims of socialism in favour of a liberal socialism.

Jean Jaures viewed Marxism as a soteriology, particularly the proposition that socialism as a fully objectivised scientific theory was replaced by Jaures' view that socialism was about morals and human values. Paul Lafargue and Georges Sorel patronised the following traditional positions in Marxian thought: historical materialism; totality; revolution; production, organisation and the relations of production; and the subordination of the proletariat that can be surmounted through the concept of working class syndicates. In Italy, Antonio Labriola focused on the historicist, anti-positivist version of Marxism with a focus on looking at social phenomena as a part of historical totalities and relating them to particular historical epochs. The three Polish theoreticians Ludwik Krzywicki, Kazimierz Kelles-Krauz and Stanislaw Brzozowski focused on the methodology of classical and orthodox Marxism – particularly historical materialism as a method to study society and social processes and a historical subjectivism of sorts in comprehending the position of being in the context of society. The core contentions of the Austro-Marxists were linking Marxian traditions with those of Kant. While accepting the basic principles including the theory of value, the class struggle and historical materialism, they did not agree that Marxism logically presupposed a materialist philosophy or that its validity depended on the philosophical arguments of Engels to which they objected as 'uncritical' in the Kantian sense. The general attitude was that of transcendentalism, critique of knowledge (rather than a scientistic-positivist world view) and theory of ethics and values and forwarded ethical socialism as a thought trend. Ethical socialism proposes that employing Kantian ethics, socialism can be viewed to have desirable values and like all ethical precepts, have universal validity. Hence, ideals of socialism can be advocated by appealing to universal human values vis-a-vis solely working class interests (Kolakowski, 1978; Craig, 1998).

Hegelian Marxism

Hegelian Marxism proposes that Marx's early writings in the late 1920s and the subsequent publication of the Grundrisse posited him as a radical Hegelian. Terms such as alienation, mediation, objectification, reification and the central concern with culture characterised Hegelian Marxism. The other terms that had an important place in the Hegelian Marxist dictionary was 'totality' (Jay, 1984b). The chief proponents of Hegelian Marxism are Georg Lukacs and Antonio Gramsci.

According to Lukacs (History of Class Consciousness, 1921), history has an inner logic that propels the human race towards its essential predetermined goal of communism. Hence as opposed to the orthodox Marxian focus on action, Lukacs proposes that the hostility towards capitalist forces and the position of labour within it would lead to a process of 'reification'. Similar to Marxian understanding of alienation, reification proposes that humans become passive spectators of the social forces that structure their lives; in the capitalist mode of production they become subjected to the hegemonic effects of instrumental rationality. Feenberg (1983) has suggested that Lukacs developed his philosophy of praxis from the methodological traces of Marx's own philosophical positions visible in his economic writings. The defining trait of the philosophy of praxis is the attempt to show that the antinomies of philosophy can be resolved only in history. For Lukacs, the crisis of reason encompasses the dominant paradigm of rationality in all its manifestations and the concept of reification is thus based on three principal sources: Marx's concept of economic fetishism, Weber's concept of rationalisation and Hegel's concept of appearance.

Gramsci did not accept Hegelian teleology of history following a pre-ordained pattern, but viewed Marxism as a humanistic philosophy aiming for a cultural renaissance. Factors of production were ordered in accordance with principles of optimality, where this meant the rationalisation and mechanisation of the productive process; and self-expression at the workplace could be achieved through democratic participation and not through transformation or humanisation of the bourgeoisie productive techniques. The prevalence of capitalism was due to the 'hegemony' – a spiritual and cultural supremacy of the ruling classes, who, through a manipulation of the mechanisms of socialisation, fossil their beliefs/ideas and hence the strategy was to be the 'battle of ideas' and 'war of positions' (Joll, 1977). As discussed by Holub (1992), hegemony and counter hegemony are chief concepts of Gramsci. Gramsci's Hegelian flavour emerges through his understanding of 'differential pragmatics' as a response to power structures that emphasise the role of the intellectual – creating dialogues that structure the conscious resolving simultaneously the antagonism and contradictions through a fetish for totality and universalism. Historicism was another aspect that characterised Gramscian thought which mean critically looking at histories and reality in a historical context.

Hegelian Marxism thus has the following characteristics: stress on praxis, subjectivity and consciousness; inertial force of the objective elements (like means of production) in social totality; recognising the primordial role of nature and its importance in dialectics; positing a normative totality in the future as the end of all alienation and reification. Further, history is viewed as an objective totality in which every particular moment appears as the self-differentiation of the universal – setting the grounds for a longitudinal view of totality (as a world view). The purpose is to invoke the totalising epistemology of the Hegelian tradition against the antinomies of bourgeoisie thought. There is the concept of the total man who is both the subject and object of Becoming, and normative totality is considered to be the telos of history (Jay, 1984b).

Later Theoretical Developments

The first domain of the later theoretical developments is the contemporary theorisations on class and class conflict. Nicos Poulantzas proposes that classes are defined by their role in the economic sphere, but they are also influenced by political and ideological elements. Poulantzas makes a distinction between the 'place' of a class in the structural relations and its position in a conjuncture. Erik Olin Wright developed the concept of class boundaries stating that some classes are inherently antagonistic or contradictory, but some classes occupy 'doubly contradictory' class locations. He explicates this notion in terms of three basic processes involved in the formation of capitalism: loss of control over the labour process by workers, the separation between the formal ownership of capital and the actual directive power in firms, and the development of bureaucratic, managerial hierarchies in industrial organisations. Harry Braverman proposes that instead of a social division of labour which is an apriori condition of all societies, capitalism introduces a technical division of labour based upon the fragmentation of craft skills. Anthony Giddens moves beyond the concept of class boundaries to introduce the concept of class structuration – accentuating the modes in which structured social forms are founded upon class relationships. The sources of class structuration are the degree of closure of mobility chances, the nature of division of labour within organisations and the authority system of the enterprise. Drawing upon Weber's notion of social closure, Frank Parkin applies the same to class societies proposing that in capitalist societies, there are two predominant modes of exclusionary closure – control of capital and control over professional qualifications and credentials (Giddens and Held, 1982).

In terms of aspects of ownership and control, Goran Therborn has suggested that some conventionally established modes of conceptualising the power of the dominant classes have to be placed in question. Three ways of relooking at the power of the dominant classes have to be examined – subjectivist, economic and dialectical-materialist. Claus Offe and Bolker Ronge have developed upon the understanding of the state within class analysis. Capitalist state is viewed at the cross-juncture of capital accumulation and democratic processes. The other arena of deliberation is class consciousness – David Lockwood has provided the three types of class outlook of workers: proletarian, deferential and privatised. Gender and ethnicity are two other domains within contemporary class analysis from a post-Marxian lens. In terms of gender, the key argument that labour force is essentially heterogeneous and the effects of this heterogeneity upon the class structure must be studied. Issues of segmented labour market, productive labour versus socially necessary labour and sexual division of labour are discussed. Marxist class analysis has also been utilised to study ethnic inequalities.

In terms of the later theoretical developments, post-Marxian thought was aligned to the antithetical philosophies including Freudianism, existentialism and structuralism. The overarching theme was the threat posed by technological progress and its indifference to spiritual needs. Whereas conventional Marxists condemned capitalism for producing poverty, the principal grievance of the post-Marxian theorists was that capitalism engendered abundance and satisfied a multiplicity of artificial wants. Further, traditional Marxism was ignoring the question of individual psychology – particularly that distorted society produced a distorted psyche whose eradication required more than simple economic changes. The main disagreement among Marxist philosophers and after Marx was over the nature of the dialectical method. Most accepted what came to be regarded as the orthodoxy shaped by Engels according to which certain dialectical principles which had been extracted from Hegel's logic constituted the most general laws of nature governing the physical and the social world. Adherents to the dialectical materialism thus conceived included the main figures of the Second and the Third Internationals, Lenin and Trotsky as well as Kautsky and Plekhanov. The other group rejected the idea of a dialectic of nature, arguing that the distinctively Marxist method was concerned with elucidating the relationship between the conscious human subjects and the objective social structures. Lukacs, Gramsci. Korsch, Sartre and Adorno belong to this vein.

Some post-Marxian theorists were Herbert Marcuse (*One Dimensional Man*, 1964) whose fundamental thesis was that modern technology, by satisfying all material desires, had removed the motives for protest or dissent in advanced capitalist societies. Hence, one-dimensional thought and behaviour is re-inforced by scientific and technological rationality in human life. Viewing science and technology as domination, Marcuse proposed that totalitarian ideas of liberty repress individual freedom. Existentialist Jean Paul Sartre combined Marxian concern for human liberation with the existential notions of freedom. Marxian notion of freedom was viewed to eventually collapse into political conformities which then become institutionalised as structures and systems. Hence, complete freedom needed existentialist overtones.

Louis Althusser synthesized Marxism and structuralism, rejecting traditional Marxian model of base and superstructure. Society was viewed as a structure of structures – economic, social, political and cultural/ideological; each structure determined by other structures and global forces. Social determination was thus in the Althusserian scheme of things complex, with interdependent structures and superstructure as intertwined with complexities of the base. Hence, there are co-existential regularities and not causal laws in society. Althusser showed that Hegelian dialectic contained implicit within it the progressive unfolding of the Absolute's self-consciousness. Any earlier version of Marxism which possessed Hegel's conceptual structures would therefore be liable to certain idealist deviations: in the case of orthodox dialectical materialism, a tendency to conceive history as a teleological process moving towards an inevitable goal, in the case of Hegelian Marxism a liability to reduce social structures to forms of consciousness.

Developing on Marxian philosophy, Korsch (1970) has discussed as to how orthodox Marxism needs to develop the understanding on the subjective pre-conditions of a revolution – stressing the need for a struggle in the realm of civil society, in culture and ideology since the power of the ruling class was protected by its ideological hegemony over all classes in civil society. By applying Marxist materialist method to the history of Marxist theory itself, Korsch proposed that as the material base of any society is in its socio-economic structure that must be overthrown in practice if the intellectual superstructure is to be overcome in history. It is only by grasping the historical relationship between the bourgeoisie revolution and its theoretical expression in idealist philosophy that the working class can tackle the bourgeoisie ideological power in practice. Mclennan (1988) has examined the debate between Marxism and pluralism – conjoining historical materialism (taken as a broadly interpreted substantive theory) to a scientific realist methodological outlook. Analytical Marxism was another genre of later theoretical developments distinguished by the use of state-of-the-art methods of analytical philosophy and positivist social science (Callinicos, 1989). The core contentions of analytical Marxism are as follows: 1) the development thesis which proposes that productive forces tend to develop throughout history and 2) the primacy thesis which proposes that the nature of production relations of a society is explained by the level of development of its productive forces.

Critical Theory

Critical theory is a theoretical orientation concretised in the Institute of Social Research, Frankfurt, spearheaded by Max Horkheimer and his associates. Frankfurt School looks at Marxism as a starting point and an aid to the analysis and criticism of existing culture and also incorporates understanding from Freud, Hegel, Kant and Nietzsche. It did not identify with any political movement in terms of either communism or democracy. Influenced by the interpretation of Marxism evolved by Lukacs and Korsch in the 1920s, especially the concept of reification as an epitome of all the problems of the modern world, it emphasised in the simultaneous independence and autonomy of theory and objected to it being subsumed under praxis. While accepting Marxian position on the exploitation and alienation of the proletariat, it did not identify with the latter in terms of its existing class consciousness as an apriori norm. Critical theory emphasised instead the universality of reification as a process affecting all strata of society and came to be doubtful of the proletariat's revolutionary and liberatory role. Critical theory provides a critique of modernity which was conceived as emerging from feudalism and the Renaissance – political economy and economic development as the foundation of the historical trajectory of modernity (Kellner, 1989).

Critical theory proposes that thought or reason is constitutive (i.e., there are limits to human reason) as well as transformative (i.e., human reason can envisage a change through history which is truly revolutionary in nature). Technology and automation draw away from humans their freedom and potential and hence restoring an 'intersubjective social action' is imperative to social change. Main concern with critical theory is the human agency and particularly issues of existence, freedom and place in the social fabric and role in social transformation. The core contentions are the concept of society as bourgeoisie, the idea that knowledge centres in production, the critique of the so-called liberal individual as autonomous and the primacy of history. Horkheimer and Adorno have further discussed that the basic forms of the historically given commodity economy on which the modern history rests contains in itself the internal and external tensions of the modern era (Lakatos and Musgrave, 1970). Horkheimer has further discussed that the task of critical theory is an acute refutation of positivism (according to which the world of appearances constitutes the structure of reality and man can only know that which is given in experience or representations of experience through linguistic communication) and the scientistic tendencies of orthodox Marxism. Critical theory is dialectical, recognising that the world of appearance is a product of human activity and that subject–object distinctions in the social world are passé (Horkheimer, 1972). The subject of critical theory is a definite individual in his real relationship to other individuals and groups, in his conflict with a particular class and finally in the resultant web of relationships with social totality and with nature. The commencing point of critical theory is abstract determinations and with the characterisations of an economy based on exchange.

There is a certain departure from Marxian economic determinism in two distinct ways: one is by establishing a correspondence with the superstructure with its inherent contradictions and viewing the social totality through the complex homologies and the second is lending greater credence to the superstructure by making everything which is subject to it in the social totality 'correspond' to itself. Whether in the guise of a form of social consciousness (a hegemonic ideology, instrumental reason, a particular episteme, logocentrism, social energia) or of some legal or political or administrative structuration (fascism, centralised planning, disciplines) the superstructure imposes conformity on all aspects of social being (Bannet, 1993).

Critical theory rests on the critique of instrumental reason which implies a critique of modes of rationality. It is a critical view of what is taken as accepted norms and forms of society – what is endorsed by media, bureaucracy, economy and cultural life, becomes rational – the dominant thought to which an individual must comply – thereby reducing his/her autonomy. Reason, according to critical theory, can function critically, but it can also become the dominant norm of society which is then controlling and hegemonic. In technical terms, this is called the 'Dialectic of Enlightenment'. The three core realms of critical theory are critique, justice and reason. Critical theory is a critique of bourgeoisie reality/society/ideals: of the prevalent mode of production and the relations of production; of the binary vision of society – into two classes; and of class struggle as eventually leading to emancipation. The task of critique in society is to find inherent structures and forces that hinder the development of forms of mutual communication. Justice as the second pillar is understood as a utopia of all communicative rationality and social action. This justice can be attained through a practical discourse proposing that those norms of justice are valid that meet with approval of all affected in the practical discourse. There is also a critique of reason moving from the conventional understanding of reason as liberation from dogma towards reason as inherently dominant (governed by instrumental rationality) and the dialectic of reason. Liberation is sought through dialectics, art and communicative action (Rasmussen, 1998). The other realm of theorisation in terms of critical theory is of art as discussed by Adorno (who supported an aesthetic modernism). Art in the notions of critical theory is a medium of expressing all that is beyond rationality and reason. Art is more than a mere representation of a society, it has not only the capacity to represent, but also go beyond that representation, hence art reconstructs. Further, mass culture was considered as not popular culture rising from the experiences and concerns of people, but a form of administered culture imposed from the above – new sociocultural forms by which neocapitalist societies legitimate and reproduce themselves. Cultural criticism and critique of mass culture were celebrated by critical theory. Further, authentic art was supposed to provide both a form of opposition to the established society and a utopian mode of reconciliation with nature. There was an alignment to surrealism by Walter Benjamin privileging the avant-garde over realism and believing that certain kinds of art provided a virtually mystical 'revelation' of truths and insights concerning social life which are hidden from the everyday consciousness.

One other task of the Institute of Social Research, under the directorship of Horkheimer, was to develop a critical social psychology. For this purpose, the Institute appointed Freudian psychoanalyst Erich Fromm (Escape from Freedom and The Sane Society as his premier works) who in his work *Psychoanalysis and Sociology* sketched the attempt to combine sociology and psychology and undertook a Marx-Freud synthesis in order the analyse the ways in which social conditions constituted the psyche and psychological factors that affected social life. However, in this vein, differences existed between Marcuse and Fromm on the employment of Freudian analysis. Whereas Marcuse employed Freud from a metapsychological point of view, Fromm made a clinical use of Freud insights. According to Marcuse, the unconscious provided integral images of happiness and liberation which allowed for a critique of existing society (creating a theory of instinctual liberation and nonrepressive civilization). Nevertheless, both Marcuse and Fromm viewed libidinal energies as a source of opposition to the existing order and privileged subjectivity as an emancipatory force. The other critical theorist Leo Lowenthal argued against dominant idealist and philological positions, instead favouring an approach that interpreted texts and determined the meaning of cultural objects within their social and historical contexts (Bronner and Kellner, 1989).

Some of the core thoughts by some proponents of the Frankfurt School such as Adorno, Marcuse and Habermas can be discussed as follows. As a critical theorist, Theodor Adorno's main proposition was that of negative dialectics – a dialectical model of negations that simultaneously constructed and deconstructed patterns of a fluid reality; there being no moment of triumphant reconciliation that traditionally captured a dialectical process. Two aspects governed Adornian thoughts – force field and constellation. By force field was meant a relational interplay of attractions and aversions that constituted the dynamic, transmutational structure of a complex phenomenon. Constellation signified a juxtaposed rather than integrated cluster of changing elements that resist reduction to a common denominator, essential core or generative first principle. Adorno rejected mass culture, bureaucratic domination and technological, instrumental reason. Aspects of prevalent epistemologies that influenced Adorno were western Marxism, aesthetic modernism, mandarin cultural despair, Jewish self-identification and deconstruction. Adornian thought thus favoured subjectivity, inserted aspects of culture and psyche in the Marxian version of totality and deliberated on culture to ultimately develop a dialectical theory of culture – the high/mass culture dichotomy and the need for an immanent and a transcendent critique to examine culture issues (Jay, 1984a).

Herbert Marcuse addressed the crucial existential question of human freedom (in his seminal work *One Dimensional Man*), drawing the critique from Heidegger's phenomenological existentialism, Freud's metapsychology, Marx's aesthetic theory and Hegelian dialectics. Concerned with the core question of human emancipation, Marcuse, drawing on Marxian understandings of communism and humanism, stresses on aspects of need gratification, aesthetic-erotic components in a nonrepressive civilisation and a new consciousness as necessary components of a liberated society. Marcuse has provided a critique of science and technology as domination – positing simultaneously a phenomenological critique of instrumental rationality. Marcuse has also simultaneously attempted to provide an aesthetic dimension to critical theory – not by art itself (as in Adorno) but the political actions which have direct effects on the material world must be progressively informed by the promise of memory and imagination conveyed by aesthetic forms (Marcuse, 1968; Ray, 1998).

Delving further into his seminal work, 'One Dimensional Man', Marcuse proposes that in the one-dimensional society, the subject is assimilated into the object and follows the dictates of external objective structures, thus losing its abilities to realize the self. Marcuse's theory presupposes the creation of a new subject with traditional features of freedom, creativity and self-determination that stand in opposition to an object-world. This bi-dimensional thought pre-supposes antagonism between the subject and the object so that the subject is free to perceived possibilities in the world that could be realised through human practice. The self-conscious subject, aware of its nature and powers, is a 'being for itself' and contains the powers of objectification in which it appropriates and makes its own ideas, forms of behaviour, objects and institutions. Essential to its freedom and self-consciousness is the awareness of independence from the object: a free subject controls the object and is able to use the otherness for its own projects; if, however, the object controls the subject, a condition of unfreedom exists. This is precisely the situation in one-dimensional society, where the object exercises control and domination over the subject. The tension between subject and object, also central to Hegel's thought, dissolves and the subject assimilates itself to the object and thus loses its subjectivity. In forfeiting its powers of self-determination and self-consciousness, the subject loses its capacity to determine its own development and instead becomes the object of domination. In losing the individuality, the one-dimensional man also loses his freedom (Ray, 1998).

Jurgen Habermas as a contemporary critical theorist conceived of his project as an attempt to develop a theory of society with a practical intention: the self-emancipation of people from domination. Influenced by Kant's propositions on critical reflection, Habermas locates the central feature of Kant's project as the recognition of the limits of reason and the simultaneous preservation of the critical-transcendental power of reason to ground claims to truth and to normative rightness. The main thrust of his work has been concerned with redeeming the possibility of an emancipator form of knowledge through the project of universal pragmatics by rendering plausible his theory of communicative action and rationality (Ashenden and Owen, 1999).

A major concern of Habermas has been the spread of instrumental reason to many areas of social life and at the level of theory of knowledge, the way instrumental reason has dominated modern thought has been investigated. Knowledge is historically rooted and interest bound. In his work 'Knowledge and Human Interests', Habermas has developed the theory of cognitive interests (or knowledge constitutive interests), the first stage in his relationship of knowledge to human activity. The theory of cognitive interests is concerned with uncovering the conditions for the possibility of knowledge – knowledge understood in light of the problems man encounters in his efforts to 'produce his existence and reproduce his species being'. The conditions of the constitution of knowledge which determines 'the structure of objects of possible experience' are the historical material conditions in which the development of the species has occurred. Humankind has interest in creation of knowledge which would enable it to control objectified processes, to maintain communication and to be self-reflective and self-determining, i.e., emancipatory. Following this theorisation, Habermas developed a theory of communicative competence that looked at the structure of speech and language as inherently containing the structures of society. An ideal speech situation would entail a discursively attained consensus of norms which aid emancipation. Further, freedom is dependent on praxis which was defined by Habermas in two key parts – instrumental-rational action (work) and communicative interaction or communicative action. Hence, Habermas's theory of social evolution claims that through work and interaction the human species evolves in two separate but interrelated dimensions, namely the development of the forces of production and the development of the normative structures of evolution. Work or purposive rational action is that dimension of activity in which the human species, through the manipulation and control of objects, produces from nature what is needed for its material existence. Language or communicative action is that dimension of activity in which the human species communicates through the use of intersubjectively understood symbols within the context of rule governed institutions. In the sphere of work, through the generation and application of technical knowledge there is development of the forces of production. In the sphere of language, through the generation and application of practical and moral knowledge there are changes in structured interaction. The theory of social evolution proposes that capitalist societies are susceptible to 'legitimation crisis' and the 'possibility spaces' of development is cumulative growth in technical and scientific knowledge and patterns of reflexivity and discursiveness in the sphere of practical life (Held, 1980).

Habermas' theory is thus based on philosophy of language – instrumental reason colonises the lifeworlds of people as it infuses society with subtle structures as in language. Social integration and communication can materialise through communicative and purposive rationality and strategic action, leading to decolonisation of the lifeworld. Habermas dealt with the core problem of what comprises valid knowledge and understanding as well as reality which was proposed to having two parts: discursive and practical. The discursive part of reality is composed by the rules of language and structure that determine reason. The practical part is governed by the discursive part. Habermas argues that the conditions of discourse (which combine the discursive and the practical) must make possible the radicalisation of arguments and lead to self-reflection and emancipation of subjects. Hence, the theoretical discourse or the discursive realm progresses from metatheoretical language criticism and a subsequent critique of knowledge. The practical part, through a grounding in theoretical justifications, moves in parallel from metaethical/metapolitical language-criticism towards the formation of a rational critical will (McCarthy, 1978; Ashenden and Owen, 1999).

In Summary

In Marxian thought, there is an epistemological shift from Hegelian idealism to a materialist conception of society and history. Hegel believed that particular entities within the world of experience are not real and the universals are not sense objects but products of thoughts, 'thought objects' and ideas. There is a view of history of human society as a dialectical movement of ideas marching towards the realisation of its essence – ideas are assigned independent existence and held as a reality. The 'Absolute Idea' is considered as the subject and the material world is placed in the position of the predicate – the real world as the external, phenomenal form of the Idea.

Marxian thought commences with a critique of Hegelian idealism, a philosophical humanist stance. In German Ideology (1845), Marx argues that 'under capitalism our social consciousness is distorted under institutions of private property, resulting in mere false consciousness, which tends to preserve rather than alter the present social situation'. Hence, it conceals the contradictions inherent in modern industrial society (Eatwell and Wright, 1999).

The key tenets of the materialist epistemology are that the economic structure of society, composed of relations of production (corresponding to a stage in the development of forces of production), underlies the legal and political superstructure (corresponding to definite forms of social consciousness). The aggregate of productive forces determine the conditions of society, and history of humanity must always be studied in relation to the history of industry and exchange. Between modes of production and forms of consciousness of which the former is the basis, there is a reciprocal action and transformation of one can alter the other. This totality in itself contains the essence of transformation – of exchange relations, value and consciousness (Choudhary, 2002).

Two important methodological dimensions to Marxian thought are historical materialism and dialectical materialism – developed by Engels and Georgi Plekhanov respectively. Historical materialism presupposes productive forces as the basis of all history and the material roots of consciousness. Through differential stages in human history, varied forms of property ownership emerges which in turn determine the nature of division of labour. It is this historical baggage of productive forces, production relations, capital and social exchange that provide a material premise for revolution and change. Dialectical materialism commences with the vantage point of 'contradiction' – as the motive force in history. The main contradiction lies in the economic sphere, i.e., between relatively conservative social relations of production and the relatively dynamic development of means of production (technology). At certain nodal points of human history this conflict is resolved leading the society to a higher state of social development in which the relations and means of production are brought to a relative harmony. This process of conflicting forces and their dynamic resolution is reflected in ongoing class struggles and revolutions in human society. Dialectic is thus not only the affirmative recognition of the existing state of things but also the recognition of breaking up of that state – considering every historically developed social form in 'fluid movement' and hence it is 'critical and revolutionary' (Kolakowski, 1978).

Moving beyond the economic determinism of puritan Marxian tenets, Gramsci and the Frankfurt School critical theorists have enlivened the deliberations by viewing Marxism as a method, critique and social theory – escalating the debates to domains of power other than class. Gramscian departures are in terms of introduction of concepts such as historicism and culture. The main theme of Gramsci's reflections is the question of the relation of human thoughts, feelings and will to 'objective' social processes – called historicism. All the concepts by which our knowledge of the world is organized are related primarily not to 'things' but to relations between the users of those concepts. Relations of production cannot be explained solely with the 'scientific' and 'objective' analysis of Marxists – culture being a hitherto ignored category.

'Cultural hegemony' in Gramscian formulations was a fundamental and prior condition of attaining political power. The working class could only conquer by first imparting its world view and system of values to the other classes who might be its political allies: in this way it would become the intellectual leader of society, just as the bourgeoisie had done before seizing political control. The proletariat needed 'organic' intellectuals" (one of Gramsci's favourite and most frequent adjectives): that is to say, intellectuals who did not simply describe social life from outside in accordance with scientific rules, but who used the language of culture to 'express' the real experiences and feelings which the masses could not express for themselves (Kolakowski, 1978; Callinicos, 1983).

The Frankfurt School proponents as philosophical Marxists introduced other dimensions to the analysis. Combining Marxian ideas of commodification of social relations and penetration of rationality into spheres of social life, Georg Lukacs has proposed the concept of 'reification' wherein social relations become 'objects' that can be manipulated. Hence, an analysis of power needs to examine these micropolitics of exchange moving beyond economic determinism (Livingstone, 1968). Horkheimer and Adorno have submitted the need to describe other historical forces that dominate human freedom and comprehend their ideological justifications. Adornian 'negative dialectics' particularly provide a constant critique of ideas, conceptions and conditions. There is also a need to see in analysis of commodity fetishism, exchange and value (parallel to Spivak's discourse on Asiatic mode of production) how 'instrumental reason' (a means ends rationality) has created binaries and invaded the human spirit (Rasmussen, 1998).

In Habermasian conceptualisations, the need is to reconcile forces of material production and political organisation within the forces of 'intersubjectivity' – the integration of the system and the lifeworld. Due to modernity, the system processes revolving around the economy and the state have 'colonised' and 'dominated lifeworld processes' concerned with mutually shared meanings, understandings and intersubjectivity. The integrative problems in capitalist societies are manifested in crises concerning the 'reproduction of the lifeworld' – that is the acts of communicative action that reproduce this lifeworld are replaced by 'delinguistified media' such as money and power that are used in the reproduction of system processes. The goal of critical theory is then to document those facets of society wherein the lifeworld has been colonised and to suggest approaches whereby situations of 'communicative action' can be reestablished. This involves a critical examination of processes by which particular view of society has been legitimized – deconstructing the same through communicative rationality (Joseph, 1988).

4

Theory and Social Epistemology–3

Structuralism, the 'Post' Genres and Feminism

This chapter examines the various domains within structuralism, poststructuralism, postmodernism and postcolonialism as social theorisations. Further, the school of subaltern studies with its varied nuances have also been discussed. Within structuralism, the positions of Saussure and Claude Levi-Strauss along with certain aspects of Durkheimian and post-Durkheimian thinking predominate. The 'post' genres have references to threefold modes of thinking – poststructuralism, postmodernism and postcolonialism. Poststructuralism is characterised by the works of Jacques Derrida and Michel Foucault. The renditions of Jameson, Baudrillard and Lyotard characterise the postmodernist school of thought. Postcolonialism takes a position, drawing from the radical legacies, of views beyond colonial temperaments and mentalities and the subaltern genre, building on critical historiographies emphasises on alternate visions of history and realities. This chapter further delves into a brief narrative history of feminism, discourses on the historiography of patriarchy and emergent genus of thought. The deliberations are in terms of comprehension of feminist ontology, epistemology and praxis.

Structuralism

Structuralism is based on the assumption that the social life is a sign system, with sign being anything that determines something else. Signs are codes that represent underlying structures and these are essentially context specific (Eco, 1973). So structuralism operates on this basic premise that the society is full of sign systems determining meanings. First meanings are established by people of specific cultures who inhabit society, this meaning is then carried forward through history and then it takes varied forms. That is how ideas get fixated and structures get established in society. Laws of communication are the laws of culture and this culture can be studied by language games in society. The main assumptions of structuralism are that all patterns of human behaviour are codes, with characteristics of language. Human beings have an innate structuring capacity which determines the limits within which the structures of all types of social phenomena can be formed. Social reality can be described as binary oppositions.

Ferdinand de Saussure and C. S. Peirce have further discussed the various kinds of signs in society – symbols (arbitrary devices such as the words of verbal language), indexes (symptoms or natural events from which we can infer other events) and icons (category of signs supposed to possess some of the properties of their referent. The semiotic roots of structuralism are sought in the works of Saussure and the anthropological roots in the works of Levi-Strauss. Apart from the two core thinkers, the other schools within structuralism are macro- and microstructuralism, structuration theory and references to structure in the works of Comte, Vico, Durkheim, Mauss and Halbwachs, Piaget and German sociologists.

Commencing with Ferdinand de Saussure, the basic contention is that semiotics covers the field of culture or social life – the task of semiotics is to isolate different systems of signification, each of them ruled by specific norms and to demonstrate that there is signification and there are norms. The semiotic approach thus signifies that any cultural manifestation can be viewed as a communication process (Robey, 1973). Language is a social system that is coherent and susceptible to explanation and understanding as a whole, syntax and semantics together constituting a group of rules imposed on individuals and to which individual thought must be submitted if it seeks expression. Second there is an element of arbitrariness of the verbal sign, the signifier, which being conventional supposes neither an intrinsic rapport with the concept which constitutes its signification, the signified, nor an inherent stability with it. Further, Saussure made a distinction between langue, the institution of language, and, on the other hand, parole, or the particular and individual acts of linguistic expression. The key principle of the structure of language is that it forms a system that is fundamentally one of contrasts, distinctions and ultimately oppositions, since the elements of language do not exist in isolation but in relation to one another (Lane, 1970).

Claude Levi-Strauss discusses social structures as systems formed by customs and the unconscious structures underlying institutions and social relations are the basic material from which the models that constitute the social structure are built. So structuralism goes beyond pure description towards a quality of rationality underlying social phenomena. Analysing myths, Levi-Strauss has proposed that consciousness of structures per se is not possible; awareness of concrete manifestations is a likelihood. With binary oppositions as core to structures, the goal of structuralist analysis is to realise the whole inventory of social relations that the unconscious reason operates on. In the semiological science of social forms, Levi-Strauss proposes a theory of social organisation wherein the primitive societies are said to be constituted of distinct and complex social forms; kinship phenomena have effects within these forms and there is a relationship between these social forms and processes of history (Jenkins, 1979). Levi-Strauss is influenced by Saussurean linguistics, primarily three principles of the tradition: language to be studied in itself before its relationship with other systems; speech as the audible structure of language to be broken down into finite number of minimal elements such as phonemes on the phonological level and elements of a language are to be defined by their mutual relationships. These relationships are of two kinds: paradigmatic relationships between elements which can be substituted for each other and syntagmatic relationships between elements which can combine together (Sturrock, 1999).

Levi-Strauss has discussed (through his analysis of the code of kinship and marriage in his first book *Elementary Structures of Kinship*) that all human social phenomena including cultural practices in any society constitute language. Hence, their regularities may be reduced to the same set of rules that define and govern language. Roland Barthes has used the term 'code' to cover all types of socially employed systems of communication – social codes having their own lexicon and vocabulary. The other emphasis in Straussian structuralism is the emphasis on wholes or totalities. The whole is explained in terms of the relationships that exist between the parts, structuralism seeking the structures not at an observable level but below or behind the level of empirical reality. Further, the relationships that exist at the observable and at the subtle levels can be viewed as binary oppositions in two senses – analogous comprising logically opposite pairs and those that are not logically pairs of complementary, exhaustive, mutually exclusive categories, but shown to be perceived as such within specific contexts. In the scheme of Levi-Strauss, structuralism focuses on synchronic rather than diachronic structures – structures being developed and constituted not by historical processes but by the network of existing structural relations. Structuralist analysis focuses on laws of transformation rather than causal analysis (Lane, 1970). Using Freudian analysis of symbolic system of dreams to reconstruct individual history, Levi-Strauss has analysed the symbolic systems of myths in order to reconstruct cultural histories and along the lines of Parsons focused on universal patterns of oppositions to explain social reality (Kurzweil, 1980). Levi-Strauss' works in the anthropological genre signify a cultural symbolism of sorts referring to a mode of thinking shared by all humans irrespective of time or place; symbols are open to a great variety of different and complementary interpretations and the systematic relationship between symbols and the abstract level of interpretation is a means of establishing these relationships rather than an end in itself.

References to structure are also found in the works of Comte, Vico, Durkheim, Mauss and Halbwachs, Piaget and German theorists. Comte saw the relationship between language and the social order and that society comprises elemental structures, static and dynamic – which are conceptually antecedent to individuals. Relations of resemblance are constitutive objects of static study, and the relationships of structure in motion are aspects of dynamic study. Vico's structuralist thought reflects in the endeavour to discern the recurrent patterns and structures of events, principle or recurring stages/phases through which history passes (moving beyond conventional and unilinear historiographies and myths as affecting the development of culture and human consciousness. Durkheim's treatment of structure refers to a form in the process of becoming and post-Durkheimian understanding by Mauss and Halbwachs has discussed (apart from the mechanical and organic aspects of social solidarity as discussed by Durkheim as structural features) the patterning of social relationships and objective manifestations of recurrent human interactions. Halbwachs has, in his work on the *Social Bases of Memory* (1925), looked at the social sources of individual memory. Through an examination of what he calls the affirmative ideal in each of the structural systems of inquiry, Piaget works towards the fundamental nature of structuralism and the common denominator in all these systems. According to Jean Piaget, a structure is composed of three key ideas – wholeness, transformation and self-regulation. Within the context of German theorisations, Marxist thinkers are concerned with analysing structures of modes of production and social formations as well as with notions of totality. Leopold von Wiese, influenced by Simmel's forms of interaction or sociation, has developed aspects of structuralism on four basic concepts – social process, social distance, social space and social formation. Social structure is conceived as an abstract model of social relations between individuals and groups, which arise from and depend upon individual interaction and constitute a representation of society that is constructed by actors themselves (Mills, 1959; Popkin, 1999; Bottomore and Nisbet, 2004).

Other versions of structuralism are macro- and microstructuralism and the structuration theory of Giddens. Macrostructuralism of Peter Blau is built on two key concepts of heterogeneity and inequality that are in turn determined by consolidation and intersection of parameters which constitute social dynamics. Nominal and graduated parameters, intertwined with inequality and heterogeneity, determine the nature and extent of social integration. The microstructuralism of Randall Collins commences with conceptions of structure as reifications and metaphors to then formulate explicit conceptions of social structure as chain of interaction rituals stretched out in time through their repetition by individuals in concrete settings. Macro dimensions of space, time and size impact on these interaction rituals. The structuration theory of Giddens communicates the duality of structures, i.e., social structure is used by active agents. And in so using the properties of structure, they transform or reproduce this structure. Structure has been conceptualised by Giddens as rules and resources that actors use in interaction contexts that extend across space and over time. Rules and resources are transformational and meditating. Institutions are systems of interaction in societies that endure over time and distribute people in space. The extent and form of institutionalisation in societies is related to structural principles which are inherently contradictory. Both the ontological security of the agents and the institutionalisation of structures in time and space depend upon routinised and regionalised interactions among actors (Giddens, 1974; Giddens, 1987; Turner, 1987).

Hence, structuralism has many connotations ranging from linguistic to anthropological towards domains of micro and macrostructural theorising and the structuration aspects. The fundamental aspect of structure remains with differential manifestations of norms and forms of the same.

Poststructuralism

Poststructuralism is a genus of thinking beyond the structuralist claims attributed mainly to the works of Jacques Derrida and Michel Foucault. It is a position between structuralism and postmodernism, with crucial phases such as critical modernism, deconstruction, Foucault's genealogy and postmodernism. Two legacies within poststructuralist thought are Saussurian and Nietzschean. The Saussurian stance is evident in Habermasian communicative rationality and Derrida's deconstruction (focusing on the aesthetics of difference, text as indeterminate and unstable, dualism of rational/irrational and discursive/nondiscursive as well as double reading). The Nietzschean stance is evident in Foucault's will to knowledge/power, transgression of discursive by nondiscursive and the text as discreet and decomposed into a relationship between body and desire (Pandey, 1995). Grenberg (1999) has proposed that both Derrida and Foucault are interested in the systematic nature of structures that are used to create meaning and order in human experience. Derrida's investigations are concerned with the matrix of language, and he shows how the concepts of society, culture and the individual are produced as a function of language. Foucault's work is concerned with the matrix of power in the social order and its role in constructing and changing concepts of society and culture. The analysis has been in terms of how factors affect the ultimate expression of power and the inevitable links between bodies of knowledge and the systems of social control. Through revisionist readings of history, Foucault has proposed that society and culture are determined by their relations to social norms and specific forms of discourse.

Commencing with Jacques Derrida (the French thinker heavily influenced by structuralism), the core proposition is that things do not have a single basic meaning and there is fragmentation, conflict and discontinuity in matters of history, identity and culture. The central theoretical concern of Derrida is deconstruction primarily concerning how meanings of 'texts' can be plural and unstable instead of fixing them to a rigid structure. The discussion of Derrida is within the overarching domain of 'Grammatology' as a type of knowledge concerning 'writing' which is a manifestation of that knowledge. Deconstruction is thus a method of inquiry, a social play of presence and absence with difference as the guiding principle. There is a search for hidden meanings of the text; texts which are stratified in the sense that they bear along with them a whole network of articulated themes and assumptions whose meaning everywhere links with other texts or genres or topics of discourse. Language in Derrida is a system of difference, 'subject' is a product of language and hence subject inspires difference. It is this play of differences which determines the identity of the subject and thus understanding of the 'text' and the structures embedded in them as essential to understanding society. There is an 'aesthetics of difference' aspect to deconstruction, positing that text (social text) is indeterminate and writ with dualisms (Doshi, 2003).

Derridaen method of deconstruction has concepts of double reading, erasure and difference (Critchley, 2007). The ethics of deconstruction purport a closure of metaphysics, and influenced by Husserl and Heidegger, a clotural reading of texts (this has reference to Derrida's texts called *Voice and Phenomenon and Violence and Metaphysics*). Closure is the double refusal both of remaining within the limits of the tradition and the possibility of transgressing that limit – a constant and essential gesture within the logic of deconstruction. A deconstructive reading shows both how a text is dependent upon the presuppositions of a metaphysics of presence or logocentrism. Further, there is a connection between deconstruction, phenomenology and the thinking of being – hence poststructuralism having a connection with writings of Husserl and Heidegger.

In 'Of Grammatology', Derrida discusses the way in which those who write about language have always privileged speech over writing and about what is at stake in that hierarchisation. Arguing that all those qualities which are said to characterise writing, as distinct from speech, turn to hold for speech also, Derrida uses Saussurian theory of linguistics to develop his theory of language. In 'Writings and Difference' he has written two views of interpretation – one retrospective, which attempts to reconstruct an original meaning or truth, the other prospective, which explicitly welcomes the indeterminacy of meaning which builds into notions of free play. 'Speech and Phenomena' is a unified work of philosophical analysis concerned with Husserl's theory of signs and in particular with the role and status in phenomenology of the notions of voice and presence. Husserl's account views signs as derivative and dependent indications of meaning, which, in turn, is seen as what is present to consciousness at the moment of utterance, Derrida shows that by Husserl's own account of time, meaning can never be a simple presence, but a part of system of 'traces' and contrasts which exceeds any present instant – technically the deconstructionist argument (Culler, 1999).

The nature of the project towards which all writings of Derrida contribute is that of readings of various texts, constructions of one's own texts and reexamining logocentrism and the metaphysics of presence. Structures are all pervasive and deterministic and drawing largely from structures of language, which exist a priori and hence prior differentiation is assumed. Structures are composed of signifying events which depend on differences, which are themselves the product of events. Difference is the key operational principle of Derrida – difference being the systematic play of differences, of traces of differences, of the spacing by which elements refer to one another. Deconstruction thus is composed of undertaking a double reading, describing the ways in which lines of argument in the texts it is analysing call their premises into question, and uses a system of concepts within which a text works to produce constructs, such as 'differance' and 'supplement' that challenge the consistency of the system (Sturrock, 1999).

Rejecting Weberian rationality, Foucault has posited economic determinism as limiting and hence advocated for a structural linguistic premise to comprehend the social fabric. Foucauldian repertoire has been constructed out of case studies made of social institutions namely the penal system and psychiatric institutions. These social institutions do not operate in isolation but are tied up to complex operations of power in our society; individual freedom further being constrained by social conditioning, hence challenging Sartrean notions of existential freedom (Strathern, 1998). The core of Foucault's poststructuralist contentions proposes that language is the basis to understand society. The meaning of the signified (object) is at the discretion and social conditioning of the individual. Binary oppositions found in language are also found in knowledge and social structure. The structure of language is a dominant one and people come into existence through language and thus one is not 'free' to think outside the rules of one's language. The locus classicus of Foucault's analysis emerges through three key discursive domains – knowledge, power and discourse. Further, his thorough critiques of reason, individual and truth emerge from his anti-teleological understanding of history rejecting its portrayal as a grand scheme or a master narrative. Foucault's earlier work is described as archaeology that sought to expose the implicit knowledge that is a prerequisite and sometimes a catalyst for specific social practices, institutions and theories. Later he adopted another approach in order to examine and explain the changes in systems of discourse and their nondiscursive practices in the social power structure – genealogy. Genealogy has focused on the historical transformations and manifestations of power and how that has affected and produced the individual as subject (Grenberg, 1999).

Knowledge in the Foucauldian scheme is primary and a domain perpetuating subjectivation of the subject. Each historical age is characterised by particular forms of knowledge which are called epistemes – means a set of presuppositions that organise what counts as knowledge, truth and reality. Knowledge and truth are not essential and ahistorical, but are produced by epistemes and, at the same time, hold that episteme together. This means that knowledge and truth are tied up with the way in which power is exercised in our age and are themselves caught up in power struggles. Power is a discursive formation manifesting as a structure of knowledge and not operating without resistance. Hence, knowledge and power are intertwined – power has a capillary form existence and is exercised through multitude of interactions at the micro level of society called micropolitics, thereby rejecting the notion that power is located in an overarching 'state'. The chief proposition is that micropolitics of power relations operate in different localities, contexts and situations. This leads to conclude that there is an intimate relationship between systems of knowledge which codify techniques and practices for exercise of social control and domination within particular localised centres. The relationship between knowledge and power manifests in the celebrated Foucauldian phrase of 'knowledge is power'. Knowledge gives rise to technologies that exercise power and the knowledge – power relationship encourages struggles at multiple levels. Truth is produced by power – interpretation tied to the operation of power and domination. Works such as Discipline and Punishment, Panopticon and History of Sexuality demonstrate this knowledge-power connection. The archaeology of knowledge and the genealogy of power operationalise social control.

Discourse is the third domain in Foucault's analysis. Power and knowledge are used to control society through discourse, and discourse according to Foucault meant social institutions, discipline and language. Discourse provides a framework of thinking given by language and conditioned by history and systems of categorisation and exclusion upon which society depends. The central problematic in Foucault is the conflict between the subject and the discourse of which the subject is a part. Proposing systems of regularities which have a decisive role in the history of societies, the archaeology of discourses seeks to discover the whole domain of institutions, economic processes and social relations on which discursive formations can be articulated.

Foucault combines traditional analysis of Marxism, functionalism and pragmatism, using them all to cut through language and arrive at underlying beliefs or structural codes of knowledge. Search for structures of knowledge has led Foucault to introduce the concept of historical blocks of time, arguing that this allows him to study 'periods dominated by a specific knowledge.' In comprehending discourse and structures of knowledge, Foucault unveils strategies that sanction 'conceptualising rituals' and divergences from conventional history. Syntax is put into historical context through the four cornered system or the 'quadrilateral of language' comprising proposition, articulation, designation and observation. There is a move away from cultural totalities, refuting continuity of history and grand theorisations (Kurzweil, 1980).

Foucault rejects the authority of both logic and conventional narrative and reaffirms the primacy of discourse. The regulatory principles of analysis of discourse as proposed by Foucault in the 'Discourse on Language' are the notions of events, series, regularity and the possible conditions of existence. These conditions of existence are not to be sought in some correlation of 'what is said' with an 'order of things' which pre-exists and sanctions one 'order of words' against another. They are to be found in two kinds of restraint placed on discourse since the time of its domestication by the Greeks: external, on the one side, consisting of the repressions or displacements corresponding to those governing the expression of desire or the expression of power, and internal, on the other, consisting of certain rules of classification, ordering and distribution and certain 'rarefactions' which have the effect of masking discourses' true nature as free play (White, 1999).

Discourse is situated and classified by reference to the epistemes referring to the 'total set of relations that unite, at a given period, the discursive practices that give rise to epistemological figures, sciences and possibly formalised systems' of knowledge. Catachresis (i.e., distinction between literal and figurative meaning of words) is the basis of all language, and discourse takes its origins in a tropological space, unfolding within one or another of the fundamental modalities of figuration in which a relationship between 'words and things' can be construed. Tropology thus constitutes the basis of what Foucault calls the 'episteme' of an age in the history of thought and expression and of the archaeological method which primarily comprises analogies and differences (White, 1999).

Postmodernism

Postmodernism is an epistemological reaction to modernism and Enlightenment rationality, providing a whole new way of thinking and being in the world. Moving away from bourgeoisie nationalisms and overarching cultures, it recognises a different cultural politics of sorts. With key proponents as Lyotard, Jameson and Baudrillard, the postmodernist stance rejects totalising macro perspectives on society and history favoured by modernity in favour of micro theory and micro politics. Modernist assumptions of social coherence and notions of causality are deferred in favour of multiplicity, plurality, fragmentation and indeterminacy. There is a simultaneous critique of the modern belief that 'theory mirrors reality', taking instead perspectivist and relativist positions, challenging a broad array of discourses and institutionalised forms of power. Postmodernism is thus a discourse of plurality, difference and multinarratives that has brought about visibility to important ideological and structural forces such as race, gender and class – by acknowledging the question of power and value in the construction of knowledge and subjectivities.

It raises questions regarding how culture is inscribed in the production of centre/margin hierarchies and the reproduction of postcolonial forms of subjugation. The understanding of reality is constructivist and contextualist, utilising methods of deconstruction and intuitive interpretation, proposing micronarratives and genealogy to replace conventional explanations. 'Binary opposites' that traditionally governed Western philosophy are challenged and in the deconstructionist sense as propagated by Lyotard, metanarratives are dispositioned as totalising. Fragmentation of knowledge and culture, unearthing domains of micropolitics, discursive domains of culture as a category of analysis (in the Jamesonian sense, postmodernism is declared the cultural logic of late capitalism and aspects of popular culture, and postmodern culture as integrated into commodity production) and transcending Marxian analysis from realms of production towards Baudrillardian realms of consumption characterise the core of postmodernism (Lash, 1990; Doshi, 2003).

Commencing with Lyotard's position, there is a writing in the wake of French post-Marxism, that is, an enormous reaction on all levels against the various Marxist and Communist traditions in France, whose prime target on the philosophical level is the Hegel/Lukacs concept of totality. Further, there is an allegiance towards Nietzschean thematics of history wherein the debilitating influence of the linearity and temporality of history and historiography is taken cognizance of, in favour of 'consuming the past' – so as to circumvent a social reproduction. This social reproduction through history and historicity arises from the notion that there is a radical differentiation between consumption of past in narrative and its storage, hoarding and capitalisation in 'science' and scientific thought: a mode of understanding that, like the first surplus on the economic level, will determine a whole range of complex and extensive institutional objectifications. The other aspect is the post-Marxian rejection of class as having a strategic position of power in the social fabric, in favour of nonclass formations such as bureaucracy and technocracy. There is a fetish for a 'consumer' or 'postindustrial' society wherein there is a shift from the older industrial technologies towards newer informational ones – where there are newer versions and the global expansion of capitalism. There is a conception of the 'culture industry' and the penetration of commodity fetishism into those realms of the imagination and the psyche (Taylor and Winquist, 1998). Difference is celebrated through notions of a 'schizophrenic ethic' parallel to the repudiation of Habermasian consensus community, in which the dissolution of the self into a host of networks and relations, of contradictory codes and interfering messages is prophetically valorised. Lyotard's ultimate vision of science and technology is a search not for consensus, but for 'instabilities' as a practice of paralogism, in which the point is not to reach agreement but to undermine from within the very framework in which the previous 'normal science' has been conducted (Jameson, 1998).

Harvey and Roberts (1993) have proposed that Lyotard's aesthetic critique of language, literature and discourse have professed him as a systematic heir of Wittgenstein's philosophy of language and bringing in of that genus of thought within the philosophy of science and technology. Drawing from phenomenology (primary influence being Merleau Ponty) and aesthetic theorisations (works of Lhote and Kaufmann), the focus is on dispelling the idealistic belief that reason has the capacity to totalise and master knowledge. For Lyotard, art and artistic creation, at certain critical moments, breaks away from the collective superego and creates a discourse to unmask the micropolitics of power. Pagan theatre (suppressed for parodying the hypocrisy of the republican order), as discussed by Lyotard in his essay 'Jewish Oedipus', is a depiction of signs being acts of representation, evoking both imaginary constructs and positioning in 'reality'. Hence, pagan and libidinal manifestations in art and society form the foundations of Lyotard's later concerns with the sublime along with the notions of 'differend' through the logic of nonconvergence as expressed in 'The Intractable'. Apart from art works, literary works are for Lyotard, a mapping of the dystopia (space for subjective dislocation common to all transhistoric individuals to which the literary craft gives expression) and in general lead to a rethinking of the spatiality of the text.

Hence, Lyotard's seminal work, *The Postmodern Condition* (1979) has obtained the position of criticising the 'order' or 'consensual' theorisations of Durkheim, Weber, Comte, Spencer and Parsons as well as a critique of conflict theorisations as positing order as a Utopia (Marx, Simmel, Mills to Marcuse and Habermas), towards an incredulity of metanarratives and the penchant for the evolutionary logic. With arguments on the state of knowledge in postindustrial societies, Lyotard contends that it is a paradigm shift from structure to culture as an analytical genus. Further, there is a fetish for annihilation from emancipatory and scientific metanarratives the locus classicus of the work lies in the argument that prevalent knowledge is a formulation of the 'discourse' – fragmentation, disjunctures and discontinuities as characterising the same.

The positions of Baudrillard develop upon two core issues to weave the postmodern theorisation – the nature of contemporary reality and notions of cultural consumption. Hence, within the frame of reference of the contemporary society as being the 'society of images' which are in effect simulations, the notions of consumer society are conceived (which involves consumption of signs and images). The three prominent themes in the writings of Baudrillard are the reality of society, the relationship between reality and representations (code, sign and image), and the consumer society. Commencing with Marxian understandings of production and production relations, Baudrillard has catapulted the understanding onto domains of consumption and relating the same to images or representations of the media society. Drawing from Saussure, linguistic structuralism is the other prominent influence in Baudrillardian scheme of things.

Hence with the cumulative influence of linguistics, philosophy and Marxian analysis of capitalism, two domains predominate in Baudrillardian analysis – simulation society and consumer society. The aspect of simulation society propounds the notion that vis-à-vis the real, it is the aspect of imagery or representation that dominates the social fabric. The social world is constructed by modes or simulations which are hyperreal. Phases of simulations and hyperreality are constructed which include the image as reflection of reality; images disguise or conceal reality; total absence of reality (signifying a simultaneous shift from a capitalist-productivist society towards a neo-cybernetic capitalist society wherein instead of production, reproduction controls society) and no relation to reality as the fourth order whence all difference is negated. The last phase is further qualified by Baudrillard as a culture characterised by transpolitical, transaesthetic and transsexual attributes. With respect to the domain of consumer society and related deliberations, within the Marxian repertoire, Baudrillard inserts the arguments of transition from production to reproduction (images and information being more important than solid commodities) and that of the cultural superstructure having a power of its own (not being a mere reflection of what happens at the economic base). Hence owing to this acceptance of the micropolitics of power, the consumer society is also influenced by signs and images which intensify social stratification. At the base of the consumer society, there is a substantial communication system of signs and images which constitute simulations. These signs and images create classes of different commodities of consumption which then determine social stratification. What is consumed is not objects but signs and consumption in the Baudrillardian scheme of things are a systemic act of manipulation of signs. Code is another core theme in his analysis wherein objects or consumption items are given signs whose value is determined by a disciplinary code. Code is a controlling system of signs which guide and control the signs, and the items of consumption are a part of the sign system. The entire class structure in the postmodern society is subordinate to signs, images, codes and simulations. If production is the key to analyse class antagonism, code constitute the dominant factor to explain postmodern society; interruptions to which can be brought about through fracturing and symbolic disorder (Doshi, 2003).

Jameson's neo Marxian stance emerges in terms of his analysis of culture in terms of late capitalism. The postmodern culture is integrated into commodity production primarily signifying that culture is commodified and subordinated to class analysis. In his scheme, the postmodern repertoire supports plurality of social groups, Marxian metanarratives and dialectics. Postmodernity is characterised by a loss of historicity and a simultaneous insertion of culture as a categorical imperative in Marxian economic determinism. This culture is commodified, is integrated into commodity production, engineers micropolitics and is represented in a text which is a structure of sign flow resisting meaning with a fundamental inner logic of transcending any canon or regulation (Kolakowski, 1978).

For Habermas, postmodernism involves an explicit repudiation of the modernist tradition – the return of the middle-class philistine ejection of the modernist forms and values and as such the expression of a new social conservatism (Taylor and Winquist, 1998). There is a penchant for the Derridaen concept of 'differance' – and a radial hermeneutics of social processes leading to a distinction between system integration and social integration – the distance being evident in the modernist period due to differentiation of the subsystems, decentering of the worldviews (Weberian disenchantment of the world) and the uncoupling of the law from morality (Jay, 1998).

Postmodernism essentially draws heavily from the Derridaen concept of deconstruction primarily concerning the shattering of the logic of key ideas (Royle, 2007). Institutions and framing creates indivisible lines and borders and boxes create structures which need to be penetrated. From language, these get reflected in the social structure and then the exercise needs to be geared towards decentering – of the human subject, institutions and logos; it is a question of the deconstruction of logocentrism or of the centrism of language in general. Deconstruction is writ by the logic of destabilisation and spectrality.

Jameson (1991) has thus proposed that postmodernism is generally viewed from an antimodernist standpoint and posits a social and political conception of a new social system beyond classical capitalism. Alliance is demonstrated towards 'populist cultures' and the need to transcend the binaries of the antithetical traditions of the 'classical' and the 'popular'. The line of argument is carried forward towards the conception of cultural mutation in which what used to be stigmatised as mass or commercial culture is now received into the precincts of a new and enlarged cultural realm.

Postmodernism presupposes a postmodern social theory which is inherently interdisciplinary combining sociological perspectives and nonsociological perspectives such as literary criticism, anthropological perspectives and the critique of modernity. Liberal postmodern theorists such as Giddens and Habermas have looked at postmodernism largely from the perspective of modernity; from the lens of Jameson it is about culture products and linked to the politics of culture and from the positions of Rosenau and Baudrillard it is about rejecting metanarratives, grand narratives and totalisations. Further, it instils a comparable critical sensibility to the spatiality of social life, a practical theoretical consciousness that sees the lifeworld of being creatively located not only in the making of history but also in the construction of human geographies, the social production of space and the restless formation and reformation of geographical landscapes: social being actively emplaced in space and time in an explicitly historical and geographical contextualisation (Soja, 1997). There is a revisioning of the ontological nexus of space-time-being and differential spatialities of real, hyperreal and virtual nature.

To further deliberate on postmodern social theory, Seidman (1994) proposes that these challenge the Enlightenment paradigm of social knowledge. Signs of postmodernity are visible in the process of de-differentiation (the breakdown of the boundaries between social institutions and cultural spheres) and the 'deterritorialisation' of national economies and cultures. Lyotard's content in postmodern social theorisation is the assertion of the decline in the legitimating power of the metanarratives. The major theme of the postmodern turn has been the decentering of the subject and the social world. Instead of viewing knowledge in terms of an ahistorical mind and proposing a language of truth and enlightenment, there is the discursive realm of dominant and subjugated knowledges, multiple subjects or producers of knowledges and the interconnection of knowledges to various axes of domination and resistance. The position of Richard Rorty also concerns the theme of decentering of culture and society, the discourse is on traditions and communities that produce multiple vocabularies of self and the world. The broader genealogy is about a new cultural politics of difference which proposes a decentred perspective of the self, wherein identities are viewed as fractured, multiple and protean. There is a shift from a language of subject-object dualism, objectivity and truth, to a perspective which asserts the interconnection of knowledge and power and which troubles the boundaries between science, rhetoric and the narrative. Anti-foundationalism and subjectivity lenses are unearthed in terms of a critique of an Archimedean standpoint theorisation for its exclusionary politics. Binaries are propositioned and transcended, and as proposed by Zygmunt Bauman, postmodern social analysis is inherently a hermeneutic inquiry. In the postmodern social theory context, two theorists James Clifford and Richard Brown have introduced rhetorical and literary aspects into the analysis. Whereas James Clifford proposes for the introduction of metaphor and allegory into social analysis, Brown – through his textualist approach – has proposed the view of society less as a social system than as a symbolic meaning produced construction rooted in historically specific linguistic and discursive practices. The linguistically organised subjective and social orders are not fixed or stable; but shifting, unstable and sites of contestation, thus paving the epistemological way for Wittgensteinian language games and a new cultural politics of difference.

Postcolonialism

Postcolonialism displays a position beyond colonial temperaments and mentalities. There is a disappointment with the politics of liberation advocating that a narrative which posits an enabling arche and a vindicating telos is no longer an adequate figure for plotting the human trajectories in society. Hence, there is instigation for different practices and re-interpretable and redeployable experiences in which the formerly silent native speaks and acts on the territory taken back from the colonialist. Embedded within it are certain dimension of anti-Westernism and reformism, moving away from the 'episode' of colonial rules. Postcolonialism is thus interested in the genealogy of contemporary culture and ideology of erstwhile 'colonies' in a nonsynchronous and nonlinear manner. It signifies a freedom from the sovereign historical force of imperialism – and its power to hegemonise everything within its dominion. Postcolonial cultures are those affected by the imperial forces from the moment of colonisation to the present days. There is a continuity of preoccupations throughout the historical forces initiated by European imperial aggression (Doshi, 2003). The core characteristic of postcolonialism is the literary content and intent – postcolonial literatures having emerged in their present form out of the experience of colonisation and asserted themselves by foregrounding the tension with the imperial power and by emphasising their differences from the assumptions of the imperial centres. There is a critically looking at of the 'institutionalisation and subsequent valorisation of English literary studies to a shape and ideological content developed in the colonial context'. Further, criticality traverses towards domains of the 'Othering of the colonised' comprising naturalising of the constructed values of civilisation, humanity, etc., which conversely established savagery, native and primitive as their antithesis and as the object of a reforming zeal.

As per Edward Said, the core premise of postcolonialism is 'constant affiliation under the guise of filiations'. It recognises that the cultural hegemony still persists despite the colonial rule being over – language being an important medium through which hierarchical structures of power are perpetuated and conceptions of 'truth', 'order' and 'reality' become established. In asserting difference from the imperial centre, issues of identity (through geographical and linguistic discourses of place and displacement) as well as the centre-periphery discourses predominate. Postcolonialism is thus going beyond the aesthetic and social values of colonialism; the formal and historical constraints that colonialism brings into the genre and the oppressive political and cultural assertion of metropolitan dominance of centre over margin. Marginality is the subject position in the postcolonial discourse and there is a simultaneous challenging of the 'cultural cringe' inspired by imperial dominance wherein native is attributed the status of 'otherness'. Disjunctures and difference dominate postcolonial literary evidences – Rushdie's *Midnight Children* and Gandhi's *Hind Swaraj* being illustrations of the same. Chakrabarty et al. (2007) have looked at the historical complexities involved in nations born under the aegis of the colonial rule evolving into postcolonial polities. Although decolonisation is a process signifying a complete cultural and institutional autonomy for the once-colonised, the nature of transition is essentially fragmentary and incomplete. For instance certain postindependence events have demonstrated the colonising tendencies that an anticolonial nationalism may display as it mutates into official nationalism with an assumption of power by the nationalists.

From the feminist lens, John (1996) has proposed that postcolonialism involves revisiting of certain theoretical constructs – a different kind of reading preparing the ground for alternate theorisations and divergences. Utilising the historical and genealogical approach, the multiple subject positions are emphasised. Hence, although postcolonialism involves a departure from colonial existentialities, the transnational nature of the 'west' as a category extending beyond geographical determinations and creating new and specific loci of power/knowledge through the manifold process of westernisation cannot be negated. Hence, postcolonialism from an epistemological point of view is a departure from universal forms and norms of theorisations towards partial and composite theories. Damodaran and Unnithan-Kumar (2000) have proposed that within the postcolonial context, discourses on modernity and state have had effects on the shifting notions of identity. Bayly (2007) has understood postcoloniality from the point of view of Vietnam, wherein legacies of colonialism and socialism have played out in ways to comprehend the moral and social ambiguities of postsocialist societies. The core contention is that several key traditions and neo-traditions of the socialist ecumene in Vietnam have endowed new life in the Vietnamese moral legacy. Viewing the lives of educated 'moderns' in Vietnam (who in the study of postcolonies have been identified as 'cultural producers'), their importance as members of a class or social stratum who play a critical role in the creation and dissemination of their homeland's official narratives (primarily narratives of nationhood and other forms of exclusive cultural identity) has been emphasised. Through personal histories and family narratives, the discontinuous nature of transition from colonial to socialist systems – a broad supralocal world of socialist views and values within the postcolonial repertoire has been identified.

Brun and Jazeel (2009) have discussed postcoloniality through the spatial politics of Sri Lanka. Highlighting the importance of space in the ethnic conflict fuelled Sri Lankan civil war, the postcolonial discourses on Sri Lankan nationhood and identity have been highlighted. Sri Lanka's continuing civil war and the postcolonial discourses on Sri Lankan nationhood and identity have been identified. Within the larger gamut of debates on locations and dislocations, postcolonialism and geographies have been perceived to be intimately linked; their intersections evoking the social, spatial and political effects of enduring colonial representations and materialities. Spatialities have been discussed in terms of cities and built spaces, diasporic productions and imaginations, commodity cultures and their concordant networks, knowledge spaces and 'foreign' interventions, landscape and sacred spaces. Ways in which essentialised difference is produced through meaningful spaces; spaces that act and therefore must be imbued with some kind of agency in Sri Lanka's contested politics of ethnicity are a subject matter of the postcolonial deliberation. Contested modes of 'Srilankan-ness' are best regarded as engagements and negotiations with the complexities of living the position of a partially objectified subject. These objectifications are lived in and through the striated spaces of everyday life, whose roots are traced through Ceylon's colonial encounter and postindependence trajectories, space becomes a part of an ever shifting social geometry of power and signification in which the material and the ideological are co-constitutive.

Dube (1997) has suggested that postcolonialism, rather than being a settled stage of history or an exclusive form of knowledge, is a critical perspective probing the contradictions and connections between the colonial state and the Indian nation, exploring the conditions and prospects of modernity and questions the projection of the West as history and destiny. The realisation of the postcolonial perspectives emerge from the subaltern perspectives – the theoretical and political emphasis being a critique of the colonial rule (and its imperial and postimperial historiography) and an interrogation of middle-class nationalism (and its nationalist and left biography). There is an emphasis on the small voice of history that scrambles authoritative pasts to the highlighting of the multiform articulations of the civil-political sphere within a colonial modernity, which exceeds the concerns of the rational and secular historiography. Further, there is an interplay between colonial power and imperial knowledge as a part of the wider excursus into the intimate enmeshments of caste, colonialism and modernity in India. Hence, within the genus of imperial anxieties and colonial contradictions, the assumptions of a stimulus response model between the coloniser and the colonised have been replaced by a more nuanced and acute conceptualisations, highlighting that at stake in colonial histories were critical entanglements in complex fields, the interplay between metropolitan and vernacular, between meaning and power. In the anti-essentialist mode, newer understandings of nation and nationalism have emerged. Historicism emerges as a methodology in the postcolonial genre – juxtaposing totalising and nontotalising trends of thought and positing universals as a part of the immanent critique on structures of domination that predicate themselves on the same universals.

Kandyil (2009) has proposed that postcolonial is about revisiting histories from the below – traditional social fabric coloured by the unquestioning adherence to the irrational ideas and beliefs that conditioned the consciousness of the lower castes in accepting their inferior status in the ritual hierarchy as a part of the natural order of things. Chatterjee (2009) has analysed the writings of Ranajit Guha from the postcolonial lens proposing that postcoloniality entailed a critique of the elitisms of colonialisms and nationalisms from the historiographical point of view. Against history, whose practices are necessarily entwined with the rationality of the state and always implicated in the practices of domination, Guha, invoking Heidegger, has proposed the concept of historicality that could recall the past in the phenomenology of everyday life. Subaltern studies project has undertaken to explore the submerged narratives of the subaltern Indian, who, far from being the metanarrative of European history, covertly inverted the tropes of that metanarrative to produce what Dipesh Chakrabarty calls 'nonmetropolitan histories'.

Focussing on postcolonial writing, Sharma (2003) has focused on images of England and the English in Indian writing in English. It explores how, despite their necessary imbrications in the colonial process and the unavoidable transformations in their social and ideological constructions, educated Indians used literary writing to resist their typification and subjectification as passive objects in the Orientalist discourse. Texts from the nineteenth century to Indian independence are read for resistance, assumption of representational authority, appropriation of language and forms, subversion of colonialist discourses and co-option and complicity. In the British enterprise of acquiring a mastery and command over Indian languages for the purpose of facilitating the governance of India, the intimate connections between knowledge and power underlined by Foucault are obvious. The conquest of India also became a conquest of narrative authority – British conquering and representing the diversity of the 'Indian' pasts through a homogenising narrative of transition from a 'medieval' period to 'modernity'. The connections between English education and British Orientalism, on the one hand, and the Indian nationalism, modernisation and Bengali Renaissance, on the other, have been studied; further, analysis discoursing on how the Indian literary production in the English language deliberately appropriated British 'technologies' and used them to resist British authority. Using novel as a sign and metaphor, Sharma (2003) argued that the appropriation and 'Indianisation' of the form and narration became the first steps in countering the control of Western discourses. This genre of narrative prose then provides a more developed historical analysis of the circumstances of economic, political and cultural domination and repression and is hence important for raising a systematic and concerted challenge to the imposed chronology of what Frederic Jameson has called 'master narratives', ideological paradigms which contain within their plots a predetermined ending. Thus, its use by the Third World resistance writers both appropriates and challenges the historical and historicising propositions, the narrative conclusions, implicated within Western tradition and its development.

Along the lines of propositions of Edward Said in Orientalism, that the Orient is essentially a construction of the West, Indian writing in English proposes representations of England as a protean construction composed of many experiences of the English in the varied contexts of the Indo-English encounter. English education (and subjectification through texts) and direct encounter with

English life constitute two poles of these constructions. The 'internalisation' or 'epidermalisation' (to borrow Fanon's term) of English literary texts, the subversive potential of the 'mastery' and appropriation of the English language, as well as the anticolonial/postcolonial resistance to dominant Western/English discourses are the foci. This has led to the emergence of colonial discourse analysis that has examined Englishness in the widest sense from its determined positions on the margins: not questing for the essence of Englishness but examining the representations it has produced for itself of its Other, against and through which it defines itself, together with the function of such representations in a structure of power in which they are used instrumentally.

Boehmer (2005) has positioned 'colonial', 'colonialist' and 'postcolonial' literatures. Whereas colonial literature is mainly concerned with writings concerning colonial perceptions and experiences, written mainly by metropolitans, but also by creoles and indigenes during the colonial times. Colonialist literature concerns colonial expansion – literature written by and for colonising Europeans about non-European lands dominated by them, embodying the imperialists' point of view. Postcolonial literature is generally defined as that which critically or subversively scrutinises the colonial relationship. Within the discourse of postcolonialism, Boehmer (2005) has proposed that cultural representations were central first to the process of colonising other lands and then to the process of obtaining independence from the coloniser. Thus, postcolonial literatures are concerned with not simply articulating colonial or nationalist preoccupations, they also contribute to the making, clarification and definition of the same preoccupations. Postcolonial critical theory is concerned with key terms such as 'subaltern', 'colonial resistance', 'writing back' and 'hybridity'. Influenced largely by poststructuralism, postcolonial critical discourse is concerned with textual resistance as well as transformations and disjunctures and connections and interrelationships between different writings. Further, postcolonialism also emphasises that the ramifications of colonialism can be traced through metaphors and representative texts, albeit through their pluralised and particularised expressions.

Homi Bhabha's writings in the postcolonial genre are a combination of Lacanian psychoanalysis and Derridaen deconstruction. He theorises colonial mimicry as the representation of the partial presence that disrupts the coloniser's narcissistic aspirations and the subjects Englishness to profound strain whereby 'the familiar, transported to distant parts, becomes uncannily transformed, the imitation subverts the identity of that which is being represented, and the relation of power, if not altogether reversed, certainly begins to vacillate' (Roy, 1998: 46). Hence, much of the recent works on colonial and postcolonial South Asia has engaged the questions of identity and difference at a broader epistemic level – this 'traffic' between identities has surfaced on debates as to how originality and impersonation functions not just for 'western' or 'westernised' subjects but across a range of identities. In the fascination of going 'native' multiple identity issues in the postmodern style have emerged.

Moore-Gilbert (1997) has proposed that postcolonial theory has methodological affiliations to French high theory – Derrida, Lacan and Foucault translating in practice in terms of works of Edward Said, Gayatri Spivak and Michel Foucault. There has been a radical reconceptualisation of the relationship between nature, culture and ethnicity, which has major cultural/political significance. Two strands of theoretical lineages emerge in the context of postcolonialism – Marxian and poststructuralist. In Said's seminal work called 'Orientalism', the abiding line of argument is that Orientalism operates in the service of the West's hegemony over the East primarily by producing the East discursively as the West's inferior 'Other', a manoeuvre which strengthens – indeed, even partially constructs – the West's self-image as a superior civilisation. Spivak (1999) has examined 'othering' in the postcolonial discourse from the Marxist and poststructuralist standpoints. Her application of deconstruction to postcolonial issues can be divided into two strands – the aversion to establish an 'authoritative truth' of the text/problem in question and as an ideology-critique. Further, in countering hegemonic discourses, two arenas in which the re-inscriptions of dominant ideologies take place are definitions of identity and the role of the hegemonic subject. Identity is understood in the Derridaen sense as discursively constructed and there are an inevitable multiplicity of subject positions with which textuality inscribes both author and reader and the subject in general. Building on theoretical premises of Foucault and Derrida, Bhabha has looked at the colonial discourse through his concept of 'mimicry'. This is understood as a form of colonial control generated by the metropolitan coloniser which operates in conformity with the logic of the panoptical gaze of power elaborated in Foucault's Discipline and Punishment. The coloniser requires that the colonised subject adopts the outward forms and internalises the values and norms of the occupying power. Mimicry expresses the 'epic' project of the civilising mission to transform the colonised culture by making it copy or repeat the coloniser's culture. The 'lack' of the coloniser's identity causes the dominant discourse to split along the axis of its power to be representative and authoritative. The other aspect of Bhabha's analysis involves looking at issues of political engagement, resistance and agency – working through the psychic ambivalence on part of both the partners in the colonial relationship. There has been a focus on the psychodynamic and the discursive spheres of colonial relations that constructs 'transitive' resistance in terms of psychological guerrilla warfare and subversion of the terms of the symbolic order which authorises the coloniser's identity.

Subaltern School

The subaltern school legacy is an interdisciplinary organisation of South Asian scholars led by Ranajit Guha commenced in 1970s. The chief purport was that of reconstructing historiographies and developing histories from the below. This involved departures from conventional brands of social histories – national narratives, orientalist images, ethnic stereotypes and Hindu majoritarianism. Subaltern studies primarily are read against liberalism and Marxism and read into the ideologies of difference and otherness. The origins of the legacy lay in accounts of subaltern lives during world wars in the form of memoirs and diaries. After the Russian Revolution, Antonio Gramsci began to weave ideas about subaltern identity into theories of class struggle. With a rapid decline in state-centred historical research, histories from the below flourished. E. P. Thompson's 1963 book 'The Making of the English Working Class' has been cited as an inspiration for the growing number of 'bottom up' studies for people whose histories had been previously ignored. Subaltern school legacy has generally been visualised in terms of three phases: the first phase of peasant struggles, the second phase intertwined with discourses on nationalisms and the literary genres and the third phase has examined the micropolitics of power and reexamined conventional hierarchies in the wake of neoliberalism and globalisation (Ludden, 2002).

The first phase was composed of studies on the peasant movements and insurgency in colonial India. The focus was on exploring the agency of individuals from the below, formation of cliques and power of specific class interests. Coupled with a parallel development of the 'Cambridge School of South Asian History', grand narratives of nationalism were the main subject of contention. The core arenas of deliberation in the first phase were debates on the role of culture in nationalism; struggle within the 'national' regimes and prominence to native culture and popular histories vis-à-vis official histories filled with elites and political parties (Guha, 1982). The second phase brought in the recognition that in the Indian context, stratification on the logic of caste and the basic socioeconomic structure of society are intertwined with nationalism. This socioeconomic structure is supported and perpetuated by the colonial/imperial regime and hence revolution and voices from the below become further complex. The core contentions of the second phase were recognition of the fact that the intensification of exploitation due to class-caste hierarchies formed the basis of second dimension of histories from the below parallel to national histories; popular resistance to state power as the prominent academic theme and a move away from the study of grand revolutions towards more localised personal resistances to the power of elites and states (Foucault's influence). The second phase was also characterised by the effects of the neoliberal regimes and globalisation – an engaging critique of the logic supporting state authority as national boundaries were collapsing under transnational flows and nation was being reconfigured, reimagined and retheorised. Hence in this phase, subaltern studies became an original site of a new kind of histories from the below – a people's history free from national constraints. This also led to a post-nationalist reimagining of the Indian nation at the margins, outside conventional nationalism. Subaltern studies thus rejected official nationalism and developed transnationally – demonstrating a sign of 'political nationalism' losing its grip on the historical imaginations as the nations were reinvented as 'imagined communities'. Further in the second phase, subaltern studies took a linguistic and literary turn, spearheaded by Gayatri Spivak that brought in the bequest of range of 'writings from the below'. Old empirical certainties of modernisation, capitalist development and national progress disassembled in the radical newness of postmodern and postcolonial writings – lending spaces for cultural studies, cultural criticism and cultural politics. This also led to the coming of age of the politics of language, media and representation.

The third phase signified a moving beyond of hard dichotomies of elite and subalterns towards domains of social histories that included more than two storeys. Further looking at other lenses (other than class analysis) gave subaltern studies an entry into 'politics' and the power to threaten the political structure. There was a shift away from subaltern politics in the vein of Garmsci towards cultural history, critical theory and representations of subaltern subjectivity in the vein of Michel Foucault and Jacques Derrida. The prominence of subaltern consciousness led to making of a theory of the 'consciousness vis-à-vis a theory of change' in terms of the subaltern episteme. The subaltern classes, specifically peasants gave way to a textuality of colonialism and resistance. This has led to the expanding of the field of subalternity towards a transnational study of colonialism with the chief focus being the dominance of colonial modernity over the indigenous culture. Hence, the discourse has catapulted onto a postcolonial critique of modern, European and Enlightenment epistemologies. This has further led to a rewriting of the nation outside state-centred national discourse that replicates colonial power/knowledge in a world of globalisation (Ludden, 2003).

Ontologically thus the subaltern school reinvented 'subalternity' by going beyond Gramscian formulations and positing it vis-à-vis colonial elitism and bourgeoisie nationalist elitism. As this too created binaries of sorts (excluding subalternities from social histories that had more than two differentiations and from political histories as discourses were solely confined to the below), in 1985 David Hardiman and other scholars broadened the scope. The shift was away from studies of subaltern politics in the vein of E. P. Thopmson and Gramsci towards cultural history, critical theory and representations of subaltern subjectivities in the vein of Michel Foucault and Jacques Derrida. Politics and representation are two aspects of subalternity that historians study in records of action and discourse – both evoking anti-hegemonic possibilities. Bernard Cohn and Gayatri Spivak have further explored the cultural perspective to the ontology of subalternity by exploring the language and textuality of discursive power.

Epistemologically, it addressed the question of subaltern consciousness as a composite culture of resistance to and acceptance of domination and hierarchy – explored through the 'colonial subject'. Hence post-colonial cultural criticism, deconstructing colonial constructions of power forms the bedrock of the subaltern epistemology. There is a certain rewriting of the nation outside the state-centred national discourse that replicates colonial power/knowledge in a world of globalisation (Ludden, 2002). This new kind of national history contains dispersed moments and fragments which subaltern historians seek in the ethnographic present of colonialism. Methodologically recuperating subaltern subjectivity entails the analytical and rhetorical liberation from its domination by the colonial archive and modernity. Writing such histories constitutes subversive cultural politics because it exposes forms of power/knowledge that oppresses subaltern people. This evokes a new cultural history which is nonlinear, capturing indigenous dissent, symbolic and vernacular.

Some dilemmas and debates that continue to persist are that subaltern political activity has not been able to detach empirically or theoretically from 'elites' – even when detached from nationalist institutions. The thorny question of consciousness centred on the 'composite culture of resistance to and acceptance of domination and hierarchy' remains. The other contradictions that exist are those of subaltern autonomy versus subalterns as a polarised social category, and subalterns as an aggregated group versus differentials within them.

History of Feminism, Patriarchy and Positionalities

The historical journey of feminism can be classified in terms of periods pre and post the world wars. Hence, categorisations can be done in terms of feminism prior to the First World War, between the wars and after the Second World War. Feminism before the First World War is precursored by capitalist development in the late seventeenth century and the worsening legal and economic situation for women. Mary Wollstonecraft's 'A vindication of the Rights of Women' (1792) during the early years of the French Revolution provides the first full expression of early liberal feminism. Main contentions of early liberal feminism are that women and men have the same epistemological resource, the human mind, and are hence equal. Women are considered as rational individuals, to have equal rights. These principles found concrete expression at the Women's Right Convention at the Seneca Falls in the United States in 1848. In

England, John Stuart Mill introduced the question of women's suffrage to the House of Commons in 1857, and his work 'The subjection of Women' was first published in 1859. The latter versions of the liberal stance arose with Betty Friedan's work 'The Feminine Mystique' published in 1963. The work led to a questioning of the socialisation and manipulation of women into believing that their fulfilment lay in the home. The advanced version of the liberal stance came with power feminism that believed women to determine their own rights and life's cartographies, incorporating the ideas of modern liberal theorist John Rawls. Gender equality was perceived to be in the totalitarian interest of the society, however the liberal stance has been criticised on grounds that there is no addressal of structures, equality and role of the state are rhetorical and multiple hierarchies of society are not viewed (Rege, 2003).

Early socialist and Marxist feminism have discussed that capitalist development not only results in women's subordination, but is also upheld by the same. This school developed an analysis that linked sexuality to economic and political issues. Family and sexual relationships, like any other form of social organisation, are perceived to be the product of a particular stage of economic development. They cannot be altered at will, but only as a result of socioeconomic change expressed through class conflict and revolution. This understanding was first developed by Frederick Engels in 'The Origin of the Family, Private Property and the State' published in 1884. Women's oppression came to be understood with differential modes of production and private property and the desire of men to pass property to known heirs made them control women. This motive was believed to disappear with the overthrow of capitalism, when women would no longer be dependent on men. Later versions of Marxist and socialist feminisms propose that women's subordination is a historically specific product of class society. There are two forces at work in history – capitalism and patriarchy. Other aspects of the contentions include the 'domestic labour debate' (changing the definition of the term value attached to the work done by women at home and relating the same to the capitalist economy); Marxist concept of alienation used to represent women's lack of control over sexuality and reproduction and connection between structural changes, kinship relations, establishment of private property and monogamous marriages and control over female sexuality (England, 1993; Peterson and Lewis, 1999; Kachuck, 2003).

Feminist positions in the 'between the wars' period highlighted significant debates – equal political rights versus welfare feminism (to protect women's roles of production and reproduction within familial and work sphere set ups) being the key. The philosophy of not just equal rights but also protective discrimination and the Russian context took forward the Marxist feminist position that women's oppression was a result of class society. Apart from looking at processes that liberate women, the need to look at the fact that questions of sexuality and family organisation would not automatically be resolved through economic change, but must be tackled directly was highlighted. After the Second World War, Simone de Beauvoir's (1908–1986) 'The Second Sex' was recognised as a landmark work. Feminity and domesticity were viewed as not natural attributes of womanhood, but artificial creations that limit women's freedom and deny them the expression of their full humanity. Woman's biology was understood to be as not all governing lending credence to the philosophical premise of existentialism and Sartrean freedom through the prism of women's experiences.

Radical feminism focuses on sexual politics, the core argument being 'personal is political' and the sex class system as recognising the multiple hegemonies of patriarchy. Male power is understood to be socially constructed and patriarchy as all pervasive and embedded in structures and social institutions. The core sites of oppression are family and domains of reproduction, forced heterosexuality and women's oppression in male control of culture, language and knowledge. Radical feminist explanation of patriarchy includes the contentions of Shulamith Firestone that women's oppression is because of reproduction and that sex class system based on relations of reproduction is the key. Not women's biology itself but the value men place on it and the power they derive from control over it is oppressive. The prominent works in the radical feminist genre have been by Susan Brownmiller, Elizabeth Fischer and Mary O'Brien. Further, in terms of the debates on reproduction, the ecofeminist stance brings in another angle in terms of reproduction being the source of women's oppression versus source of superior womanly values (Stanley, 1990).

Postmodern feminism commences with propositions entailing a rejection of a search for truth and certainty, arguing that it is now meaningless in societies that are increasingly characterised by fragmentation, diversity and transience. Labels such as 'woman' can conceal the multiplicity of particular experiences and what needs cognizance is identity politics and micropolitics of power. Power is constructed through language, knowledge and sexuality and has multiple manifestations. This has further led to the development of the conception of feminism at intersectionalities taking into account the vantage points of women at the interconnections and interactions of different forms of oppression; intertwined with dimensions of colonialism, imperialism and nationalism (McCann and Kim, 2003; Rege, 2006).

The epistemological journey from liberal to postmodern feminist stances can be categorised in terms of the first, second and third waves of feminisms – each with their own agendas for women's emancipation. In general the three major assumptions of feminism are as follows: gender is a social construct that oppresses women more than men; patriarchy shapes these constructions and women's experiential knowledge best helps us envision the future of a nonsexist society. Further, the agendas are the task of critique and the task of construction and the recurrent themes include reproduction, representation and the sexual division of labour. The first wave feminists were those in the nationalist movements largely in search of new political identities and emancipation. Significant events in the first wave genre included the work of Mary Wollstonecraft who talked about the psychological and economic damage to women by their forced dependence on men and exclusion from the public sphere. Feminists in that period championed the abolition of slave trade and were active in food boycotts supporting the principles of emancipation, unity and benevolence. In Britain, the first wave was signified by the works of Josephine Butler and the Married Women's Property Act. In Australia and New Zealand, gender issues were brought to light through social reform movements. In China and Egypt, issues of gender were brought to light in 1912–1919 after national change. In the United States, nineteenth-century feminism focused on suffrage primarily through the endeavours of women such as Elizabeth Cady Stanton and Susan B. Anthony. The Seneca Falls Convention, 1848, sought to apply the American Declaration of Independence to women. In 1869, National Woman's Suffrage Association was formed; in 1888, the International Council of Women took shape in the United States. Other significant work included Charlotte Perkins Gilman's 'The Man Made World' (1911) who adopted the socialist feminist position and emphasised on the economic independence of women. In 1833, in Great Britain, the

Co-operative Women's Guild discussed suffrage issues, and in 1874 the radical working-class feminists formed the Women's Protective and Provident League. In 1903, the Women's Social and Political Union (WSPU) was formed by Emmeline Pankhurst and her daughters in Great Britain. In 1908, the WSPU ensured limited franchise for British Women aged 30 and above by 1918 and full suffrage by 1928. The second wave of feminism commenced in the 1960s whence the Women's Liberation Movement (WLM) in the United States extended the terms politics and economy to sexuality. Aspects of 'personal is political' and a new vocabulary of sexual politics were emphasised. In the United States, WLM and radical groups such as the Red Stocking were concerned with reproductive issues and the ubiquity of patriarchy. The significant work of this period was Simone De Beauvoir's 'Second Sex' and in the primarily liberal vein, Betty Friedan's 'The Feminine Mystique' (1963) that described the frustration of white heterosexual middle-class women without careers locked in domesticity. In 1966, Friedan founded the National Organization for Women. In Great Britain, significant events in the second wave included the First Women's Liberation Conference at the Ruskin College, Oxford, in 1970, that forwarded the socialist and liberalist demands for equal pay, 24 hours childcare, free contraception and abortion on demand. In 1972, the Organisation for Battered Women Refugees in Chiswick, London, was formed, and in 1974 the Working Women's Charter was formulated. In 1976, the "Organisation of Women of Asian and African Descent" in Britain was formed. The UN declared the decade for women from 1975 to 1985 which led to several significant developments such as concepts of engendering development (WID/WAD/GRAD) and governance. The period from the 1980s onwards has witnessed the third wave genre focusing on multiple histories, forms and norms of patriarchy, issues of identity, difference and fragmentation (Bryson, 1999; Rege, 2003; Kachuck, 2003; Acharya, 2004).

Feminist Ontology

Feminist ontology comprises an 'engendered' nature of reality and a certain construction of 'womanhood', 'gender', 'hegemonic institution of patriarchy that permeates all spheres of the social fabric' and subjugation of women that exists at subtle, metaphorical, surreal, real and hyperreal levels and contexts. How are then women posited in the brouhaha of the social fabric that is inherently writ with antagonisms and contradictions is the dimension that is discerned. This thus lends space to unearth the regime of patronage and exploitation and unveil the existential spaces for women (Stanley and Wise, 1992).

Facets of feminist ontology that prevail in literature include feminist realism and critical realism; engendered phenomenology; feminist subjectivity and the social construction of gender; feminist materialism; feminist poststructuralism and discourses on subjectivity; postcolonial narratives (decolonising the woman subject); culture, micropolitics and feminist ontology and feminist postmodernism. The ontological stances portray essentially a sort of feminist repertoire on the stage of ways of seeing and viewing the woman self and the world.

Feminist Realism and Critical Realism

Feminist realism as an ontological stance is essentially critical in its approach. Then the truth of reality becomes multidimensional, and the woman's view is the dimension of truth that is most sought after. The introduction of the 'so-called personal' into the scientific objectivity of truth exposes dimensions of criticality and relativism – through uses of accounts of 'experience' of women – persistently undermining the masculine myths of neutrality of truth positions that characterise discourses. Reintroduction of personal voices is a way of reinstating 'truth claims as relative and engendered' – a way of disseminating authority and decomposing the false universality of patriarchal institutionalised meanings of truths. Critical realist and relativist positions that give credence to the 'woman subject' – her views, opinions, sense of being and becoming – provide spaces then for her voices and discourses. Feminist ontology thereby incorporates the qualification of 'relativism' in a realist domain – wherein the conditionalities and positionalities of women determine truth contexts – a landmark departure from one-sided scientific realism and objectivity (Broadbeck, 1968; Roy Bhaskar, 1975; Hardin, 1991).

Engendered Phenomenology

Another dimension of the relativist position in feminist ontology is an engendered phenomenology – to comprehend the differential nature of consciousness that emerges with essentially distinct nature of hierarchy/subjugation and experiences therein. The key deliberation in phenomenology is the critical interaction between the phenomena (the act/event/essence) and the noumena (the actors/precipitating factors/subjects) and the difference that emerges with each changing domains (Schutz, 1952; Craig, 1998). The engendered phenomenology position of feminist ontology posits the argument that subjugation is essentially differential and the 'vindicated subject' is also in many shades of differential consciousness. The points of alignments (of the act and the subject) determine the critical consciousness of that woman subject. To understand and internalise the fact that all 'essences' (of acts and subjects) are not 'essential' but 'differential' and that this difference is determined by encounters with cultures of consciousness and is the key component of engendered phenomenology. This gives spaces to view each 'woman subject' singularly (detached from essentialisms) and examine hegemony of patriarchy through the noumena of the subject (incorporating consciousness, institutions and subjectivities).

Feminist Subjectivity and the Social Construction of Gender

The diametrically polarised positions on discourses of truth and consciousness (which are transcendental in their compositions) are the determination of subjectivity through the lens of social construction (Berger and Luckmann, 1966). That all positions and identities are socially constructed, determined by conditions of language, structure and culture is the key deliberation embedded herein. The composition of the subjective ontology of women is in the following manner – subjectivity determined by language games, subjectivity determined by structure and subjectivity determined by culture. Feminist subjectivity determined by language games is a transcendence of the rules of language (which is structured, hierarchical and determined by popular domains and discourses) to lend a voice to the subaltern woman subject. The structural determinant involves a transcendence of the stratification embedded in the structure (of the social fabric) and the cultural determinant is (under the understanding of the structural conception of culture in sociological terms) about traversing norms embedded in the cultural hegemony which only facilitate a routinised transfer of norms, forms and power which are essentially hierarchical. The three domains combine to present a subjectivity (engendered) that is created through a deconstruction of popular social construction (D'Souza and Pereira, 2002; Kachuck, 2003).

Feminist Materialism

That the nature and culture of existence of women is socially determined (by the prevalent norms and conditions developed through historicity) and is the ontological stance of feminist materialism (Rege, 2003). Two concepts predominate herein – historicism and dialectics. Historicism purports that the soci (onto) logical status of a woman (the securities and insecurities embedded therein) is historically determined, in a truly Engelian-Marxian sense through the varying modes of production and relations of production – the radical overtones also appending elements of sexuality and reproduction. Hence, it is this sociohistorically determined and constructed baggage of oppression that needs to be addressed to reaffirm ontological security in various regionalised contexts. The modicum of attaining this security is through a process of engendered dialectics – attempting to address the antagonisms and contradictions embedded in patriarchy through a series of contradictory movements to eventually attain a synthesis of sorts. Historicism and dialectics collate to form this feminist materialist ontology wherein women's nature of being and existence is not just an outcome of acts of domination to be addressed by differential truth claims and consciousness. Instead it is a historically determined and structurally organised phenomenon that is deeply embedded and hence needs to be addressed through dialectics of positioning and repositioning of women to dodge historical baggage – reconstructing historiographies in the process (Ludden, 2002).

Feminist Poststructuralism

One of the key ontological anchor domains of feminism is the poststructuralist discourse (addressing what Rosi Braidotti sums together as one word 'Foucaultlacanderrida') – which opens up debates about the meaning of the category 'woman'. The fact that any notion of fixed identity category is problematic is a testimony to the proposition that categories under consideration are a constantly shifting signifier of multiple meanings with multiple embedded layers. Hence, the woman is a subject who is constrained by power structures – she becomes an 'effect of language' (language as determinants of and determined by social structure) and 'positioned by discourse'. The subjectivity of women is fractured and fragmented due to competing discourses at the societal level and the disruptive impact of the unconscious at the cognitive level (Lacan's psychoanalytic viewpoint). What needs to be taken cognisance of is the illusory character of the notion of a unified and coherent self of the woman. Rather what is evident is the contradictory dimensions of her identity writ with antagonisms and contradictions of the competing claims of all pervasive patriarchy at the structural level and dimensions of hegemony precipitating onto the cognitive level. To comprehend that the woman subject is at the locus classicus of multiple hegemonies and layers of domination is the heart of the poststructuralist lens (Sturrock, 1979; Doshi, 2003; Kachuck, 2003).

Postcolonial Narratives

The other lens to comprehend women and their corresponding ontological status is to view the same from the lens of colonial/postcolonial narratives. That colonialism/imperialism carries a certain baggage of structures, cultures, norms and forms (Craig, 1998) leading to (in many ways) decentring of the woman subject by injecting newer ways of exploitation/domination and differential binaries. The differential positionalities that colonial narratives bring in towards indigenous women are precisely what postcolonial narratives intent to address. The ontological position of the woman herein is that of a 'decentred, fractured and fragmented subject' – the causative factors for the same being the multidimensional reach of colonialism/imperialism. The woman subject is also a product of multiple binaries of race, caste, class and nationality/ethnicity and sexuality – all an outcome of the gendered hierarchies embedded in the colonial cultures. Hence, the postcolonial narratives attempt twofold ontological tasks – 'decolonising the woman subject/violated woman subject' and 'reinstating an ontological security in various regionalised contexts'. The first one is an account of viewing the context-specific condition and position of women (the nature, norms and forms of hegemony) and not succumbing to grand narratives. The second is a reassertion of the woman as a being in and for herself – not captured by a colonisation of sorts.

Culture, Micropolitics and Feminist Ontology

The other crucial lens of determining feminist ontology is the interplay of 'culture' and 'micropolitics of power' (Kachuck, 2003). That is, how the nature of being of a woman is impacted by culture (the structural and critical conception of culture and not merely the instrumental one) and the micropolitics of power (reproduced by multiple structures and has multiple forms – as in the Gramscian, Foucauldian and the feminist materialist sense). The nature of cultural hegemony is embedded in the socialisation processes – the norms, forms and relations of transferring roles and engagements, determining the freedom over sexuality (or whether freedom exists at all in a truly Sartrean sense) and the nature of emancipation sought by women – whether negotiation, reconciliation, realignment or deconstruction. Hence, enveloped within the above cultures (norms and forms) is the woman's identity and sense of emancipation (ontological security/insecurity). To comprehend that power is all pervasive and manifests in any situation of evident or subtle binaries is the crux of micropolitics. Feminist ontology views the nature of existence of women as an outcome of 'binaries' and 'power domains'. This power is not just of patriarchy as an overarching institution, but also multitude organs systems and structures that support the patriarchal regime such as the family, jurisprudence, governance and society at large.

Feminist Postmodernism

Feminist ontology quintessentially epitomises the postmodern legacy which questions the possibility of the authenticity of experience and the unified woman subject on the origin of all meanings for the lifeworlds of women – emphasising rather on 'intertextuality' of cultural representations, styles and modes of experience. The violated woman's nature of being is not a unified entity determined by some contexts (of ethnicity and nationality alone), but a fragmented and at times fractured selfhood at the juncture of several overlapping categorical imperatives of race, caste, class, patriarchy, ethnicity and nationality (if nationality as a concept exists in the postmodern repertoire. Her diametrical opposition to the liberated woman is in itself hegemony of sorts. Ontology in the feminist postmodern sense is regionalised, transcending grand narratives of conceptions of woman's being towards more discontinued senses of her existence. Binaries of all nature are also a determinant of feminist ontology – where women's nature of being is determined by overpowering oppositions and in the quest of transgressing/annihilating the very same dualities. Being determined by the dual nature of realities and attempting to transcend the same is the essence of ontologies of women in the postmodern (beyond Enlightenment) sense. Difference is the third guiding principle of feminist ontology from the postmodern lens (Doshi, 2003; Raheja, 2003). The difference principle guides analysis and interventions through its emphasis on differentials (of contexts, norms and forms of patriarchy) and the faith in social construction and cultural constitution of the embodied subjectivity of violated women.

Feminist Epistemologies

Feminist epistemologies are a complex composite of instrumental, classical and critical approaches to comprehend knowledge of feminist subjectivity. The instrumental approaches introduce an element of logic to comprehend equity and justice within the feminist repertoire (White, 1991). The classical approaches of liberal, socialist, Marxist and radical are at once emancipatory and critical. The further critical approaches (can actually be called the classical critical) of poststructuralism and postmodernism unveil further elements of subjectivity and criticality in feminist worldviews – discussing episteme of understanding violence, oppression and various dimensions of women's positionality and conditionality (Kachuck, 2003). Apart from the aforementioned conventional classification, epistemologies also assume hybridised versions combining differential and at times juxtaposed stances. The view is deterministically critical (at times with radical overtones) drawing from puritan and pragmatic tenets to achieve emancipatory ideals. Feminist epistemologies can thus be discussed in terms of the instrumental approaches, classical positions, critical theory approaches, poststructuralist and postmodern lenses, and hybridised epistemologies.

Instrumental Approaches

Instrumental approaches propose that similar ontological entities (men and women) warrant similar epistemological positionalities as they are endowed with the same epistemological resource – the human mind. Hence, even in a linear and logical frame of reference, the illogic and undesirability of subordination of women is evident. From the critical realist lens women are crucial elements of the real world and hence have equal stake in the same. The view of 'truth claims' (of norms, forms and totality) solely from the male perspective is unreal – the feminine lens as equally crucial and critical. The critical realist vision incorporates all dimensions of reality to determine 'truth claims of real' – even if those dimensions may be conflictual and contradictory. The eventual positionmay be that of Meta Reality where all existence (men and women) collides to become essences that are truthful and pure. The fact that the assertion of woman is made is adequate grounding for it to be an instrumental approach. From the logical positivist view point, even in a linear and systemic view of the world, logic (encompassing suppositions, propositions and affirmations) deems equity – gender equity as being one dimension of justice (Hardin, 1991).

Classical Positions

The classical positions of liberal, Marxist, socialist and radical have crucial significance. These epistemologies have twofold sets of propositions – one defining the nature of domination and subjugation of women and the second determining emancipatory ideals. The liberal feminist epistemologies governed by Sartrean and Rawlsian ideas of freedom and justice propose an equity in the sphere of rights and opportunities (Gorowitz, 1975; Pandey, 1995) as emancipatory for women. Curtailing of that equity is defined as dominance/hegemony. Whereas the Marxist epistemology deliberates on hegemony in the sphere of production and capitalist production mode being the answer, the socialist position discusses both realms of the woman's world – production and reproduction, and issues of dominance, invisibility, informalisation and homebasedness, thereby leading to a denial of 'spaces' for women. Reasserting spaces is the pathway to transcendence, the radical epistemology focuses on sexuality – the 'sex class system' (along the lines of the economic class system) as being the reason for hegemony. What is addressed is the patriarchal control over female bodies and sexuality; the answer lying in either transgressing the control through redefining sexuality or simply resisting patriarchal control by assertions and negotiations.

Critical Theory Approaches

Feminist criticality in terms of critical theory approaches employs a subjectivity lens that is grounded in dimensions beyond deterministic ones – thereby portraying a differential viewpoint of looking at societal reality from an engendered lens. This moves beyond conventional stratification approaches that views hierarchy from a singular standpoint (of either class or race/ethnicity) towards multiple manifestations of power, antagonisms and contradictions (Held, 1990). In the sense of critical theory, even patriarchy as a hegemonic institution has multiple forms that need to be countered. Hence, epistemologies need to be characterised by a marked shift from visions of one-dimensionality (Marcusian term) and a deterministic approach towards a fetish for seeking difference. Particularly what is of concern is how the unconscious enters politics and how the understanding of the woman self and sexual identity changes the understanding of the conventional stratification of class. It is essentially through a process of negative dialectics (Adornian term) that 'women subjects' are created through processes that are social class related and sexual-political. What is then tackled are largely the monoliths – which negate difference; posing of simple dichotomies between equality and difference and instead emphasise on the importance of understanding the dominated woman subject within the context of the prevailing social and political thought (Rasmussen, 1996).

Poststructuralist and Postmodern Epistemological Repertoire

In the poststructuralist and postmodern epistemological repertoire, woman's subjectivity is discursively produced in social institutions and processes. Here language and discourse are central since no directly knowable reality exists, because the very language that is used to describe the social world at the same time inscribes and constructs it. Further, women's representation of their own experiences of subjugation is mediated through their habituation of discourses. Hence, whether patriarchy in itself is comprehended as hegemonic or inevitable and imperative is determined by language and discourse. Hence, the critical approaches of poststructuralism and postmodernism provides a different point of view to knowledge of violated woman's subjectivity. There is an emphasis on deconstructing the discursive practices through which the social world is portrayed in texts, thereby challenging even the category of 'woman' which in itself is historically and discursively constructed and relative to other categories which are also in modes of transition. There is a certain reexamination of the changing nature of social identity and political consciousness which is to be reexamined in the light of woman's experience. Postmodern feminist epistemologies further challenge the essential and inevitable in favour of reconstructing historicity, systems, structure and sexuality through the lifeworlds of women to then comprehend the complex and omniscient nature of patriarchy – which in itself is comprehended as being fluid (Rege, 2003).

Epistemological Hybridisation

Several conditions pre-empt 'epistemological hybridisation' – going beyond the phallocentric denials of legitimacy of gender as a category of analysis towards crucial questions of construction, examination and institutionalisation of difference within feminist discourses. Some illustrations are socio-political and geographical locations, questions of difference (class, ethnicity, faith and nation) experience and historicity. The politics of location (socio-political and geographic) unearth questions of historical, geographical, cultural, psychic and imaginative boundaries which provide ground for political definition and self definition of violated women. It is in reality the 'politics of space' and the interplay of 'culture, space and power' which determine the existential realities of women (Stanley and Wise, 1992). They cannot be explained solely by conventional epistemologies but require a more grounded theory approach (Eagleton, 1991).

The questions of difference form another dimensions of conditions pre-empting/pre-disposing hybridisation. Difference is an outcome of categorical imperatives that determine differential nature of subjectivities/conditionalities/positionalities. Class as an epistemic category of difference is classically deterministic in the truly Marxian sense wherein the latter dimension of the binary (the lower class/proletariat) is more prone to oppression (the nature of oppression also being intensive). Ethnicity as a category pre-empting difference affects situations of oppression in a culturally pre-disposed manner, wherein experiences of subjugation are intertwined and/or materialised on the basis of ethnicity, manifesting at cognitive (psychic) and structural social levels. Faith similarly brings in another angle to the lens of difference – either determining or pushing boundaries through its politics of culture and beliefs.

The colonial narratives of nationhood reinforce essentialist domains of the institution of patriarchy. Ideals of nationhood endorse the pro forma of patriarchy which requires consequently reformulated engendered epistemologies to tackle the same. Experience is a baggage of historical interconnections of notions of identity/identity politics, colonisation/decolonisation and equality/inequalities – located through the politics of space and geographies. Experience is subjectivity that is moulded through historicism and culture (Gramscian legacy) reproduced in reformulations which determine them. Altering experiences amount to altering subjectivities and subsequently the episteme which determine those subjectivities, thereby calling for grounded theory. Further, the embedded mainstreaming in conventional histories that govern discourses determine women's oppression through their invisibility, thereby leading to curtailing of voices and informalisation/domestication (in the public-private work domain).

Hybridised epistemologies take multiple forms ranging from dual to multiple combinations of instrumental and classical epistemologies to critical ones. The amalgam depends on the nature, norms and forms of domination and emancipatory ideals/visions. Generally within the overarching poststructuralist and radical tenets, hybridisation assumes the form of toning through classical and instrumental stances. The instrumental perspectives of logical positivism and critical realism bring in concepts of truth and justice to realise the egalitarian vision – logic being the governing principle and deontological and teleological ethics (ethics as absolute ends and ethics as means) as being the value base. The classical perspectives of liberal, socialist, Marxist bring in their own elements into an essentially radical and poststructuralist repertoire. The liberal lens is that of epistemological equity along the lines of Cartesian Cogito (existence precedes essence) (Popper, 1972) but from a feminist lens accounting for women's experience, hence stating that women's existence and experience precedes their essence.

The Marxist stance is a clear rendition of the sphere of production and sexual domination as perceived to be an outcome of the economic class system. The element that Marxian stance brings to the rendition is that of 'class hierarchies subsuming sexual inequities' – hence abolition/annihilation of class (in an economic deterministic fashion) would reinstate egalitarianism. The socialist stance moves beyond the sphere of production towards the sphere of reproduction, thereby bringing in elements of sexuality into the discourse on inequities and institutions. Herein emancipation is a simultaneous annihilation from both the sex and economic class systems through the elements of liberation and Sartrean freedom that re-instates the power of choice. All the aforementioned strands of emancipation emerging from classical perspectives collate to form engendered and hybridised epistemologies. The essentially radical garb highlights dimensions and angles of sexuality and sex class system as oppressive. Poststructuralist lens then brings in elements of subjectivity (woman's subjectivity) and elements of Foucauldian micropolitics, Lacanian psychoanalytical manysidedness (exploring hitherto unexplored domains of sexuality) and Derridaen deconstruction (wherein social reality is fragmented, writ with discontinuities; and history and culture are no longer sole determinants of contemporary realities). These amalgamate to form hybridised versions of epistemologies which are essentially engendered – thereby preparing a stage for feminist praxis.

Feminist Praxis

This comprises addressing hegemony, structure and systems by employing the normative and ideational stance of the subjective epistemology. It is this very ethical backing that transforms practice into praxis – loaded with colours of ways of seeing and viewing and envisaging an engendered world. The prime purport is to understand 'how' – normatively and strategically – issues of hegemony (which is posited as multisystemic), structural antagonisms and contradictions are addressed. The key domains of praxis that emerge are addressing issues of patriarchy and women's oppression through the complexities of social categorical imperatives of caste, class, gender and faith; conceptualising 'work' through the existing systems of governance and jurisprudence and addressing how an engendered lens of praxis emerges, which is a transcendence from just working with women. The first domain involves a comprehension of patriarchy and domination from multiple epistemic lenses and the complexities that arise due to social hierarchies that cause multiple jeopardies. Hence, it is a refocusing of sorts depending on the extant conditionality – positionality of women. The second domain is a strategising which occurs in the meso- and macrodomains with other stakeholders in the process – the prime objective being that of instilling an engendered stance. The third is about transforming a 'working with women' position towards a graduated feminist praxis – informed at the epistemic and ontic levels – permeating onto praxis (Reinharz, 1992).

Feminist praxis is thus about addressing hegemony, structure and systems. It is largely an outcome of hybridised epistemologies which are engendered and indigenous – taking into account elements of grounded reality. The grounded theory flavour thus emerges with several ingredients drawn from the varied episteme. Epistemes have in them embedded elements of praxis – as epistemology is a natural precedence to methodology, predisposing its repertoire in many ways.

Feminist praxis has multiple levels of operations as well as multiple domains of interventions. The levels range from household, family and kinship to systems, structure and society – capturing thus within its fold micro to macro ranges of action. The domains are cognitive (in the Peter Blau's microstructural, Blumer and Kuhn's ethnomethodological and Mead's behaviouristic sense), real (Tarksi's real spaces of interaction), structural (Randall and Collins macrostructural and Marxian notions of structure) and systemic (the macrosociological conceptualisations of systems as encompassing economic, social, political and social geographical domains of interaction) (Garfinkel, 1967; Barnes, 1982; Guba, 2002).

As praxis has largely a Marxian and structural connotation, extant literature on feminist praxis can be categorised into the following:

- Puritan radical and poststructuralist forms of praxis
- Problematising positivism and realism through the radical domains of praxis
- The unblemished postmodern repertoire
- Hybridisation and Indigenisation: Grounds to incorporate multiple episteme translating onto praxis
- Angles of the liberal feminist epistemology in the radical and poststructuralist stance
- Positions of Marxist feminist epistemology enmeshed with radicalism and poststructuralism
- The amalgam of socialist feminist epistemology with an essentially radical rendition
- Toning the radical, poststructuralist and the postmodern: Operating within boundaries of institutions

Puritan Radical and Poststructuralist Forms of Praxis

Radical and poststructuralist praxis involves elements and tenets of addressing the establishment – extant institutions and inequalities embedded in them – patriarchy being the primary one. The radical stance addresses the sexual inequalities and works towards unearthing the roots of sexual subjugation and oppression. The radical stance of praxis carries the prime quality of addressing the sex class system by taking views of woman's sexuality that are essentially polarised and diametrically opposed to mainstream established views which carry with them the historical baggage of oppression and invisibility of women and their sexuality choices. Hence, strategies of praxis assume the form of addressal of establishment (even in situation of working with them, such addressal would involve addressing inherent inequities) negotiations for space and realignment of sorts. The poststructuralist form of praxis operates on the key domain of deconstruction aligning to subjectivity motives of violated women. Subjectivity is a contextualised, regionalised and un-routinised construction of a woman's lifeworld and notions of sexuality. Deconstruction of set patterns of reality is the prime operating principle – with alternative views of re-negotiating her space as primordial. Radical and poststructuralist forms of praxis operate in unison to promote a heterogeneous vision of the establishment – addressing deconstruction and reconstruction (Krishnaraj, 1992).

Problematising Positivism and Realism through the Radical Domains of Praxis

Translating onto praxis involves a re-instatement of binaries in worldviews which are hierarchical and a sense of being prosaic about extant realities, institutions and inequalities. Patriarchy is then assumed to be an integral element of the structure which is pre-endowed providing little space for change and transformation. The radical dimension of praxis attempts to address the norms and forms of the institution of marriage and family, kinship; systems of society, economy and polity; structures of law governance and administration so as to reinstate engendered subjectivities to a scientistic way of operation. The realist epistemologies bring with it the discourses on truth and absolute truth as given and empirically evident and verifiable (Sayer, 1984). The radical feminist lens to the realist conception of truth posits women's voices as premier in the construction of 'truth' – the version being composed by elements and dimensions of her experience of oppression. Hence, the radical feminist version of realist truth is that woman is the truth teller (and one who constructs it based on sensory perceptions, cognitive understanding and experience) and then it becomes reality as opposed to the rhetoric (as specified in Morgan's 1984 essay 'Sisterhood is Global'). Hence, problematising arises from a repositioning – the different ways of seeing.

The Unblemished Postmodern Repertoire

The postmodern stance brings with it three elements in praxis – celebrating difference, comprehending micropolitics and negating essentialisms in favour of understanding contextualities and intersectionalities created by categorical imperatives of caste, class, ethnicity and faith. Difference is the key organising principle of the otherwise disorganised (epistemologically) postmodern repertoire (Doshi, 2003). The denials of universals in experience, norms and forms of subjugation and the individualised differentials embedded in women's subjectivities (which is also in turn socially constructed) is the summum bonum of difference. Experience of oppression among women thus becomes ahistorical – history and culture as categorical imperatives rather than governing principles in defining the experiences of domination.

Micropolitics in a truly Foucauldian sense (Pandey, 1995) is the comprehension of multiple domains of operations of power and hegemony, not singularly governed by an overarching patriarchal institution – but that patriarchy manifests in all forms of regimentation and binaries and the very way the world is constructed (social world) and systems and structures operate and function. Micropolitics endows patriarchy with the quality of not just male dominance and power, but also an effervescence that is evident in all material relations of production and reproduction and materialist conception of history. Essentialisms in defining the women's subjectivities are thus negated – the woman being defined by a cross-juncture of class, faith, ethnicity and caste – to determine the nature and extent of differential jeopardies.

Hybridisation and Indigenisation: Grounds to Incorporate Multiple Episteme Translating onto Praxis

The key arguments that warrant thus the complex tackling of feminist praxis are hybridisation and indigenisation. This emerges from the classical opposition between history and histories, thereby challenging an implicit assumption that pluralism is an adequate substitute for political analysis of dependent histories and larger historical configurations. The need to recognise essentially the importance of twin elements of hybridisation and indigenisation emerges from the fact that there exists a historical and cultural relativism in experiences of domination – culturally and socially construed and historically mediated. From the critical hermeneutics point of view, when stances of radical, poststructuralist and postmodern coagulate/amalgamate, different episteme for 'feminisms' are born which make the praxis hybridised, contextualised, regionalised, un-routinised and indigenised. Critical hermeneutics is thus a critical interpretation of what emerges as 'essences' from radical, poststructuralist and postmodern which provides an epistemically informed ground for hybridised praxis – drawing from strands of each (Craig, 1998). The context and the social and geographical space in which violence against women is construed and constructed – which is relative, historically mediated and spatially defined – provide an argument for indigenisation.

Angles of the Liberal Feminist Epistemology in the Radical and Poststructuralist Stance

The hybridisation in praxis comes from the amalgam of strands of classical epistemologies so as to tackle the 'real' and 'tangible'. This hybridisation also provides a sense of the pragmatic in interventions. Liberal feminist epistemology with its emphasis on equity, freedom and political liberalism (in spheres of public and private domains of the woman) is an underlying philosophy. It operates as an outcome of interventions in many spheres of a woman's life (wherein equity, freedom and justice are the prime moving and motivating factors) and is a desirable reality (Kachuck, 2003). Further, what the liberal feminist epistemology brings to praxis are bounds of rationality – operating within given spheres and domains and extant institutions both at macro and micro levels. Several instances of interventions reveal an alliance to extant structures (of society) and institutions (of marriage, family and kinship) wherein women's sense of utopia is created in the form of an equitable reconciliation, realignment and negotiation of spaces within existing family and household domains. It is a resettling in of sorts within the overarching liberal framework of human freedom, individual space and rights – reconciliation and arbitration with all cartographies of patriarchy (mapping within the household and kinship domain and systems and structure outside) being the key operating strategy.

Positions of Marxist Feminist Epistemology Enmeshed with Radicalism and Poststructuralism

In feminist praxis, the essence of Marxist feminist epistemology – especially the emphasis on class analysis and historical materialism (Kolakowski, 1986) – is another dimension that features across (giving also an element of historical mediation to structures of family and kinship). This aspect of hegemony embedded in 'class' and 'historical determinism' of institutions and inequities (the proposition of Andre Beteille) feature systematically. Class gives an affinity towards the subalternity of women in multiple domains – the class analysis also brings in dimensions of layers of inequity for women (patriarchy being one overarching layer). However, whether emancipation from class hegemony would lead to emancipation from domination is a matter of studied empirical verifications. Historical materialism brings in two dimensions – one, the historical constructions of the structures of family and kinship; and the second, the subsequent domestication, informalisation and homebasedness of women and their work that provides a premise for subjugation and inequities. This historical construction also provides credence to view 'histories of subjugation of women' and not just one singular history writ with baggage determined by realms of production. The strategies that are then forwarded are emancipation from class hegemony and baggage of historical determinism.

The Amalgam of Socialist Feminist Epistemology within an Essentially Radical Rendition

The softer element in dealing with women's position in domains of production and reproduction emerges in the socialist feminist stance – wherein the Marxian analysis also enmeshed with comprehending the spheres of reproduction. This runs through feminist praxis in varied formats – particularly in defining and determining the conditionalities and positionalities of women. What the socialist feminist repertoire brings in is a cumulative understanding of women through twin domains of production and reproduction. Hence, it opens up sites in parallel for oppression as being the domains of household, work and sexuality. Equity and fair negotiating spaces being the governing principles (Fonow and Cook, 1989), the socialist feminist lens tones down the radical renditions of deconstruction and realignment (to structures and institutions), towards a stance warranting reconciliation, arbitration and adjudication. This reposes a faith in the responsiveness of the superstructure (the institutions of law, police and governance) towards the changing role of the base (emerging from the changing/altering nuances of the categorical imperatives of class, caste, ethnicity and faith). Hence, negotiating spaces with law/legislations, governance/administration and the police systems to reinstate an engendered vision, but operating largely within their norms, is the socialist angle to the repertoire.

Toning the Radical, Poststructuralist and the Postmodern: Operating within Boundaries of Institutions

The arenas wherein radical quests are toned include determining the desirable realities for women, aligning to given structures, institutions and superstructures (operating largely within their frame of reference) and accepting grand narratives, universalisation and essentialisms in some spheres – such as accepting the notions of 'sisterhood' and lending credence to the aspects of organisation and cooperation and shared visions and goals for action. The desirable realities of women emerge generally as obtaining an equitable negotiating stance (in the metaphorical sense) in the household and family domains and retaining those set-ups. Much of feminist praxis also draws from existing legal and governance framework, thereby displaying a key alignment to the superstructure, but nevertheless retaining spaces for engendered changes. The sense of the collective brings notions of essentialisms and universalisms (as micronarratives then get subsumed under grand imagined and constructed realities). This is accepted at one level to further the perpetual vision of emancipation, thereby departing from perpetual erasures (Dews, 1987).

An Indigenous Version of Feminism through Women's Histories and Voices

Elaborating on feminist praxis further, the alignment with Third World 'stories' of women (in the nature of the subaltern) and a dialogue that discusses the space created within the women's movement in the indigenous context deems deliberations. In particular this involves a reexamination of the subalternity of women and examination of the nature of assertions, negotiations, reconciliations and deconstruction of hegemonies through the feminist lens. How subalternity further intensifies the nature of subjugation/marginalisation by providing a lens of reconstructing historiographies (of women) and examining subcultures and microcultures to unearth a woman's view to the world and society – which is essentially egalitarian and engendered – is the key area of exploration. Stories of alignment, coalition, collectivisation and organisation that give shape to 'movements' that address issues of subjugation and sexuality and the nuances and nature of assertions/insertions therein are discussed. Shades of oppression that exist are unravelled and asserted in different pro formas, thereby lending a differential flavour to the various angles of the women's movement. The varied histories and voices of women lead to the varied nature of insertions into the women's movement – the premier junctures into the waves of the movements being that of assertions of equity, rights, access to knowledge; sexuality and sexual politics and difference (as a nonessentialist principle). At every stage of the wave of the women's movement, there are different conceptualisations of the nature of oppression which are construed, constructed and placed for discourse. Hence, the (soci) ontic component (the prevalent waves of the women's movement) leads to the (soci) epistemic component (the faces of violence) and thereby lead to the action element (the nature and approach to emancipation). The waves/iterative stages can be discussed thus:

- Assertions of equity
- Case for equitable access to knowledge as a means to emancipation
- Assertions of rights in the social sphere
- Assertions of rights in the domestic sphere
- The domain of sexuality and control over spheres of reproduction
- Dimensions and debates on motherhood and related discourses
- The difference principle for assertion of rights
- Feminisation of the Rawlsian principle (of greater equity for the multiple disadvantaged): Rules of intersectionality

Assertions of Equity

Drawing from the essentially liberal framework and political liberalism, the Archimedean standpoint of feminist assertion is the principle of equity. This also characterised the first wave of the women's movement, wherein aligning to and drawing from Enlightenment rationality and the construction of logic – all epistemological and cognitive equities – are inherently equitable. With that premise the feminist constructions emerged with the alignment of equity for women, as all grounds of inequity were illogical and nonscientific/irrational. Hence as inequity between sexes could not be proved (except on biological grounds), the case for gender equity was projected. All negations of the norms and forms of this equity lead to the construction of subjugation within this framework, the basic premise being inequity. Equality as a governing principle then subsumes under it an equitable access, opportunity, diffusion and attainment of all aspirations and rights, a negation or a denial in any of the aforementioned spheres would lead to constructions of oppression, which deems quests for emancipation. The quest for equity is to be realised by equal opportunities, rights and access to social and political participation.

Case for Equitable Access to Knowledge as a Means for Emancipation

The furthering realm in the assertions of equity is a certain degree of credence endowed to the quintessentiality of 'knowledge' for emancipation (coming from one angle of the entire Foucauldian knowledge/power discourse and from the other as the liberal-functionalist view of the emancipatory potential in education). Any denial of access to the sphere of 'knowledge' would amount towards a construction of violence/subjugation. This denial of access to education or affirming access but towards unequal systems of education leads to (in this frame of reference) a social reproduction of inequities – economic, social and cultural. The economic reproductive model of Gramsci emphasises on class inequities as emerging from unequal domains of knowledge – precipitating then onto gender equities. The social reproductive model of Bowles and Gintis focuses on social inequity as emerging from unequal domains of knowledge, precipitating then onto gender inequities and the cultural reproductive model of Bourdieu with similar preambles and precipitations (Rege, 2003). These inequities then become the constructions of oppression for women, as denial of access to knowledge or unequal access to unequal realms of knowledge for women would then endow with inequitable negotiating grounds. Hence, emancipation in this frame of reference is the access, diffusion, availability and attainment in the knowledge domain as a means to what can be construed as empowerment.

Assertions of Rights in the Social Sphere

There is a certain degree of alignment to the socialist feminist framework in determining assertions in the social sphere – particularly in the domains of women's work, visibility and social negotiating space. Dimensions of denial of the social space, domestication, invisibility of women's work and informalisation are comprehended as violence – a curtailment of the free expression of women's potential and capabilities in the social sphere. Drawing from the seminal work of Ester Boserup and subsequently Polanyi, this dimension of assertion of rights in the social sphere, hints at a certain macroeconomic role of women and their work in the larger developmental processes. This is conditioned by patriarchy on the one hand and global political economy dynamics which are driven by hegemonic ideologies on the other (Krishnaraj, 1992). Hence, subjugation/violence is construed as the subalternity of women perpetuated by regimes of patronage and exploitation in the work sphere, which then have implications for the conditions and positions of women. The pathway to emancipation is the recognition of the nuances of women's work – both in the household and social domains and the nature of entitlements that women need to be endowed with or are rightfully within the realm of women's existential realities. Beyond recognition it is also visibility, equal negotiating spaces in both spheres of woman's existence and notions of egalitarianism that govern pathways of assertion.

Assertions of Rights in the Domestic Sphere

Within the range of women's movement, the sphere of the 'household' and 'family and kinship relations' feature in a subtle manner perpetually dissolving the public-private dichotomy, politicising the personal and unearthing the subjectivity realm of women through dialogues on equity; discourses on sexuality and sexual politics and in the further amalgamated realm of discourses on identity politics (Smart, 1989; Hardin, 1991). Dialogues on equity are composed of the preliminary nature of assertion of woman's spaces – metaphorically projecting the undesirability of any forms of overt and covert violence. Further, inequities in the household domains are construed as inequities in the (soci) ontic realms – which then portray claims for engendering paradigms. Discourses on sexuality and sexual politics form the core of violence and oppression in the domestic sphere, touching realms of production and women's control over their own bodies – their very conception of selfhood. Deconstruction of the patriarchal norms and forms of control in the realms of subjective sexualities (differential perspectives of women over their own bodies and the notions of dimensions of reproduction) is the key to emancipation. The third realm of discourses on identity stem from amalgamated dialogues in equity and sexual politics – towards also embedding the idea of difference. This endorses the fact that equity and sexual preferences are not uniform and essentialist but changing with different cultural connotations. Taking into account these differentials is the essence of culturally informed poststructuralist feminist praxis (Grenberg, 1999).

The Domain of Sexuality and Control over Spheres of Reproduction

The very fundamental question of biology and the social construction of the same into the sex class system writ with hierarchies, antagonisms and contradictions is the essence of the rendition. Whereas globally discourses on gender, body and sexuality have assumed poststructuralist dimensions of subjectivity domains to unearth differential hegemonies, in the indigenous context the focus is on autonomy, freedom from subordination and unravelling the micropolitics of power that curtail choices and freedom (family and kinship as one key domain). Autonomy is the quest to determine one's sexual orientation independent of dominant trends, freedom to determine sexual connections (albeit within legal limits) and the power to resist sexual control. Freedom from subordination stems from this power which can manifest within institutional limits (such as marriage and family) and within larger social domains (such as situations of sexual abuse and rape). The very instance of institutional limits and social domains endows the qualification of power within sexuality, and emancipation is also an emancipation of those social boundaries in a postbinary, postmodernist sense. The micropolitics of power manifests in multiple domains of sexuality – orientation, preference and fulfilment. Violence and subjugation can thus manifest in all the domains and hence praxis is suitably moulded in a nonessentialist manner (Berg and Acharya, 2003).

Dimensions and Debates on Motherhood and Related Discourses

The extension of discourses in sexuality and spheres of reproduction are further interluded with the entire gamut of discourses on motherhood within the feminist movement in the indigenous context. Several subjectivities of women persist in their 'motherhood orientations' within the largely deconstructionist framework of revisiting conventional norms and forms of institutions of marriage and family (Kachuck, 2003). Although motherhood is also a social construction within the larger frame of reference of gender discourses, it is one notion that reaches the realm of 'non-negotiables' in terms of emancipation of women from violence and subjugation (within the larger discussions on sexuality and sexual politics). Elements of ownership, attachment and retention of filial/maternal ties feature in an essentially deconstructionist frame of institutional realignments (breaking away from conventional family norms). Hence in the indigenous context, feminism in the radical poststructuralist sense possesses constructivist overtones which are construed by institutions and discourses on 'motherhood'. The construction of motherhood as also a social construct brings in a different dimension to the entire discourse on poststructuralist contentions and notions of power. Motherhood emerges as a 'second nature' element to women even in the context of violence – thereby redefining power hierarchies, conceptualisations of power within sexuality domains and bringing in the understanding that power persists and manifests only if perceived.

The Difference Principle for Assertion of Rights

The poststructuralist turn of praxis in the indigenous context, colliding with the third wave of the global feminist movement, operates in the principle of difference – negating essentialisms in favour of multilayered existentialities of women created by categorical imperatives of caste, class, ethnicity and faith. These play a major role in comprehending the complexities created for women – the double, triple and multiple jeopardies as explicated in literature. Particular kinds of categorical imperatives create certain nature of realities which deem a certain nature of negotiation of rights and hence aspects of the postmodern feminist turn to the praxis legacy are evident. The brouhaha gets intensified with the categories of culture, politics of location and politics of experience (Lakatos and Musgrave, 1970; Grossberg and Nelson, 1990; England, 1993) in the indigenous context. Culture brings different connotations of violence/subjugation and constructions of meanings to the act of violence/oppression. The layers which are prominently unearthed are an unquestioned acceptance to the act of oppression (as what ought to be), subversiveness (as violated women perceive self to be powerless), hidden revolt (unexpressed claims and desires) and propensity for action (expressed through an alliance with and collaboration with extant interventions). Politics of location or social geographies bring in another dimension to difference – wherein spaces (rural/urban) play a crucial role in construing histories of 'hegemony' and perceptions thereof. This culture and politics of location then account for the politics of experience in the regionalised context.

Feminisation of the Rawlsian Principle: Rules of Intersectionality

John Rawls (1971) in his seminal work titled 'A Theory of Justice' attempted to make the conflicting alternatives of liberty and equality as compatible. Two principles of justice have been derived and defined – principle of equal basic liberty and the difference principle combined with the requirement of fair equality of opportunity. They are to govern the assignment of rights and duties and to regulate the distribution of social and economic advantages and benefits. Differences to be to the greatest benefit of the least advantaged and attached to positions accessible to all under conditions of fair equality and opportunity. In his later work titled 'Political Liberalism' (1993), Rawls re-affirmed the Kantian interest in developing and exercising individual moral powers of rational autonomy and fair dealing. Hence, he advocated ideals of relativity in lieu of a search for universal principles of justice. Further, he advocated a 'justice as fairness' principle positioning a political conception of justice rather than a comprehensive moral conception – moral ideals nevertheless backed by spirit of democratic and aligned culture.

Incorporation of culture and politics of difference in viewing the indigenous context of feminist praxis leads to an emergence of the prominent strand of feminist political liberalism – also called the feminisation of the Rawlsian principle. With intervening categorical imperatives in determining the existential realities of women, 'intersectionalities' emerge which determine the levels of vulnerability. Retaining the poststructuralist turn of subjectivity and the postmodern turn of difference, intersectionality warrants a particular kind of political positionality of women which deems 'differential justice'. Within the jurisprudential context, the entire locus of justice would then be based on domains of intersectionalities. Rawlsian principle of justice is based on the overarching principle of equity and desertion (meaning deserving) – the difference element coming in with the stratification existing within the social fabric which alters the face of justice (as curtailing social reproduction of inequities then becomes the prime motive). To have preferential and compensatory equitability measures for those at the junctures of multiple vulnerabilities is the crux (Gorowitz, 1975; White, 1991). In terms of engendered praxis, this manifests as advocacy and assertions/negotiations for favourable laws and a reconstruction of rights – a feminist jurisprudence beyond protectionism and compensation (Smart, 1989).

In Summary

Structuralist epistemology, some key proponents of which are Saussure, Levi-Strauss and Wittgenstein, uses linguistics as the vantage point of all social analysis – language being the surface manifestation of fundamental mental processes which in turn are manifestations of general patterns of social and cultural organisations (Saussure). Borrowing from the twentieth-century linguist Roman Jakobson, Levi-Strauss has harboured the notion that mental thought underlying language occurs in terms of binary contrasts – which in turn are organised by a series of 'innate codes' used to generate many different social forms (Hawkes, 1997).

Durkheim's structural analysis concerns structural differentiation in view of cognitive processes through the lens of ritual activities and social solidarity. Social structure as an emergent reality sui generis is understandable in terms of its own dynamics – the macrostructural norms of size, differentiation and integration as guiding points of analysis (Turner, 1987). The other school of thought is influenced to some degree by Wittgenstein's Tractatus Logico-Philosophicus (which posits language as representing facts of the world sharing a certain logical form – logical propositions of language {language games} being a picture of the world) (Coward and Ellis, 1977; Strathern, 1998). It proposes a microstructuralism of sorts in the sense of collective structural force operating through individual consciousness – the mind organising microfoundations of structure. Epistemologies emphasising systems, reality as organised in terms of binary opposites which in turn are within the bounded rationality of language generally, form the core of structuralist thought.

The structuration thesis of Giddens as a variant of structuralist thought is a 'sensitising conceptual scheme' (post the conundrum of poststructuralism), in Roy Bhaskar's (2002) style of Meta Reality containing the dialectic of self-realisation. The key concept is structuration which is intended to communicate the duality of structure. That is, social structure is used by active agents; and in so using the properties of structure, they transform or reproduce this structure. Thus, the process of structuration requires a conceptualisation of the nature of structure, of agents who use structure and of the ways that these are mutually implicated in each other to produce varying patterns of human organisation (Turner, 1987).

The poststructuralists contest those very domains of language, logic and binary oppositions guided by notions of Sartrean freedom, which then take the 'postmodern turn' (Lyotard's conceptualisation) under the influence of Nietzsche. Foucault's poststructuralist discourses feature prominently herein in terms of his contestation of Sartrean freedom ('Existence precedes essence. And essence means real or ultimate nature of a human being. Essence or meaning of things was not determined by outside force. Meanings are constructed by individuals who filter the world through language. Individual has the freedom to determine his actions.') (Cumming, 2003; Strathern, 1996). Foucault contested the existential freedom given by Sartre to the individual and argued that individual freedom is limited or constrained by social conditioning which surrounds the individual – the micropolitics of power.

Foucault's epistemology revolves around the central argument of 'knowledge is power', truth tied to the operations of power and domination and that power, knowledge and truth are interconnected through discourses and texts. The poststructuralist essence is unearthed through his propositions that language is the basis to understand society. The meaning of the signified (object) is at the discretion, and social conditioning of the individual and binary oppositions found in language is also found in knowledge and social structure. The structure of language is a dominant one and people come into existence through language. Thus, one is not 'free' to think outside the rules of one's language – a framework of thought given by language and conditioned by history. Each historical age is characterised by particular forms of knowledge – called epistemes – periods of history organised around and explicable in terms of specific world views and discourse, showing that the way in which people make sense of their world depends on an order of reason and sets of discursive formations (Sturrock, 1999; Henry, 2002)

Derrida's poststructuralist contentions commence with the Archimedean standpoint that things do not have a single basic meaning and there is essentially a fragmentation, conflict and discontinuity in matters of history, identity and culture (Pandey, 1995). The core to his epistemology is 'deconstruction' stemming from an understanding as to how meanings of texts can be 'plural' and 'unstable' instead of fixing them to a rigid structure. Manifesting through grammatology as a type of knowledge that views writings as setting up particular constructions of reality and that these constructions are always tied up in history, society and politics. Deconstruction is a method of inquiry with difference as the basic guiding principle stratifying the 'hidden' meanings of texts that carry baggage of discourse (Callinicos, 1985; Doshi, 2003).

Postmodern theorising brought in a stress on subjectivity and derivativeness of meaning replacing philosophical conceptions of the subject, representation, causality, truth and value with a perspectivist orientation. As discourses on plurality and difference, there is a celebration of difference and a critique of representation and reason. Conceptions of Lyotard (The Postmodern Condition, 1979), Jameson and Baudrillard heavily influenced by Nietzsche's work on fragmentation of the inexplicable, focused on rejection of metanarratives and limitations of knowledge production within hegemonic norms and micropolitics of society. In Jameson's analysis of culture in terms of late capitalism, postmodern culture integrated into commodity production – culture which subordinates class analysis. Thus, postmodernism signifies the cultural logic of late capitalism – characterised by postindustrial regimen wherein the globalised market economy is the repository of power. Focusing on a post-Marxian analysis of consumption, Baudrillard conceptualisation of postmodern society is a social stratification based on 'consumption of signs and images' that in turn reproduce social categories. Hence, signs and images represent an ontology which is metaphorical and hyperreal governing the palpable and real (Best and Kellner, 1998).

An important dimension of contemporary thought is the postcolonial discourse – the history of which does not reflect a linear development, easy periodisation and thematic concerns that go beyond political oppression and subordination to presumably aesthetic concerns – all interrogating the so-called 'imperial structures'. Alongside, forwarding the need to historicise, there is an intertwining of culture and literary history to political happenings. This polysemic construct, the chief proponents of which are Gandhi, Said, Spivak, Nandy and Aijaz Ahmad, has 'resistance', 'retrieval', 'transgression', 'confrontation' and 'opposition' as its key concepts.

Attributed to scholars such as Ranajit Guha, Spivak, David Hardiman and others, the subaltern thoughts' key preoccupation is reconstructing historiographies – endowing a view from the below, employing Gramsci's ideas of 'cultural hegemony' as a standpoint of analysis.

Feminism as a social theorisation genre provides a way of looking at the world that sees women's issues and inequalities between men and women as central political issues. There are, however, variations in interpretations on the nature and causes of women's inequality, subordination or oppression, and hence feminism contains several competing epistemic strands. Feminism can be understood in terms of feminist ontology, epistemology and praxis. Feminist ontology refers to an engendered view of reality, epistemology as an engendered construction of knowledge and methodology in terms of praxis.

5

Positions Emerging from Religion and Faith

Literal and Critical

The quintessentiality of religion as a social institution and as a social categorical imperative is evident through a plethora of instances and manifestations of the same in the social milieu through historicity. Religion has at once a theological premise and a social one; in that it operates at the philosophical-metaphysical level as well as at the socio-ontic level. At the philosophical-metaphysical level, there are propositions, tenets and premises that are of the order of cosmology and theism. At the socio-ontic level, there are manifestations at the structural and functional domains and phenomenologies of sacralisation, ritualisation and routinisation (from the structurationist standpoint). The complexities get further intensified as religion has a historiographical presence – commencing with the theistic positions of the Greek philosophers, Latin tradition in Christianity particularly St. Augustine, Bonaventure and Aquinas, Judaic theologians, Gnostics and the Islamic theologians: Averroes and Avicenna as systematic commentators on Quranic expositions, within the global context. Other domains include the Mazdaaic religion as a mystical theology of Iranian and Persian origins and subsequent manifestations, dissensions and sectarian developments in all organised forms of religion symbolised by syncretic and pluralistic tenets. Hence, ranging from the development of secret societies based on a unified mystical experience, brotherhood associations based on ecumenical leanings, the move have been towards organised sectarian developments such as Protestant theology within Christianity. In the Indian context, there has been a sojourn from the Vedic thought towards post-Vedic developments, differential versions of Hinduism as drawing from Vedic and post-Vedic developments towards agnostic and logical empiricist traditions of Jainism and Buddhism. Syncretism and theistic existential humanism are evident in Sikhism and the Bhakti-Sufi developments and manifestations. Other significant domains of deliberation in the arena of religion are the amalgamating and pluralistic influences of globalisation; new religious movements with a combination of surreal, mystical, transcendental, world affirming and world negating positions; and spirituality as a transpersonal and supramental arena of deliberation – having a predominant aspect of its origination in theism.

Although the metaphysical and the cosmological-transcendental domain preclude discourses on religion, the social and the moral-ethical aspects cohabit in terms of deliberation space. Social domains pertain to the role functions of religion in time-space contexts, myths, rituals, hagiographies (Houtart and Lemerciner, 1984; Campbell, 1988) and the intertwining of religion as a categorical imperative with other categories of caste, class, gender and power in the communal/ethnic contexts. Whereas morality is a subject matter of creating praxis-oriented binaries (socially appropriate/inappropriate), ethics prescribe positions – deontological ethics being apriori positions and teleological ethics being relational domains governing social operations. Hence, the social and moral-ethical domains of religion combine to lend the social negotiating space to religion as an institution interspersed with other social institutions and structural entities.

Social work epistemology is concerned with identification of the normative-ideational basis of social work which has praxis leanings. The Archimedean standpoint of this identification can be anchored with theological discourses – historically and historiographically. The core components of social work being welfare (as manifested through altruism and philanthropy) and development (as manifested through the triad of equity-rights-justice); the textual, symbolic and metaphorical renditions in religion lend an epistemic base to the same. The embeddedness of the 'social' in religion has, apart from rituals and the institutionalisation of the sacralistation genre, references of the order of social commitment, equality tenets and social justice. Social commitment manifests in terms of altruism and philanthropy, and equality tenets and social justice in terms of prescriptions and ascriptions on the social order. Religion when examined from the approaches of structural functionalism and phenomenology (Madan, 1991) has references of the order of value base, ethics, moral order, altruism, philanthropy and desirable world view. Criticalities and deconstruction in the poststructuralist genres also simultaneously coexist with the postmodern repertoire of difference gaining precedence over linear tenets.

This chapter is thus an attempt at simultaneously comprehending the nuances of religion, faith and their connections to social work – both literal and lateral. In the realm of discussions on positions and social work, theological discourses emerge as one of the core vantage points – religion being the categorical imperative under consideration. Commencing with a conceptual comprehension on religion, theism, theology and faith, this chapter discusses the theoretical positions and forms of religion as a preamble. Focusing primarily on organised forms of religion and subsequent manifestations, global and Indic conceptualisations and positionalities of organised forms of religion in terms of genesis and textual traditions, medieval manifestations, institutional developments and postmodern/poststructuralist influences have been discussed. Further, global and indigenous facets of discourses on religion from an engendered lens as a crucial positionality have been deliberated. As the connections are sought with social work, within textual traditions and organisational dimensions, discussions have then been catapulted onto synthesising the 'social' in the global and indigenous discourses on religion. The critical domains emerge with the politics of conversion, assimilation and adoption as visualised through pluralism and syncretism. In the macro sphere the role of religion as a public institution, relegated to the private realm by Enlightenment rationality's penchant for pure reason, has been discerned through post 'modernity' discourses on religion and civil society. The culminating level of discussion is on comprehending communalism and the communal agenda as the critical realist manifestations of the social domains of religion – the postulates, facets, phases and faces. The emergent epistemes, epistemologies and vantage points have then been consolidated to build an understanding of religion for social work. Textual embeddedness provides testimonies to altruism and philanthropy as well as a moral and value orientedness. Engendered discourses, pluralism and syncretism blend 'positionalities, alterities and subalternities' – a differential voice and lens in understandings of religion – which can systematically be linked to positions in social work from a theistic lens. Spaces for heteronormativities and hypernormalities are also simultaneously provided through the concerned discussions. Communalism brings in structurally, psycho-analytically and sociologically the domains of the 'critical' and through the range of deliberations on 'othering' and 'otherness' a juxtaposition of the radical with the social.

The broad purport of the chapter is to build an academic discourse on positions in religion and faith and social work. The fact that a gamut of literature is available on religion and the allied discourses, linking the same so as to build a consolidated understanding for social work is an imperative towards which some endeavours have been made. The literal positions look for references on the social in religion and faith, and the critical positions such as communal discourses provide the lens of critique to religion as a social category.

Meaning of Religion, Theism, Theology and Faith

Religion has been explained from the ontological-epistemological, philosophico-theological, sociological, psychological and anthropological viewpoints with explanations of the metaphysical, theological, functionalist, structuralist, phenomenological, feminist and postmodern/poststructuralist veins (particularly those that discuss religion in the macro sphere). Miall-Edwards (1963) has proposed that from a historical-psychological point of view, religion becomes a fact of human life. From the metaphysical point of view, there is a certain relation of the religious experience to the real truth and nature of things. Isherwood (1954) has proposed that approaches to religion can traverse from theological to psychological, literal to figurative and intellectual to empirical. It provides the experience of truth that is then related to self-knowledge and that is further related to the larger integration with the Self or Being. The approaches of effecting influence are from authoritarian to inward and provincial to universal.

Theism is an argument for the existence of God, the ontological argument which has been provided by Anselm, cosmological argument by Aquinas and teleological argument by Kant (Macgregor, 1964). The core contention in theism is divine ascesis – the metaphysical simplicity of God and his existence and there are propositions surrounding this divine personhood. Aquinas's interpretation of this divine simplicity is based on the deontological Aristotelian constructions of apriori existence of God and the Neoplatonic formulations of being-in-itself which does not require attributes for its description and hence its existence is apriori – that is Godhead. The other aspects of the doctrine of divine simplicity include God's identification with all the intrinsic properties, ontological neutrality and contingent divine volition and knowledge. The second titan within theism oriented discourses is the explanatory relationship between theistic and moral facts. Threefold accounts are prevalent herein – Quinn's account of immediate divine causation, the natural law theory that provides a mediated theistic explanation and an unmediated constitutive explanation by an appeal to divine command and divine motivation.

Hicks (1937) has discussed the philosophical bases of theism with an ontic bases in religious experience and the notion of divine immanence. The cosmological argument celebrates the conceptions of the 'first cause', further explicated by Martineau in his conceptions of theism as the basis of creative activity of the cosmos and encompasses the Aristotelian notion of the doctrine of God and the world of creation. The teleological argument, employing Hume's distinctions between 'relation of ideas' and 'matters of fact', proposes that theism implies that the existence of God is to be conceived of as a 'matter of fact', wherefrom there are implications for living organisms and evolution. The moral argument connects 'existence' and 'subsistence' within the realms of being and combines aesthetics of the process as the basis of theism.

Cosmological theism, in the understanding of Laird (1940), is the contingent existence of the world on Godhead. The related discourses pertain to 'creation' (as becoming from beingness), eternity (as cognition and not conjecture), ubiquity of the divine (the traditional metaphysics of spatiality of Godhead, its substantiality or quasi substantiality) and omnipotence. Theism's existential support is sought through the teleological argument (or the argument from design).

Theism also simultaneously proposes deliberations on 'consciousness' – which is meaning-conferring and object constituting. There is a systematic noesis-noema correlation reaffirmed by the perceptual and the hermeneutic models. Mohanty (2009) has linked theism's core apparatus to Heideggerian discourses on 'being-in-the-world', Kantian pure reason and rational theology, and Husserl's transcendentalism idealism. Some of the important contentions then surrounding theism are transcendental consciousness, transcendentalising the natural and an ontological attitude which is hermeneutical in nature. There are alignments to idealism within theism – shaped by conceptions of the intentional acts and the correlate intended objects, the core of the noesis-noema scheme. The proposition is that the world is a correlate of consciousness which is essentially theistic in nature. This consciousness surfaces within the intentional content as a constitutive sense and points to an intentional experience of sorts which eventually transforms into transcendental metaphors and aphorisms.

Theology is primarily aimed at an understanding of the nature and attributes of God and the God's relationship to the world and its inhabitants (Flint and Rea, 2009). There is a certain focus on the epistemology of religious beliefs and the meaningfulness of religious discourse along with a discussion on divine attributes and arguments for the existence of God. The Deistic school has affirmed theological propositions by the arguments that God exists and there is a divine revelation in which the Bible plays a crucial role. Theology finds epistemological resort in the finitude of human comprehension and infinitude of God as proposed in Leibnizian discourses and Aquinas's claims that some truths of God exceed the power of human reason. There are references of God's incomprehensibility and subsequent references on 'demonstration' – a propositional knowledge that then circumvents ontological and epistemologies mysteries surrounding God's existence. The quintessential characteristics of Godhead are omniscience, immutability and omnipotence. Theological doctrines also discuss domains of omnipresence with problematisations on account of simplicity, multilocation, containment, timelessness, incorporeality and collocation. Deontological morality as emerging out of discourses of Aristotle, Aquinas and Kant (as emerging from arguments of pure reason) and the utility-oriented consequentialism of Bentham and Mill also have theology as its crucial vantage point. Open theists curtail this unconditional God providence with the temporality of the divine being propositions and other theologians posit the debate of providence between God's free knowledge and natural knowledge (Flint and Rea, 2009). Misra (1971) has discussed the systematic theology of Paul Tillich to propose that it is ontological and technical reason that guides revelation and hence theology. In the Indic context, theology demonstrates alignment to consciousness discourses as well as deliberations on 'reality', 'being-ness' and 'becoming' aligned to the Absolute. Theories of causation, the dialectic of human reason and the logic of the infinite further characterise the same.

Plott (1987) and Copleston (1993) have proposed that the word 'faith' has its origins in post-Aristotelian philosophy particularly the school of cynics, neo-Pythagoreans and the Jewish-Hellenistic school of philosophy. The concept was used then by St. Augustine to explain the proof of God from eternal truths and the attributes of God. John Scot Eriugena II utilised the term *faith* in understanding the knowledge of God in affirmative and negative ways Ockham used it so as to explain the metaphysic of essences. Nicholas of Cusa's principle explaining the infinity of the world, man as the microcosm and the relationship of the God to the world called 'coincidentia oppositorum' elucidated the quintessence of faith. From the Renaissance Scholastic school, Francis Suarez used the term 'faith' to explain God' s existence, essence and relation of beings with attributes to God. Locke proposed faith as that principle that determines the knowledge of the existence of God. Hume has contended faith to be a supra-empirical belief explaining the existence and nature of God. Kant in his discourses on religion as rational theology proposed that faith is an underlying factor that can be described as teleological ethicotheology – encompassing the theological and ethical dimensions within it. The idealist schools comprising J. Caird, Bradley, Bosanquet and Royce visualised faith as a metaphysical conceptualisation enveloping discussions on the Absolute, God and Religion; the meaning of Being and the meaning of ideas; the finite self and the Absolute and the social aspect of morality and discourses on immortality. Henri Bergson from the positivist vein presupposed faith as encompassing religion and mysticism. Teilhard de Chardin proposes faith to be religiosity with a worldview and Gabriel Marcel proposes that faith as existential religiosity – one is outwardly directed and the other as possessing inward contentions.

King (1928) has proposed that as opposed to the standard medieval neo-scholastic thinking, 'faith' is not simply higher than reason; for, even on a supposedly 'natural' level of reason and evidence, what is at stake is an absolutely evident, not a simply evident, basic trust/mistrust – a trustingly accepted or a nihilistically rejected 'grace'. Even the fact that God exists is accepted not strictly on the grounds of proof or evidence from pure reason as natural theology claims, but on a ground of trust itself grounded in reality. As opposed to the Protestant-Barthian dichotomy, it must be stressed that faith is not against reason. What takes place on the level of reason in everyday thinking, in occupation and the sciences, and in philosophy is not simply irrelevant for faith or opposed to it in advance but is determined by the dialectic of affirmation and negation, basic trust and basic mistrust, justification and rejection. According to Berger (1961), 'faith' is grounded in reality itself – meaning a move away from the historical-psychological interpretation of religion, to trust in God as presupposed by trust in God. Nadel (1954) has discussed the capacity of faith as to furnish the view of the world of experience which intelligence is driven to demand; its capacity to announce and maintain moral values, its competencies to hold together societies and sustain their structure and its capacities to furnish individuals with specific experiences and stimulations.

As the cartography of the constructs of religion, theism, theology and faith is multifaceted and the contours are blurred, for the purpose of academic praxis and terminological consolidation which then facilitates epistemological credence, they have been assumed to be intertwined at several critical junctures. Hence, the epistemic treatment on religion and religiosity that ensues would find the boundaries fuzzy at several vantage point, critically delineating them wherever essential.

Theories of Religion: A Broad Spectrum Review

In examining the theoretical repertoire of religion, several binaries are encountered, which have been outlined by Kunin and Miles-Watson (2006) as those pertaining to transcendence/humanism, essentialism/reductionism, insider/outsider and unilinear evolutionist/multilinear relativist. Theorisations on religion have revealed several genres of epistemes commencing from historiographical, phenomenological towards anthropological, sociological, feminist and psychological.

The first epistemological renditions on religion, however, are sought in the writings of Greek philosophers and subsequent thinkers in the Ecclesiastical and Continental genres who have discussed the following components of the same. God and nature discourses are prominent, with metaphysics and mysticism as the underlying tenets. The chain of thought cultivated has been represented here. Dwight (1822) has proposed that that the attributes of God are the attributes of nature and that the earth is the 'being and agency of God'. Ward (1889) proposes that nature is Gnostic and teleological, implying substantial causes and constant relations among various natural entities.

The stance of natural theology visualises God in nature (Bell, 1836; Seeley, 1882) and along the lines of Hume refers to the phenomena of nature as arising from a 'principle being' – God (Crombie, 1829). Drawing from Hegel and Berkeley, Haley's (1836) definition is that of a metaphysical view of the world, a realistic monism, i.e., regarding the events in the existential world as the result of the actions of the Absolute and proposition of a dualistic theism – reverence of God and nature. Substantive arguments of the scholastic theology of Aquinas propose that God and nature are inseparable and that it can be proved through the argument of infinite motion and the carrying of potentiality into actuality, the consideration of efficient causes and the first efficient cause as God or primordial nature (along with parallels sought in the philosophy of nature and theism and the teleology of immanence) (Caldicott and Mackintosh, 1904).

There exist Kantian notions of the dialectical illusion in all transcendental arguments for the existence of the Absolute as co-terminus with nature and theologist Mansel's notions of the Absolute as equated to Acosmism. Mansel envisaged the argument that the Infinite Absolute and finite nature are inseparable correlations intrinsically bound up together, one of the them is giving us the cause and the ontological ground and the other the phenomenal manifestation. This idealism has elaborated the conception of an Absolute which embraces the relative as a living element of itself, an infinite which fills the finite with meaning and takes it up organically into its own nature (Caldicott and Mackintosh, 1804). The thesis of surrelativism postulates that all natural beings are relative and there exists simultaneously a wholly nonrelative abstract being – God, responsible for the existence of nature (Hartshorne, 1948).

A combination of dynamical Spinozism and empirical Gnosticism of Hume proposes that natural reality or the natural world represents inexplicable successive changes in the appearances of the Absolute (Fraser, 1895). An adaptation of Leibniz's theodicy combined with the proposition of Mill (1874) proposes that 'Nature' is the sum of all natural phenomena along with the divine causes, which produce them. Philosophical theism combines a two dimensional cosmological argument – an existential assertion that the natural world exists and an inference by complementary relation that the natural world or nature is a causal conclusion of the Absolute or a divine Being (Physicus, 1878; Max Mueller, 1889; Laird, 1940; Galloway, 1948; Hick, 1963). Along the lines of Emerson's works there is a contention that the Universe (Cosmos) has a divine soul representing 'order' (James, 1941) proposing thus a cosmic consciousness – consciousness of life and order of the universe (Bucke, 1901). Tenets of natural theology postulating that nature is a means to knowableness of the infinite being and the world as the self-evolution of the Absolute being (Lindsay, 1897) form another realm of metaphysical understandings. Kierkegaard's stance is that the Absolute entity is instrumental in the totality and order of the Universe (Lieuw, 1933).

Hicks' (1989) understanding of theology concentrates on the naturalistic definition of religion combining the phenomenological aspects dealing with dimensions of the sacred and the other cosmological arguments; the premier tenets being – Nature as the perfect being or a reflection of the perfect being – the Absolute; the Kantian notion to say that cosmic force exists is to affirm that certain concepts such as that of the infinite personal creator of the universe are substantiated; the idea of 'existence' of nature as integral to the concept. Thus according to Hicks (1989), the core contention is religious realism (religion understood as a varied human response to the transcendent reality and on Kantian lines taking full account of the subjective contribution to all awareness), which is analogous to epistemological critical realism (critical differentiated from naive realism in taking into account the conceptual and interpretative element within sense perception).

Reat and Perry (1991) have proposed that religion is based on certain design arguments falling in the realm of scientific metaphysics (term coined along Kantian lines by Tennant (1930)). The design arguments are the coincidental obtaining of a variety of cosmic circumstances as preconditions of an orderly universe producing life; moral ideals and notions of moral interconnectedness embedded in human-nature relationships; the universe (preconceived as infinite) is knowable and intelligible only to some extent to the human mind; naturalistic worldview that includes interpretation of the phenomena of interface of religion and nature in its totality; emphasis on natural meaning of natural experience (meaning understood both in a relational and practical context) and ethical and aesthetic meaning of natural experience, thereby substantiating the sacredness arguments. Burghart and Cantlie (1995) have applied the Kantian epistemological model to the epistemology of religion proposing that categories [Forgie (1997) prefers to call them category analogies] of religious experiences are culture relative and there is a need to understand 'real nature' as personal is the basis to religious experience. [This view was further developed by Forgie (1997) who characterized it as Hyper Kantianism.]

The other Archimedean standpoint of religion-related theorisations is signified by the evolutionary logic tracing the development from magic to religion to science. These unilinear evolutionary models underlie the works of Freud and Jung which emphasise on the external etic as opposed to the internal emic perspective. The core debate herein is the role of religion in relation to either individual or society. In this genus of thinking, Durkheim has viewed religion as relating to social solidarity abiding by the functionalist argument. Freud, James, Otto and Schleiermacher have placed a stronger emphasis on the relationship between the religion and the individual and their approaches are characterised by an essentialist view of religion. Whereas William James views religious experience as arising from the human rather than the transcendent order simultaneously taking the positivistic view emphasising on the regenerative role of religion, the indologist Max Mueller associates the origins of religion with natural phenomena. Rudolf Otto emphasises on the faculty of the holy in relation to the transcendent that forms the basis of religion and Frederick Schleiermacher has proposed that religion arises from the aesthetic faculty rather than the rational. A differential perspective herein was the Marxian one which focused on religion as expression of false consciousness and alienation.

The phenomenological genre has looked at religion in a less essentialised and more nuanced sense. Bianchi has defined religion as both analogical and dialogical and Eliade's focus is on the unifying transcendent experience emerging from religion. Elaborating further,

Rennie (1996) has proposed that Eliade's conceptualisation of religion can be pronounced as creative hermeneutics incorporating interpretative strategies such as hierophany, the sacred and coincidentia oppositorum Heirophany is the perception of the sacred; the sacred is equated to the real and accorded an ontological status – an ur-datum which is also the presuppositional given of Eliade's hermeneutics, a notion which is more adjectival rather than substantial; and, the sacred and profane are presupposed in a dialectical relationship with each other. The domain of coincidentia oppositorum propounds that myths reveal more profoundly than any rational experience the actual structure of divinity which transcends all attributes and reconciles all contraries. The core herein is that religious symbols and symbolism are capable of revealing a modality of the real or a structure of the world that is not evident on the level (plane) of immediate experience – a modality of the real which is inaccessible to human experience. Further summarising, Rennie (2001) has proposed that the aspects of subjectivity, hermeneutics and phenomenology in the study of religion provide the core emic lens and grounded theory analysis.

Other phenomenological theorisations include those by Gerard Van der Leecuw who has focussed on nuanced theology emphasising on the essence and manifestation of religion and by Segal who views religion within the bounds of culture. Anthropological theories have arisen from the engagements with the practice of religion, pronouncing culture as an important categorical imperative of analysis. Unilinear evolutionists such as Taylor and Fraser who have viewed religion as a quintessential vanguard of the civilisational cycle are pioneers within the anthropological purview. Functionalists such as Malinowski and Radcliffe Brown have viewed religion as serving the function of social regulation with the latter's theorisation as developing a trajectory that would culminate into French structuralism. Clifford Geertz and Edward Shapiro have proposed religion as a means of constructing the cosmos and a system of meaning that develops lifeworlds. Whereas Evans-Pritchard's analysis is that of a combination of a functional and structuralist one in comprehending religion, Talal Asad's approach is more culturally contextualised, with leverage on domains of power and authority in comprehending religion. Another specific conceptualisation within the anthropological fold has been by Melford Shapiro who has combined Freudian presuppositions about the role of religion and place of God combined with Geertz's explanation. Religion herein ultimately arises from the Oedipus complex and the projection of the father onto a transcendent level. In the phenomenological discourse domain, Kaufman (1958) proposes religion as representations of subjective truths and revelation. Employing the arguments for the proof of existence of God as proposed by Plato, Kant and Aquinas, revelation has been further explicated as aligned congruently to reason and not wholly naturalistic.

Philosophical discourses on religion form a crucial body of deliberations through historicity. Primarily epistemological and ontological in nature, they form a crucial body of deliberations within the theoretical realms of understanding. Aquinas's explanations, in the vein of theology, commenced with the inevitability of God's existence, Godhead's instrumentality in all creation and that his existence and essence are not distinct (Kenny, 1980)

Webb (1926) has discussed that the Kantian understanding on the philosophy of religion is chiefly concerned with the impression of design made upon us by the spectacle of nature. There is an inevitable recognition that there is the hand of God in the order and harmony of the Universe, akin to the Newtonian system. In the Critique of Pure Reason, there are three well-known arguments for the existence of God. The first is the physico-theological proof, that is, the argument from design. The second is the cosmological proof which argues from the existence of things which are contingent, that is, which we can conceive not to exist and so are impelled to ask why they exist, to the existence of a necessary Being on which they depend, and which itself cannot be conceived not to exist. The third and last is the ontological proof which infers from the fact that we can form the notion of a most perfect Being the existence of this Being, since, existence being itself a perfection, without which such a being would be less perfect, the notion of a most perfect Being that did not exist would be self-contradictory.

In his Transcendental Dialectic, Kant gives an account of the illusory reasonings which owe their origin on an attempt to employ the categories of understanding beyond the region of possible experience by means of the senses to which they alone are applicable. The illusory reasonings as described by him are concerned with three ideas – the third idea is of God as the Supreme Being in whom all possible perfections are united in a concrete individuality; in view of this attribution to it as concrete individuality, this is distinguished as the Ideal of Pure Reason. Kantian rational theology provides proofs of existence of God. Religion and rational theology are perceived as the source of existence of morals and ethics.

Greene and Hudson (1960) discuss Kantian thoughts on religion within the limits of reason alone. With the Archimedean standpoint of debates between the original predisposition to good in human beings and the propensity to evil in human nature, aspects of the personified idea of the good principle and the objective reality of that idea are prominent. God is the entity that ultimately distinguishes between good and evil with the purport of establishing/founding the kingdom of God on earth. Church as an institutional entity facilitating the ethical commonwealth and that this ecclesiastical faith is further transgressed by pure religious faith. Further relevant propositions are the Kantian conceptions of the nature of the knowing process, the distinction between the phenomena and noumena, treatment of the rationalistic proofs of God's existence and his own moral argument to God freedom and immortality. Further, Walker (1978) has discussed that in the Kantian frame of reference, moral imperatives emerge as categorical imperatives; religion operates primarily within the limits of reason and pietistic and sanctimonious religiosity predominate.

The locus of analysis of the sociological approach is the focus on religion as a social institution and a methodological atheism of sorts wherein the supernatural or theological explanation is replaced in favour of a more humanistic or social explanation. The prominent sociological conceptualisations are by Peter Berger, Hervieu-Leger, Parsons, and Stark and Bainbridge. Peter Berger has proposed that religion is related to worldviews – proposing a system of meaning and meaning construction. Beliefs have been conceptualised by Hervieu-Leger proposing religion as a chain of memory. Parsons focuses on the element of need fulfilment as the core locus classicus of religion and Stark and Bainbridge focus on the element of religious commitment.

The feminist approaches address the concept of consciousness in religion and discuss the domains of false consciousness that religion engineers as aligning to the Marxian paradigm and the related 'gendering' phenomena precipitated thereof. Within the feminist schemata, essentialism is challenged in favour of feminist diversity and the engendered viewpoint – incorporating the experiential and personal approaches in the study of religion are emphasised.

Within the domain of psychological approaches, the individual and belief systems within the ambit of religion are the locus of analysis with a focus on individual experiences and conventional public symbols. Jung's theory of collective consciousness and archetypes proposes a psychic universalism embedded in religion, wherein McIntosh's schema theory argues for more open-ended structures. Another theorist Peter Hill applies cognitive theory to the area of religious experiences. The focus is on the issue of attitudes, i.e., judgements attached to an object and their role in relation to conscious and unconscious control. These experiences become a means of categorising different forms of religious experience on the basis of presence or absence of conscious control. Maslow's analysis has focussed on the experiential basis of religion rather than the structural construction of religion by beliefs and institutions.

Fromm (1950) has examined the connection between psychoanalysis and religion. Commencing with the analysis of the Freudian conceptualisations of religion as an illusion, and Jung's interpretation of religion as phenomenological; psychological understandings on religion have been forwarded. In Fromm's conceptualisation, religion is any system of thought which gives the individual a frame of orientation and an object of devotion. The psychoanalytic approach to religion aims at understanding of human reality behind thought systems. It inquires whether a thought system is expressive of the feeling which it portrays or whether it is a rationalisation hiding opposite attitudes. Furthermore, it asks whether the thought system grows from a strong emotional matrix or whether it is an empty opinion. Leuba (1972) has discussed, in particular, the psychology of religious mysticism. The focus has been on the origin, nature and functions of God ideas: of the beliefs in personal immortality and of the mystical beliefs and practices – mysticism as a cognitive yearning for the incomprehensible. Deliberating further on psychoanalysis and religion, Zilboorg (1967) has employed Freudian psychological determinism to understand the psychic apparatus of religion.

Hence, conceptualisations and theorisations on religion propose the following broad facets and postulates – largely discussed as apriori and ontological arguments. The immanent sacred is predicated on the intimacy of being and the cosmos (Bataille, 1992) highlighting 'adaptive divine cosmologies' and 'traditional concepts of the divine' (Wainwright, 1918) and the postmodernist conception of mysticism not requiring 'experience' in order to explain relationship of being and natural phenomena (Cupitt, 1998). The ontological argument of Ulrici that God is the creative author of the world/nature. Taking the conditioned atoms (which he postulates as the last elements of natural existence) as given, Ulrici necessarily presupposes an 'unconditioned' as the ground of their conditionality and existence. Thus, the conception of the conditioned powers of nature and their efforts lead to the disclosure of an unconditioned cause mediating and determining all that is existential. Through this the nature side of divine essence is derived, or as it has been termed Nature in God.

The stance according to Gunther Theile is that the basis of all things or natural beings are natural substances as causa sui. This existence of the natural substance is connected with the necessity for an Unconditioned – the Absolute substance that is perceived as the sole instrumental cause of the world. The ontological notions of the French School of theology (particularly Malebranche) that the idea of the Infinite nature is the proof of existence of the divine being and the entire proof consists in rising from the finite to the infinite by the negation of the limits of the Infinite, thereby proposing an underlying unity between God and Nature. The ontological stance of the Italian School of theology (particularly Giobert) that Being creates existences in the natural world and the idea of the Being which is really innate as instrumental in the creation of infinite beings. The stance according to the British philosopher Caird is that the ontological argument consists of the notions that the conscious life of beings is based on the notions of the Absolute being, which is not merely a subjective notion or conception, but which carries with it the proof of the existence of the Absolute being and its connection with the universe (Lindsay, 1897).

Indian theorisations on religion align to understandings of Madan (1991, 2004), Saraswati (2000) and European indologists. Pereira (1976) has proposed that from the standpoint of European indologists, there are three genres of theology – of difference (difference as real and identity unreal); of identity (identity is real, difference unreal) and difference in identity (both are real). Theology as proposing a posteriori implications for pluralistic and syncretic discourses by endowing standpoints from the critical hermeneutics of the Bhakti genre has been discussed by Robertson (2006). Whereas Madan (1991, 2004) proposes a structural functionalist and phenomenological approach to religion, Saraswati (2000) aligns to the multi-epistemic STOPA model (sacred space, time, object, person and arrangement), within the sociological understandings of religion, intertwinings of domains of caste, class, gender and ethnicity and the hierarchicus sentiment.

Forms of Religion

Forms of religion have been discussed by Miall-Edwards (1963), MacGregor (1964) and Mensching (1976) as derived from varied theoretical postulates on religion and by Saraswati (2000) and Madan (1991, 2004) in the Indian context. Miall-Edwards (1963) has, looking at the historical development of religions, proposed that the types of religion are tribal, national and universal – tribal religions aligning to animism and totemism; national religions aligning to polytheism and universal religions concerned with moralisation of Gods and movement in the direction of monotheism. These typologies have congruence with a journey traversed through the anthropological conception of religion to the psychical origin and development of religion. MacGregor (1964) has discussed types based on the basic conceptions of God and perceptual efficacies of the Absolute Being – dynamism, animism, polytheism, pantheism, dualism, evolutionary naturalism, humanism, agnosticism and theism. Mensching (1976) has proposed a detailed typology of religion with a sevenfold classification based on differential criteria which include nature religion-culture religion; dynamistic-animistic-theistic religion; demanding-granting religion; revealed-book religion; natural-founded religion; mystic-prophetic and missionary-non-missionary-wandering religions.

According to Saraswati (2000) the basic forms of religion are simple, complex and mixed. The characteristic features of the simple forms of religion are belief in the divinely given form of life; ahistorical, unfounded, unformulated; belief and practices transmitted orally, from one generation to the next; religious experience, interwoven with aesthetic experience, shared collectively in such performances as ritual dance and festivity; and essentially descriptive. Complex and organised forms of religion are characterised by pride in historical origins; 'founder' attributed with divine powers, often recognised as the Incarnation of God, the Son of God, the Messenger of God; personalism signifying faith organised around the personality of the founder; textualised knowledge of beliefs and rituals concerning scriptures, containing the sacred words of God, or his representative, worshipped as a deity; and around the body of original doctrine, new doctrines added up in course of scholastic development. Mixed forms of religion are characterised by explanations of simple and complex forms of religion. Whereas tribal religions can be attributed the quality of simple forms of religion, organised forms of religion are characterised as complex. Madan (1991, 2004) has corroborated the aforementioned categorisation with an emphasis on the domains of ritualisation, sacralisation and rites of passage from the functionalist, structuralist and phenomenological standpoints.

Global Conceptualisations and Positionalities of Organised Forms of Religion

Global conceptualisations of organised forms of religion encompass discussions on Judaism, Christianity, Zoroastrianism and Islam along with Sufi manifestations. Apart from these there are forms of Japanese, Chinese, Korean, African and Latin American religion that further deem deliberations. What has been discussed here are the core thought processes that demonstrate an allegiance to social work such as discourses on morality, ethics, beingness and cosmological doctrines. The origins, medieval manifestations, modern faces and postmodern flavours within each have been addressed from the standpoint of journeys in social orientations.

In terms of organised religions, Judaism has demonstrated existence since historicity with doctrines having Neoplatonic and Kantian overtones. Jewish thought proposes that in terms of moral operations, there is a bridge between divine omniscience and human freedom. Morality is autonomous and heteronomous and hence moral order is divinely ordained and governed by rationality. Influences of Neoplatonic doctrines are apparent in discourses on Universal soul, intellect and nature; morality is defined when by actions and deeds the individual soul strives to unite with the Universal soul to return from the ephemeral world of multiplicity to the divine world of unity (Cohn-Sherbok, 1999). Isaac Israeli, the first Jewish Neoplatonic thinker, proposed the doctrine of equality of beings and the postulate of 'emanationism' wherein forms are created by the will of God, thereby providing the framework for theistic existentialism (Glustrom, 1966).

Apart from works and renditions on the Torah (as the book of the Moses) and the repertoire of the Old Testament, there are propositions and interpretations of Jewish Philosophers such as Ibn Gabirol, Maimonides and Joseph Albo who have provided relevant insights. Ibn Gabirol has discussed notions of form and matter, conceived as both independent universal principles and as present in every object. Spiritual matter precedes and underlies all physical form is believed to emerge from God's will and matter from His essence and hence all beings are designated as 'becoming and potentiality of God'. All discrete physical existence is unified in the supernal realm, to which the individual soul, through ethical behaviour, yearns to return and hence there is a focus on practical morality. Further, human beings represent the pinnacle of creation and there is a need for a teleological ethics so as to attain felicity of the soul – which is the larger human endeavour. Maimonides has discussed the aspects of practical ethics within the Judaic canonical literature that conform to rational and political laws and that the 'highest human good' can be attained by prophecy, divine providence and divine laws. Divine laws elaborate human felicity by proposing of a perfection of the soul through a moral order. Taking the deliberation further, Joseph Albo (Spanish Judaic philosopher) has deliberated on how morality and values are juxtaposed at the juncture of natural, conventional and divine laws. 'Zohar' as central work in the literature of the Jewish Kabbalah (Jewish theophilosophical texts believed to provide esoteric information about the universe and humanity's place therein) has core relevance apart from the Torah and the Testament having a combination of practical and metaphysical tenets of the order of ethics and cosmology. In Zohar, people are made in the image of God and originate from Godhead itself, having the power to influence and act in the divine realm of good and ill. Through devotion, prayer and fulfilling the social obligations in the commandments, people become active participants in the mystery of unification (Glustrom, 1966; Cohn-Sherbok, 1999).

Alignments within Christianity can be traced to the early Greek and Latin traditions. Early Greek tradition in Christian philosophy proposes that moral tenets arise from the notion of 'people' as diffusions of God. There is an ontological link between God and the temporal products, creation of matter and reality (*Origen*). There is a linking of moral freedom with ontology so that the reality that we know is an expression of the ethical disposition of beings that inhabit the same. The Latin tradition within Christianity commences with St. Augustine's propositions of linking God, souls and humanity, to then construct the contingent soul towards a matrix of morality. Morality is at the crossroads of divine foreknowledge, public good and free will (Popkin, 1999). Holscher (1986) has discussed the Augustinian arguments drawing from ecclesiastical leanings regarding the existence of an incorporeal and spiritual substance in man, i.e., the spiritual substantiality of man's soul. Rational spirituality is a positive characteristic of the soul and there is the cogitare-seipsum argument for the spirituality of the soul – proposing that the soul is the self-conscious spiritual being and possesses characteristics of substantiality to the degree of perfection not found in the body. Developing the analysis on Graeco-Roman Christianity, Cochrane (1972) has proposed that the arguments from Augustus to Augustine were primarily centred around reexamining the tenets of scientistic naturalism in favour of a worldview based on the vision of Christ. In that sense theism, cosmology and the principle of divine providence form the key tenets. Hence, in the vein of Augustine there is a substitution of the embodied for the disembodied logos and a Christian historiography that claims to establish a concrete principle of interpretation in lieu of ideologies classicism.

Gnosticism within Christianity holds the fundamental cosmological belief that the world is to be composed of spiritual human beings. The causal principle of the spiritual world is the unknowable being and all moral order focuses on redemption from the alienation of the spiritual being and moving towards the Gnostic. Medieval Christian thought owes its repertoire to Bonaventure and Aquinas. Bonaventure has proposed that the knowledge of the soul is 'true knowledge' that can be known through ethically guided behaviour. Aquinas's seminal principle being the creation for 'action' and 'ethical action' is a dimension of the proof of existence of God. 'Everything we know of acts within a moral frame and purposefully, and thus there must be some being who directs the purposes to the ends and this being is called God.'

Modern manifestations of Christianity are visualised in the writings of Continental theistic philosophers who propose a moral order that establishes a correlation between human quest and divine graciousness. Altruism is viewed as a practical manifestation of a sui generis region of human experience, whose presumptive reference is the theos (Popkin, 1999). Hayes and Gearon (1998) have adopted a historical-critical approach to biblical exegesis so as to discern alignments between praxis, morality and theology – based on the unifying theological theme based in the texts examining the relationship between God and God's people. Links are established between Christology, Catholic biblical sources and ecclesiology – recognising the different models of the Church in contemporary theology balancing different models of Jesus while retaining Jesus' paradigmatic status as the second person in the Trinity. Further in terms of contemporary developments, there is also a revisiting of Christologies in the light of discoveries in cosmology as well as connections and organic interlinkages between humanity and divinity as a central Christological question. These discourse have also catapulted onto realms of morality, particularly the concept of agape and social principle centring around domains of dignity, communitas, common good, distributive justice, participation, subsidiarity, altruism and philanthropy.

In the Indian context, Christianity has assumed Thomist, neo-Thomist, Protestant and conventional ecclesiastical forms and has also assumed in the critical historiographical vein, a subaltern temperament and postulates of liberation theology. Clarke (1998) has positioned discourses in Indian Christianity by examining theology as the critical and constructive reflection on the dialogical symbolic interaction of the community in its effort to make sense of, find meaning in and determining order for living collectively under the divine. Further, the proposition is that in order for Indian Christian theology to be dialogical, inclusive and liberative, it is determined that the religious world of the subaltern be re-collected and remembered.

Protestantism as a significant branch of development as a departure from Roman Catholicism and mainstream Christianity has, apart from differential ritualistic, monastic and ecumenical stances, floated missionary attitudes at the juncture of orient/occident tendencies, Anglicism and secularism (as a departure from dogma and orthodoxy) (Copley, 1997). However, the domains of 'cultural conditioning' and 'contextual hermeneutics' and in some situations colonial epistemologies have to a great extent shaped the faces of Protestantism and their missions.

Islamic thought owes its genesis to the epistemes of Persian thinkers such as Avicenna and Averroes who have delved into the metaphysics of Quranic tenets. There is a belief in the exclusive efficacy of God of whose direct intervention the events of nature are alleged to be the overt manifestation or occasion (Fakhry, 1958). Islamic worldview proposes a discontinuous and discrete worldview – thus lending credence to tautological inference and categories of causality based on an elaborate metaphysics of knowledge – thereby defining issues of 'identity', 'self' and 'continuity of consciousness'. There is a metaphysical justification of the supernatural and its incursion into the domain of the real. There is an allegiance to the atomic composition of bodies, atomic character of time and the existence of void – all having their substantial sources to God. Theistic logic is predominant signifying the 'maxim of admissibility' – meaning that whatever is possible in reason is possible for God. This omnipotence of God culminates in the repudiation of the natural efficacy of 'secondary agents' both animate and inanimate. Modes of relationship of reciprocity, antecedence and consequence and cause-effect domains all assume the apriori existence of a Godhead.

Averroes has however proposed an ontological re-assertion of 'beings' – re-positioning the sole credence to Godhead. Although Being and order of the universe are constituted by Godhead, there is a certain anthropomorphic emphasis in that pure immanence is assumed to not exist. Manifestations are more an outcome of 'act potency', teleology and rationality. According to Fakhry (1958), Averroes has proposed an integral acceptance of the hylomorphic dualism of Aristotle, leading him to the endorsement of the allied Aristotelian notion of the eternal Prime Matter which is the abiding substratum of becoming and change in the universe. There is a certain determinism which balances the effective providence view with the rational-pragmatic role of beings in the universe.

Corbin (1960) has discussed the symbolic, mystical and angelic aspects of Avicennian thought – a core Gnostic thinker in the Islamic vein. Cosmology characterises his thought with parallels drawn towards Greek philosophical thinking of Aristotle and Plotinus. Other doctrines include those on Self and the necessary Existent that depart from the conventional genre and align to a predominantly ontic and mystical domain. Examining the metaphysical content of his thought, Morewedge (1973) has discussed that there is a primary analysis of nature, of being, its application to numerous things and an introduction to the exposition of substance. Being-ness is deliberated upon and in particular the relation to universality and particularity apart from other categorical imperatives governing existence. Qualities and attributes of being and Necessary Existent are explained. Whereas 'being' is contingent on unity-plurality, priority-posteriority, finitude, cause-effect, potentiality-actuality, the Necessary Existent is united, singular in essence, eternal and absolute. There is a certain sense of 'emanationism' – proposing that all 'beings' emanate from the Necessary Existent. Avicenna then in his metaphysical work Dânish-Nâma-i'alâ'î (*The Book of Scientific Knowledge*) discusses the conditions in which it is possible for the 'being' to connect with the Necessary Existent. Along Spinozan lines, there is a distinction between essence-existence and description of the soul-self substances. The Necessary Existent is portrayed as normative and the ultimate being which exists apriori to all categories, substances and bodies (material substances). Hence, drawing from core Quranic tenets, the metaphysics of Avicenna is a systematic exposition into theistic cosmology – combining the systematic theology of Paul Tillich and the natural theology tenets of Continental philosophers.

Whereas traditional Islamic tenets aligned towards the Quran, Sufism focussed largely on illumination and mysticism (Khan, 1995). Direct communion, alignment and affinity with the Absolute, of the being, is a manifestation of essence, existence, being-ness and a statement towards addressing the hegemony of ritualisms and orthodoxy. Schisms within Sufism differ in their approaches towards the axiology of attaining the Absolute and the nature of the union; but the core structurationist elements of human agency, actors, role manifestations, cartographies and symbologies remain similar. Further, Sufism in terms of its transcendental tenets and intentions has demonstrated parallels with Upanishadic tenets, cultivation of human emotions to achieve direct allegiance with the Absolute and a penchant for syncretism.

Zoroastrianism as a historically evolved faith in Iran, traversing space and time, has manifestations in the Indian context with interpretations from the Gathas embodied in the scripture Zend Avesta. The Avesta is divided into two groups – the first group comprising the Vendiad, the Visperad and the Yasna; the second group comprising the minor prayers and the Yashts, called the Khordeh Avesta or the abridged Avesta – prayer book for the laity in use today by the Parsis who practice the religion. In terms of the first group, the Vendiad is a compilation of the religious laws and the priestly code prescribing various purifications, penalties and expiations; the Visperad is a collection of litanies, invocations and homage to the lords and the Yasna is composed of hymns or songs including the five hymns or Gathas written in a special dialect – the metrical Gathas that constitute the oldest as well as the most important part of the whole Avesta (Nariman, 1999). Elements of nature worship, divinisation and sacralisation of nature, practical metaphysics and discourses on morality and teleological and deontological ethics encompass the gamut of deliberations on Mazdaism. The quintessential 'good' is posited vis-a-vis the 'evil' which needs to be addressed and this is done through the cognition of the six abstract attributes of God – truth or righteousness, good mind and the prudence to select the good path, the divine utopia of universal happiness, pious mindedness, perfection and immortality.

As per Mazdean scholars such as George Dumezil and Will Durant, dualism and dichotomy characterise Avestan thought – with privileging of eschatologies and soteriologies of the propriety over the imprudent. This chain of thought further perpetuates discourses of self and linked deliberations and discursive domains. The recognition of the transcendent reality and the capacity of the human individual to intuit it by ethical life are the core of the theosophy (Toot, 1957). The postulate of righteousness translates into domains of altruism and philanthropy – the core of Zoroastrian teleological ethics, with the puritan deontological ethics delving into moral domains of conduct and pragmatic conduit. Other aspects include self-realisation through sublimation and prescription of paths of goodness, wisdom, divine knowledge, divine love and endeavours of union with the Absolute – that address simultaneously the issues of 'evil' by a metaphysical alignment to the benevolent divinity (Toot, 1957). Commenting on the ethical domains of Zoroastrian thought, Marwaha (2006) has further synthesised the elements of self and soul and the five constituting elements of the theology of praxis being the body, breath of life, soul, prototype image and the guardian spirit. These elements intertwine to define selfhood, praxis and the ethical repertoire through the prism of duality as the underpinning hypothesis of Mazdean thought – the binary category of the 'good' privileged over the other.

One position on the new religious movements by O'Connell (1999) proposes that the initial surge of socio-religious reform has transposed and channelled into an ongoing movement, sect, caste or other identifiable communities. Cohesively these form the basis of comprehending new religious movements, the nouveau dimensions manifesting in themes of sociocultural orientations and control of sacred spaces, functioning of religious leadership (Long, 2003), formations of religion-social propositions of reform, protest and millennial revolt and modification/hybridisation of sacred texts and rituals. According to Harvey (2000), the diversity and complexity in new religious movements arises from existential principles manifesting in praxis as persons, powers and gifts with underlying themes as human and other-than-human encounters, emerging from a dialectic between religion, traditions, change and continuity and social geographies and bio-regions. The modes of expression demonstrate steps towards liberation and postcolonialism – determined in effect by cosmological and social orders in which they are located (Beckford, 1986). Habib (2007) has proposed that the roots of religion as philological and historical-anthropological with the 'text' being the Archimedean departure point of assertions of difference.

Looking at the apparent, erotic and esoteric interpretations of texts, the submission is that the new religious movements code texts with multilayered and multifaceted meanings, connecting the disconnect between practice and texts, simultaneously making assertions of religious textuality as being an expression of class divided society. McDaniel (1989) has explored the domains of religious ecstasy within the context of the Bhakti and post-Bhakti and neo-religious/faith traditions. Based on hagiographies written by devotees, the emphasis on expressionism, co-existence of apparently conflicting propositions, antagonisms and contradictions and re-interpretation of texts sometimes through a hitherto unexplored and subaltern perspective, historiography and sensibility is the summum bonum of the new religious movement genre.

Religion in the Japanese, Chinese and other South East Asian contexts focuses on domains that align to a theocentric value theory (MacGregor, 1964). In the context of Chinese religion, there is an emphasis on the perception of the concrete which builds into a nondevelopment of abstract thought, emphasis on the particular, conservatism expressed in exaltation of antiquity, fondness for complex multiplicity expressed in concrete form, formal conformity, tendency towards practicality, individualism with a simultaneous reverence for hierarchy and nature and syncretic as well as conciliatory tendencies. Japanese religion dwells in particular on the acceptance of phenomenalism and nonrationalistic tendencies. In general the focus of South East Asian religion is that of consciousness of the individuals, discovery of the Absolute in beings and a certain sense of submission to the religiously charismatic individuals.

The core of ethnic religions of the African and Latin American contexts has dimensions of impulse and form, sense of the numinous, astral relationships, immortalised life and sacralisation (Mensching, 1976). There is a certain combination of archaic spirituality and Christianity tenets (Armstrong (1976), a certain alignment with the Hegelian scheme of things, Kantian practical reason that proposes connections with the infinite and Diderot's natural religion (MaxMueller, 1972).

Indic Conceptualisations and Positionalities of Organised Forms of Religion

The repertoire of Indic conceptualisations commences with the Archimedean standpoint of the Vedic renditions catapulting onto further classical exegesis of the Brahmanas and Aranyakas, Upanishads (major and minor Upanishadic versions), Epic literature, Dharmashastras and the Arthashastra, Puranic injunctions, Agamic literature, Tantric epistemes and Dravidian classical metaphysical literature. The sophisticated ontologies and epistemologies find spaces in the six Indic philosophical schools – Mimansa, Nyaya, Vaisesika, Sankhya, Yoga and Vedanta (Radhakrishnan, 1940). Jainism and Buddhistic tenets form another domain of the gamut of the conceptualisation with classical canonical and noncanonical literature as the commencing point. Whereas in the Vedic genre, postclassical thought finds historiographical continuity through the Bhakti tradition and subsequent ecclesiastically inclined modernists, 'modernity' in itself has subsequent syncretic and pluralistic manifestations in the form of amalgamated and hybridised metaphysics. Jainism and Buddhism seek their postclassical and modern manifestations through schisms and differential metaphysical orientations in the phenomenological vein.

The other vanguard of Indic religious schemata is visualised in Sikhism, the debut version of syncretism in the genus – with its own versions of theistic metaphysics, existentialism and structuralist interpretations of 'text-context' within the inherently theological discourse. Institutional developments and subsequently the poststructuralist-postmodernist disjunctures have brought in aspects of communitas, bonding-bridging capital, competing theistic agendas and equalities and theological antagonisms and contradictions within an essentially the (onto) logical framework. The lens of deconstruction and difference have thus provided penetrating insights into the differential facets and postulates of Indic faiths – hybrid, amalgamated, syncretic and aporetic versions (personal mysticism and institutional facades) which contribute towards the Indic theo-existential brouhaha. Indic religions are defined as those having their archaeology and genealogy in the Indian subcontinent through historicity (Madan, 2004). The core content of Indic thought is primarily the stress on universals and the concept of unity, primacy of Universal self over individual self and a transcendence component from the objective natural world (Weiner, 1964).

The core vantage point for a discussion on Indic religions commences with Vedic literature and allied scriptural leanings emerging from subsequent texts. Through deification of the cosmos and nature, the Vedic Samhitas (Rigveda, Samaveda, Yajurveda and Atharvaveda) contain readings wherein celestial, atmospheric and terrestrial deities are venerated and the cosmogenic process is explained (Macdonnell, 1960). Skolimowski (1993) has proposed that postulates expressed in the Vedas realize the divinity that is close to Plato's conception of knowledge as culminating in arriving at a Godhead and notions of continuously evolving universe as supported by the Epicurean philosophers of the Democritus school. The Brahmanas and Aranyakas extol philosophies that precipitate ethics through an elucidation of the cosmotheandric experience and the quintessentiality of primordial nature and the subtle elements, which lead to the evolution of the gross elements (Satyashrava, 1955). The Aranyakas or the forest treatises also contain descriptions of the rituals of worship and also the mystical and symbolic interpretations of the rituals (Biswas, 2000). The Upanishads extol ecosophies through metaphysical discourses on Brahman (cosmos) and primordial matter (Prakriti). There are eighteen principal Upanishads and several minor Upanishads (or neo-Upanishads) discussing 'being' and Absolute Being as well as soteriological discourses in a multitude ways. Neo Upanishadic philosophy is paralleled to Neo-Platonism with predominant interest in pragmatic epistemology and axiology (Mahadevan, 1998). Of the minor Upanishads containing discourses on cosmology twenty-four minor Upanishads classified as Samanya Vedanta Upanishads deal with the general Upanishadic doctrines on cosmology, primal substances, primordial nature and gross and subtle elements. Epic literature is composed primarily of the two major epics Ramayana and Mahabharata, the readings (basically of a descriptive nature) extol a moral interconnectedness in terms of human-cosmos relationships, teleological and deontological ethics of praxis.

According to Kane (1970), an amalgamation of soteriological and morality based discourses are available in the Dharmashastras (classical canonical texts expounding laws). The Gautama Dharmasutra and Apastamba Dharmasutra propose a spiritual reconnection of 'beings' with the cosmos by emphasising upon intrinsic value propositions. The Baudhayana and Vasistha Dharmasutras forward propositions that could be paralleled with the Gaia hypothesis, particularly teleological Gaia emphasising upon a worldview with a purposeful teleology – cosmocentrism. Proposing sectarian developments (conception of the cosmology integrated with the triadic deities; i.e., the cosmos (Brahman) is equated to Brahma, Vishnu, Mahesh or the divine feminine principle), the core readings of the Puranas are composed of theories of creation proposing divine cosmologies along triadic lines, discussions on the primal, subtle and gross elements as proposed by the philosophical schools – particularly the Sankhya school; and pragmatic aspects of cosmological consciousness, moral interconnectedness and sacredness dimensions (Tagare, 1978). There exist around eighteen Puranas and their corresponding Upapuranas combining tenets from animism and monotheism (revolving around the particular deity of worship from the triad or the divine feminine principle).

Possessing a time period parallel to the Vedas but being differential in orientation and content (Santideva, 1999), the Tantras (incorporating Agamas and Samhitas) incorporate the same self/other, spirit/matter distinction, associating the feminine and nature with materiality typically leading to an ontological devaluation of both. According to Kinsley (1998), Tantric literature provides visions of the divine feminine. This notion departs from the traditional conceptualisation of the divine feminine as self-sacrificing. This postulate has been supported by readings from primary sources such as the Damara Tantra, Devi Mahatmya, Kaulajnananirnaya tantra, Kulacudamani nigama, Mahanirvana tantra, Pranatoshini tantra, Vamakeshvara agama and Yoni tantra. Scriptures in Dravidian languages support the Advaita stance as discerned through the sutras of Siva jnana bodham and Panniru Thirumurai. The postulate of nonduality between the 'being' and 'cosmos' can be suitably interpreted to provide for metaphysical tenets. Such descriptions are found in the mystical renderings of Tirumular, Nayanmar, Alwars and Nammalvar's Thiruvaymoli. The epistemological stances of Ramalinga swamigal, Ramana Maharshi, Thyagaraja, Vemana, Basavayya and Raghuvendra can also be interpreted to provide for cosmological readings with variations as visualised in Advaita tenets discussing the relationship of 'being' and 'cosmos'.

Outlining the core tenets of the six philosophical schools, the nucleus of Nyaya school lies in constructions of valid knowledge through logical criticism; the other domains being the object of knowledge, sources of valid knowledge, nature of the physical world and a syllogistic analysis of the individual soul, liberation and God. It provides proof of existence of Godhead through inference, syllogism, induction and causation. The logical progression of the individual soul consciousness towards this Absolute being is described. Vaisesika propositions are the analysis of the varied aspects of reality, categories and qualities of substance and the concept of creation and annihilation of the world. It proposes an atomistic pluralism, God as the efficient cause of the world and substances and categories as subsequent manifestations of the same. Sankhya abides by the dualistic principle and theorisation pertaining to the cause and effect of creation – Prakriti being the unconscious principle and Purusa the conscious; which are also the sources of valid knowledge contributing to the process of evolution of the universe and the pragmatic duality oriented conceptualisations of liberation and God. It describes the cosmic evolution, mergers of human attributes that facilitate transcendence and an ontological dualism between spirit and nature. The Yoga school is primarily consciousness driven, the consciousness being of the theistic existentialist nature with the ultimate purport being the knowledge and concept of God. Further, whereas Mimansa has a ritualistic orientation to attain the theistic utopia of divinity and the knowledge of the Absolute, the Vedanta school emphasises on transcendence with its philosophy of monism, discourses on the soul, self and Absolute being; with manifestations of the supreme self, consciousness and transcendental dialectic and deductions as the summum bonum of the theo-analytical trajectory (Tigunaut, 1983; Potter, 2001–2008). The full-fledged emphasis on transcendence emerges in the Vedanta school and its variations.

MaxMueller (1973) has discussed that the key in Indic philosophy are the immortality of the soul, metaphors such as phenomenal reality, concepts of Atman-Brahman and eschatology. Outlining certain key domains of classical Indian philosophy, Krishna (1997) and Mohanty (2000) have discussed that in the Indic scheme of things the ontological and epistemological principles interact to form predispositions which in turn give rise to categories determining existence – spiritual attainments being one of them. Herein the central metaphysical issues are the problem of causality, existence of an external world, whether the world is real/unreal, identity and difference issues, and absolutism versus non-absolutism. The abiding principle is however the propensity of linkages between entities such as self, world, Absolute and soul liberation.

More detailed renditions with epistemic comparisons drawn towards the western repertoire and highlighting the nuanced contents of the philosophical musings can be presented here. The Nyaya school has been compared to the dialectics of the Aristotelian School (Colebrooke, 1977). The epistemological variations within the Nyaya school through a series of propositions and syllogisms aim to arrive at a consciousness of existential nature (Randle, 1976). This dimension also emerges in a study on cosmology by Mukhopadhyay (1995) who looked at the Tattvachintamani text of Gangeshopadhyay of the Nyaya school propagating that creation presupposes existence of primordial stuff or matter (bhuta) which is divine and which cannot be structurally, conceptually or physically broken into simple units of matter.

The Vaisesika school (parallels found in the philosophy of the Greek philosopher Democritus) discusses primal substances, matter and atoms. Reality consists of substances that possess qualities. Substances are substrates of qualities but are distinct from qualities that they possess. The Vaisesika sutra enumerates that the substances (Book I, chapter 1) defines attributes of primal substances (Book II, chapter 1) and also defines and explains the various phenomena of nature. Another Vaisesika text Padarthadharmasangraha defines various attributes of primal substances (chapter III, 20–25) and the creation of gross natural elements from primal substances (Radhakrishnan, 1957; MaxMueller, 1973). Combining the aforementioned two systems, Lalye (1995) has looked at the Nyaya Vaisesika system (particularly the text – Siddhanta muktavali) taking into account God as the efficient cause who keeps order in nature along with discussions on the traditional five elements, their level of experience and the correspondence with modern physics.

The Sankhya school [parallels found in Pythagorean philosophy (Colebrooke, 1977)] is known for the theory of evolution. Prakriti or primal matter is the basis of all existence. As the changing object, Prakriti is the source of the world of becoming. In it all determinate matter is implicitly contained. The third section of the Sankhyakarika describes the primal nature as the root matter. The Samkhya Pravachana Sutra maintains that Prakriti is the state of quiescence (equilibrium), the disequilibrium of which is responsible for the evolution of five tanmatras and the gross elements, thereby displaying holistic ecological ethics in the process of evolution (Pereira, 1976). Examining the ecological implications of the Sankhya doctrines, Rege (1995) propagates that it presupposes a basic ontological division between minds, which are characterised by consciousness, and material things, which are characterised by extension and motion; the ultimate constituents of all entities being Prakriti (nature), Guna (attributes) or a substantive entity. The Yoga school contains a pragmatic epistemology (Desai, 1972; MaxMueller, 1973) which through its doctrine of unification of the consciousness reveals an embedded universal consciousness. The Yoga sutras of Patanjali contain references on Prakriti, revealing that the basis of Prakriti is Chitta, the common existential element in all beings (Rocher, 1985). The Purva Mimansa sutras contain theological treatises describing modes of animistic forms of worship and veneration of nature's forces (MaxMueller, 1973).

The Vedanta school consists of different interpretation of the Upanishads and the Brahmasutra providing multiple theses on Brahman (the substratum of the microcosm and macrocosm of the universe) (Parthasarathy, 1983). Bertocci (1985) finds parallels of Vedanta in Greek philosophy particularly Aristotle's ontology (primal substances as prime movers of the world) and Plato's three independent and coeternal metaphysical ultimates: Demi Urge, eternal form and receptacle; the interaction between them produces a world of time and space. There are also parallels to the normative implications of Gestalt's principle of organic wholeness variously manifesting itself as configurations and form a totality (Minakshi Sundaram, 1985).

The variations within the Vedanta school provide multiple worldviews ranging from cosmocentrism to ecocentrism, displaying various shades of ecological ethics through spiritual cosmologies. The discourses also contain the relationship of the individual soul in existential beings to the cosmic soul, the unity or duality between which form crucial points of departure (Gandhi, 1970). The stance of Ramanuja states that the cosmos is an adjectival determination of the Absolute and hence possesses divine connotations – the Vishishtadvaitic stance (Thibaut, 1962; (Rangacharya and Aiyangar, 1961). The Vallabhite interpretation is known as the Siddha dvaita or pure nondualism. The stance is that the relationship between the Absolute and the world is that of the relation between the whole and the part and thus the cosmos is divine (Date, 1973; MaxMueller, 1973). The Dvaitadvaita stance of Nimbarka maintains that the relation between the Absolute and the cosmos is that of independence and dependence – cosmos is a subordinate existential reality of the Absolute. Duality is thus different as well as nondifferent from the nondual independent reality; different as possessing a dependent subordinate existence and nondifferent as possessing no independent existence; each 'being' representing an existential counterpart of the spiritual being (Gandhi, 1970; Colebrooke, 1977). Madhvacharya's stance is that of Dvaita – the Absolute and cosmos/world/phenomenal world are different, the Absolute being the instrumental precipitating factor, thereby providing for a spiritual cosmology. The Avibhagalaksana of Vijnanabhiksu proposes a nonduality of empirical reality that appears as a differentiated plurality in its manifest form. The example cited is that of Prakriti or primordial matter in its transcendental form as a nondual basis of the differentiated world of experience. Nonduality (Brahman) in the transcendental state also translates to nonduality in the metempirical state, thus providing a basis for holistic ecological ethics or ecocentrism (Van Buitenen, 1971).

The critical hermeneutics of Sankara's thesis of Advaita forwards that the Absolute along with the phenomenal consciousness create the cosmos, which is divine and not differentiated from the Absolute. All existential beings form the Absolute (Brahman). Brahman is the material cause and through the instrumentality of the phenomenal consciousness evolution takes place – thus providing for a divine cosmology. Brahman is thus considered to be the material and efficient cause of empirical reality. The commentators on the Sankarabhashya of the Brahmasutra (Vachaspati Mishra, Vignaraja and Bhaskara) propose that Advaita envelops the transformation of Brahman into metempirical reality postulating both difference and nondifference as the essential relation between Absolute and the phenomenal world. The finite world is regarded as an integral expression of the Absolute (Radhakrishnan, 1923; Thibaut, 1962; Gupta, 1996; Chattopadhyay, 1978; Comaer, 2000). Among the refutations to this trend of thought, Nelson (2000) forwards that Advaita presupposes a wholesale objectification and radical ontological devaluation by its thesis of transcendental dualism that is world negating.

The focus of canonical and noncanonical literature within Jainism focuses on a metempirical reality and ontologies of nonabsolutism (or Anekantavada) as a metaphysical metaphor for equality. Within the context of Jainism, refined aspects have emerged through the abiding tenets of multiperspectival stance of understanding reality through evidence and logic, equity and universality of soul. There are references to 'body' and 'soul' denoting 'substance' and 'quality' attempting to attain nonsubstance that is multiple in nature (Barlingay, 1992). Two major categories of literature within Jainism are Agam Literature, which are texts that are sacred books of the Jain religion, and the non-Agam literature. Differences exist among the four major Jain sects (Digambara Jain, Svetambara Murtipujak, Svetambara Sthanakavasi and Shwetambar Terapanth) on the validity of the documented Jain scriptures. The general content of Jaina epistemology which is uniform is that Jiva (soul) exists in the world in contact with Ajiva (matter). This contact/association perpetuates the cycle of birth and death, which, as a process, could be curtailed by a course of discipline leading to nirvana (salvation). As a 'realistic thought', it accepts the findings of Vedanta, but seeks to reorient a logical attitude, accepting 'contradictions' as the true meaning of reality. There is a focus on sense perception, deductive reasoning, hypothetical reasoning and inference to understand the merger of self and Absolute Self. Hence, through a postulate for incorporating all possible angles of vision into a synthetic approach to reality (syadvada), Jainism takes the position between logical rationalism and logical empiricism proposing that 'reality of the world must be set alongside the subject who perceives it as real'. Jaina episteme thus includes understandings of sense perception and deductive reasoning; knowledge by acquaintance; importance of pramana or valid knowledge and importance of evidence-inference – belief and a distinction between direct and indirect cognition. The fundamental position is expressed by the equation 'pramana' (evidence) added to samayoga (incidence and co-incidence) is equivalent to jnana or knowledge (Folkert, 1993; Jaini, 2000; Balcerowicz, 2003).

Developed as a primarily agnostic tradition, Buddhism, in the course of its proliferation, developed schisms manifesting itself into approximately nineteen schools geographically spread out – the prominent ones being Sthaviravada, Sarvastivada, Mahayana, Sautrantika and Madhyamaka. Later on syncretic trends were visualised and differentiations within schools is fundamentally epistemological in nature (Davids, 1997). Buddhist canonical literature comprising Silas, Parayanas, Nikayas, Jatakas and Dhammapada and Abhidhamma books pronounces the general content of Buddhistic thought which includes four bases of self-possession, right exertions, bases of power, five faculties and strengths emerging therefrom, seven factors of enlightenment, four truths and the eightfold path (Warder, 2000). Other aspects of Buddhistic thought are the impermanence principle of the existential material world, knowledge through sense-perception and experience, knowledge of objective facts and theology to be replaced by science of causation.

Buddhistic thought is thus characterised by a certain pragmatic agnosticism. 'Being' is perceived to be subjective and reality exists only if it is empirically verifiable – inherently reality being dynamic in nature. The core proposition is that 'beings' are impermanent and the evolutionary process is continuous, and the merger of being and Being is possible only if it is empirically verifiable. This merger (process of actualisation) is interpreted differentially by different schools of Buddhism as Nirvana, subjectivism and nihilism (Yoshinori, 1995).

Systematic renditions of nontheistic spirituality are further found in Buddhistic tenets. Apart from the theory of dependent origination and self-nature exchange, Ichimura (2001) has discussed the dimensions of Buddhist critical spirituality through the concepts of 'Prajna' and 'Sunyata'. Prajna is the transcendental knowledge and sunyata is the nonduality proposition, both also being key schemes of the Mahayana tradition. Critical spirituality herein implies the transcendental knowledge or insight into the nonduality of all existence. For the Yogacara Buddhists, the ultimate spiritual context is the insight of nondifference of self, matter and the material world of existence.

Two domains that characterise Buddhistic thought across its global (Indian, Chinese, Tibetan and Southeast Asian) manifestations are meditation and emptiness. Meditation signifies a nondiscursive awareness of present reality emphasised peculiarly in the Abhidhamma books and a remodelled version in the Zen tradition. This meditation is a metanoia of thinking, a conversion within the reflective thought that signals a return to the authentic self – which is not only a path to enlightenment of the mind, but it also effects a transformation of the affective life at its very roots. Liberation from attachment is the foundation for a range of psychological, epistemological and ontological theories. The Mahayana movement in India and its acculturation in Tibet and China have expanded the tradition of detachment and articulated itself across the whole range of thought giving rise to the dominant intuition of emptiness (sunyata). The teaching of emptiness was given a firm logical underpinning in the Mulamadhyamakakarika of Nagarjuna, who subjected basic Buddhist concepts to a radical logical analysis, with a purpose of demonstrating the emptiness of all things. Since all things arise of dependent co-origination, all things are empty of self-nature or own being; emptiness is the true nature of the real, which cannot be grasped in our own words or concepts but only in the meditation that leaves thought behind. The other school of the Mahayana tradition is the 'mind only' school founded by Asanga and Vasubandhu – looking at facets of Nihilism, but rooted in the doctrine of mind. Nothingness and emptiness parallel Western epistemological discourses on being and essences and forms the sublimated component of actualisation (Yoshinori, 1995).

Bhakti, as a medieval manifestation and subsequent modernist developments influenced by enlightenment rationality, has unveiled several facets of religion. Devotional literature, the semantic-linguistic-historical analysis of which provides the base reveals several domains of Bhakti tradition in its early history of Krsna to its modern adaptations in nineteenth and twentieth-century culture (McGregor, 1992), forms the fundamental rendition. Allegiances are drawn towards the ontology and ideation of St. Bonaventure and Gabriel Marcel, with a focus on rediscovering the philosophy of presence and emphasis on transvaluation (Plott, 1974). Parallelism and diffusion characterise the spread of the Bhakti genre (Marulasiddaiah, 1996) with an alignment to the understanding emerging from Weberian understanding of the religion of the nonprivileged class drawing from Nietzschean understanding of the sentiment of resentment. Traces of congregationalism, salvation and rational ethical religion are identified. Further Lorenzen (1995) has drawn from the Dumontian understanding to interpret how Bhakti is a modified and subaltern replication of the upper class belief, articulation of social ideology and formation of community identity as key processes in the evolution and definitions of the saguni and nirguni traditions. Expressed principally through the hagiographies and genealogies of teachers and disciples, Bhakti symbolises subaltern historiographies, reexamination of authority and manifestations of dissidence.

Drawing upon Hobsbawm's analysis of invented traditions, Lorenzen (1995) has comprehended the variations in the Bhakti genre as those establishing or symbolising social cohesion, real or artificial communities; those establishing or legitimising institutions, status or relations of authority and those inclined towards building a sense of communitas and bonding type of social capital. The religious vocabulary of the Bhakti genre has been constructed by protest-oriented socially conscious canon of poetry (Hawley and Juergensmeyer, 2004).

Some of the key affinities emerging from Bhakti are rejection of degenerated forms of ritualism and re-instating divinity; focus on love and service (Vallabha devotion and Bengal Vaishnavism); erotic love and supremacy of the devotional sentiment. There is a certain denominational name of God, an overarching Divine Principle which reveals itself in form and mode and a lateral movement from 'ego-centrism' to 'theocentrism' is facilitated. Bhakti genre finds parallels in Charles Hartshorne's neoclassical theism where one includes contingency, becoming and variability in divine nature, without, however, diminishing the metaphysical perfections of the divine such as constancy and necessity. Further, nuances within the

Bhakti understanding include aspects of disembodied spiritualism (drawing from the Puranic, Agamic and the Tantric traditions) and holistic realism. Mysticism characterises another domain of Bhakti – delving into the psycho-somatic structure of the individual. Transcendence of language, subject-object duality and pervading levels of existence – gross, physical, vital and subtle so as to attain Godhead – are other domains. Categorical imperative of sameness-oneness, time, space, objecthood, subjecthood and related thought constructs concretise the tenets of Bhakti – retaining voices from the below and syncretic sensibilities (Sundararajan and Mukerji, 1997).

The modernist genus of religious thinking in the Indic context is characterised by critique of 'world negation' and renunciation tenets and the extant social structure and stratification. Identification of theological sources on universal love and compassion (Ramalingar); relating art and aesthetics to mystical/spiritual experiences (Tagore); creative experiencing of mystical experiences through the divine play of the Absolute and the divine feminine (Ramakrishna); direct nondualistic experiencing of the Ultimate Reality which signifies a substantial monism (Vivekananda); insightful connections with the divine and an annihilation of the gross material self (Krishnamurthi); ascetic austerity for divine realisation (Sivananda); supramental manifestation and realisation through integral yoga (Aurobindo Ghosh) and pragmatic spirituality emerging from moral categories of praxis such as nonviolence and peace (Gandhi) are some key facets of modernist versions of Indic thought (Sundararajan and Mukerji, 1997). Theistic humanism further characterised the thought trends of the Brahmo Samaj, Arya Samaj and renaissance inspired social reform in Maharashtra (Tarkhedkar) and Karnataka (Veerasaivism and the Dasa saints). Certain elements of connections with the notions of the 'personal God', and divine ontologies and epistemologies emerging therefrom are core to the postulates. Syncretism and pluralism within the Indic modernist trend emerges from Kabir's mysticism, Thomistic Christian tradition particularly the amalgamated tenets of Syrian Christianity and Sikhism. Emphasis of Sikhism is on the centrality of the transcendent, focus on the inner subjective experience and alliance with notions of the Absolute and Infinity and prescription of pathways to attain the same.

Syncretic and pluralistic thought (primarily the alignment of the Bhakti and Sufi traditions as well as developments in Sikhism), institutional manifestations (institutional, medieval and contemporary of the traditional Indic, pluralistic Indic and syncretic Indic genre) and post 'modernity' neo-religious thought trends characterise developments in the Indic lineage. As discussed by Iraqi (2009), the nonconformist Nirguna Bhakti Saints who came to prominence in medieval and central India in the fifteenth and seventeenth centuries redefined traditionally institutionalised religions with their own personal syncretic leanings, advocated a philosophy of praxis and consolidated voices of protest in the social, political and administrative spheres. Sikhism as a syncretic manifestation of an institutionalised form of religion has built its theosophy on the basis of prose hagiographies of its pioneering and subsequent saints proposing equity, justice and an organic connection with God or the Supreme Being (not based on any intermediary conditions). Mysticism and piety in the context of Sikhism has implied holy name incantations and reminiscences, devotional music and social service – the last element being the summum bonum of egalitarianism and justice. Sufi thought (within the Sunni and Shi'ite Islam) in the indigenous context is largely concerned with ascetism, religious discipline and theological speculation, centred on religious teachers, pirs and shakirs and organised into orders, silsilahs or tariqahs, that is paths to truth. Sufism implies an affective union with and total absorption of God wherein the mystic undergoes a moral transformation. Attainment of an intuitive apprehension of God and a further apprehension that all existing things are in some sense one with God governs the core of the thought. Sufis however differ among themselves in this interpretation of the unity of being and underwent transformations with colonial developments and postcolonial manifestations – with differential norms and forms as per the regional contexts (Jones, 1989).

Subsequent institutional manifestations, based on the organisational and institutional manifestations of the eighteenth and nineteenth century transitional and acculturative socio-religious reform, have asserted the post 'modernity' realm – translated faith-based ideational frameworks (derived from traditional scriptural authorities or modified versions as derivative of conventions and developed by a charismatic teacher/seer (Copley, 2000) into the apparently 'secular' notions of social service delivery. The postcolonial and postmodern flavour emerges from the amalgam of the Orient and Occident, voices of radicalism intertwined with theological discourses (such as the assertions of the Bhakti saints in the liberation theology vein questioning basic categorical imperatives and hierarchicus of caste and class) and nouveau reassertions of assimilative traditions such as the Swadhyay and the neo-Vedantic movements. Communitas and anti-structure along Turnerian lines and generation of social capital of the bonding and bridging nature characterise these renditions (Pandya, 2006).

Engendering Discourses on Religion: Global and Indigenous Facets

The dialogue on engendering discourses on religion commences with propositions pertaining to re-reading, re-conceiving and reconstruction traditions (Juschka, 2001). Re-reading implies that all textual materials are read in a manner so as to reveal androcentric tendencies which assume only the male as subject. Re-conceiving texts entails the act of looking at noncanonical sources, of looking outside the normative in order to historically conceive the tradition. Reconstruction is a bipolar categorical imperative of deconstruction – attempting to revisit stances which imply an embedded patriarchal hegemony in matters of theology and faith in arenas of text, traditions and rituals.

The facets of discussions within the ambit of engendering discourses on religion include citations and references on women in religious texts and traditions, discussions on the divine feminine principle or the feminine in divine soteriologies in the indigenous context (include studies and renditions on Úâktism and the Vaishnavi) and a feminist poststructuralist deconstruction of extant norms, forms and manifestations of religion and related discourses (the critical theory approach to the Nityasumangali tradition/Devadasi conventions being a predominant discursive rendition).

Vaishnavi literature discusses the phenomenon of goddess worship and the divine feminine energy within an essentially patriarchal locus classicus (Rosen, 1996). Whereas rebellion and pushing boundaries is characteristic to Mirabai, ecclesiastical leadership is particular to women within Gaudiya Vaishnavism of the Chaitanya movement of Bengal (feminist critics have however viewed this as a hidden agenda of subtle hegemonies of women – elevating their status as spiritual exemplars and ensure confinement to domesticity negating personal-political spaces). Within the Bhakti tradition, there are two models of feminine behaviour – women saints who defy societal norms and the ordinary woman who follows her 'stridharma'; the comparison is further sought to two basic types of Goddesses – the solitary Goddess of the folk tradition and the goddess consort of the classical tradition. Srivaishnavism, based on the hymns of the Alvars and the writings of the Acaryas, has explicit positions on gender inclusivity, universality and equality; women having access to the path of salvation and the lover-beloved relationship within bounds of feminist theology as the prominent discourse.

With respect to the position of women vis-a-vis religions across the world, Sharma (1987) has, employing the phenomenological and historical method, discussed the ideological issues concerning the position of women in world religions. Gross (1987) has examined the life crisis and periodic religious rituals of women and issues and patterns of inclusion/exclusion therein. Further, within an overarching modicum of sacredness, participation of women in men's religious lives and the quintessentially consort role played therein and the fabric of co-participation in myth and ritual are examined. Young (1987) has examined nature of references to women and feminine ideals in the textual traditions of Hinduism along with providing a critical view of role and position stereotyping of women across scripture translating then onto praxis. Buddhist doctrinal gender equity and egalitarian ascetic order with spaces for women ascetics has been deliberated by Barnes (1987) with feminine principle elucidated for both the clergy and laity women. Women's position in the Confucian order as instrumental in maintaining the harmonious social order has been discussed by Kelleher (1987) and Reed (1987) has deliberated on divine soteriologies within the Taoist traditions. The sacred quality of the female creative power and the description of being and nonbeing with female imagery are characteristic of the rendition. Role categorisations and straitjacketed spiritual orientations as text prescribed characterise Judaic (Carmody, 1987) and Christian traditions (Ruether, 1987) as well as Islam (Smith, 1987).

Within engendered discourses on religion, two other prominent strands that emerge are pertaining to the veneration of the divine feminine or Saktism and various nuances within the same and deliberations on fundamentalism and spaces of gendered hegemony-subordination. Humes and McDermott (2009) have reexamined texts, rituals and traditions to unveil various domains that pose questions towards the androcentric biases embedded therein. Some aspects of Sakta explorations (South Asian Goddess) include reexamination of Vedic texts for cosmogenic conceptions that might differ from male myths of Purusa and Prakriti; the Srivaishnava tradition with Pancaratra theological principles and the Pancaratra meditational icon of Sakti from the Kushan period and the ontological status of Lakshmi; and, revisitations of Sita as a female protagonist by subverting the traditional hagiography of Ramayana. The other domain herein is the Tantric tradition, with historical, field-oriented and textual perspectives on 'sacrifice'. Art history also simultaneously offers historiographical and hagiographical analysis of representations of divine feminine images and a critical reflection of altering nuances across ages.

The core themes of deliberations within Sakta discourses are veneration of the divine feminine and associated characterisations of fertility, chastity and reproduction, feminine mystique and power, and psychoanalytic sublimation of the sexual energies. Criticality underlies presuppositions on all of the above – with postulates such as adoration of divine females does not necessarily translate into empowerment of women; metaphors that draw comparison between soil and women, link procreative power with social power as inherently perpetuating binaries and the need to employ critical hermeneutics in comprehending divine feminine eschatology and soteriologies – particularly visualised through the feminist materialist critical renditions on Nityasumangalis or the temple girls/women.

Pertaining to 'fundamentalisms', authors, such as Hawley (1994), have viewed its intimate connections with constructs such as gender. Viewing fundamentalisms as representing the same basic constellation of responses to the stresses of post-Enlightenment modernity, propositionists herein believe that the identity of woman figures critically in the fundamentalist discourse. There are several vantage points of viewing the interlocking – literature having aspects of 'otherness', 'nostalgia' and the 'religious machismo' as prominent. 'Projection of the other' is perceived as a rubric for describing the relationship between the threat of modernism and the perceived need to control women (with traditional religiosity visions of domesticity and chastity). 'Nostalgia' implies a bringing together to the centre of religious experience, the more broadly felt adult need to solidify ties with a nurturing childhood. Motifs of otherness and nostalgia, as prominent features if fundamentalist consciousness, reinforce each other and converge in the gender ideology – reconstructing the past and reformulating the present. The connection is further compounded by the concept of 'religious machismo' – translated as the necessity of 'maleness' to reassert in the face of adversity.

Hence, the above conceptual deliberations have portrayed the linear positivist connections between religion and women, towards more critical spaces reviewing androcentrisms in traditions, texts and rituals and the poststructuralist attempts at deconstruction. Veneration of the divine feminine principle has been juxtaposed with embedded hegemony in the wake of fundamentalisms as well as a critical visioning of the divinity metaphors per se. That there is a proximity of women to religion and at once an embodied antagonism and contradiction that is perennially to be grappled with is the core contention.

Synthesising the 'Social' in Global and Indigenous Discourses on Religion and Faith: Textual Traditions and Organisational Dimensions

Whereas cosmological and metaphysical arguments predominate discourses on religion within the phenomenological frame of reference, the structural-functionalist and hermeneutic domains highlight the category of 'social' explicitly. This is further catapulted by discussions within the poststructuralist frame of reference – highlighting the deconstructionist role of religion on the one hand and the domains of power and violence embedded within faith discourses on the other – manifesting then onto praxis. The categorical imperative of the 'social' can be discussed from the vantage points of textual embeddedness; theories of origination and the role functions of religion at differential temporal junctures (Houtart and Lemerciner, 1984); myth, ritual and hagiographies (Campbell, 1988); and norms and forms of praxis projected then onto organisational and institutional manifestations – generating then a faith-embedded social capital. 'Social' is then further intertwined with categories of gender, caste/race, class and ethnicity, further then proximate to domains of 'power', 'contradictions' and the categorical imperative of 'communal'.

With respect to textual embeddedness and discovering the category of 'social' within theology, several approaches are prevalent.

The fact that textuality implies an apriori existence of the 'culture of the text' is a postulational given-ness within the operational frame of reference. Houtart and Lemerciner (1984) and Sutherland et al. (1988) have discussed the systematic evolution of the sense of the 'text' within religion from the social anthropology standpoint – texts largely as testimonies of the sacredness construct – deliberating on, as proposed by Saraswati (2000), domains of sacred space, time, objects, persons and arrangements. Aspects which are promulgated are those pertaining to lifecourse rituals, lifeworld definitions, rites of passage and mythic metaphors feeding into personal mysticism in the micro-meso sphere. At the macro level, texts lay down social hierarchicus (a Dumontian legacy), social epistemes (drawing from theodicy) and construct social and symbolic meanings of existentialist, exchange and interactionist genre. From the epistemological point of view, there is a certain social edifice definition that is generated providing schemata of lifeworld definitions, deontological and teleological ethics; furthered by literal, semiological and metaphorical understandings of myth and meanings. This implies that the category of social is also intertwined with the moral (in the Kantian sense, cosmology, the taxonomy of the social and the moral coexist) and ethics thus form an integral part of the definition of the social. Hence, the justification for theistic existentialism gains ground in the construction of the social – as the theistic realm encompasses within its fold deliberations on normative and ideational forms.

Three key vantage points of examining the text traditions for social leanings are the approach of the apologetics (Jennings, 1985; Shorter, 1988), linguistic and literary interpretation, semantic and semiological interpretation, feminist interpretation; postcolonial and poststructuralist revisiting and deconstruction of texts and the postmodern brouhaha of difference as the abiding principle. The approach of the apologetics defines scriptures and traditions as possessing the quintessential base for definitions and straitjacketing of the 'social' and all spheres of influence that accompany the same. In that sense, it is a linear and positivist approach to textual exegesis. The linguistic and literary interpretation of texts is 'literal' and characteristic of Indologists and Ecumenical scholars who have interpreted Indic texts and ecclesiastical sources from syntactic and literary history point of view (MaxMueller, 1973). There is a syllogistic search for the dimensions of 'social' and associated references which are comprehended through facet analysis. Collectively literal meanings of social and society are generated, governed by underlying tenets of theism and theology. Critical readings of the 'text' are characteristics of the remaining genres of interpretations. The semantic and semiological interpretations draw from Saussurean linguistics and Straussian developments subsequently – exploring metaphors and dichotomised categories that signify the social in discourses. Feminist lens is a larger endeavour towards engendering textualities – revisiting and reconstructing apparently known realities (Juschka, 2001). The post 'modernity' lens – characterised differentially by postcolonial, poststructuralist and postmodern repertoire – implies (as commenced by Gadamerian hermeneutics) a questioning of the limits of crosscultural understanding and the textualist bias in religion and employing a cultural relativism, emphasising on the diversity, fluidity and complexity within as well as between texts and prescribing a reification of their differences (thereby avoiding a monadic essentialism) (King, 1999).

Theories of origination and the role functions of religion at different temporal junctures discuss the social theology aspects of religion. Toynbee (1956) has discussed how the category of social was more deeply embedded in the successive progression of forms of religion at different temporal junctures. Whereas worship of nature phenomena was more naturalistic, impersonal worship of a universal state as a deified institution manifested through parochial community worship and ecumenical worship (idolisation) inserted the social domains in the discourse. Subsequently, realms of personal worship of a deified ruler of the universe and the epiphany of higher religions and religious institutions have further revealed aspects of faith-embedded social capital. Further through human history, Smart (1969) proposes that the prominent dimensions of religion are ritual, mythological, doctrinal, ethical, social and experiential – gradually revealing that from the abstraction of the mystical the episteme of the social is an imperative in the historical progression of religions. This social category reveals itself through themes elaborated by Madan (2004) as sacred places and performances; spiritual power and charisma; piety and passion; traditions of oral narratives and canonical texts; religious creativity and social change; and interrelationships between religion, politics and society. This aspect has been further developed in discussions on political theology (Vries and Sullivan,

2007) largely comprehended as a convergence of politics and theology through three intervening imperatives of systematicity, dispassionateness and neutrality (dealt with in detail later on the macro influences of religion).

Within the context of myth, ritual and hagiographies, the category 'social' is unveiled through the historical, existentialist, transcendental, hermeneutic and eschatological domains (Kachapally, 2005). In the vein of Levi-Strauss and Saussure, myths are signs and symbols that constitute as metaphors for a larger system of signs and structures in society (Sturrock, 1979). Within the context of religion, myth, ritual and hagiographies signify a practical manifestation of tenets embedded in religious thought and hence lend meaning to the understanding of 'social' differentially in different contexts. Pannenberg has proposed that myths signify a transcendence of the real and a source of sublimation of the actual through spaces that are historically constrained. Hence, a kind of radical historicality unveils the 'social' in myths as metaphors. Tillich proposes that myths and rituals curtail an existentialist nemesis – providing pragmatic spaces for 'untold and unexpressed' desires of the human mind with religion as the backdrop. Rahner proposes these as phenomena within the domain of structural anthropology – the social aspect being unveiled through a transcendence of sorts from objective and apparent domains towards their transcendent meanings and causes. Critical hermeneutics of Paul Ricouer build on the linguistic analysis of Wittgensteinian language games in interpreting symbolic and mythic structures. This aspect is also parallel to Schleiermacher's and Dilthey's understanding of myths and rituals as grounded in the philosophical affirmation of the identity of inner realities – understanding involving both comparative and divinatory phases (Rennie, 1996). From the eschatological point of view (which is concerned with soul discourses), Schleiermacher and Kant have proposed that soul journeys unravel domains of the 'social' through intervening instrumentalities of myth, ritual and hagiographies. Whereas Schleiermacher proposes that they provide aesthetic sensibilities that translate practical/actual meanings into soul discourses that then implicate on the 'social' (Crouter, 1997); Kant proposes in his transcendental philosophy that myths and symbols signify a paradoxical coexistence of transcendence and immanence of God – transcendence revealing God's hidden nature and immanence being the moral law which govern 'social causalities, spaces and time' (Palmquist, 2000).

Organisational and institutional manifestations generate a differential normative and ideational culture, defining and redefining the 'social' within religiosity discourses. Bawa (1993) has undertaken a meta-analysis of the role of religious/faith-based organisations in terms of genres of social faces/facets of the organisations. In the positivist frame, proposed role is that of awareness and conscientisation through an instrumental knowledge of existing structures. Through the viewpoint of phenomenology and critical hermeneutics, their role would signify the mapping of differential domain of consciousness and charting identities in those domains. Going into the specificities of the phenomenological and hermeneutical standpoints, the proposition is that in the hermeneutic frame their role involves the dialectical-dialogical mediation between stakeholders in the development process. Particularly in the critical hermeneutic stance of Apel and Habermas, their role is emancipatory – that is, an appraisal of the existing state of affairs in view of the standards that derive from the knowledge of something better than already exists as a potential or tendency in the present. Applying the Husserlian phenomenological method, the role of religious/faith-based institutions has been construed as the progressive deepening of the human spirit in its openness to social existence and consciousness. It involves the re-mapping of subjectivity within the subject-object nexus of the meta-psychologies of self – largely in the intersubjective frame.

In the Marxist and critical theory frame, the role of the institutions is synonymous to emancipation from hegemonic forces. Critique and dialectics are Archimedean standpoints. Through the visions of the critical theorists, particularly the frameworks of Adler and Gramsci, their role is engagement in transcendental dialectics (what ought to be) and propositions of a release from hegemonic forces. In the modernist frame, particularly the stance of Nietzsche, their role is realised through the critique of modern reason. Combining the discourses of Foucault and Habermas, their role is perceived to be a critique of power – to take position on the ways in which power effects the presuppositions and consequences of the practice of critique. In the poststructuralist and postmodernist frames, the role of institutions involves challenging the hegemony of structural discourses; working towards a societal condition which marks the end of grand narratives and the favouring of a socially and linguistically decentred and fragmented subject; and in Baudrillardian frame moving towards a radical semiurgy, the constantly accelerating proliferation of signs produce simulations creating new forms of society, culture, experience and subjectivity.

Some empirical literature highlighting the element of the 'social' within the faith/religious organisational discourse is of the vein of studies on their role in the macro sphere and how there is a translation of faith leanings into the apparently secular agenda of service delivery. Particularly convexing onto the Indian context, there are studies by church historians and those on Indic faith-based organisations since historicity unveil social historiographies and contemporary orientations.

Studies by church historians provide historical and descriptive accounts of churches and socio-religious organisations set up by Christian missionaries in India, their soci (onto) logical space and stake in the macro-processes of development. There are also studies by Church historians on the missionary organisations in South Asia. These studies are largely descriptive accounts examining the role of churches as religious organisations in the meso- and macro-processes of development. From the point of view of religion as ideological apparatus, Seybold (1971) and Rodrigues (1989) have examined the role of the Catholic Church in Dakshineshwar Kannada. Lapp (1972) has examined the Mennonite Church in terms of its community-based initiatives and corresponding social stake. Wiebe and Peter (1977) have critically examined the role of Catholic churches in rural Tamil Nadu from the antagonistic perspectives of simultaneous emancipation and re-hegemonisation. Forrester (1980) has presented a detailed study on Anglo-Saxon Protestant Churches in India, highlighting their stake in welfare initiatives protruding onto their social stake in development processes. Biedelman (1982) has studied the East African Evangelical Church, its Episcopal legacy and the role played in community outreach by the church organisations in the southwestern parts of the Indian subcontinent. Correspondingly the conversion hegemonies have also been highlighted. Immanuel (1984) in his doctoral thesis has presented a historical account using secondary data and in-depth interviews of American Missionaries in South India. The meso implications in terms of the missionary Churches' role in social reform/transformation have been highlighted.

Further, the proselytisation aspects have also been brought to light. In a similar vein, D'Souza (1982) has examined the growth and activity of Catholic Churches in North India and Saxena and Mishra (1987) have examined the roles of Christian Missionary organisations in Chhattisgarh. Studying the dynamics and reciprocal exchange of church and community in Goa from a cultural anthropology perspective, Robinson (2004a) has undertaken the social stake of the church as a faith-based organisation in civil society – in terms of how church articulates and maintains local systems of power and hierarchy within a village community (what makes the Goan case particularly interesting is the manner in which inequalities of social status characteristic of the caste-based Hindu social order are reproduced in Christian society but not without contestation).

Studies on Indic faith-based organisations include descriptive accounts of socio-religious organisations highlighting their ideological underpinnings, social outreach and implications. In terms of studies on religious organisations, Kennedy (1925) has made a case study of the ashram of Chaitanya Mahaprabhu as a potential site for socio-religious transformation. Kopf (1979) has made a case study of the Brahmo Samaj – from the institutionalist perspective – the organisational structure and agency effecting upon societal structure and human agency. Murray (1980) has made a pan-Indian study of Ashrams as religious organisations – viewing their religiosity in ideological underpinnings, organisational functioning translating onto social pervasiveness. Pimpley and Sharma (1983) have presented a descriptive account of the role of Arya Samaj in eradication of untouchability in Punjab. Tambiah (1985) has made a study of the socio-spiritual dimensions of the Theravada Buddhist societies – social transformations as effected by the spirituality contentions in Theravada Buddhism.

Sullivan (1985, Brooks (1989) and Sullivan (2000) have presented ethnographic case descriptions of the Hare Krishna movement – its inherent structure, ISKCON as an organisation with spiritual-religious leanings and teleological ethics of praxis and the meso-social interventions in the area of education and health care and macro-interventions in the arena of ecological consciousness and a corresponding lifestyle. In the Indian context, Ramakrishna Mission as a faith-based voluntary organisation has been maximally visited in terms of empirical explorations from multiple standpoints. This predominance can be attributed to the correspondence between Vivekananda's practical Vedanta and nationalist discourses. Few of the theoretical perspectives and arenas of visitation in the context of studies have been specified thus: Gupta (1973) has viewed, from a historical-materialist perspective, Ramakrishna Missions ideational transformation from an autology of renunciation characteristic of traditional Vedic tenets to a mission of faith-inspired altruistic service. Linking sociology of religion to that of knowledge, the key arenas of investigation have been on the processes through which Vivekananda's ideas have been formulated, accepted and institutionalised; the positionality of Ramakrishna Mission against the historic situation of India and the permeation of the organisational ideals onto other dimensions of society. The earlier studies have largely adopted the functionalist paradigm converging the stances of Weber, Durkheim and Malinowski. Ramakrishna Mission has been considered as a response to the missionary challenge to the late nineteenth-century India, and Vivekananda's Practical Vedanta as facilitating the Westernisation of Hinduism (Datta, 1954; Majumdar, 1965; Roy, 1970).

At a higher level of generalisation, the mission has been viewed as a prototype of the native response to the Western challenge, leading to or re-instating tradition (Singh, 1973); modernity (Srinivas, 1966) or to a tradition-modernity synthesis (Saran, 1969). (These stances reflect the normative-ideational positions of authors on the ideological niche of the Mission-precipitated from the Hindu social reform agenda, and the corresponding implications) (Heimsath, 1964). Morearty (1975) has, adopting the historical method, studied the ideological leanings and organisational culture precipitated by Hindu social reform, drawing parallels between symbolic transformations beckoned by the Brahmo Samaj and Ramakrishna Mission – both signifying a neo-Vedantism of sorts with elements of praxis embedded in them as portrayed through their social face.

Further, according to Madan (2004), the aforementioned discussions have centred around a macro positioning of the Mission in the context of change and continuity. The theoretical considerations therein have been guided by the criteria for assessing the rationality content of a given religious organisations: first, how far does the organisation signify a differentiation from the society into one of its independent but interacting sub-systems; two, to what extent does the movement act as a leverage for inducing rational changes in a total society. The locus classicus implicitly laying down these criteria has been Weber's Protestant ethic thesis that demonstrated the internal autonomy and the rationalising implications of the Reformation. Since then the thesis has been worked out more systematically by Parsons and Bellah who have posited differentiation as the master key to unlock evolutionary processes and Protestant missions as ideal types of pre-modern religious organisations.

Reviewing the teachings of Swami Vivekananda, and adopting the method of historiography, Basu (2002) has highlighted the reflection of the complex relationship between nationalism and modernity in the colonial world of nineteenth-century Bengal. The birth of the Ramakrishna Math and Mission and Vivekananda Kendra has been intimately associated with the growth of Indian nationalism. Further, the examination has viewed ways in which Vivekananda's neo-Hinduism emerged as a powerful ideology of Hindu nationalism – combining the European Enlightenment ideals of modernity and rationalism with the Hindu doctrine of Advaita Vedanta. This new nationalist idiom provided the forum for the reconciliation of the conservative and radical reformers. It also permitted the accommodation of the European Enlightenment values of rationality but without disturbing the ancient spirit of Hinduism (Beckerlegge, 2003).

Some other descriptive case studies on contemporary faith-based voluntary organisations have been done by Juergensmeyer (1991) on Radhasaomi Satsang, Taylor (1987) on the Satya Sai Baba Seva Mission, White (1992) on the Sai Baba Seva Sansthan and Williams (1984) on the Swaminarayan Sansthan. Falling within the purview of discourses on the sociology of religion, these case studies have from a largely structural-functionalist perspective, laid a dual emphasis on the spiritual-theological and social service aspects of the organisations. Further, a focus has also been on the stake of the organisations in civil society attributed further credence by the nature of people's adherence to them. Adopting a case study approach, Malkani (1989) has presented a socio-historical account of volunteer social service initiatives of Bharatiya Swayamsevak Sangh – a faith-based voluntary organisation professing the ideals of universal brotherhood and peace expressed in the basic tenets of 'vasudhaiva kutumbakam' – with specific reference to its Nairobi chapter.

Conducting an ethnographic study of South Indian Temples, Appadurai and Breckenridge (2004) have addressed the question of the nature of interrelatedness of religion, society and institutionalised authority – looking upon the South Indian Temple as a well-defined sacred space in which different aspects of society are uniquely synthesized in cultural and structural terms. Temples have been perceived as significant institutions in the redistribution of ritual, symbolic and economic benefits in society. The social functions of the temple flow from the many functions and ordered meanings that are associated with it. Other recent studies include those by Khan (2004), who has, in the context of shrine as a faith-based organisation discussed the intertwining of socio-religious and political lives of Muslims. The data have been drawn from a study of the famous holy shrine at Hazratbal where a holy relic of Prophet Muhammad is venerated by the devout on two auspicious days every year. Khan (2004) has described the arrival of the relic in Kashmir and the manner of veneration which sets Kashmiri Muslims apart from orthodox Muslim communities elsewhere. The approach adopted has been systemic: social reality is seen to comprise different interrelated or overlapping subsystems, such that one is not reducible to any one of the others (reductionism), or conversely the foundation or cause of the others (determinism). Faith does not exist sui generis, prior to society, but is socially constructed (Madan, 2004).

Understanding 'Pluralism' and 'Syncretism'

Discourses on pluralism and syncretism have penetrated into analysis of religion and faith in a historiographical fashion, intertwining domains of religion and culture as a paradigm shift from solely structural analysis. Quinn and Maker (2000) have proposed a singular and unified ontic realm of discourses with the Ultimate Reality or the sublime as the locus classicus of analysis. With aligning and associative perspectives of scepticism, exclusivism and inclusivism, pluralism tenets draw from Hicks' epistemology that advances and defends the hypothesis of a noumenal and transcendent divine reality (in itself infinite and unknowable) underlying and serving as the ultimate referent of the diverse phenomenal religions (viewed as culturally shaped; and differential conceptualisations of and response to the divine noumena). The other philosophical leaning of pluralism draws from Wittgensteinian perspectives on the nature of religions, conceiving them as cultural linguistic systems (language games), making possible corresponding forms of life, experience and expression. The system of thought is structured around the practical soteriological aim of encouraging and regulating transformation of the self in relation to differing conceptions of the ultimately real (Dean, 1997).

As an ontological postulate, the pluralist hypothesis rationally requires the postulation of a divine noumenal reality underlying and unifying the diverse phenomenal religions through a common ultimate referent (for their differential conceptions of the Real). Epistemologically it is a deconstruction of the absolute claims to truth within the theistic domains. Methodologically there is a proposing of a 'revisionist' conception of and approach to religious diversity – involving the notion that the same soteriological process of human transformation takes place within the contexts of the differential religions and cultural traditions – and then adopting as a methodological assumption the basic religious conviction that religious experience and thought mediate real contact with the higher reality – also called in-principled veridicality of religious experience and thought. Religious pluralism pre-empts a distinction between divine-in-itself versus the divine as humanly experienced parallel to Kantian noumenal-phenomenal distinction. Kantian 'category analogues' suggest the distinction between the conceptions of the Absolute and the Real as personal versus non-personal functions. Pluralism is an infiltration of the domains of 'personal' into apparently differential domains of the non-personal. In Kantian terms, the noumenal exists independently of our experience of it and accordingly the phenomenal world is the same as the noumenal world in pluralistic discourses – human consciousness imbibing unity and difference simultaneously (Quinn and Maker, 2000).

Pluralism also implies a critical and comparative hermeneutics (Piet and Prasad, 2000) and ethical lineages which are comparable (Billimoria et al., 2007). Along the lines of Immanuel Levinas, pluralism implies a placement of religious ethics in interlocutionary relation to the other. It is this experience of alterity as the pre-linguistic basic form of knowledge which may be the origin of transcendence. This transcendence is the ontic precursor towards the epistemic realm of pluralism – translating into metaphors of tolerance, equity and theistically emanated social justice. Further, the deeper basis of pluralism is theistic existentialism and phenomenology which examines myth, symbols and meanings. Dean (1997) has proposed that religious pluralism posits second-order questions of a hermeneutical nature drawing the epistemic base from theoretical alignments of phenomenology, existentialism and poststructuralism. Pluralism in the theistic domains thus posits an epistemological relativism and a certain philosophy of worldviews situated symbolically in congruence with one another. Pluralism is essentially a dialogical dialogue in the quest for truth arrived at through a mutual encounter of religions and hence it is called pluralism de jure, primarily signifying a co-existence of juxtaposed worldviews. Propositional truth is considered relatively less crucial, and criteria for metaphysical truth which includes transcendental and pragmatic matters may be applied to ascertain truth claims within an inherently plural religious scenario. Gadamerian hermeneutics provide the base for comprehending pluralism – primarily Gadamer's concepts of the horizon of understanding as open-ended, the dialectical structure of experience and the conversational or dialogical structure of the hermeneutical process implying an openness to truth claims of other religions and the possibility of transformation. Phenomenologically, pluralism demonstrated its stances through differentials in mystical experiences associated with religion and the quest for seeking discernable and subtle congruence relationships therein.

Comparative studies in the arena of religion have emphasised pluralistic tenets and aligned to assimilation and adoption-related discourses. Smart and Murthy (1996) have compared the western philosophical tradition of the Greek philosophers, Wittgenstein and Schopenhauer to Indic thought, particularly its theistic tenets emerging from Upanishads. Connections are sought between Wittgensteinian thought and 'svatahpramanyavada' – on the connections between language and reality and the position that this connection is internally metaphysical in character. Further, areas of congruence between the Vedas and the Torah have been discussed with particular reference to the totality of the Word which is the essence of Ultimate Reality; knowledge, which is identified with the creator principle as the immediate source of creation; divine language which constitutes the archetypal plan from which the creator structures the form of creation and the concrete corpus of oral and/or written texts. Parallels are also sought between Vedanta and Aristotle in the domains of self-realisation. Rational reconstruction provided by Eudaemonism (Aristotle's Nicomachean ethics) being the argument that 'good for man consists in his happiness or well-being largely obtained by self-realisation' is linked to Indian moral thought emerging from the canonical texts. Congruencies between Hegel and Madhyamika dialectics are visualised particularly notions of truth and concepts of dialectics. Derrida's play of difference has been linked to Nagarjuna's dialectics and Hegelian nullity of differences. Focussing on comparison, Neville (2001) has proposed that the facets of comparison within the religious domain are unity, ontological status, value as the phenomenological vantage point emphasising praxis and causation. From these vantage points, he has examined that the Chinese religion offer a world friendly vision of the human condition, a vision of interactive and process rather than individuality and substance, and a vision of body-mind unity wherein one's conscious perceptions of self and the world determine the degree of human enterprise. There are aspects of obligation to nature and society, realisation of oneness with the cosmos and transcendence. Buddhistic thought on the other hand focus primarily on doctrinal evidence of the four noble truths emanating from canonical evidence. Judaic thought has emphasised on the linkage between God and Universe by the Torah and the order of the universe as having implications on the human condition and Islamic thought has focused on maintaining the God-human disjunction and the linkages between the transcendental and the historical.

The argument and postulates of pluralism also imply dimensions of conversion, assimilation and adoption. Whereas assimilation and adoption has implications of exchange and transformation, according to Robinson and Clarke (2003) the experience of conversion traverses the terrain of multiple and diverse possibilities that focus on new boundaries, identities, beliefs and practices. There thus exist a range of contexts in which novel forms of piety and modes of religious dissent and desertion take place. Indian discourse on pluralism emerges from Gandhian tenets particularly through the epistemic category of religious tolerance (Chakrabarti, 1989) and the multidimensionality of truth. The other representation arises in the repertoire of acculturative social reform (Oomen, 2004) wherein ecumenical and oriental leanings visualise a confluence. Other nationalist thinkers such as Tagore and Nehru also aligned to Gandhian categories and the acculturative tradition in social reform in defining versions of pluralism – natural theology and systematic amalgamation of theistic tenets being the positions respectively (Chatterjee, 2009).

Syncretism as a theoretical category implies a cultural reciprocation and a mode of cultural synthesis, the fundamental source of which is social tolerance. The emergence of syncretism has partly been from a culture of dissent and signifies religious ideas and cultural traits that mediate between diverse ethnic communities, religious communities, sects and cultural regions and give rise to a complex unity (Das, 2003). The epistemological alignments of syncretism are critical theory tenets and subaltern propositions. Along Habermasian lines it proposes a critique of instrumental reason (which colonises the lifeworlds of people as it infuses society with subtle structures as in language) and posits social integration and communication through communicative action. Along subaltern lines there is a certain assertion of native cultures and popular histories which have a sense of amalgam vis-à-vis Puritanism and along Gramscian lines an insertion of culture in the schemata of analysis. There is a challenge posited to the socioeconomic structure and caste-class hierarchies perpetuated by imperialism/colonialism – most syncretic shrines symbolising a re-assertion of new cultures and identities as forms and modes of dissent from the hegemonic mainstream.

Hence, pluralism and syncretism within the ambit of religion make assertions of spaces and voices and at the same time posit an epistemological hybridisation through a confluence of multiple tenets.

Post 'modernity' discourses on Religion and Civil Society: The Macro Sphere

Within the macro sphere, there have been renditions on the post 'modernity' discourses on resurgence of religion-oriented discourses in the public sphere after 'modernisations' last whistle' (in the vein of the writings of Arjun Appadurai and Veena Das) (Robinson, 2004b). In the context of the United States, this was stimulated by political economy forces and the Whitehouse resolution of lending credence to religious and faith-based institutions in the public sphere (Wuthnow, 1998; Carlson-Thies, 1999).

Brandon (1965) has discussed the macro role of religion as a pragmatic operationalisation of the divine teleology – visualised best in the Gnostic conceptualisation of spirit-matter distinction; matter serving as a vanguard of spirit prolegomena of divinity. This manifests in terms of the revelation of the divine purpose in the category of the 'social' contingent on the temporal and the social. Jennings (1985) has viewed the macro implications of religion from the point of view of linguistically of religious experience (ontological and aesthetic) – signifying a shift from theism-oriented theology discourses towards structuralist and deconstructionist approaches to language and experience so as to understand novel aspects of the religious discourse. There are assertions made of the order of kerygmatic and doxological discourses (do do with the meaning and existence of God) that move beyond conventional theology to project the 'political image of religion' – which is then called political theology.

Plant (2001) has discussed the domains of political theology within the realms of liberal society. Political theology is defined as contextual-classical, attempting to relate classical Christian theological tradition to a contemporary situation. Based to some extent on Hegelian phenomenological conceptualisation of God, self and the other, political theologies main contention is the definition of selfhood and identity emerging from theism albeit within the gamut of the social categorical imperative. There is a certain dialectical and teleological historiography within political theology which defines a theologico-political self-consciousness and individual freedom. Some aspects of Shorter's (1988) analysis of religion as a cultural system and that political theology is an inculturation of the socio-political categorical imperatives within an essentially theistic analysis can be visualised herein. Hence, political theology is a poststructuralist rendition manifesting through grammar and language games of an inherently theistic discourse.

Vries and Sullivan (2007) have provided a detailed deliberation on political theology. In Platonic terms, it indicates a conjunction by simple juxtaposition, Calvinistic subordination of the political to the theological and a Hobbesian subordination of the theological to the political. From the Spinozan 'Theologico-Political Treatise' viewpoint political theology implies an interdependence between natural religion and a democracy favourable towards the freedom of thought. In the amalgamated understating of Locke, Kant and Voltaire, political theology pre-empts tolerance and is based on three core imperatives – of systematicity, dispassionateness and neutrality. Further there are also tenets of Rawlsian political liberalism imbibed within it. Foucault and Debord have conceptualised theoscopy as political theology, mapping the theological origin of modern power. Particularly Foucault's political theology is preoccupied with notions of examining the theological notions of modern power. Power in the schema of Foucault has four types of theological connections – historical derivation, structural isomorphism, self-referential knowledge and paradigmaticity. Writings of Guy Debord have deliberated on the notion of political theology – both in terms of derivation (the historical genealogical descent) of the spectacle out of a medieval religious world and in terms of an isomorphism between part theocracies and the spectacular present. Debord's notion of spectacle carries in it a theory of representation and a theory of time and history wherein the spectacle is viewed not merely as an expression of a disenchanted, secularised, reified society with a religious past, but also perfection and visualised realisation of the potentialities of such a past. This then informs the modalities of the present which are theologically implicated within the realms of political economy and dynamics embedded therein. Liberation theology as an organ of political theology posits the view that the relationship between theology and praxis is dialectical – there being a primacy of orthopraxis over orthodoxy. The church is visualised as an institution that makes sociocultural freedom possible, the starting point being the reaction to the concrete expression of oppression, inimical to the gospel.

Wolfhart Pannenberg has combined the hermeneutical epistemology of Gadamer with a detailed account of theology and science to position political theology. Pannenberg's theology is founded on the perception of revelation itself as history (understood in a hermeneutical sense) wherein God is indirectly revealed in his concrete dealings with humans in history. In this conceptualisation of political theology, knowledge of the social world is historically and hermeneutically mediated. The question of what constitutes humanity and theologically propelled social exchanges is construed in the basis of post-Heideggerian accounts of human identity – incorporating coherence rather than correspondence view of truth (Stewart, 2000).

Political theology is thus influenced by poststructuralism and postmodernism. Kamitsuka (1999) has developed the discourse drawing from postliberal, revisionary and Latin American liberation theological perspective – offering proposals on the theological method and doctrine responsive to the intellectual, pastoral and sociopolitical challenges of contemporary culture. There is a certain recasting of inter-movement politics/polemics in order to forge a theological approach in order to promote what are often considered to be competing values among three theological movements – solidarity of the oppressed (liberationist), redescribing the Christian communal sense of the scripture (postliberal) and fully critical reflection (revisionist). There is an advocating of an apologetic strategy entailing coherentist and consensus elements for justifying Christian claims in a pluralistic public realm. It provides a model for reading scriptures theologically which addresses the challenges of poststructuralism in a globally diverse Church. Role theory is used to adjudicate doctrinal disputes on the relationship between salvation and political liberation simultaneously providing methodological 'virtues' for theological practice rooted in practical judgements.

Ward (1997) proposes that political theology as a macro proforma of theology is a representative thinking of late modernity, depicting the apotheosis of a liberal tradition and concerns as modernity's enlightenment rationality rhetoric (relegating theological discourses to the background). Political theology according to Ward (1997) affirms a radical immanentism – a nihilistic monism or ontology which is at odds with what is a search for transcendentalism empiricism in postmodern thinking; representing a kind of nomadic ecstasy and radical antinomianism. In the post 'modernity' vein thus, theological discourses of the political genre having macro intentions and implications have their own spatiality and temporality (own personhood and body) (Coakley, 1997) and their doctrines of creation and incarnation moving beyond the anti-theologies and humanisms of modernity.

There have been few systematic studies to examine the role of religion through the prism of individual and institutional actors, within the macro sphere. Within the largely structural functionalist frame of reference, critical realist and poststructuralist stances on the role of religion have emerged – lending credence to the thesis of religion as one of the locus classicus of civil society (Anhelm, 1999). Studying the role of churches in eradicating apartheid in South Africa, Johnston (1994) has proposed that the unfolding abandonment of apartheid in South Africa illustrates transformational potential of the religious factor. Further, the case study mentioned that the reversal by the South African Dutch Reformed Church of its stand on Apartheid has effectively removed the theological justification for such a system for most Afrikaners. Luttwak (1994) has illustrated descriptively the role of the church inspired moral re-armament movement as instrumental in

Franco-German reconciliation in the wake of World War II. Nichols (1994) has undertaken a similar study of Nicaragua wherein a third party mediation on the part of Moravian Church and other religious officials was involved in helping resolve a major conflict between the Sandinista regime and the East Coast Indians. Studying the role of Church groups in the Nigerian civil war, Sampson (1994) has proposed that although the Nigerian civil war was settled at the battlefield instead of at the bargaining table, the efforts of the Quakers in that conflict may have contributed to what was a remarkably conciliatory aftermath.

Employing the case study design, Steele (1994) has undertaken a study of churches in East Germany (most particularly Lutheran) that provided the instrumental forum for civil opposition, which led to the country's peaceful and political revolution in 1989. The study has also explored the spiritual dimension of the churches' role in addition to the political aspects. Wooster (1994) has undertaken the case study at Philippines reflecting a situation in which the temporal power of the Roman Catholic Church was brought to bear in diffusing a potentially violent transition from the Marcos to the Aquino's regime. Kraybill (1994) has elucidated the case relating to Rhodesian independence that illustrates the impact of several religious actors in bringing about a negotiated end to a civil war and facilitating a peaceful transition of power.

Johnston and Sampson (1994) have also cited the examples of spiritually motivated individuals operating on a personal basis – thereby illustrating the transformational dimension of faith. These range from an inspired initiative in one part of Southern Sudanese Guerrilla leader that contributed to the breakthrough settlement in the North in 1972, to the personal contribution of a Catholic Cardinal in Rome to relieving the persecution of Christians in East Germany, to the role played by the Chairman of the US Joint Chief of Staff, acting in the capacity as a member of a prayer following group in resolving border dispute between two African countries.

Reviewing the findings of the aforementioned seven case studies, Johnston and Sampson (1994) have proposed that personal interviews have been the principal method of inquiry for the case studies. Evaluation of the impact of the spiritual dimension has required a more subjective assessment on the part of the individuals interviewed. Beyond the subjective aspects of the analysis, other elements convey a wide and complex array of involvements. Some case studies, for example, suggest that resources from within the local religious community should be tapped (Philippines, East Germany, Nicaragua, South Africa and Rhodesia/Zimbabwe). Other cases highlighted the value of involving key people from outside (France/Germany and Nigeria). In some cases religious actors worked within the political process (Nicaragua and Nigeria), in others they remained external to it (France/Germany, Philippines and South Africa). In East Germany, church members operated outside the process during the initial stages of revolution, but later assumed roles integral to the political transition from within.

The gamut of literature demonstrating the political, poststructuralist and the reformist face of religion emerges from the new religious movements (Beckford, 1986) across the globe. Another angle is projected through discourse on Hindu nationalism and the exchange between state and the Hindu religion in the nineteenth century and onwards (Hansen, 1999; Jaffrelot, 1993; Zavos, 2000). Hindu nationalism is visualised as one of the several contingent outcomes of a protracted struggle over the definition of Indian nationhood and involves the creation of a common narrative of subjugation and a strategy of benchmarking the Indian identity, with roots in colonial politics and jurisprudential claims. As proposed by Jaffrelot and Hansen (1998), the facet of political theology in the indigenous context is the mapping of postcolonial trajectories and cartographies of democracy against the backdrop of Hindu nationalism.

Comprehending Communalism and the Communal Agenda: Postulates, Facets, Phases and Faces of the Critical

When doctrines of epistemological and ontological pluralism do not naturally translate into inter sectarian tolerance, the communal agenda is forwarded (Malik and Reifeld, 2005). This is signified by a relationship between different religions in a shared social space which is characterised by antagonism rather than by creative coexistence; reducing the complex network of different religious attitudes to lead to systems such as 'Huntington's clash of civilisations'. This is also a marked departure from the liberal separatist model towards a communitarian model – thereby moving from a systematised religious pluralism towards a religiously segmented society (concept given by Tilly, 1978, cited in Malik and Reifeld, 2005, developed in the context of religion-state relationships in Western Europe).

The conceptualising of communalism serves as a crucial titan in problematising the connections between theology and society. Particularly the focus is on understanding how communalism is 'explained' by theorists and the relevance for practice. The expositions commence with the arguments of the Gyanendra Pandey of the subaltern studies group, who, drawing on the discourse theory of Foucault and Said, has shown how the colonial narratives of communal riots have created timeless narratives of religious communes locked in perennial conflicts which explains the 'construction' of communalism. This is pragmatically symbolic of Foucault's treatment of modern power through four types of theological connections which are historical derivation, structural isomorphism, self-referential knowledge and paradigmaticity (Vries and Sullivan, 2007). Edward Said has further proposed that countering communalism is based on the recognition of 'multiple definitions', that is, 'when differences are recognised then individuals can be secure in their own identities and develop progressively larger identities'.

Aligning to the socio-economic explanations genre, Ian Copland (study of Muslims in Hyderabad during the British rule) and Paul Brass (study of Muslims in the United Province) have proposed that it is not backwardness of one community but economic disparities between two communities that lead to communal disharmony. Other genres of explanation include the cultural which concern aspects of identity and otherness within communalism discourses; the psychological, linking communalism to aspects of psyche and unconscious; and the sociopolitical viewing conflict as a form of sociation along the lines of Georg Simmel. Within the cultural explanations genre are theorisations of Mark Juergensmeyer, who has (drawing from the explanation of Berger and Luckmann (1966) proposing that identity is a phenomenon that emerges from the dialectic between individual and society), discussed that the central question in the study of communalism is how religion gets implicated in identities. Identity is constructed not by essential characteristics but instead by a set of relationships to the 'other' or whatever is not the self. This 'other' as per anthropologist Jean Francois Kervegan acquires an ontological status and a radical 'differential' – violence then becoming the logical form of action to counter the same (Heehs, 1998).

Within the psychological genre, there are theorisations of Rene Girard and Sudhir Kakar who have provided psychoanalytical explanations of communalism. Contentions of Rene Girard propose that violence and religion are inseparable and the object of religion is that of transferring the community's essential internal violence to an emissary victim. This 'displacement' is a defence mechanism and a simultaneous projection of the internal conflict onto a significant other. Sudhir Kakar has proposed that communal conflict draw from repositories of unconscious images of demonising the unavowable 'other' which in turn brings in an increase in the sense of well-being in the narcissistic realm. The sociopolitical explanations of communalism emerge from theorisations of C. A. Bayly and Habermas. C. A. Bayly's explanation derives from phenomenon in the eighteenth and nineteenth century period, wherein syncretism was evident and local out breaks of violence between the communities for political, economic and cultural reasons led to 'primordial conflict' which through historicity manifested and assumed communal overtones. Habermasian explanations are of the order of 'conflict of lifeworlds' which elucidate the dissensions of communal order (Heehs, 1998).

Armstrong (2001) has proposed communalism and fundamentalism to be a spiritual crisis of the modern world. The collapse of piety rooted in myths and cult during the Enlightenment forced people of faith to grasp for newer ways of religiosity. Along the Nietzschean lines of thinking, without Godhead there is a sense of infinite nothingness and modernity perpetuates that sense through a fetish for science. This sense has pervaded three core fundamentalist movements with communal overtones have been the Protestant fundamentalism of the United States, Jewish fundamentalism in Israel and the Islamic fundamentalism in Egypt and Iran as responses to modernity. Ward (1997) has proposed that communalism represents the apotheosis of a liberal tradition in religion and affirms a radical immanentism.

Discussing the episode of the Somnath temple and popular construction of history of Islamic invasions and related impact on the same, Kumar (2008) has proposed that rather than providing popular communal overtones, the event can be viewed as a medieval lexicon of power. This manifestation of power is a systematic practice of iconoclasm, appropriated images and secondary signs. What Somanth symbolises and proposes as an explanation of communalism is the colonial perception of antagonistic duality of Hindus and Muslims and a religious nationalism projecting a particular view of the past as opposed to a rational-historical inquiry, simultaneously recreating grievance genealogies of predictable nature. Ali (2003) has proposed American imperialism as fundamentalist and building into communal politics and Bhagwan and Feldhaus (2008) with a radical humanist view of religion posit devotionalism as an arena for communitas and hence commune as a precursor to communalist politics.

Khan (2004) has examined the shaping of religious identities in South Asia and more particularly in Northern India. She has argued that the perception of Islam and Hinduism as two monoliths and perpetually antagonistic faiths coexisting uneasily in South Asia has become so deeply ingrained that the complexity of the historical fabric is often neglected. The idea of communalism is thus that of an 'imagined community' constructed in opposition to an entity perceived to be in opposition to the 'significant other'. Such constructs enable to address the question of identity versus alterity and examine broader issues of self and other – both at individual and collective levels and reexamined naturalised categories of communities. There is a certain logical positivist either/or logic that is embedded in communal thinking – demystified by concepts such as transcultures (developed by Cuban sociologist Fernando Ortiz in the 1940s), syncretism, liminality (concept in psychology to refer to in-between structures of consciousness) (Van Gennep and Victor Turner) and contact zones.

In Summary

For social work epistemology and praxis, the following aspects of the discussions on religion, faith and social work thus hold significance:

Religion, theism, theology and faith are terminological constructs which are distinctive in terms of their epistemes but intertwine from the praxis lens. Theoretical stances are multiperspectival, ranging from historiographical, phenomenological towards anthropological, sociological, feminist and psychological. For social work, these offer understandings of the order of historical legacy of origin of philanthropy, altruism, value base, morals and ethics; understandings of the aspects of ritualisation, sacralisation and myths/metaphors which qualify the social fabric; and the institutional, engendered and psychoanalytical lenses of a social categorical imperative that pervades all domains of society – the locus classicus of social work renditions.

Forms of religion are simple, organised and complex/mixed – each offering positionalities in terms of worldviews and visions of social existence (deontological and teleological ethics) and transcendence. Global conceptualisations of organised forms of religion encompass discussions on Judaism, Christianity, Zoroastrianism, and Islam along with Sufi manifestations. Apart from these, there are forms of Japanese, Chinese, Korean, African and Latin American religion. Each possesses core thought processes that demonstrate an allegiance to social work such as discourses on morality, ethics, being-ness and cosmological doctrines. New religious movements as subsequent manifestations of original religious formulations manifest in themes of sociocultural orientations and control of sacred spaces, functioning of religious leadership, formations of religion-social propositions of reform, protest and millennial revolt and modification/hybridisation of sacred texts and rituals.

Traditional Indic conceptualisations possess a combination of transcendental and social-moral tenets, and Bhakti traditions propose aspects of syncretism and a fetish for subalternity – both being critical constructs for social work episteme. Subsequent institutional manifestations, based on the organisational and institutional manifestations of the eighteenth and nineteenth-century transitional and acculturative socio-religious reform have asserted the post 'modernity' realm – translating faith-based ideational frameworks into the apparently 'secular' notions of social service delivery. The postcolonial and postmodern flavour emerges from the amalgam of the Orient and Occident, voices of radicalism intertwined with theological discourses (such as the assertions of the latter Bhakti saints in the liberation theology vein questioning basic categorical imperatives and hierarchicus of caste and class) and nouveau reassertions of assimilative traditions.

The dialogue on engendering discourses on religion commences with propositions pertaining to re-reading, re-conceiving and reconstruction traditions. Conceptual deliberations have portrayed the linear positivist connections between religion and women, towards more critical spaces reviewing androcentrisms in traditions, texts and rituals and the poststructuralist attempts at deconstruction. Veneration of the divine feminine principle has been juxtaposed with embedded hegemony in the wake of fundamentalisms as well as a critical visioning of the divinity metaphors per se. The understanding for social work praxis emerging is a proximity of women to religion and at once an embodied antagonism and contradiction that is perennially to be grappled with.

The core category of 'social' in religion which has a direct connivance with social work is discussed through textual traditions; myths, rituals and hagiographies; and organisational dimensions. Aspects which are discussed are those pertaining to lifecourse rituals, lifeworld definitions, rites of passage and mythic metaphors feeding into personal mysticism in the micro-meso sphere. At the macro level, texts lay down social hierarchicus, social epistemes and construct social and symbolic meanings of existentialist, exchange and interactionist genre. From the epistemological point of view, there is a certain social edifice definition that is generated providing schemata of lifeworld definitions, deontological and teleological ethics, furthered by literal, semiological and metaphorical understandings of myth and meanings. Theories of origination and the role functions of religion discuss the social theology aspects of religion. Organisational and institutional manifestations generate a differential normative and ideational culture, defining and redefining the 'social' within religiosity discourses.

Discourses on pluralism and syncretism bring in aspects of culture into the deliberation – pluralism implying an epistemological coexistence and comparison along with dimensions of adoption, assimilation and conversion. Syncretism as a theoretical category implies a cultural reciprocation and a mode of cultural synthesis, the fundamental source of which is social tolerance. The emergence of syncretism has partly been from a culture of dissent and signifies religious ideas and cultural traits that mediate between diverse ethnic communities, religious communities, sects and cultural regions and give rise to a complex unity. Both pluralism and syncretism pose as complex realities and a hybridisation of the social fabric – the very edifice of social work.

At the macro level, within the post 'modernity' genre, assertions are of the order of political theology – a contextual-classical version of religion which employs theological tenets to address contemporary issues. Liberation theology being one such version, globally there are also a range of studies that have looked at the church-state-civil society connections to visualise the social manifestations of religious institutions.

Communal domains signify a relationship between different religions in a shared social space which is characterised by antagonism rather than by creative coexistence. Discussions on religion are incomplete without comprehending this angle and for social work praxis it assumes significance as an 'issue' and as a defining quality of the social reality. Communalism represents the apotheosis of a liberal tradition in religion and affirms a radical immanentism.

This chapter has thus dealt with the varied dimensions of religion and faith – attempting to understand the domains of theorisations, nuances, manifestations, developments and antagonisms-contradictions. The 'social' dimensions of religion and the congruent linkages for social work have been sought. As an Archimedean standpoint for normative-ideational lineages of social work, religion and related discourses assume significance – an aspect that this chapter has endeavoured to address.

6

Modern and Postcolonial Positions

Social Reform, Gandhi and Nationalism

This chapter examines the interrelated domains of social reform, Gandhian thought and nationalism – the modern and postcolonial positions. In terms of history, this spans the period from the nineteenth century to the middle of the twentieth century in the Indian context, leading simultaneously to several normative and ideational developments – acculturative, assimilative and transformational. What is attempted here is a mapping of the trajectory of the much celebrated social reform endeavours in the Indian context, the emergence of Gandhian thought and ideals and the juxtapositions, polarities and polemics with the subaltern visions and the grand narrative of the nation-state. Cumulatively they assert a basket of 'modern' and 'postcolonial' positions that reveal the indigenous flavours in terms of episteme, praxis and positionalities.

Social Reform: Genesis, Facets and Legacies

Social reform, also known as socio-religious reform in the Indian context, advocated modification in social behaviour and justified such advocacy by one or another form of religious authority and built an organisational structure that it maintained over time. Two broad types of reform movements prevail: transitional, that had their origins in precolonial world and arose from an indigenous form of socio-religious dissent, and acculturative, that had their origins within the colonial milieu and was led by individuals who were a product of cultural interaction. With beginnings in the nineteenth century, social reform signified the coming together of the occidental ideas with the oriental with two prominent forces at work – the indigenous (comprising the English-educated elite) and foreign (comprising the utilitarians and the evangelicals). According to Andre Beteille, social reform attempted to establish a harmony between morphological or existential order and normative order through threefold ways: complete rejection of extant normative order and establishment of the new one, slight modifications and retaining of the extant normative order. The overarching key tenets that prevailed in terms of social reform were synthesis and syncretism in religion, religion of praxis for the extant moral order, values such as rationalism, individualism and humanism, liberal ideas of democracy, reason and rationality. The three core regions for the renaissance of social reform in the Indian context were Bengal, Maharashtra and Karnataka.

British rule established and introduced a capitalist economy, a new administrative system and English education in the early nineteenth century. Consequently an educated class emerged in urban areas comprising the upper-caste Hindus, who advocated alterations in the social fabric advocating a gradualist approach. Herein social reform meant infusing the existing social structure with new ways – the society being preserved while its members being transformed. The reformers either revolted individually or formed associations which were generally of three types: general or voluntary associations, caste reform associations and religious reform bodies (generally called samaj). The main thrust remained in terms of rejuvenating Hindu religion and society to counter the impact of Western culture and the efforts of proselytisation by Christian missionaries (Heimsath, 1964; Shah, 2004). The other viewpoint on this aspect proposed that the innovative potentiality of Hinduism was more responsible for its rejuvenation rather than the impact of other religions and cultures. Further, as the traditional social structure and religion were not able to cope with the new economic structure which was based on individualism, the reformers strove to extend the principle of individual liberty to the sphere of religion. Social reform among the Muslims began with the Aligarh Movement led by Syed Ahmed Khan, the main thrust being to persuade the Muslim landed gentry to take an English education and an urge to generate a separate and independent status for the Muslims (Shah, 2004). The social reform movements among Hindus and Muslims contributed to the development of nationalism along regional and religious lines. The study of social reform is akin to the study of social histories – along the lines of Hobsbawm, the social being an adjunct to the economic and studies mapping political protest (Pruthi and Devi, 1999). Further, the discursive field of social reform is inhabited by fundamentalisms, ascendant Dalit movements and movements within Islam such as the Tablighi Jamaat. The focus is on striving to realise a realm beyond power and impotence, domination and submission and allow beings to 'be'. There is a certain sense of Habermasian practical discourse wherein actors are engaged in moral argumentations about the foundations of life, thereby leading to a democratic transformation of modes of power and authority (Giri, 2008).

Regional manifestations and flavours of social reform can be discussed through the transitional and acculturative movements in Bengal and Northeastern India, the Gangetic core, Punjab and the North West, Maharashtra and the South. Social reform in Bengal and Northeastern India followed two main channels: one rural and Islamic and the other Hindu and urban. Among Bengali Muslims, the Faraizis and allied movements were transitional in nature, owing nothing in their leadership or membership to the colonial milieu. Speaking from their traditional role of ulama, Islamic leaders addressed primarily a peasant audience. They drew on Islamic schools of philosophy and theology outside South Asia. The essentially acculturative, Hindu socioreligious movements, the Brahmos, Ramakrishnas and the followers of the neo-Vaishnavas drew symbols, concepts and scriptural legitimisation for the long history of protest within their religious heritage as well as elements of Western civilisation. Roy adopted some concepts of ethics, theism and rationalism from the West and Sen conscripted Christian symbols. Led by members of a rising educated elite, the Hindu movements of return adopted an imported organisational structure. In terms of the reaction to Christianity, the Brahmo Samaj sought equivalence, while the followers of Vivekananda and Sen proposed Hindu superiority. Ramakrishna Mission integrated the Hindu faith ideational elements with the secular motives of social service delivery. Both sets of movements strengthened religious consciousness as well as defined and redefined boundaries that took communal formulations (Jones, 1989).

In the region of the Gangetic core (comprising Bihar and Uttar Pradesh), the Muslims at the end of the nineteenth century had produced socioreligious movements through which four ideological approaches and concomitant patterns of action were clearly discernible. The Tariqah-i-Muhammadiyah attempted to re-establish Islamic supremacy through war and adopted an egalitarian approach. The Deobandis and Ahl-al-Hadith focused on the role of the Ulama as the natural leaders of the community. The loss of political power was dealt with by creating an Islamic community that would retain its cohesion through an appeal to the individual's conscience rather than state authority – under the guidance of the ulama. On the other hand, Sir Syed Ahmed Khan envisioned the reemergence of a bureaucratic and administrative elite who would cooperate with the British Indian government using the backdrop of Western education. Lastly the Barelvis defended orthodoxy in an alliance with the hereditary pirs of the countryside. The Hindus of the Gangetic plain on the other hand created two types of socioreligious movements – both acculturative and one defensively orthodox. Influenced by the Brahmo Samaj, the first turn was towards traditional institutions, with the Radhasoamis refurbishing the authority of the guru. Appealing to a rising vernacular and literate group, the endeavour was towards spiritual enlightenment and creation of a new psychosocial order. The Bharat Dharma Mahamandal aligned to the traditional varnasrama dharma and defended religion based on pre-British elite of aristocrats, priests, landlords and merchants (Jones, 1989).

Punjab has unveiled a differential flavour in the genus of social reform – the chief Arya Samaj movement paralleled with the Singh Sabha Movement and sectarian developments of influences of Christianity and the Ahmadiyah movements. Social reform as an agenda has however dominated the Arya Samaj context – reinstating equality within an essentially Hindu repertoire based on Vedic tenets (Puri and Judge, 2000). Further, the diversity of the religious communities in Punjab led to a greater number of socioreligious movement apart from divisions within and among the religious communities that appeared repeatedly. The two Sikh transitional movements grew from the crisis within the community and by the British conquest of the Sikh kingdom. The major Sikh acculturative movement, the Singh Sabha, was bifurcated between a pre-British elite centred in Amritsar and a new rising group at Lahore. Punjabi Hindus, to preserve the Hindu sentiments, founded the Lahore Arya Samaj in 1877. This aspect was in conflict with the Brahmo Samaj, orthodox Hindus and the Dev Samaj. Punjabi Muslims were influenced by movements of return from the Gangetic basin and orthodox Muslim leadership of Mirza Ghulam and the sole truth claims of the Ahmadis. Socioreligious reform movements in Punjab adopted Western organisational techniques through which they created a wide variety of institutions – missionaries, tract societies, parochial schools, centres of worship and associations. Religious identity and transboundary communal consciousness was developed on the basis of a combination of symbols based on language, script and religion (Jones, 1989; Shah, 2004).

Maharashtra's social reform was also deeply intertwined with academic and journalistic writings through which the radical and revolutionary tempers were unearthed. Further, Wagle (1999) has discussed that a historiographical and historic-literary analysis reveals several facets of social reform in the state. There were aspects of change-oriented agendas of reformers; transformations of political ideologies and practices; the transformative writings in Marathi periodicals and English newspapers and influence of Western medicine, science, history and literature on Maharashtrian intellectuals. The transitional socioreligious reform movements that developed in the central belt, and Maharashtra is composed of the Swaminarayan Sampraday, the Satnamis, the Manav Dharma Sabha and the Prarthana Samaj. The Swaminarayan movement had a Brahman leadership, supported Hindu ideals and emphasised on a moral code parallel to the Bhakti genre. Satnamis were largely a lower-caste group with voices of protest. The Manav Dharma Sabha, Oriyan in its origin, had members from Brahmin communities as well as Hinduised tribals. This movement attempted to create a form of religion that bridged the gap from formal Hinduism and the tribal hill people at the edge of the Hindu world – drawing in history of religious teachings. The acculturative movements in this region were the Paramahansa Mandali and the Prarthana Samaj. The other religious community in this region was that of the Parsis and the acculturative movement Rahnumai Mazdayasnan Sabha that looked into re-shaping the religion to adjust to the colonial milieu (Jones, 1989).

The south is composed of a combination of the Hindu and the Christian communities at the time of the nineteenth-century reform. Christianity in the South was further propelled by the missionaries, even prior to the establishment of the colonial milieu. According to Nadars, Christianity was an ideology that provided them with an arena for social mobility through a rejection of the caste system.

Three areas of Christian-Hindu strife (where Hindu orthodoxy reacted sharply to Christian challenges) emerged: among the Nadars of Tinnevelly within the British-controlled territory, with the members of the same caste in the princely state of Travancore and finally in the latter half of the nineteenth century in the Telugu-speaking districts north of Madras, where the Protestant missionaries were active. Another prominent socioreligious movement in the South was the Theosophical Society which drew on centuries of socioreligious dissent and protest within the Western civilisation. They borrowed non-Western symbols and ideas as part of their ideology and followed them back to their sources in Egypt and South Asia. They patronised Hindu-Buddhist symbols and deployed them to support their doctrines which led to a legitimisation of indigenous orthodoxies. This was juxtaposed with the movement of Swami Narayan Guru of Kerala that initially resorted to Brahminical Hinduism in the socioreligious endeavour to uplift the status of the Izhavas, but later rejected the same (Jones, 1989). The twentieth-century face of social reform contained aspects of competing nationalisms and heightened religious conflict. The growth was through emigration, conversion and transnational developments of socioreligious reform movements – Arya Samaj, Ramakrishna Math and Mission and Ahmadiyah Movement being important ones in question. Further by independence, these movements inhabited a complex ideological world as secular motifs of nationalism, socialism, communism and fascism were available to justify social change.

Scholars have also problematised social reform by initially equating social reformism to ideals of individualism, egalitarianism and humanism as also by a cultural nationalist impulse to restore the pristine values of Indian civilisation. It is especially valorised as the redeeming aspect of several modern religious reform movements, which are otherwise judged to have been compromised by the tendency to divide along communal lines. However as Uberoi (1996) discusses, the problematics emerge through the largely upper caste and elite class allegiance of the reformers which reinstates newer regimes of patronage and exploitation; the positionalities and views on women as essentialist and from an androcentric viewpoint; the role of Christian missionaries in providing institutional models for reformist emulation (in sharp contrast with the official imperial policy) as being writ with ambiguities and contradictions; and the tension between social reform as being a process of incremental betterment of society vis-à-vis it being a very limited and specific phenomenon spanning the century prior to the end of the first world war. Further, particularly in view of the issues of women (incidentally which were a prominent agenda of social reform), several disjunctures emerged. After the upsurge of interest on women's issues at the time of the social reform in the early decades of the twentieth century, the concern was reactivated only with the advent of the second wave of international feminism in the 1970s. This decline of interest in the women's problem paralleled the rise of the nationalist movement on the one hand, and of lower caste, peasant and tribal movement on the other: in either case, the women's question was coopted into a larger political project. Further, the grand narrative of social legislations that accompanied social reforms has been problematised as being essentialist, statist, patronising newer hegemonies along with jurisprudential issues of action and implementation. Using the philosophical theorisation of Hegel which visualised the facilitating of the transition from the 'personalistic' towards the 'objective' by civil society as the mediating institution, Chatterjee (2010) has undertaken an interrogation of the fundamental categorical imperative of the 'scientific' domain of the normative-ideational postulate of 'helping' that is done through a re-visiting of the rhetoric of the nineteenth-century social reform as the Archimedean standpoint for rationalistic praxis. By tracing the personal histories of the three conventional doyens of Bengal social reform – Roy, Keshub Sen and Brajen Seal using a 'personalytical approach', the point is that there are contradictions between the personal-mystical (examining the life histories) and the public-objective (in terms of official histories of their work in the arena of social reform). Hence, the connections between self-transformation and social transformation (which incidentally is also a Gandhian endeavour) then become rhetorical.

Gandhi and Gandhian Thought

Gandhian thought can be understood in terms of his political ideology, spiritual and ethical concerns, moral philosophy and praxis. The core of the thought which is essentially eclectic can be derived from his writings and collections of talks/speeches – a systematic documentation of which is available in multiple forms. Whereas the summum bonum of his political ideology encompasses arguments of nonviolence, Satyagraha (quest for truth), civil disobedience and emancipation from colonialism, his spiritual and ethical concerns discuss the ethics of frugality, equality and transcendence. In terms of praxis the lens encompasses aspects of sarvodaya, self-sustenance and reliance and focus on constructive action with 'rural' as the locus classicus of understandings. Amalgamating multiple normative and ideational influences the chief among them being Rousseau, Tolstoy, Vedanta (transcendental monism), vaishnavism (God personification), work ethics of protestantism and theosophy, Gandhi has submitted certain concepts based on metaphysical propositions. These include – satya, ahimsa, moksa, tapas, Satyagraha, swaraj and swadeshi, hence catapulting metaphysical propositions to have ethical-political implications as well as bound up with religious beliefs. In that sense, Gandhi was pre-Machiavellian in the intertwining of religion with politics. Posing limitations to reason and Western scientism, Gandhi's focus nevertheless remained developing a moral law and ethics of praxis rather than personal salvation alone through political disengagement. The overarching amalgamated political ideology was socialist, communist, liberal, reactionary and revolutionary (Iyer, 1973).

Gandhian thought can be further discussed in terms of his theistic ideas, moral propositions and ethical legacies, political ideologies and social theorisations. In terms of his theistic ideas, Gandhi aligned to the idea of an apriori existence of Godhead, the ideas of God being assimilated from Vedic, Upanishadic and Vedantic tenets, the indeterminate absolute proposition of Sankara's Vedanta and subsequently the contrary propositions of Vaishnava teachers (Ramanuja, Nimbarka, Vallabha and Madhva) who propounded that liberation is possible through God propitiated by devotion and self-surrender. Further, Gandhi also assimilated the ideas of Jaina tenets of anekantavada and syadvada in his understandings of Godhead – which can culminated in a comprehension of God being an all pervasive reality immanent in man and also in the world and like Whitehead, described God from both the primordial and the consequent aspects. Further akin to theistic realism, Godhead is equated to truth and truth claims and in that sense there are elements of absolutism and universalism in Gandhian thought. The other domains of his theistic ideas are a penchant for religious unity (seeking commonalities of tenets in all religions), naturalism (a reverence to nature and equating the same to Godhead) and theistic existentialism (Datta, 1953).

In terms of the moral propositions and ethical legacies, Gandhian thought aligns to the tenets that morality is the essence of religion – love, knowledge of self and others, free will, soul force, work by self-surrender and dynamic humility and peace as further dimensions of the same (Kim, 1996). Within the moral repertoire, discourses on truth and nonviolence predominate – ahimsa, Satyagraha and sarvodaya being the core moral vernaculars. Gandhian ethics provide a language of nonviolent relationality in the public domain, of moral internationalism based on the notion of compassion for and connectivity with strangers and the language of soul force based on truth and love. This ethics of nonviolence (ahimsa) as viewed by Gandhi (2009) is not only rooted in the indigenous context, but also constitutes a transcultural nonviolent ethics of the everyday that is eminently translatable across a range of political sites. It is an ethics of relationality across strangeness and difference as against an orientation that valorises propinquity and sameness to mark human sociality. Gandhi's anti-imperial, nonviolent energy is refined and filtered through acts of relational embodiment – his experience of vegetarianism, his quirky experiments with alternative medicine and his renowned fasts (Shetty, 2009; Suhrud, 2009). The three key sites of sociality, professional relationality and discursivity that were crucial in shaping Gandhi's ethical orientations included his friendships in various ashrams, his practice as a lawyer in colonial South Africa and his English rendering of the Hind Swaraj and the tensions involved in the translations thereof. In terms of moral propositions, there are fundamental and absolutist moral beliefs and along Kantian lines a belief in the universalisability of the categorical imperative of duty.

Political ideologies demonstrated a clear alignment to socialism with concepts of trusteeship as the abiding tenet of political organisation. The core term of Gandhian political thought was 'swaraj', which meant self-rule and, in a stricter political sense, a sovereign kingdom's freedom from external control. This philosophy related spiritual and political freedom or swaraj to a perception of unity or oneness of life and an enlightened self-restraint (Dalton, 1998). As expressed in Hind Swaraj, the Gandhian concepts of swaraj and Satyagraha were related to the emphasis placed in employing the right means to attain an end. In terms of analysing Gandhian political ideologies, Dalton (1998) proposes similarities between Gandhian political idealism and Plato's thoughts. Plato views freedom in the same dual sense as liberation of both self and system and he also identifies freedom with both self-restraint and self-realisation. The logical relationship between genuinely free individual and community is evoked (the fact that freedom also has certain constraints in the societal context), which is also visualised in Gandhian thought. Although Plato and Gandhi align in conceptions of power, the ideal state conceptions of Plato and Gandhian notions of democracy differ. The purpose of political leadership was perceived by Gandhi along Platonic lines as that of reinstating moral values. This leadership was further qualified by James Burns as transformational leadership – combining tenets of swaraj and Satyagraha (also labelled by Gandhi as heuristic because it employed the power that encouraged reflection an reexamination of motives, needs and interests) towards the ideal of inclusivity.

Combining several utopian ideals in his sense of polity and politics, Gandhi, as discussed by Hardiman (2003) has advocated a radical style of politics that fought the many insidious divides found in societies. This divisive politics involves defining the antagonist as the 'other' who is seen to stand apart from the community to which the 'self' is perceived to belong. The core contention was resistance of such divisive politics, of nationalists who posited a polarisation with the coloniser through assertion of a warped sense of masculinity through assassinations, instead arguing for feminine principles of nonviolent opposition and civility. Gandhi never sought to evolve a grand political theory, but through a dialogic scheme his 'truth' worked out as praxis and it was understood that it had to evolve constantly in relation to his and other people's experiences. In terms of his contentions on nationalism, it was incorporative (broad and catholic) and recognised simultaneously the vital need to nurture a dynamic political space that was separate from state power and which could act as a check on that power. Private property, held in a spirit of trusteeship, provided one such counter position. Gandhi combined liberalism, anarchism, decentralisation, self-determination and self-rule in his political positions. Incorporative nationalism combined understandings from the subaltern classes and a quest for revolution. Hegemony of a particular class was denied and, along

Gramscian lines, argued that the elite and subaltern classes structure their discourses in relationship to each other through a 'series of negations'. Further the Gandhian stance has been the ideational back up for several political assertions manifesting through new social movements operating in a number of discrete spheres. A similar thought is found in the writings of Foucault - particularly the argument that hegemonic power is dispersed throughout the social formation in various sites, with each sit expressing a a particular relationship of domination and subordination. The Gandhian position is reflected in the fact that transformation is sought not through direct capture of state power through elections, but through attempts to transform the nature of politics itself. In intertwining politics with religion, Gandhian thought is akin to Emerson and Mazzini (Iyer, 1973). Religion was further understood by Gandhi in the Augustinian sense as a spiritual commitment which is personal. Hence, what predominates is a theological worldview within the realms of realpolitik.

In the realm of social theorisations, Gandhi at once demonstrates an alignment to structuralist and postcolonial propositions. Gandhi further was sceptical of the unilinear vision of history and state-centred narratives in favour of ethics and myths (Ashis Nandy has argued that Gandhi valorised myth over history, thus adopting a 'traditional' Indian stance towards the past) and that were considered to be more deterministic in developing a critique of colonialism (Hardiman, 2003). The postcolonial flavour of Gandhi arises in his transcultural androgynous protest against the excessive aggression of British colonialism holding in trust a peculiar form of ethically potent 'weakness' (metaphor for nonviolence) to which according to Nandy (1983) a violent world may have to return. The structure is evident in Gandhian notions of society and the colonial state. In the Hind Swaraj (Gandhi's most prominent postcolonial text), the dualism of the coloniser-colonised is discursively unearthed; notions of fair and just governmentality evoked by the anticolonial nationalism is discussed and notions of authentic selfhood at the very disjunctures and discontinuities of colonial temperaments are debated.

Problematics to Gandhi's positions have been by the subaltern groups, particularly Dalits in the Phule-Ambedkarite vein, who visualised Gandhi's claims to equality as rhetorical, subverting assertions of depressed castes under the garb of nationalism. Hence, although equality was accepted within the Gandhian repertoire in theory, in practice, it perceived the other as merely an object of consciousness and not another consciousness (Ganguly, 2009). Further, Hardiman (2003) has deliberated as to how patriarchy was rooted in the familial practice of Gandhi and that it remained an abiding sentiment from the feminist and psychoanalytical point of view despite the fact that women were encouraged to take active part in the campaigns for civil resistance.

Nationalism

Nationalism as an ideological position demonstrates an allegiance to the idea of the nation-state – spatially and metaphorically. Literature on nationalism has provided theoretical renditions and political economy discourses at the epistemic level and, in the indigenous context, discursive realms intertwining categorical imperatives of ethnicity, religion, caste and class with the conception of the nation-state.

Theoretical renditions and political economy discourses on nationalism can be discussed as follows: Hayes (1931) has traced the historical evolution of nationalism identifying the forms as humanitarian, Jacobin, traditional, liberal, integral and economic. The proponents of humanitarian nationalism were Bolingbroke, Rousseau and Herder. Bolingbroke proposed a nationalism based on theistic naturalism – that nationality came directly from the God of nature as also aristocratic – depending upon the patriotism of the nobility, church and masses. Rousseau drawing upon his central doctrine of social contract (proposing a principle of popular sovereignty) laid the foundations of a democratic nationalism. Herder proposed a cultural nationalism providing an exposition of what most basically distinguishes one nationality from the other – territoriality and culture being two aspects. Jacobin version of nationalism is the French vision developed on the basis of humanitarian democratic nationalism of Rousseau and focused on extending the liberty-equality-fraternity goals of the French Revolution. To some extent Jacobin nationalism was also religious and missionary and deployed militarism to realise visions and goals. Traditional nationalism is based on the ideas of Edmund Burke, Vicomte de Bonald and Friedrich von Schlegel. Burke's nationalism proposed that the idea of a nation was divinely ordained and providential and abided by the tenets of aristocratic nationalism. Bonald proposed that nationalism constituted threefold 'marks' – a public religion also simultaneously tolerant of minority dissent, permanent social distinctions and an executive authority vested in the monarch. Schlegel on the other hand was a proponent of cultural ethnocentrism and romanticism as aligned to the sentiment of nationalism.

The proponents of liberal nationalism were Bentham, Guizot, Welcker and Mazzini. Bentham's nationalism was influenced by his abiding ideas of laissez-faire, utilitarianism and liberty championing thus 'an individualism based on enlightened self-interest', ignoring of the social contract, natural rights and other metaphysical conceptions and instead stressing a practical utility and a penchant for systematic, logical and consistent reforms and a passive policeman state with a government which should allow individual wide liberty-political, economic, religious, educational and military (Hayes, 1931). Guizot and Welker corroborated the Benthamite stance in the context of the practical politics of France. Mazzini, within the liberal nationalist genre and in the context of Italy, proposed a 'law of nationality' – nationalism consists in the work of humanity which God had prescribed to each people and that along with rights, duties are important to realise nationalist goals. Integral nationalism is focused on national integrity and the increase of national power and is concerned with the consolidation aspects of nations that have already attained political independence. The economic face of nationalism is juxtaposed vis-à-vis economic liberalism. Adolf Wagner, a German economist of the historical school and a proponent of the economic version of nationalism, discussed that natural rights and natural powers of an individual are conditioned by the national state which in itself is a historical product.

Hobsbawm (1990) proposes that nationalism signifies a principle which holds that the political and national unit should be congruent; nations are formulations of nationalisms and not vice versa; the national question is situated at the point of intersection of politics, technology and transformation; and nations are thus a dual phenomenon constructed essentially from above, but which cannot be understood unless analysed from below (hence distinctions sought between official ideologies of the state and individual ideologies and that national identifications as non-deterministic, not solely constitutive of individual identities and temporally non-static).

Based on Gellner's definition of nationalism as a congruence of power and culture, Aloysius (1997) has looked at the sociological treatment of the concept of nationalism. Initially within the realms of political theory and history, sociology of nationalism has looked at problematisation of the concepts related to nationalism and shift its emphasis from state, ideology and movement to nation as a distinct social category and particularly in the aspect of its becoming, i.e., the transition from premodern to the new cultural/political totality. As a theory of cultural power, the sociology of nationalism is a study of social change from the perspective of movements of power and power positions within society affecting its structure and culture. This internal approach to the study of nationalism as a specific form of social change is the core contribution of the new sociological approach.

From an anthropological viewpoint, Gupta (2000) has looked at nation-state as a cultural phenomenon rather than lineaments on the map. Commencing with a premise that a clear conception of cultural membership can determine space, this conceptualisation has been extended to include the cultural membership of the nation-state and the territorial space that such membership connotes. Hence, nation-states are bound by strong sentiments of identity that are best understood as a cultural phenomenon and root metaphors. These sentiments need to be buttressed by structures of governance which bring people together by keeping alive the principles of citizenship and fraternity. State formation herein is largely pertaining to territorialisation and citizenship. While the concept of territorialisation refers to the boundaries between cultures for the purpose of exclusion of alien cultures from structural power, citizenship is the affirmation of inclusion via membership in the share of the same power.

Elaborating on the Marxist theory of nationalism, Davis (1978) has discussed that nationalism entails the concept of nation in the Marxist repertoire which signifies a specified territory and a consciousness of itself as a nation akin to class consciousness. Nations are formed from states, in struggle against foreign oppression and then by first attaining cultural solidarity and then a political expression of that solidarity. Marxian version of nationalism was concretised through the ideas of Lenin and Rosa Luxemburg. Lenin emphasised on the right to self-determination of nations and the role of bourgeoisie in building modern nations. Luxemburg on the other hand viewed the role of bourgeoisie as minimal and emphasised instead on the concepts of federation and autonomy in nation-building. Stalin included culture in his definition of nationalism and the materialist conception of history wherein he viewed nations as historically evolving. Like Lenin, Stalin too focused on the role of the bourgeoisie in nation building and the historically predisposing factors as being primarily economic. He saw the restrictions on suppressed nationalities as being imposed by the bourgeoisie of the dominant nation as a part of the struggle with the bourgeoisie of the oppressed nation. Trotsky focused primarily on the economics of nationalism (economic factors as overriding in determining the stability of the nation-state) and distinguished between nationalism of the colonial bourgeoisie and proletariat. Hence, a Marxist treatment of nationalism is a dialectical journey showing how nationalism arises in history, under what conditions, its relation to democracy, socialism and specifically Asiatic mode of production, class struggle and proletarian internationalism.

Further, the bourgeoisie nationalism that was patronised by Lenin and Stalin was critiqued by latter theorists such as Frantz Fanon and Amilcar Cabral. Based on the experiences of the Algerian resistance movement, Fanon discussed the role of several classes in bringing about revolution for two core privileges in the realm of the colonial regime: economic privilege and the national privilege. But unlike the orthodox version of Marxism wherein the proletariat and peasants would have a role in the revolution, Fanon recognises the role of the lumpenproletariat in the process. Cabral (from the erstwhile Portuguese colony, now known as Guinea-Bissau at the western end of sub-Saharan Africa) has discussed the importance of culture in building the process of national consciousness, and the process of national liberation is the process of restoring history. This is contrary to the Marxian proposition that class struggle is the motive force of progress, instead arguing for a position that the level of productive forces is the driving power of history. Class struggle would emerge after the anticolonial struggle, and the petty bourgeoisie would be instrumental in nation formation (Davis, 1978).

From the post-Marxian viewpoint, Giddens (1985) has distinguished between traditional states and modern states, the core characteristics of modern nation-states being identified as: emergence of administrative orders of high intensity, polyarchy (derived from the administrative concentration achieved via the expansion of surveillance and from the altered nature of the dialectic of control which this produces), systemic relations with other nation-states, intertwining with capitalism and industrialism, industrialisation of war (creation of a world military order that crosscuts the division between the first, second and third worlds) and transborder operations. According to Giddens, there are four 'institutional clutterings' that are associated with modernity and nation-state: heightened surveillance, capitalistic enterprise, industrial production and consolidation of centralised control of means of violence. Hence, there is a significant shift from traditional Marxian societies which are class divided and segmental in character.

Chandra (1979) has mapped the colonialism-modernism-nationalism trajectory in the Indian context. The development of nationalist sentiment has been against the backdrop of the structure of colonialism, the process of its evolution and deconstruction through anticolonial propositions. Colonial historiographies and policies and their critique provided the core agenda of anti-imperialists and nationalists. Developing further on this premise, Ganachari (2004) has proposed nationalism as a renaissance sentiment that arose through English education and Western ideals and led to the eventual indictment of the colonisers. Demystifying imperialist dominations or colonial constructions such as the 'white man's burden', nationalism as an ideational entity was based on the unified notion of nativity and sense of territorial and cultural allegiance. In the Indian context such understandings were promoted by Naoroji, Ranade, Joshi, Gokhale, Iyer and Dutt through the locus classicus of the Indian National Congress as a political entity. Revolutionary cultural nationalists such as Tilak, Pal and Lajpat Rai further affirmed the contention that Indian nationalism was linked to Macaulay's early nineteenth-century fetish for impregnating the colony with Western, scientific and rational education. In that sense, Indian nationalism is perceived by imperial historians as renaissance gift of Western enlightenment to the colonies, albeit containing factions of patrons and clients. The other characteristics of nationalism in the Indian context were an anti-establishment stance (as demonstrated through Gandhian Satyagraha), use of religious, cultural and historical iconographies taking sometimes the forms of 'invented traditions' (Tilak and Gandhi); inverting the logic of colonialism by indigenising development and notions of modernisation in the postcolonial era (Nehruvian paradigm of development that aligned to Rostow and Mahalanobis that economic growth would lead to social development) and harbouring on the Indic spiritual franchise (Tagore, Vivekananda and the Vedantic missions).

Dube and Banerjee-Dube (2006) discuss that the idea of nationalism is intertwined with the conception of modernity and colonial modernity in particular. Colonialism and modernity are comprehended as dominant European projects of power/knowledge. There is the politics of exclusion/inclusion with the impulse of the modern nation and the colonial state towards excluding subaltern subjects and colonised people and the simultaneous drive of including them at the margins of the authoritative grid of civilisation. The notion of nationalism is entwined with the colonial interplay of power and difference, of convergent divergences, of the fabrication of the colonised as a primitive outsider who had to be forged as the improved insider within the space of the empire and the time of the nation, and the colonial quest of building a residual civil society in the colony.

Other domains of contemporary global discourses on nationalism include aspects of ethnic nationalisms challenging the polyethnic constitution of the liberal democratic idea of the nation-state. Wieland (2006) has, utilising the situative-primordial approach to ethnicity proposed the idea of ethno-nationalism which is based on an organic and ethnic ideal of the nation. This variety of nationalism does not fall back on the state as the integrating factor – rather the state is the consequence of a preceding process of ethnic and parallel cultural homogenisation of a people as a community. There is also a parallel process of construction and instrumentalisation of ethnic groups that takes place in state formation.

Intertwining of religion with ideational entities of nationalism and nation-state has resulted in the emergence of certain chain of arguments by scholars in the Indian context, some of which have been highlighted here:

Satyamurthy (1994) has discussed that in the indigenous context, anticolonial nationalism has forwarded aspects of democratic pluralism, secularism and reformist egalitarianism. Further, the nationalist discourse commencing from the early responses of Indians regarding European entry into India was dominated by political and cultural consideration rather than solely economic ones. The early generations of Indian elite who came into contact with the colonial power readily acquired the alphabet of

Western thought that led to a social layering that was mediated through political norms of civil society set by elites (which established its distance from the majority of the people by means of a high literary culture). The discourse on nationalism in India was thus founded on the vision of representative figures thrown up by a syncretically minded elite. Gandhi, faced with the two entirely separate worlds of high and low culture, forged a new configuration of nationalism based on a composite culture. Hence in the Indian context, nationalism assumed the following key formations: Gandhian (based on an anticolonial consciousness), Nehruvian (based on rationalistic ideals of secularism), ethnic (based on communal identifications and belongingness) and radical (based on anti-imperialist sentiments and dealing with questions of poverty and social justice).

The symbiosis between national and communal identities in the nineteenth century resulted partly from the consciousness of belonging to a 'nation' on the one hand and to reformed Hindu and Muslim communities on the other. Awareness of being Indian was attended by a new appreciation of what it meant to be Hindu or Muslim, an appreciation that would eventually fuel antipodal constructions of 'the nation' by the intellectuals of the two communities. The tendency to view nationalism, not as an alternative principle of social cohesion but as one that coexisted with and depended upon traditional social cohesive units like the religious communities can be ascribed to the fact that colonialism probably fuelled the traditional social units as opposed to its modernisation venture. The inability to view communal consciousness and nationalism as binary categories had also to do with the premodern nature of Indian social formation, since 'traditional' ideologies are typical accompaniments of premodern social structures (Barlas, 1995).

The genesis of Indian nationalism has been traced to various periods in history. Some claim that there was an existing national unity in precolonial times created by the fourth-century Hindu Gupta dynasty; nationalist historians trace it to the 1857 revolt which they depict as the national war of independence and some trace its genesis to the Orientalists' attempts to educate the British. The strands of nationalist discourse have also been taken to be religious in their imagery and focus – Gandhian version of the same being an important one in question. Gandhian nationalism was interwoven with religiosity – rejecting the hegemonising discourses of colonialism necessarily entailing the rejection of secularism with its claims to universality. Gandhi's attempts to elevate nonviolence and class harmony to political virtues (drawing from religion) put an end to agrarian discontent and conceived of a politics wherein peasants are distanced from the nation-state and at the political margins. Further in the Indian context, nationalism has assumed a majoritarian Hindu face (invocation of the community ideology taking the shape of secular nationalism), while the Muslim has been looked at as a 'communal aberration created by imperialism to fracture the secular national identity' (Khan, 1989, cited in Barlas, 1995). Further as discussed by Panikkar (2007), the emergence of Indian nationalism is seen as a political articulation of the anticolonial consciousness further complicated by the intertwining of culture discourses. The religious politics of both pre- and post-independence periods have construed notions of cultural nationalisms. The nationalist cultural strategy was based on a dual struggle, simultaneously against the colonial and the traditional; cultural nationalism signifying a resistance against the colonial culture and struggle against the indigenous. Hence, cultural nationalism is posited vis-à-vis anticolonial nationalism (which focused primarily on political mobilisation and did not devote adequate attention to the issues raised by the Renaissance) which marginalised the cultural question. Communalism is said to thrive in this cultural vacuum, by interpreting and appropriating culture in an entirely ahistorical fashion and making it the sole basis of nationalism.

Van der Veer (1994) has looked at religious nationalism as separatist nationalism and in the Indian context it is not a product entirely of India's colonial past and that religious identities are not 'primordial attachments' inculcated by tradition, but product of changing identities spread by institutionalised devotionalism and shaped over time by pilgrimage, migration and media. How Hindu and Muslim identities are transformed in the colonial and postcolonial periods is the discursive field within which the arguments are placed. Religious nationalism then becomes distinct concept vis-à-vis Western nationalisms based on discourses of modernity. The crux of religious nationalism is that it combines the antihistorical features of religious discourse with an empiricist search for facts influenced by orientalism. In the nineteenth and the twentieth centuries, religious nationalism has built on forms of religious identity and modes of religious communication that are themselves in flux. What Van der Veer (1996) points out is that there is a reformist religion of the bourgeoisie and the religion of the 'other half' and a connection between them which is linked with antagonisms and a 'laicisation of organisation and leadership'. Further, the sacredness of the languages of the scriptures, in the context of religious nationalism, attributed to national languages – a form of 'laicisation of sacred communication'.

Discussing Hindu nationalism as a specific form of religious nationalism, Jaffrelot (2007) proposes that it emerged as an ideological reaction to European domination marking a transition from reform to revivalism. Initially based on the ideas of Roy and Sen, this thought trend was further capitalised by Dayanand Saraswati whose revivalism trend inaugurated a specific combination of stigmatisation and emulation of the threatening 'other'. Latter developments included the Hindu Sabhas and the Hindu Sangathan movements and the Maharashtrian crucible of Hindu nationalism spearheaded by Savarkar.

For the subaltern groups, nationalism turned out to be an antidemocratic discourse, a means of neutralising them by defusing their class demands and absorbing them into dominant class parties. Chatterjee (1993) has further discussed the counter arguments to nationalism in the following manner: Drawing from the arguments of Anderson (1983), he has discussed that nations were not determinate products of given sociological conditions such as language or race, but rather 'imagined communities' that came into existence through institutional forms. However, an aberration from the Andersonian thought is that nations in Asia and Africa have been posited not on an identity but on a difference with the 'modular' forms of national society propagated by the West. Second, as a colonial import, nationalism was not only a form of the modern state with egalitarian intentions, but rather an agency that retained the premise of inequality through the power of the 'rule of colonial difference' – preserving the alien-ness of the ruling group. Third, anti-colonial nationalists in India, dividing their culture into material and spiritual domains, normalised the aspirations of the various marginal groups that typified the spiritual sphere. Fourth, nationalism has been viewed as a project of mediation through three themes: appropriation of the popular (through which the popular enters the hegemonic national discourse as a gendered category), classicisation of tradition (predominantly Hindu with Islam being an alternative vein and this classicisation being a prior requirement of sanitised popular traditions) and the hegemonic domain of nationalism itself (wherein the legal-institutional forms of political authority that nationalists subscribed to were entirely in conformity with the modern disciplinary forms of power).

In Summary

This chapter has dealt with two ideational pursuits that are considered to be the vanguards of social change episteme and praxis – social reform and nationalism. The Gandhian discourse at the cross junctures of the two posits related ideological stances. Social reform, primarily understood as a nineteenth-century phenomenon in the Indian context, has two broad formations: transitional and acculturative. With reform agendas as visualising change universally, the geographical manifestations have unearthed differentials. The stances have been pro-establishment and colonial towards developing an anticolonial consciousness by celebrating indigenous sentimentalities. The discussion has examined reform endeavours in Maharashtra, Bengal, Punjab and the South with variations therein. The problematics associated with social reform in terms of its elite bias, acute emphasis on religion, androcentric bias (dealing with the women's questions primarily from a patriarchal lens) and ambiguity in terms of the role of missionaries and personal-public polarities have also been highlighted.

In terms of Gandhi, the main philosophical tenets of truth and nonviolence have been placed in a discursive plane and deliberated. The transcultural and transnational implications of the nonviolence relationality along with critique arising from the subaltern groups have been presented. Nationalism as an overarching temporality (as an outcome of modernity and hence parallel to the legacies of reform and Gandhi) has been discussed in terms of its forms and norms in the global scenario, its alignments with modernity and intertwining with domains of power and culture. In the indigenous context, the anticolonial consciousness precipitated through nationalism and versions of ethnic and religious nationalisms deem deliberation.

7

Social Justice and Human Rights Discourses

Traversing Modernities and Postmodernities

This chapter examines the varied philosophical and ideational positions within two core domains interfacing with social work – social justice and human rights. Deliberations of social justice have unearthed references to justice in Greek philosophy and seventeenth-century philosophers such as Locke, Rousseau and Hume and later thinkers such as Thomas Paine, Spencer and Kropotkin. The versions of political theorists of the twentieth century in United States and Britain as well as key figures such as John Rawls, Freire and Martha Nussbaum have been deliberated. A similar journey through historicity has been undertaken in the realm of human rights – commencing with classical, modern and contemporary thinkers. Further, indigenous perspectives and also non-Western strands have been mentioned. The endeavour in this chapter has been to examine the development of epistemologies on social justice and human rights – to then determine the flow of epistemes. Praxis domains in terms of meaning, instruments and constitutional provisions have been only mentioned – the central argument being the normative and ideational dialogues. Further, justice seems a wider rubric subsuming within it the discourse of human rights – as would be evident in the overlapping epistemes through historicity.

Social Justice

The realm of social justice includes multiple perspectives and theorisations extant and deliberated through historicity. Some general conceptions of social justice are social justice as a system of distribution and retribution that is governed by valid moral principles (identified by Mill as generosity and beneficence); social justice as rules of conduct which are universalisable; social justice as having at its centre notions of distributive justice and hence comparative allotment; equality of treatment as a prima facie requirement of justice; liberty, subsuming the claims of desert, and equality (Frankena, 1962; Brandt, 1962).

The first mention of justice was found in the *Trial of Socrates*, Book I of Plato's *The Republic* and Book V of Aristotle's *Nicomachean Ethics* as also the Melian debate in Book V of Thucydides' *The Peloponnesian War*. Earlier figures who espoused the concept of justice in myriad ways included John Locke, Rousseau, Thomas Paine, Thomas Jefferson, Dubois, Mill, Tamir and Kymlicka, who focused on elements of difference as discrimination and the need to reinstate justice by minimising difference. John Locke (1632–1704) was an early defender of representative government and his book 'The Two Treatises of Civil Government' presented three important claims: natural equality of men, priority of rights, equal subjection of law and presence of an impartial judge (Freund, 1962). Rousseau proposed the concept of social contract and general will that underpinned his conceptions of social justice. Commencing with the conception of social bond, Rousseau makes a distinction between natural liberty and civil liberty. The social contract transforms the absolute right under the former to civil liberty that is limited by the general will. Freedom is inalienable, but the need to preserve freedom goes hand in hand with the striving for equality. General will is thus an embodiment of equality – transcending differences and aspiring towards common good. Theorist of the French Revolution Thomas Paine used the idea of equal rights to challenge differences rooted in birth and status, rejecting the idea of naturalising aristocracy. Theorist of the American War of Independence Thomas Jefferson built on the Lockean belief of equality and independence and governance as instrumentalising social justice by the emphasis on life and liberty – challenging differences particularly that arose in terms of race and colour. However, Jefferson affirmed that the principle of equality can serve a purpose only when it is used by particular groups to demand equal rights and equal treatment. Similar vein of affirmations on justice were made by W. E. B. Dubois in his deliberations against racism. Mill's utilitarian theory of justice is aggregative, focussing on performance of that action which leads to the greatest happiness of all. Existing forms of exclusion and differentiation as manifestations of 'natural' differences are questioned to reinstate an egalitarian thinking through democratic patterns. Tamir and Kymlicka have argued that social justice discourses need to incorporate dimensions of culture within the understandings of nation-state – particularly negating the hegemonies of dominant cultures and recognising minority cultural rights. Minority cultural rights interrogate liberal philosophical beliefs and more directly the nature of the homogenising agenda of the nation-state. Hence, in employing the liberal conception of equality to identify unfairness and discrimination in cultural practices, the contention is that equality of treatment requires that one takes cognisance of the cultural contexts of experience and action (Mahajan, 1998).

Other thinkers included David Hume, Spencer and Kropotkin who discussed justice from particularistic viewpoints. David Hume's thinking about justice is found in two places – Book iii of the *Treatise of Human Nature* and the *Enquiry Concerning the Principles of Morals*. Justice is discussed in the treatise in the context of an inquiry of the nature of virtue. In Hume's view, the concept of justice is intimately bound up with that of property. The rules of justice are conventions whereby material goods are ascribed to particular individuals; and the virtue of justice consists in respecting this ascription. Human conventions are sole origins of justice, rights and property and hence justice is an artificial virtue. Justice is a respect for the rights of others provided that an individual's right is an ascription of a good to a person in accordance with the rules of justice (present possession, original possession and prescription with respect to property). Further according to Hume, justice and public interest may be contradictory; but justice in an egalitarian society essentially meant the respect for the established rights of others. Hence, Hume theorised in a society in which traditional status and aristocratic virtues (as opposed to bourgeoisie ones) were considered more important and hence his notions of justice emerged from rights (Miller, 1976).

Spencer's theory of justice emerges from his moral philosophy, particularly his moral philosophy and proposed three components in the ethics of social life – justice, positive beneficence and negative beneficence; justice thus being an important moral principle. The fundamental principle of justice as expressed by Spencer is that 'each individual ought to receive the benefits and evils of his own nature and consequent conduct'. Hence, justice is identified with a distribution according to desert (interpreted as achievement). The threefold justification of his distribution according to desert is: on the grounds that its implementation serves general happiness, on the grounds that it conforms to the laws of life, and on the grounds that it gives each individual what he deserves. Spencer's secondary principle of justice is derived from his understanding of equal liberty stated as 'every man is free to do which he wills, provided he infringes not the equal freedom of any other man'. Kropotkin's theory is based on needs and further on his moral theory centred on the division between three levels of moral activity – mutual aid, justice and self-sacrifice. Drawing from ideals of egalitarianism, his conception of justice was distribution according to need. The main argument in support of this is that all available resources are the collective work of humanity and thus should belong to the society as a whole. Individual appropriation is unjust and from the social point of view it is only individuals' needs that can give them a just claim to a share of resources (Boulding, 1962; Vlastos, 1962). The subject matter of justice, according to Miller (1976) is the manner in which benefits and burdens are distributed among sentient beings – the aggregative and distributive political principles (Gewirth, 1962). Social justice, as discussed by Miller, has three broad elements – rights, deserts and needs which are conceptually distinct.

The other class of theorists have built on the element of difference/diversity and its reaffirmation to conceptualise justice. These include works of twentieth century political theorists in United States and Great Britain: John Calhoun, Arend Lijphart, Michael Oakeshott, Chantal Mouffe, John Gray, A. O. Lovejoy, Bhikhu Parekh, W. E. Connolly and C. Schmitt. John Calhoun has forwarded the notion of a concurrent majority, as unlike Rousseau's propositions, he did not believe that a general or common will would emerge in the course of negotiations. The majority and minority have deep differences that cannot be transcended. Arend Lijphart has proposed the concept of consociational democracy, moving beyond Hobhouse's notion of organic liberalism and hence advocating the schema that ensures that the will of diverse groups is accounted for in the political process. Consociational democracy of Lijphart can be defined in terms of four characteristics – government by a grand coalition of political leaders of all significant segments of the plural society; mutual veto or concurrent majority rule which serves as an additional protection of vital minority interests; proportionality as the principal standard of political representation and autonomy of all political segments. Michael Oakeshott, Chantal Mouffe and John Gray have been proponents of the concept of civil association negating the substantive notion of common good and common purpose in favour of diversity. The contention is that the political needs to embody a mode of civil association, specifying practices that must be adhered to, while performing any self-chosen action. The definition of politics as a civil and associational relationship is considered to be an essential condition for the protection of individual liberty. Michael Oakeshott thus defined the political as a civil condition, building upon which Chantal Mouffe has argued that the notion of civil association creates a public space without imposing any single way of life. John Gray has proposed that this supports communitarian ethics – a crucial domain of social justice. A. O. Lovejoy has built on this notion of difference in the discourse on justice – individual, epistemological and moral. Instead of looking at difference as inequality (as understood by liberals), Lovejoy builds on the Romantic emphasis on the creativity of nature – thus attributing a positive value to difference and diversity. Hence, rejecting hegemonising cultural differences based on ascriptive cultural attributes and notions of universal/transcendental truth, this version celebrates difference in a de-sacralised world, thus giving space to the ideals of self-determination and choice. Voices of cultural plurality as the mainstay of justice moving beyond traditional liberalism have been presented by Bhikhu Parekh and W. E. Connolly. Liberal individualistic ethic is considered to be insensitive to cultural plurality and probably also assimilationist in nature. Parekh presents the idea of cultural pluralism and is interested in identifying the limits of permissible diversity. Connolly speaks of 'agonal politics', a terms derived from Nietzsche wherein a conception of democracy that incorporates cultural pluralism demands an ethico-political spirituality. C. Schmitt has proposed that through the twin ideas of representation and free expression social justice is reinstated as difference then enters into the discourse of democracy (Mahajan, 1998; Shah, 1998).

Positive discrimination is another realm of discourse in the arena of social justice discussed by political theorists in United States: James Nickel, Paul Taylor, Alan Goldman, Ronald Dworkin, Glenn Loury, Nathan Glazer and Iris Marion Young. James Nickel and Paul Taylor have critically examined the agenda of positive discrimination by making use of community identity (which is believed to legitimise discrimination). Nickel maintains that race and gender are not relevant categories; the subjects of affirmative action are 'victims of discrimination', which Taylor refutes based on their relevance according to the principles of compensatory justice. Alan Goldman questions the idea of group-based compensation reinstating however the indeterminacy of 'fairness' in the repertoire of social justice. Ronald Dworkin, while defending positive discrimination as a tool of social justice distinguishes between equal treatment and treatment as an equal. Glenn Loury and Nathan Glaser argue for positive discrimination from a pragmatic contemporaneous standpoint rather than adopting the historical materialist perspective of hegemony through historicity that needs rectification. Iris Marion Young discusses that social justice is instrumentalised through a politics of difference – group-specific strategies add to democratic accountability and promote justice better than a homogeneous public, thereby transcending the language of integration-segregation (Cohen et al., 1997).

John Rawls is an important figure in the arena of deliberation of social justice. Rawls' proposed a contractual theory of justice vis-à-vis the utilitarian proposition which he believed did not examine the distributive character of justice (the concern that each individual to receive his due as the utilitarian pre-occupation was with the aggregate positions) (Ray, 2000). In his seminal work, *A Theory of Justice* (1971), he presented an elaborate social contract argument and attempted to strike a balance between liberal thinking and equality. Two principles of justice that are derived are: the principle of equal basic liberty and the difference principle combined with the requirement of fair equality of opportunity. The debates that this work prompted were those of utility versus rights, libertarian versus egalitarian notions of distributive justice and criticisms of communitarian nature (discussing whether the Rawlsian liberal is committed to the conception of the person as unencumbered and antecedently individuated and prior to society and hence proposing an abstract conceptions of justice). In his later *work Political Liberalism* (1993), Rawls has re-interpreted justice as fairness as a distinctively political version of liberalism – formulating the 'conception of justice for specifying the fair terms of social co-operation between citizens regarded as free and equal'. Herein Rawls has secured an 'overlapping consensus' in a pluralist society, linking social justice firmly to institutional stability and social unity despite moral, religious and metaphysical disagreements among citizens. Political conception of justice attempts to harmonise juxtapositions and contradictions by balancing viewpoints and existential positions (Sushila, 1990). There are thus three elements in the political conception of justice: balance is struck between the Kantian interest in developing and exercising the moral powers of rational autonomy and fair dealing and the positionalities of individuals as citizens of an democratic culture; there is no longer a search for universal principles of justice but rather relative positions and justice as fairness assuming political overtones rather than comprehensive moral conceptions. Political liberalism implies a political constructivism – the concept of overlapping consensus and his two basic principles derived through the method. The principles of justice are the outcome of a process of choice conducted in the original position behind a veil of ignorance – the original position is a device of representation to help focus our moral ideas (modelling fair conditions under which representatives of free and equal citizens are to specify the terms of social cooperation). Intuitive ideas that are rooted in liberal culture determine justice – two core ones being the view of society as a fair system of cooperation and a conception of person as possessing two moral powers (abilities to device one's own conception of good and seek cooperation with others).

Critics of Rawls can be divided into four categories: liberal, neo-conservative, anarchist libertarian (minimal state) and the Left (which includes orthodox Marxists and Democratic socialists). The contentions of the liberal critics are that Rawlsian theory lacks the conception of a community and that social unions are essentially individualistic. Further, tacit preference is endowed to economic efficiency over claims of equality – particularly the contention that differences in wealth status and power are functionally necessary in a modern industrial society. Neo-conservative critique of Rawls centred around the scepticism towards his emphasis on egalitarianism as utopian, instead accepting the ethics of liberal capitalism. Anarchist-libertarian critique pose contentions to the Rawlsian role of state in ensuring re-distributive justice, instead arguing for the importance of a materialist conception of society and history (Robert

Wolffe) and the reality of the minimal state and market dynamics and individual autonomy as more predominant than real. The general tone of the left criticism of Rawls is that he is an essentially liberal thinker. According to left thinkers such as Macpherson, Rawls used two contradictory models as far as human individuals are concerned – the rational man, one with his own life plans, and the concept of good which seems egalitarian but is in reality bourgeoisie. Such an individual in Rawls's society desires maximisation of individual liberty and accepts the class divided society as inevitable. Hence, the inevitability of class divisions in society is at the base of Rawlsian deliberations, to which the left thinkers pose a critique. Further, his emphasis on the market and the assumption of the apriori existence of inequity which continues and may not necessarily be annihilated is critiqued (Sushila, 1990).

Another important figure in the arena of social justice deliberations is Paulo Freire (Brazilian educationist), who in his seminal work 'Pedagogy of the Oppressed' (1970) proposed four key tenets in the struggle for social justice: literacy or the way we read the word and the world; critical consciousness; the creation of liberation and escalating economic production as people come to understand their surroundings. Freire combines Hegelian dialectics Marxist (social democratic and historical materialist) and catholic/ecclesiastical views for organising social change. Through the amalgam emerges Freirean conceptions of dialectical materialism, importance of ideology and leadership, importance of dialogue and love, the lighthouse part played by history, the necessity of political parties as agents of change and liberation linked to intensified national economic development. The route to equality is through dialogues and discourse, emic view of oppression and organic leadership (along Gramscian lines). In that Freire has adopted a dialectical view of the unity of the construction of knowledge and social change. Further, the role of language in social and political reconstruction and the inseparability of power from the education process are recognised. For revolution to reinstate social justice, Freire has deliberated on dialogue and consciousness. Dialogue signifies the connection of the knowing with what is coming to be known – negotiation of reality, struggle for a new understanding of reality and the subsequent recreation of reality through knowledge. To enhance dialogue, the strategies suggested are research into the spoken language of the subjects; selection of generative words; selection of codifications into which generative words can be fitted, that is, representations of typical existential situations of the group which open perspective for the analysis of regional and national problems; and subsequent elaboration of agendas. Consciousness implies 'intentionality' towards the world and a discovery of truth which overarches ahead of understanding. There is a sense of denouncing and working against a dominant ideology. Critical consciousness is a particular and derivable way of addressing and recreating reality. Ideology lies at the base of critical consciousness resulting in overcoming the oppression of cultural silence and resulting in a language of critique and possibility. Through the human construction of ideology driving social practice and the critically consciousness, dehumanisation comes to an end. The core is class struggle and linkages of elements of literacy, consciousness, production and revolution in envisaging emancipation (Ramos, 1996).

Contemporary liberal theory has examined the concept of social justice from the lens of 'difference'. Essentially two kinds of differences are perceived: individual and collective. When differences between communities result in discrimination and social exclusion, the principle of equality comes to the fore in liberal democratic theory. When dealing with individual differences, the principle of heterogeneity becomes salient. Equality and heterogeneity provide the conceptual foundation for a liberal democratic theory to accommodate diversities within the framework of social justice. Initially the principle of equality is employed to question the arbitrary exclusion and discrimination in the public domain (Mahajan, 1998). Theorisations on social justice have also moved beyond Rawls such as those of Nussbaum (2006) who has suggested that there is an inherent limitation in the social contract theory as it is premised on the idea of a contract for mutual advantage among approximate equals. She has demonstrated that it is unable to address questions of justice between unequal parties. Rather she has developed a theory of social justice based on the 'capabilities approach' which she placed generally within the tradition of liberal conceptions. The capabilities approach according to Nussbaum has been used as a philosophical underpinning for an account of core human entitlements that should be respected and implemented by the governments of all nations as a bare minimum for what respect for human dignity requires. Central human capabilities are identified, arguing that all of them are implicit in the idea of a life worth human dignity. The capabilities are then presented as the source of political principles for a liberal pluralist society; they are set in the context of a type of political liberalism that makes them specifically political goals and presents them in a manner free of any specific metaphysical grounding. The capabilities then become the object of overlapping consensus among people who otherwise have very different comprehensive conceptions of good. Hence, human dignity is here an intuitive idea and is pursued distinctly for each and every person. Further, the approach uses the idea of a threshold level of each capability; beneath which it is held that truly human functioning is not available to citizens; the social goal should be understood in terms of getting citizens above this capabilities threshold. The capabilities approach is believed to be in favour of crosscultural norms and pluralism. Hence, commencing from the Aristotelian/Marxian conception of the human being as a social and political being who finds fulfilment in relations with others the core is human dignity. It denies that principles of justice have to secure mutual advantage, favouring instead a deontological conception of justice and that benevolent sentiments are apriori in their account of people's relation to their good (as the capabilities approach in its conception of the person incorporates the ideas of fundamental sociability and of people's ends including shared ends).

Human Rights

The complex domain of human rights has several faces and manifestations – revealed through the classical, modern, contemporary and the non-Western perspectives on human rights. Human rights are norms for social protection requiring compliance from the state (Gupta, 1996; Sharma, 1997) – the philosophy of human rights addressing questions about the existence, content, nature, universality, justification and legal status of human rights. However, the stance remains that the philosophy of human rights is derivative from extant epistemological positionings – as also overlapping with contentions of social justice. What is attempted here is to highlight those domains of thought of philosophers and thinkers which expound tenets on 'rights'. Further, in the renditions of rights there have been distinctions on natural rights, moral rights and rights which have all built into the understanding of human rights. Some underpinnings of human rights philosophy are moral universalism versus moral relativism – moral universalism posits the existence of rationally identifiable transcultural and transhistorical moral truths which further posit the existence of a moral community comprising all human beings; moral relativism holds the opposite view. Relativists view morality as a social and historical phenomenon and hence rights are differential in an essentially plural and multicultural society.

The classical perspectives on rights have been deliberated by Plato, Aristotle, Cicero, Aquinas and Hugo Grotius. Plato in his Republic has discussed the universal rights of human beings by virtue of being human beings and that is above the laws of individual states. Aristotle in his *Nicomachean Ethics* has expounded an argument in support of a natural moral order. This natural order is supposed to provide the basis for all truly rational systems of justice. Aristotle proposes that the 'natural' is that which has the same validity everywhere and does not depend upon acceptance. The criteria for determining a rational system of justice pre-exists social and historical conventions; natural justice pre-exists social and political configurations. Cicero in his work 'On the Laws' argued that human beings are created in the image of God and in that sense they are unique among material beings in possessing higher reason. This reason gives rise to rights to which all rational human beings are naturally bound. St. Thomas Aquinas in his *Summa Theologica* purported that basic human needs such as self-preservation required fundamental rights. Viewing law as an ordinance of reason, he looked at law as involving rules to mandate or prohibit certain behaviours. Law is to be directed for common good and its promulgation presupposes the existence of a lawmaker in God. Positing four kinds of laws: eternal, natural, divine and human, he emphasised that from the precepts of natural law, human reason can proceed towards the other domains of law – particular human, hence making a case for human rights as natural rights. Hugo Grotius in his work 'The Law of War and Peace' argued for natural law with characteristics of ethical objectivism, ethical universalism and deontological standing – hence rights to human beings were essentially natural rights (accruing by virtue of being human beings) (Copleston, 1993). Late medieval philosopher Ockham also discussed the natural right to property of man – he speaks of right as being a legitimate power, a power in conformity with the right reason (distinguishing between legitimate powers which are anterior to human convention from those which are dependent on human convention).

The modern perspectives have been forwarded by Thomas Hobbes, John Locke, Spinoza, Immanuel Kant, Edmund Burke, Thomas Paine, Rousseau, post-Kantian Idealists, Marx and Wollstonecraft. Thomas Hobbes, in his work *Leviathan*, proposed that in the positivist frame of reference, rights are to come from the state and hence rights require laws to protect them. He founded a contractualist theory wherein the way to preserve the natural rights of human beings was to align to the sovereign state – thereby laying the foundations of a social contract between the governed and the governor. Hence, he saw that there was one covenant by which a number of men hand over to a sovereign the 'rights' which they enjoyed in the state of nature. John Locke's central argument was that natural rights naturally accrued to human beings independently of the political recognition granted to them by the state – in that sense the understanding was liberal. These natural rights flowed from a natural law which had theological origins. Human beings were endowed with thus a right to self-preservation and a means to contain the same was personal property. Locke saw that the duty of self-preservation that human beings had towards God entailed the existence of basic natural rights to life, liberty and property. The role of the state was thus viewed as upholding of the natural rights of individuals. Spinoza's political theory resembles that of Hobbes – with contentions on natural law and natural rights albeit taking the stance of theological determinism – men to act according to divine ordinances or universal Nature. In his Theologico-Political treatise, he discusses that the purpose of civil society is peace and security of life and thus 'that dominion is the best where men pass their lives in unity and the laws are kept unbroken'. Further, 'the most rational state is also the freest, since to live freely is to live with full consent under the guidance of reason' – a sort of arrangement which Spinoza found most apt in democracy, a constitutional form that guaranteed rights and peace (Copleston, 1993). Another mention of rights is found in the philosopher of French Enlightenment Voltaire, who, in his Treatise on Metaphysics, discussed the importance of universal natural laws. God has endowed man with certain inalienable feelings which are eternal bonds and give rise to fundamental laws of human society. Voltaire adopted a traditional (but not dogmatic) and deterministic position with regard to human liberty in the psychological sense and simultaneously also defended political liberty. Like Locke, he proposed a doctrine of human rights that ought to be respected by the state – rights taking into account individual liberty of thought and expression within the larger gamut of a benevolent monarchy. Philosopher of the German Enlightenment Christian Wolff based rights on man's duties and the position of natural equality of all men. Hence, there are universal natural rights which are different from acquired rights. Acquired rights are sourced from the state which has the role to promote common good. Wolff conceded to the government wide powers of supervision with a view to the physical and spiritual well-being of the citizens. Common good is interpreted in terms of human perfection and not in purely economic terms. Nations are to be regarded as 'individual free persons living in a state of nature' – and thus just as there is a natural moral law which obliges individual men and gives rise to rights, so there is a natural law of nations which gives rise to equal rights. Nations as a whole thus possess the right of compelling individual nations to fulfil their obligations towards the greater society (Copleston, 1993). Further, two important British Empiricists Bentham and Mill proposed the principle of utility (greatest happiness of the greatest possible number) as the basic principles of morals and legislation. Bentham further juxtaposed notions of common good and political self-interest and laid the foundation arguments of political reform, abolition of monarchy and universal suffrage as ensuring rights. Mill follows Hume and Bentham in rejecting the theory of 'abstract right as a thing independent of utility' as also natural rights. The principle of utility in Mill's opinion demands that every man should be free to develop his powers according to his own will and judgement, provided that he does not do so in a way which interferes with the exercise of a similar freedom by others. Balancing the free development of individuality as also common good is the key ingredient of rights from a utilitarian standpoint (Copleston, 1995).

The central themes expressed within Immanuel Kant's moral philosophy such as the ideas of equality and the moral autonomy of rational human beings have important bearings on the philosophy of human rights. The ideal is that of a potentially universal community of rational individuals autonomously determining the moral principles for securing the conditions for equality and autonomy. This then provides the means for justifying human rights as the basis for self-determination grounded within the authority of human reason. Moral principles are identified (which are considered to be universal) that are to be within bounds of rationality (so as to ensure common good) – which Kant labelled as categorical imperatives. Hence in the

Kantian repertoire, rights emerge from reason and rationality and not divine providence. Edmund Burke's thoughts on human rights emerged from his understandings of the French Revolution and reinstated the role of the state in ensuring 'liberty and the rights of man'. Hence in his conceptions, pure liberalism with a diminished role of the state would be too open to market ambiguities – welfare state being crucial to ensure rights. Thomas Paine in his work 'The Rights of Man' proposed that human rights originate in nature and thus rights cannot be granted by a political charter – the role of the state being to safeguard the individual and his/her inherent and inalienable rights. Rousseau's social contract theory encompasses the instrumental conception of rights within the larger framework of welfare and common good – the understanding which then built into the contractualist theory of justice. Rousseau proposed that in the state of nature, there is only natural and physical inequality – due originally to the development of our faculties but then rendered permanent and legitimate by the establishment of property and laws; whenever it is not proportionate to natural and physical inequalities, it is at variance with natural right. In Social Contract, he further deliberates that in the original state of nature there is complete freedom (which also posits inequalities) which is then curtailed by the social order which is a sacred right that is the basis of all other rights – founded nevertheless on agreement and convention. The state then becomes the source of justice and the basis of all rights.

Post-Kantian idealists such as Fichte, Hegel and Schelling have discussed the concept of moral rights. From an ethical idealist standpoint, Fichte's theory of rights emerge from the practical deduction of an absolute ego as an infinite striving towards self-realisation through free moral activity and the non-ego or the world of Nature as a means or instrument for the attainment of this end. In his 1796 work Basis of Natural Rights, Fichte opined that the theory of rights and political society to be deduced independently of the principles of morality. One main reason why Fichte made this distinction between the theory of rights and political theory on the one hand and ethics on the other is that he looks on ethics as concerned with interior morality, with conscience and with the formal principles of morality, whereas the theory of rights and of political society is concerned with the external relations between human beings. Fichte did not agree that the doctrine of rights is applied ethics. Having a right does not imply an obligation to exercise it and the common good may demand on occasion a curtailment of or limitation on the exercise of rights. Moral law may add further sanction to rights, but it is not their initial source. Hegel synthesized the concepts of rights, interior morality and society in the general concept of man's ethical life. In his *Phenomenology of Spirit*, Hegel has discussed two realms of spirit – objective and subjective. The first phase of Hegel's objective spirit is the sphere of rights. The person, the individual subject, conscious of his freedom must give external expression to his nature as free spirit; he must give himself an external sphere of freedom and he does this by expressing his will in the realm of material things which are instruments for the expression of the rational will. This 'will' can be withdrawn or exercised as man's labour is external but total relinquishing of rights is not possible as moral conscience and religion are a part of man's internal nature. The concepts of abstract rights and of morality are thus for Hegel one-sided notions which have to be unified on a higher level in the concept of ethical life. In the dialectical development of the sphere of objective Spirit, they reveal themselves as moments or phases in the development of the concept of concrete ethics. Schelling's commencing point in the idealistic repertoire is the quest of the ego is self-determination and self-realisation which can be attained through concrete action in the world. The system of rights and the state are the conditions of moral action built by human beings on rules of rationality. Hence, rational laws of society support moral actions which become the basis for rights and political society (Copleston, 1994). Marx viewed rights in a different framework – equality being more important than liberty and the singular fundamental right being that of revolution. The work of Mary Wollstonecraft 'A Vindication of the Rights of Women', apart from spearheading the understanding on feminism, also looked at rights within the political context (as suffrage issues were the starting points) and viewed rights as the vehicle for effecting political change (Copleston, 1995).

Nineteenth-century writings of Auguste Comte and Durkheim also contain mention of rights. Comte rejected the idea of natural rights and the liberal conception of man as an individual is an abstraction. Prominence according to Comte was to be given to duties rather than rights. Society does endow rights to individuals as an agenda of common good, but these do not exist independently of society. In the industrial society envisaged from a positivist frame of reference, there would be a moral regeneration wherein the welfare and rights of humanity as a whole would override individual private interests. Rights would accrue to humans as a part of society performing their duties. Durkheim holds the case for individualism vis-à-vis a conformism to the dictates of society taking resort to the utilitarian principle. In positioning the notion of rights, society gets precedence over the individual only if the contentions of society and the moral laws are utilitarian. Society's real interests are nevertheless to assuring rights to all individuals as this is effectively in the essential interest of the society (Copleston, 1995).

Some prominent contemporary perspectives have been presented by H. L. A. Hart, Maurice Cranston, Joel Feinberg, Thomas Pogge and Richard Rorty. H. L. A Hart argued that the sole natural right was that of freedom which accrued to humans on grounds of morality guaranteeing them choice and autonomy. Maurice Cranston viewed an exchange relationship between rights and duties – both jointly building into the 'real' nature of human rights. Commenting on the nature and value of rights, Joel Feinberg has argued that claims make a prima facie case for rights which are then examined for validity according to a system of moral rules and legal principles – a claim when validated becomes a right. He also maintains the 'doctrine of logical correlativity of rights and duties' – stating that all duties entail other people's rights and all rights entail other people's duties. Thus, a valid claim is one that necessarily entails corresponding duties. In terms of the moral value of rights, Feinberg connects the idea of rights with notions of human dignity, self-respect and respect for others. To respect an individual's dignity is to recognise them as having rights which means to recognise them as being in a position to make and assert valid claims. Thomas Pogge differed on the contention of natural right being a social right. Social rights according to him are construed rights – the moral and political responsibility of guaranteeing which is on legal and political institutions of society. The diametrically opposite view from the mainstream appeal to reason for human rights has been taken by Richard Rorty who has argued that human rights are not exactly based on the exercise of reason but rather the sentimental visions of humanity. Human rights according to Rorty are not rationally defensible but rather based on moral beliefs and practices – they are better served by emotional appeals to identify with the sufferings of others than by arguments over the correct determination of reason (Gupta, 1996).

Non-Western perspectives on human rights are those by Confucius (focus on equality and nondiscrimination), Dalai Lama (focus on equity, freedom and liberty as also freedom from oppression), Kwasi Wiredu (human rights to examine cultural contexts of freedom and liberty and hence making a case for cultural relativism in the Akan perspective on human rights) and Abdullahi Ahmed An-Na'im (who has examined religion as the basis to ensure personal liberty, freedom and hence human rights). However, the fact remains that Western philosophy has provided the edifice for the mainstream renditions on human rights. Contemporary indigenous discourses on human rights have looked at several issues: the need for alternative reading of histories to reexamine the origin of human rights (the real originators being people in struggle and communities of resistance rather than the conventional authorship endowed to the west) and the politics of human rights (which treats human rights languages and logics as an ensemble of means for the legitimation for governance and domination). Baxi (2006) has outlined certain theoretical considerations that govern contemporary human rights discourses: genealogies of human rights, 'modern' and 'contemporary', their logics of exclusion and inclusion and the construction of ideas about 'human'; realities of overproduction of human rights norms and standards creating governance as well as resistance overload that complicates emergences of human rights futures; development of postmodernist suspicion of the power to tell large global stories (meta-narratives) that convert human rights languages into texts or tricks of governance or domination; emergence of the politics of difference and identity, exposing both emancipative and repressive potential; resurfacing of arguments from ethical and cultural relativism interrogating the politics of universality of human rights in ways that make possible in good conscience, toleration of vast stretches of human and social suffering; conversion of human rights movements into human rights markets and transformation of the paradigm of the UDHR into a trade-related market friendly paradigm of human rights ushered in by globalisation, ideologies of economic rationalism, good governance and structural adjustment.

Contemporary epistemology of human rights is writ by plurality and multiplicity of expressions of human rights as ethical imperatives, as grammar of governance; as languages of global governance; as insurrectionary praxis; as juridical production and as culture. Hence, human rights as ethical imperatives imply the view of human rights as ethical values that ought to inform individual and collective action. The definition of these values range from deontological to teleological. This discourse on natural rights arises both within the traditions of theistic and secular natural law thought. As the grammar of governance (encompassing governmentality and subjection), they offer conceptions of good governance that seek to assure overall human rights integrity of state apparatuses and conduct and at the meta-level these languages and logics address the problems of legitimacy of the power to rule. In terms of their role as languages of global governance, whereas on the one hand they provide languages of universal acquiescence, and on the other, there are several crucial and critical issues raised. These include the hegemonic singular conceptions of good governance; seismic shifts in the languages of global good governance signified by large-scale narratives of 'westernisation', 'modernisation', 'development' and 'globalisation' (embodied for instance in the turgid prose of the World Bank, marking a transition from the structural adjustment conditionalities to poverty reduction strategies); the political economy dynamics writ in the international consensus of human rights and issues of human rights, shared sovereignty, itineraries of partnership between global civil society and good governance and domains of resistance. Human rights as insurrectionary practice look at the Foucauldian micropolitics of power, unearthing the dominance of the oppressor and the problematic inherent in the binary of the oppressor and the oppressed. As juridical production, the emergences of human rights in terms of breaks, discontinuities and fissures in the canonical narratives of state sovereignty and legitimacy are the core. International relations and organisations from this lens are perceived to be having a dialectical relationship between power and resistance at the level of agency and structure. Lastly, in the discourse on human rights as culture, raven with contestations on 'universality' and 'particularism', human rights are conceived as cultural systems. In that sense human rights are described as 'cultural software' – a set of mechanisms of hermeneutic power that make, in a constantly dynamic way, new understandings of what it means, and ought to mean to be human (Balkin, 1998, cited in Baxi, 2006). These societal human rights cultures relate to global cultures of human rights – this mutuality of determination marked by both submission and struggle. Hence, human rights discursivity in the contemporary times is marked by complexity and contradiction between the statist discourse of the educated and the subversive discourse of the indigenous (Baxi, 2006).

Broadly thus, the ways that have shaped the contemporary theory and practice of human rights are fragmented universality (particularly in the neo-colonial context, newer ways to contain the sovereignty of the Third World have been discovered; creationist logic of self-determination that gave language to the aspiration of politics of identity and difference of new nations curtailed under global political economy dynamics); cold war naturalisation of human rights violations; the Marxian critique; and the Foucauldian episteme – recognising the multiple matrices of violence within which the contemporary paradigm of violence emerges. According to Baxi (2006), an interpenetration of ideological positions, politics for human rights and the worlds of power which then signifies the global institutionalisation of human rights embedded in the postmodern politics of identity and difference.

In Summary

Social justice is viewed historically commencing from Plato's principle of justice as governed by the ideal of equality and Aristotelian 'isotes' (geometric equality and proportionality proposing that 'equal' (just, fair) distribution of persons with unequal merit would have to be unequal). Contentions of Mill (social justice as any system of distribution and redistribution that is governed by valid moral principles) and Hobhouse (social justice as the test of operative consistency and method of synthesis of rights and duties) are dealt with. A discussion is undertaken on Hume's rights-based principle, Spencer's desert-based principle and Kropotkin's need-based principles of social justice. In the deliberations, two key theorists are dwelt on – John Rawls and Paulo Freire.

Rawls' principles of 'equal basic liberty' and 'difference' principle form the core. Further, the discussion is centred on the latter works of Rawls reaffirming the Kantian interest in developing and exercising individual moral powers of rational autonomy and fair dealing. Hence, it signifies not a search for universal principles of justice albeit a recognition of ideals of relativity. Freire's arguments through his pedagogy proposes four keys in the struggle for social justice – literacy (the way we read the word and the world), critical consciousness, the creation of liberation and escalating economic production as people come to understand their surroundings. The key elements of Freire's construct – dialogue, discourse and critical consciousness – form the key discussion points. Ideology in the Freirean notions lies at the base of critical consciousness and results in a language of critique and possibility. Critical consciousness leads to critical social justice that addresses hegemony – working against the dominant ideology and recreating reality. This further would lead to re-orientation of production through a new concept of distribution, development of critical awareness and revolutionary action (Gorowitz, 1975; White, 1991).

In the realm of human rights, the key discussion is around the amalgamated stance of human rights as in inclusive ideology – combining the epistemes of secular humanism, liberalism, democracy and socialism. Further, the renditions in literature have been on natural rights, moral rights, abstract rights and rights in general – all building into the understanding of human rights. The classical and modern philosophers viewed human rights as natural rights with differentials in terms of the role of state. Classical philosophers comprise deliberations by Plato, Aristotle, Cicero, Aquinas and Hugo Grotius as also Ockham. The modern perspectives are by Thomas Hobbes, John Locke, Spinoza, Immanuel Kant, Edmund Burke, Thomas Paine, Rousseau, Marx and Wollstonecraft. The central themes expressed within Immanuel Kant's moral philosophy such as the ideas of equality and the moral autonomy of rational human beings have important bearings on the philosophy of human rights. Some prominent contemporary perspectives have been presented by H. L. A. Hart, Maurice Cranston, Joel Feinberg, Thomas Pogge and Richard Rorty. Further, there are non-Western perspectives and the contemporary version of human rights that calls for alternative readings of conventional human rights histories by placing the concerns and interests of 'people in struggle and communities of resistance' at the centre stage. Further, feminist and postmodern understandings have posited a critical lens onto gendering, universalisms and essentialisms that pose antagonisms and contradictions within the rights repertoire.

8

Movements

Subaltern Voices and Praxis

This chapter looks at assertions in the realms of praxis that have revealed multiple standpoints – emerging from positions of ideologues in the process. The examination is simultaneously indigenous and transnational – both the renditions woven intermittently. Commencing with Dalit movements and assertions, the chapter goes on to examine the positionalities of tribal movements in the indigenous context. The manifestations of women's movement have been mapped in their transnational/global and Indian formats – focusing on the visions, versions and strategies. Prominent ecology and environment discourses that feed into the environmental movement trajectories have been looked at. In the vein of contemporary social movements, queer theorisations and sexuality discourses that form the realpolitik of alternative sexuality orientations have been deliberated. Further, some dimensions of disability discourses have also been mentioned – the voices of disability providing differential assertions in the social domain.

Dalit Movement and Assertions

Dalit movement can be examined from the standpoints of origin, ideologies and discourses along with stances of the key ideologues, organisational structures and practices. The Bhakti movement carries the first instances of the subaltern voices through the endeavours of saints of the syncretic traditions such as Kabir and Nanak; saints aligning to existence of the margins such as Eknath and saints who belonged to the subaltern strata such as Chokhamela (Zelliot, 1992). The origins of the Dalit movements can be traced to the early protests in the caste *sabhas* and the social reform movements. During the nineteenth and twentieth centuries, the practice of untouchability was contested and the so-called untouchables came to mobilise themselves on the basis of common exclusion. There was not 'one' reform movement at this time, but many different groups were protesting against untouchability and its practice. The caste *sabhas* were the first most conscious efforts to mobilise around a caste hierarchy – some inspired by tenets of equality in the Hindu social reform, whereas the others by the Bhakti movement – denouncing hierarchy between men and emphasising a personal relationship with God. Caste federations had broader social outreach and were formed around a *varna* identity instead of a *jati* identity – composing thus not of members of one endogamous caste group but of multiple groups based on a supposed sharing of interests and status attributes, giving rise to its own symbolism. Hence, it is not in the local caste associations mobilised on the basis of one endogamous *jati*, but in the geographically and also identity-wise broader caste federations, mainly mobilised around the experience of exclusion, that we find resemblance to the Dalit movement. Jyotiba Phule's Satyashodhak Samaj established in 1873 brought non-Brahman activists in western India together around the critique of caste as the political unconscious of Hindu society. Phule was uneasy with the alignments of secular and ritual power that British colonisation enabled. His unease coalesced around his representation of the new Brahman who was able to parlay his monopoly over ritual and scriptural knowledge into an exclusive claim upon Western education and employment in the colonial bureaucracy. One of Phule's most significant responses to the colonial context, in which Brahminical hegemony was both transformed and exacerbated in novel ways, was to take control over the language and politics of (re) naming a central element of the anticaste discourse. The category shudra-atishudra was the end result of Phule's effort to produce a new ethical community, which would be a political constituency united in the struggle against Brahmanism (Bhagavan and Feldhaus, 2008).

In terms of autonomous Dalit movements, the forerunners in terms of organisational structure and content were to be found in the Adi movements of the 1920s – the attempt being to move away from Hinduism towards an aboriginal faith (*Adi Dharma*). In the 1930s, the autonomous anticaste stand crystallised – the social organisation within the autonomous anticaste tradition was then linked to the

Independent Labour Party at the national level, while the social organisation of the Hindu caste-reformers was linked to the Congress Party. The controversies between B. R. Ambedkar and M. K. Gandhi were crucial in the formation of the anticaste position. The idea that the Depressed Classes were to be separated from Hinduism and the Hindu community was represented by B. R. Ambedkar (Zelliot, 1992). In the opposite camp, M. K. Gandhi argued in favour of the inclusion of the Depressed Classes among the Hindus and caste reforms. The distinguishing feature of the autonomous Dalit movement in the 1930s was that although it took shape as a political force at the same time as the non-Brahmin movement, the working class and peasantry movement, it remained unabsorbed by the Congress. Three pan-Indian organisations then emerged to deal with caste issues – the Depressed Classes Federation, which was Ambedkarite and connected with Ambedkar's Independent Labour Party; the Depressed Classes League, which was Gandhian and connected with the Congress Party; and the Depressed Classes Association, which was linked to the Hindu fundamentalists in the Hindu Mahasabha (Louis, 2003; Hardtman, 2009).

Postindependence and through constitutional protection obtained by the scheduled castes, newer developments were ushered. Despite constitutional safeguards the Dalits continued to experience caste discrimination in civil society in the same way as during the colonial rule. Hence in the 1960s and 1970s, this was brought to light by the Dalit Sahitya and the Dalit Panthers in Maharashtra. Commenting further on Dalit literature, Limbale (2004) positions it as erasures and assertions, establishing the Dalit subalternity not in a traditional colonial structure, but in the caste-based social, cultural and economic structure of Hindu society. This inferior location of the Dalits is not only spatial but also normative – inherited from birth and sanctioned by sacred authority. Dalit Sahitya explores as to how literature in the high tide of Brahmanism shows that the alterity of the subaltern is replicated in culture, to show that the Dalits do not have a voice or presence. However, the modern and contemporary periods have been marked by reformist liberalism – literature having moved from erasure towards containment. Unable to imagine the untouchable 'other' out of existence, Brahminical literature sought to confine it within a discourse marked by 'sympathy and compassion' (Limbale, 2004). Dalit literature is marked by a wholesale rejection of the tradition, the aesthetics, the language and the concerns of a Brahminical literature that carried within it signs of the caste-based social and cultural order – the speaking subject being the erstwhile untouchable other. Dalit literature is further characterised as purposive – the purpose being revolutionary, transformational and liberatory. There is a preference towards an identity-based approach to caste politics vis-à-vis the Marxism's class-based approach (Sharma, 2006). The figurative embodiment of language in the Dalit discourse and the correlation of the figurative aspect with the embodied states make it possible to imagine a selfhood and social collectivity that could further destabilise the traditional political order.

The prominent and influential Dalit discourses are Dalit Buddhism, Dalit Christian theology and the Dalit political perspective along with assertions of gender within the repertoire of the Dalit movement. Dalit Buddhism is the outcome of the famous mass conversion to Buddhism in Nagpur in 1956 led by Babasaheb Ambedkar. This conversion spread rapidly to areas where Ambedkar's political party, the Scheduled Caste Federation, had some influence. Dalit Christian theology is a reaction against the dominant Hindu culture, and it demands social justice within the Christian Church. However, Indian Christian theology is found to be insensitive to caste issues – hence, Dalit Christian theology is a twin protest against the caste system and the Hindu culture and also criticises the missionaries and the upper-caste Indian Christians for not having taken care to train a Dalit leadership in proportion to their numerical strength within the Church. The general tendency and direction of religious transformation could be described as from 'transcendental-experiential' to 'ethical-instrumental'; from 'individual-salvational' to 'collective-celebrational' and from passive submission to and acceptance of the religiously given to the active appropriation and construction of religious symbols and worldviews (Webster, 1999).

The Dalit political perspective is essentially anti-Gandhian and challenges the dominant narrative of Indian nationalism. Within an essentially Dalit counterpublic, the alternative to the dominant narrative is presented as opposing Hinduism/Gandhism/Congress (Pai, 2002). Further through the influence of Ambedkar in Punjab, the transnational face of the movement emerged through the Dalit movement in Britain where the first Punjabi immigrants arrived in search of a better life by the end of the 1950s. Scholars such as Mark Juergensmeyer have described this phenomenon as 'migration fever' and although many features of the traditional caste system broke down through the process, the rules of endogamy were still strictly followed in the diaspora as well as the subcontinent. There was an intensification of intercaste competition for status, and many settlers were obsessively concerned with issues of rank. Many of the so-called untouchables who arrived in Britain from Punjab had been touched by the Ad Dharm movement in India and belonged to the Ravidasi community. One of the agenda of the transbordered discourse is to translate caste discrimination into an international discourse. Assimilation is simultaneously strived for in a wider egalitarian culture as well as in the religious and political hegemony in which the caste hierarchy is found to be fundamental. The National Campaign on Dalit Human Rights played a crucial role – positioning the Ambedkarite discourse in the global context and combining it with the international language of human rights. The other component is that of Dalit feminism which is viewed as different from Brahmani feminism as Dalit feminists do not see themselves as a part of Hindu culture and the all-inclusive demands of the Brahmani feminists. Dalit women are perceived to be 'thrice discriminated' – on the bases of caste, class and gender.

The organisational aspects are related to the cultural flow of meaning that takes place within the movement. The two broad categorisations of Dalit movements that have been identified are reformative movements and alternative movements. The reformative movement attempted to reform the caste system to resolve the problem of untouchability – the subcategorisations being the Bhakti movement, neo-Vedantic movement and the Sanskritisation movement. The alternative movements attempted to create an alternative sociocultural structure wherein caste domination is eliminated and social justice is ensured – subdivided as the proselytisation movement and the secular movements (Sharma, 2006). The movement's core role has been the creation of the category of the 'Dalit' – an inaugural political subject in modern Indian political life. There is an important negotiation of modernity and democracy, one that departs from other countercolonial nativist modernity that do not adequately engage with the concerns of caste (Bhagavan and Feldhaus, 2008). Contemporary concerns are around the scepticism towards comparing race and caste (which as an outcome of the colonial period is inherently hegemonic) and that mainstream Dalit movements essentially rely on the narratives of the elites. The latter problem according to scholars can be circumvented by turning away from the political sphere to other facets of everyday life – most notably the poems and writings that the common Dalits celebrate. Further, there is a quest for a transnational political space to reinstate justice. However, some authors (despite the scepticism) have drawn similarities between Dalit consciousness to Black consciousness as a transborder agenda – looking at parallels in forms and norms of acquiescence and protest (Michael, 1999).

Dalit activists value conflict differently and contextually – differentiating between perspectives of their 'main opponents' who circulate their messages in the public sphere and of their Dalit opponents who circulate theirs within the common alternative counterpublic. Conflicts are given different values depending on whether they are interpublic or intrapublic. Dalit activists could be understood in line with Butler (1999) who has undertaken a discourse on performative acts and gender constitution. The bodies of Dalit women and men have not only been regarded as false unreal and unintelligible, but also ritually impure. In performativity (in repetitive practices and rituals), untouchability has been created and recreated over generations. Untouchability has further been effective through its naturalisation in the context of the body, understood as 'a culturally sustained temporal duration' or embodied habitus in the line of Bourdieu. When at a point in history Dalit activists are about to deconstruct an image of the material bodies of Dalit women and men as impure and reconstructing it as human, women are accused of being immoral and thus deprived of constructing a so-called femininity and men are accused of economic irresponsibility and thus deprived of creating a so-called masculinity. Hence, oppression comes not from ascribed gender identities in a heteronormative society, but through 'prevention from constructing gender identities'.

There have been variations in terms of constructions of Hinduism across movement ideologues – Phule took the position of Hinduism as Brahman exploitation based on the Aryan race theory; Pandita Ramabai and Tarabai Shinde viewed Hinduism as inherently patriarchal; Ambedkarian standpoint of Hinduism as counter revolution and the Dalit Panthers' stance of looking at Hinduism as feudal backwardness (Omvedt, 1995). In terms of general movement trajectories of the Dalits, the following domains emerge: interrelating and forming a counterpublic over vast geographical areas; differentiating between interpublic and intrapublic conflicts; using negative symbols such as anti-Gandhism internally and externally for their own benefits; redesigning and contextualising messages, from the local to the global levels; and flexibly organising and reorganising movement networks (Hardtman, 2009). Cultural politics is another dimension to the Dalit discourse – transformative effects of aesthetic and poetic expressions and identity, subjectivity and embodiment discourses in the 'ambivalence of belonging' being primary deliberations. The focus has nevertheless predominantly been on looking at the movement in terms of relative deprivation and social mobility (Louis, 2003).

Tribal Voices, Understandings and Assertions

Tribal movements have essentially been revolts against the state. Gough (1979) has given a fivefold classification of the tribal movements based on five types of action in terms of goal, ideology and method of organisation: restorative rebellions to drive out the British and restore earlier ruler and social relations; religious movements for liberation of a region or an ethnic group under a new form of government; social banditry; vengeance for collective justice and mass insurrections for redressal of particular grievances. Gough's classificatory scheme contains the descriptive historical details about the insurgent tribes whose relation with the British rule was generally defined by rebellion. The history of tribes in the Indian context has been fight against the sovereign in defence of autonomy, social and cultural freedom. The location of the site of the crisis core in the case of tribal collectivities shifts to the site of confrontation between the tribes and the state. Many accounts such as those of Guha (1983), Praharaj (1988), Natarajan (1979), Arnold (1982), Sinha (1984), Paul (1989) and Guha (1989) are of the struggles of tribal groups against the expanding political control and interference of the British. Assertions of social, cultural, economic and political autonomy constitute the kernel of the tribes' stake in most of the rebellions and revolts during the British period, contemporary faces being those of subnationalist and autonomous movements' nature.

Tribal movements have essentially been of nonclass and non-materialistic nature and largely in the defence of the community movements, i.e., for the preservation of the social, cultural, symbolic heritages and the system of their control and power. In the north-eastern part of the subcontinent, tribal assertions have largely been around issues of identity, culture, ethnicity and subnationalism. In the other regions, assertions have largely been of a political nature: assertions forwarded to the establishment for visibility, justice and rights – to existence, nature and equity.

Women's Movement: Some Transnational and Indigenous Discourses

Women's movement has multiple interpretations of its Archimedean standpoint – the institution of patriarchy. Traditionalists viewed patriarchy with arguments of 'anatomy as destiny' and the natural corollary of sexual division of labour as fulfilling functionalist norms. Engels gave an explanation to patriarchy from the historical material standpoint – women's subordination as emerging from the modes of production as developed historically as well as the patriarchal monogamous family structure. His explanation was viewed as economic deterministic because a material basis of patriarchy and women's subordination was sought – class hierarchy overriding women's questions. Structuralist Claude Levi-Strauss viewed women's subordination and patriarchy as crucial to the formation of culture in which sexual division of labour was normalised. Incest taboo was viewed as the root of all social organisation and commodity exchange of women as crucial to women's subordination. Radical feminist explanation of patriarchy was in the form of a sex class struggle and socialist feminist explanation combined Marxian and radical feminist positions. Patriarchy is viewed as a system of struggle between women and men changing historically with the modes of production. Economic class system and sex class system are viewed as two contradictions: patriarchy is viewed as related to the economic system of relations of production but not in a causal manner. They acknowledged the influence of other forces such as ideology in shaping patriarchy: patriarchy not consequence of private property alone and hence will not disappear when private property is established. Patriarchy predates class and kinship and family are viewed as the main sites of women's subordination. Mies (1981) has taken up nature/culture/human dichotomy, analysing all men's and women's interaction with nature and how in the process they build their own human nature to explain origins of patriarchy. Men's possession of technology and arms dominated over women's productive capacities, and through violence, permanent relations of exploitation and domination between sexes were created. Latter theorists emphasised on the importance of history in the understanding of patriarchy. Appropriation and commodification of women's sexual and reproductive capacity by men lies at the foundation of private property, and patriarchy is believed to precede private property and class. Patriarchy is then essentially understood as male control over fertility, sexuality and labour power. It is a structural system of male dominance with differential conceptualisations (Heath, 1984; Boone, 1990).

The discussion of the women's movement in the international/transnational context can be undertaken in terms of the three waves – the first wave spearheaded after the French Revolution and with Wollstonecraft's work 'A Vindication of the Rights of Women' (1792) in London and the writings of John Stuart Mill. This gave rise to the liberal genre feminist thinking, succeeded by Marxist-socialist thought inspired by writings of Engels and Marx. Wollstonecraft's work concentrated on describing the state of ignorance and servility to which women were condemned by social custom and training. Her acute question: 'how many generations may be necessary to give vigour to the virtue and talents of the freed posterity of abject slaves?' still has relevance. Other parallel eighteenth-century works included 'The Gleaner' by Judith Sargent Murray and 'Alcuin: A Dialogue' by Charles Brockden Brown in the United States. In France, Condorcet championed the cause of political equality of the female sex and the playwright Olympe de Gouges proclaimed a 'Declaration of the Rights of Women'. Wollstonecraft's work however had significant implications for the women's cause – Susan B. Anthony's feminist newspaper 'The Revolution' published it as a series in United States in the 1860s. John Stuart Mill's important work has been 'The Subjection of Women' (published in 1869) wherein he emphasised that the subtle and pervasive social conditioning is the means by which women are prepared to accede to roles as the servants of men.

Liberal feminist thought in the first wave thus focused on issues of suffrage and equality. Some of the main contentions were a conscious stand in opposition to male defamation and mistreatment of women – a dialectical opposition to misogyny; a belief that sexes are culturally and not just biologically formed – that women were a social group shaped to fit male notions about a defective sex; and an outlook that transcended the accepted value systems of that time by exposing and opposing the prejudice and narrowness and a desire for a truly general conception of humanity (Kelly, 1982). The Marxist flavour to the movement emerged with the writings of Engels, particularly the important work published in 1884 titled the 'Origins of Family, Private Property and the State'. In the light of the work of Lewis Morgan (American-born anthropologist), Engels viewed the patriarchal family as only one of the number of possible variations. He applied the insights of historical materialism to the analysis of the economic basis of domination of women by men and identified the existing monogamous family structure as the instrument for the exercise of male supremacy. The work 'Origins of Family, Private Property and the State' offers the basic Marxist explanation for the oppression of women – rooted in the twin facts of private ownership of property and the exclusion of women from social production. Family and monogamous marriages were viewed as instrumental in perpetuating the domination (Moi, 1989).

Early renditions on class analysis to comprehend women's oppression revealed the following flavours. Examining the relations of production entered into by women, Delphy (1970) has shown that family itself as a site of economic exploitation: that of women. Having shown that domestic work and child rearing are, first, exclusively the responsibility of women, and, second, unpaid, she concludes that women have a specific relationship to production which is comparable to serfdom. She proposed a need to analyse the relationship between the nature of domestic goods and services and their mode of production According to her explanation, all contemporary societies, including socialist ones, depend on the unpaid labour of women for domestic services and child rearing. They are furnished within the framework of a particular relationship to an individual. They are excluded from the realm of exchange and consequently have no value. Whatever women receive in return is independent of the work which they perform because it is not handed out in exchange for that work (as a wage to which their work entitles them), but rather as a gift. Husband's only obligation (which is in his own interest) is to provide for his wife's basic needs, in other words he maintains her labour power. The nature of women's work is thus to produce goods and services that have only 'use-value' and no 'exchange-value'. It is not the nature of the work performed by women but their relations of production which explain why their work is excluded from the realm of value. The nonremuneration of the wife's work by the household head is not only limited to products consumed within the family (child rearing, domestic services) but also apply to products destined for the market when they are produced within the family, and to work done by other family members. Women's production has an exchange value except when they work within the framework of the family – to which the unpaid labour of the housewife has been limited. Appropriation of the labour power of women diminished with their participation in work albeit only partially, as certain work such as domestic chores and raising children were still relegated to women – at times manifesting as double workload. Hence, there are effectively two modes of production in society: industrial and domestic – the first giving rise to capitalist exploitation and the other to patriarchal exploitation.

This analysis was fed into the women's liberation movement in the West that surrounded issues of class – or what Morgan (1970) calls the caste and class analysis. The contention could be that women could be class enemies but remain caste sisters. Women function as a class because they class-climb or class-descend via men. Women from the working-class background have been alienated by what seems to be a middle-class movement. The demand was that of wages for housework leading to an analysis of the relationship of unpaid domestic labour to capitalism; and later on an attempt to relate capitalism and patriarchy, a relationship is sometimes discussed in terms of the metaphor of marriage.

The second-wave feminism, commenced sometime around the 1960s, primarily concerned with sexuality and issues of reproduction, brought in another realm of understanding to the discourse of the women's movement through the writings of Simone de Beauvoir, Betty Friedan and European feminists. Existential, psychoanalytical and radical feminist thoughts dominated the scene. Further, advanced renditions of socialist and Marxist feminists were also viewed. Early on sexuality was the core contention – Kate Millett's sexual politics theory viewed the relationship between sexes in a political light. Politics here was viewed as a system of power structures and hierarchies whereby one group is dominated by the other. That the relationship between sexes throughout history has been that of domination, and subordination – an 'interior colonisation' of sorts governed by birthright priority logic of social order whereby male rules female – is the contention.

This phase also marked some crucial deliberations on issues of sex and gender and the social construction discourse. Learning was viewed to be a primary factor in sex linked behavioural differences; no specific correlation between sex-linked traits and incidences in sexes makes the case for cultural determinism vis-à-vis biological – learning or rather social learning being more crucial than genetics. This was the commencing argument for sex-gender renditions in the second wave and subsequently paved the way for radical thought. Margaret Mead proposed that different societies define masculinity and femininity differently, emphasising different qualities, interests and occupations as 'male' and 'female'. Hence, what can be inferred is that gender is social/cultural rather than based on sex traits.

Psychoanalytical feminism owes its allegiance to the writings of Freud – albeit not looking at Freudian theory as a biological deterministic account of the influence of biology on women's lives. Feminist critique is levied around Freud's phallocentrism – the contention that female psychological development is predicted on a high regard for male anatomy and women defined in terms of what they lack in relation to men. There is an exclusive focus on sexuality in defining subjectivity. Contesting male interpretations and usage of meaning, feminists have made a case for how psychoanalysis is a male discourse that serves to repress the feminine and to shape femininity not in itself but in accordance with male desire (Sayers, 1979). Chodorow (1978) used the psychoanalytical framework to analyse mothering – particularly why women want to mother. She rejected the two standard explanations that women are destined to be mothers by nature and that women are conditioned to be mothers by society. According to her, any theory of mothering based on the notion that women embrace, as their own, a set of socially constructed and validated feminine gender roles is flawed because it relies on the idea that gender roles can be freely chosen. Femininity is not a way of being that a girl deliberately decides to assume; rather, it is a slow, gradual process that seizes the psyche of a girl before she is self-consciously aware of herself as a girl. The desire to mother, like the desire to be feminine, is implanted in girls before they become women. Thus, mothering has little to do with conscious choice and much to do with an unconscious desire to mother.

To explain why so many women are able to empathise with children, Chodorow (1978) analysed the pre-oedipal stage which is sexually charged for boys in a way it is not for girls. In this stage, the son seeks to separate himself from his mother in order to not risk his father's wrath; this separation is traumatic. What makes the process less painful is his dawning realisation that power and prestige are to be had through identification with men – in this case, the father. Social contempt for women helps the boy define himself in opposition to the female sex his mother represents. For girls, penis envy arises both because the penis symbolises male power and because it is the sexual organ that apparently satisfies her mother. Her turn to her father is both an attack on her mother and an expression of love for her. Girls do finally transfer their primary love from a female to a male object, this transfer of love is never completed, whether a girl develops into a heterosexual woman or not, she will tend to find her strongest emotional connections with other women. This development has its social implications – the separation of the boy from his mother is the source of his inability to relate deeply to others, an inability that prepares him for work in the public sphere, which values single-minded efficiency, a down-to-business attitude and competitiveness. The girl's oneness with her mother is the source of her capacity for relatedness, a capacity that is necessary for her role as nurturant wife and mother in the private sphere. Feminine personality comes to define itself in relation and connection to other people more than masculine personality. Chodorow's conviction is that the oppression of women originates in the female monopoly on mothering – proposing dual parenting as a solution (Chodorow, 1994).

Irigaray (1981) posed a feminist critique of psychoanalysis through the critique of the phallocentric bias of language and subjectivity. It was the disquiet with the appropriation of the symbolic by 'Man' such that woman is always defined in terms of how she satisfies male desire, that compelled Irigaray (1981) to engage with language and its role in defining subjectivities. Psychoanalysis has been used as an important tool in this resistance to patriarchal discourse. Psychoanalysis takes the male/masculine as norm; subjectivity is always 'masculine' and femininity can only be considered as 'lack' in relation to a masculine subject. Luce Irigaray developed a psychoanalytic and feminist critique of phallocentrism saying that female psychology is not to be explained in response to male anatomy. Femininity, she says, is essentially constituted by female biology, by the 'two lips of the female sex'. Freud says that there is only one libido and it serves both masculine and feminine functions. She maintains that women have a 'specific female desire', and that Freud's rejection of the notion of a female libido is simply an effect of his patriarchal attitudes. Further, Irigaray posits that language is ill-fitted in the articulation of female sexuality because it assumes 'a unity in the subject', whereas there is always 'a plurality in feminine language' – this plurality being a necessary consequence of her equation of the female sex with its 'two lips'. Irigaray argues that it is the language generated by male-dominated society that is responsible for women's alienation from their sexuality. Further, the way forward that has been suggested is for women are to assert their biologically given essential femininity.

Poststructuralist Jacques Lacan emphasised the Freudian contribution of the initial bisexuality of a child and the recognition of a precarious psychic process in the definition of masculinity and femininity rather than any biological nature. However, Lacan furthered constructionist positions and the role of the symbolic in his shift from the centrality of anatomical difference in the acquisition of psychic sexual identity to the linguistic structure of the unconscious where there are repressed meanings as well as an imaginary structure of subjectivity. According to Lacan, the predominance of the paternal figure is normative rather than natural and is achieved through a play of language, symbol and metaphor, which define subjectivity as a child enters the realm of speech, law and sociality. Since women have little or no access to the symbolic order, they have even little access to language and its meaning (secured through difference – binary oppositions in which one term privileged, the other defined by absence) – leading to the primary exclusion/absence of the (m) other/feminine (Boone, 1990).

Existential feminism drew from Simone de Beauvoir's work 'The Second Sex' and was influenced by Sartrean thought. de Beauvoir (1953 trans.) adopted the ontological and ethical claims of existentialism and held that from the beginning, man has named himself the Self and the woman the 'Other'. If the Other is a threat to the Self, then woman is a threat to man and if man wishes to remain free, he must subordinate woman to him (like Blacks being subordinated by

Whites, poor by the rich). But women's oppression by men is unique because unlike oppression of race and caste it is not a contingent historical fact, an event in time which has been contested or reversed; and women have internalised the alien point of view that man is the essential, woman the inessential. In becoming the Other, women accept not only being different and separate from man but also inferior to him. Although biologists, psychoanalysts (Freudians) and Marxists have important things to say about the causes and reasons for women's condition, but none of them, according to de Beauvoir, explains why woman, not man, is the 'Other'. Biology identifies the basic difference between male and female as one rooted in the reproductive roles of males and females. These 'reproductive' facts that violate and alienate a woman from her body may make it harder for a woman to become and remain a Self, especially if she has a child. Although biological and physiological facts about woman – such as her primary role in reproduction relative to man's secondary role, her physical weakness relative to man's physical strength and her inactive role in heterosexual intercourse relative to man's active role – may be real enough. But how much value we attach to these facts is up to us as social beings. Hence, according to de Beauvoir biology does not provide the adequate answer. The psychoanalytical explanation is as follows: that woman is a creature who must struggle between her 'viriloid' (expressed through clitoral eroticism) and 'feminine' (expressed through vaginal eroticism) tendencies. To win this battle – to become normal – she must overcome her 'viriloid' tendencies and transfer her love from a woman to a man. de Beauvoir (1953) conceded Freud's genius but she rejected his idea that sexuality is the ultimate explanation for why things are the way they are as simplistic. Freud's theory of women's 'castration complex' was not perceived by her as an adequate psychological explanation for their inferior and subservient social status.

With respect to Marxism, as de Beauvoir saw it, the relations between men and women will not automatically change if we move from capitalism to socialism. She gave the following arguments instead: as civilisation developed, man discovered that one of the best ways to control woman is to construct myths about her. In man's myths about woman, two things are stressed: what man wants from woman is everything that man lacks and woman is a chameleon whose being is as mutable as nature. Thus, men's writings created different images of the 'ideal woman' and each one urged women to deny, forget or negate themselves. In addition to idealising/idolising the self-sacrificial woman, man's myths about woman betrayed a fundamental ambivalence about her nature. Women, on the other hand, were unable to reject the myth as also internalise them. Further, de Beauvoir proposed that if a woman wants to stop being the Second Sex, the Other, she must overcome her circumstances, have her way and her say as much as a man does. Three strategies that they can employ for this as suggested were: (1) women must go to work – though work is oppressive and exploitative in a capitalist world, through this, a woman 'regains her transcendence' and 'concretely affirms her status as subject'; (2) women can become intellectuals as intellectual activity, after all, is the activity of one who thinks, looks and defines, not the nonactivity of one who is thought about, looked at and defined and (3) women can work towards a socialist transformation of the society. Like Sartre, de Beauvoir held out hope for an end to the subject/object, self/other conflict among human beings in general and between men and women in particular. She also believed that one of the keys to women's liberation is economic and that the social space for this project needs to be cleared.

Radical feminists have looked at women's oppression as the most fundamental form of oppression. Reproduction is viewed as the cause of women's oppression: Shulamith Firestone claimed that patriarchy is rooted in the biological inequality of the sexes. She said that the original class distinction is between men and women and used the term 'sex class' to define this unequal structure. Considering the relations of reproduction, not production to be the driving force in history, Firestone believed that since the roots of women's oppression are biological, women's liberation required a biological revolution. Women must seize control of the means of reproduction and she says that what makes this biological revolution possible is technology. Firestone believed that when women and men stop playing substantially different roles in the reproductive drama, it will be possible to eliminate all sexual roles. When technology is able to perfect 'artificial' ways for people to reproduce, the need for the biological family will disappear and with it the need to impose genital heterosexuality as a means of ensuring human reproduction. Homosexuality would then no longer be viewed as alternatives to the norm of heterosexuality – the categories of homosexuality and heterosexuality would be abandoned and institutionalised sexual intercourse with males and females playing specific roles would disappear. The biological family's demise as a reproductive unit would also spell its demise as an economic unit. Hence, if technology can eliminate the role of woman-the-reproducer, it can eliminate the role of man-the-producer. When there would be no longer distinct productive and reproductive roles, it will be possible to overcome all of the relations, structures and ideas that have always divided the human community. She also proposed to explode masculinity and femininity, but was convinced that this explosion would not occur unless humans abandon patriarchal reproduction as well as capitalist production. She also said that the joy of giving birth – invoked so frequently in this society – is a patriarchal myth and biological motherhood is the root of further evils, especially the vice of possessiveness that generates feelings of hostility and jealousy among human beings. According to Firestone, the vice of possessiveness – the favouring of one child over another on account of it being the product of one's own ovum or sperm – is precisely what must be overcome if we are to put an end to divisive hierarchies (Moraga and Anzaldua, 1981).

Further, radical feminists have made a case for and against biological motherhood and also posed a critique against contracted/surrogate motherhood. Ann Oakley proposes that motherhood is a myth based on the threefold belief that 'all women need to be mothers, all mothers need their children, all children need their mothers'. The need to 'mother' owes nothing to women's possession of ovaries and wombs; and everything to the way in which women are socially and culturally conditioned to be mothers. There is no such thing as a maternal instinct either. Mothers are not born; they are made – based on the cultural assumptions that children need biological, not social mothers; that children, especially young children, need the devoted care of their mothers much more than that of their fathers and that children need one nurturant caretaker (preferably the biological mother), not many. Patriarchy has kept women convinced that mothering is their one and only job which denies them access to the public realm of culture – denying them also the right to have gynocentric wants and needs (Mitchell and Oakley, 1976). Rich (1976), on the other hand, made a distinction between the experience of mothering and the institution of motherhood as the difference between *women* deciding who, how, when and where to mother and *men* making these decisions for women. By institutionalising biological motherhood, patriarchy does its best to corrupt any relationship that could exist between mother and child. As Rich saw it, if women took control of childbearing and child rearing, more mothers would be able to experience biological motherhood on their own terms. The solution to the pains of childbearing, according to her was not technology, but rather for a woman to ride with, not against, her body. Dialoguing on contracted/surrogate motherhood, radical feminists propose that when society encourages a woman to rent her womb, it comes dangerously close to dehumanising reproduction by turning it into a mode of commodity production. As only women can give birth, appeals for contracted mothers can constitute something like a 'compassion trap' for women.

As a part of second-wave ventures, the new women's movement which started in most Western countries in the late 1960s and early 1970s was a protest by a new generation of women against male-dominated or patriarchal society. The branch of the movement called women's rights movements worked predominantly for political reforms by means of traditional pressure groups tactics. Women's liberation movement however focused on – consciousness raising groups, experiments in new ways of living, creating a counter culture and creating alternative institutions. In Spain, the women's movement did not emerge until 1975 after the death of Franco. In Ireland, the dominant Catholic and conservative forces have given little room for the movement to develop. In Turkey, the women's movement emerged in the late eighties. In 1970s, the abortion issue was an important demand of the women's movement – legislation responding by giving women the right of decision and hence control over their own bodies. The Italian movement was the most impressive in Europe, considering that it was up against a strong Catholic Church allied with the governing Christian democratic party. In Ireland, a Catholic stronghold, the abortion law was not liberalised, rather made more difficult by the 1983 amendment to the constitution forbidding abortion. In countries such as Scandinavia and the Netherlands, new abortion laws were passed between 1975 and 1985 after a period of intense emotional debate. For the first time in history, feminists forced the state and the public opinion to acknowledge not only the specificity of women's condition of existence, hitherto ghettoised into the family, but also the fact that women are not objects. In case of France, the feminist discourse was much more radical, refuting the notion of women's natural function and replacing it with that of free and unconditional choice of women. In Germany, there was the phenomenon of 'neue Weiblichkeitsmythos' (new myth of femininity) in recent feminism. Even during the first wave of the feminist movement, the focus in the same way shifted from equality to positive evaluation of differences between women and men, stressing women's special role as mothers. During the interwar period in Germany, this trend turned into a reactionary and biodeterministic direction. Further, the movement deliberated that the interaction with the establishment would lead to a de-radicalisation of the movement. However in terms of interaction with established politics, three signs have been observed here: (1) the ideas of the movement become absorbed by society and different important sections of it; (2) leaders of the movement are co-opted into mainstream politics and society and (3) women succeed in getting access and influence (Dahlerup, 1986).

The third wave centred around multiple identities, multiple histories and assertions had some prominent writings by Sherry Ortner, Christine Delphy, Judith Butler, bell hooks, Patricia Collins and literature of Black Feminists, Third World feminists and ecofeminism. Particularly, there has been a shift from women-oriented discourses towards gender discourses, hence paving the way for advanced renditions on gender. Ortner (1974) has explained the universality of female subordination through three types/forms: explicit devaluation, implicit devaluation through symbolic devices and socio-structural arrangements. Universal or explicit devaluation of women is through biological determinism – women associated with nature and men associated with culture – culture being self-conscious/purposeful/ritualistic and not passive. Since women are considered part of nature, culture finds it 'natural' to subordinate them; further, women are closer to nature but not nature themselves, they have an intermediary status as being less transcendental of nature than men are.

Delphy (1990) posits that there is an unexamined presupposition that sex precedes gender and political contradictions are produced by our desire as women to escape domination on one hand and our fear that we might lose what seem to be fundamental social categories on the other. Delphy argues that gender precedes sex –

'sex is a sign but has historically come to acquire a symbolic value since it does not distinguish just anything from anything else, does not distinguish equivalent things, but rather important and unequal things'. According to her, sex and gender are both social concepts; hierarchy forming the foundation for all differences. Further according to Delphy, women and men constitute opposing classes. She commences her argument with the point that until now, there has been an unexamined presupposition that sex precedes gender. This is theoretically unjustifiable as it prevents us from thinking gender in an open and unbiased way. Refuting Mead's propositions of naturalisation of sexual division of labour and combining Parsonian role theory (proposing that roles are socially ascribed), she rejected the stance of sex as the container and gender as the content and that the container is invariable because it is a part of nature and nature 'does not change'. Gender according to her preceded sex and sex in itself is a social division having attained a symbolic value since it distinguishes not equivalent, but unequal things. Delphy is further interested in looking at 'women as a class' – at the cross-junctures of patriarchy and capitalism as two class systems both of which need to be viewed independently. Discussing bourgeoisie (middle-class) women and working-class women, Delphy posits that it is as women that bourgeoisie women are vilified – seen as having no right to their privileges because they derive them from men. Similarly, working-class women also are not viewed as independently oppressed, but as deriving their oppression from men. The very analyses that deny women common class position rely on that class position – their common dependence on men – in order to deny it.

Using the phenomenological theory of 'acts', that seeks to explain the mundane way in which social agents constitute reality through language, gesture and all manner of symbolic social sign, Butler (1990, 1993, 1997, 1999) has discussed gender as a performative act. Gender is not a stable identity from which various acts proceed; rather an identity tenuously constituted in time – an identity instituted through a stylised repetition of acts. It is instituted through the stylisation of bodies and hence the mundane way in which bodily gestures, movements and enactments of various kinds constitute the illusion of an abiding gendered self. It is hence not a substantial model of identity, but rather a conception of a constituted social temporality. Body is 'a historical idea' rather than 'a natural species' – an active process of embodying certain cultural and historical possibilities (a complicated process of appropriation). That the body is a set of possibilities signifies: that its appearance in the world, for perception, is not predetermined by some manner of interior essence; and, that its concrete expression in the world must be understood as the taking up and rendering specific of a set of historical possibilities. Body not merely a materiality, but a materiality that bears meaning, and the manner of this bearing is fundamentally dramatic, i.e., body is not merely matter but a continual and incessant materialisation of possibilities. Body is a historical situation and is a manner of doing, dramatising and reproducing a historical situation – the 'stylistics of existence'. This style is never fully self-styled, for living styles have a history, and that history conditions and limits possibilities.

Hence, gender is considered an 'act' which is both intentional and performative, where 'performative' carries the double-meaning of 'dramatic' and 'non-referential'. The body is invariably transformed into his body or her body, the body is only known through its gendered appearance. The body becomes its gender through a series of acts which are renewed, revised and consolidated through time. From the feminist point of view: the gendered body is the legacy of sedimented acts rather than a predetermined or foreclosed structure, essence or fact, whether natural, cultural or linguistic. The heterosexual contract is a reproduction of a given culture taking place through instating sexual reproduction within the confines of a heterosexually based system of marriage that guarantees the eventual reproduction of that kinship system. Association of natural sex with a discrete gender and attraction to the opposing sex/gender is an unnatural conjunction of cultural constructs in the service of reproductive interests. Gender reality is performative means that it is real only to the extent that it is performed.

Respecting the multiple identities genre, hooks (1981) and Collins (1986, 1990) have brought in the discussion on the Black feminist discourse. hooks (1981) proposed that at the priority of the Black feminist thought is not a restoration of equality with men as much as it is the inherent inequality which is perceived and experienced with their White counterparts. According to her, equating feminist struggle with a countercultural women-centred world erected barriers that closed the movement off from most women. Hence, there needs to be a shift from a women-centred space towards issues of identity. Racial hierarchies need to be taken cognisance of, in an essentially class hierarchy-prone mainstream feminist movement. Collins (1986, 1990) has argued as to how Black female intellectuals have made creative use of their marginality – their 'outsider within' status to produce Black feminist thought that reflects a special standpoint on self, family and society. Three characteristic themes in such thought have been explored: (1) Black women's self-definition and self-valuation; (2) the interlocking nature of oppression and (3) the importance of Afro-American women's culture. Self-definition involves challenging the political knowledge-validation process that has resulted in externally defined, stereotypical images of Afro-American womanhood. In contrast, self-valuation stresses the content of Black women's self-definitions namely, replacing externally derived images with authentic Black female images. Attention to the interlocking nature of race, gender and class oppression is a second recurring theme in the works of Black feminists. The Black feminist attention to the interlocking nature of oppression is significant as this viewpoint shifts the entire focus of investigation from one aimed at explicating elements of race or gender or class oppression to one whose goal is to determine what the links are among these systems. The first approach typically prioritises one form of oppression as being primary, and then handles remaining types of oppression as variables within what is seen as the most important system. The oppression experienced by most Black women is shaped by their subordinate status in an array of either/or dualities. Afro-American women have been assigned the inferior half of several dualities, and this placement has been central to their continued domination. For example, the allegedly emotional, passionate nature of Afro-American women has long been used as a rationale for their sexual exploitation. Similarly, denying Black women literacy – then claiming that they lack the facts for sound judgment – illustrates another case of assigning a group inferior status, then using that inferior status as proof of the group's inferiority. Finally, denying Black women agency as subjects and treating them as objectified 'others' represents yet another dimension of the power that dichotomous oppositional constructs have in maintaining systems of domination.

A third key theme characterising Black feminist thought involves efforts to redefine and explain the importance of Black women's culture. In doing so, Black feminists have not only uncovered previously unexplored areas of the Black female experience, but they have also identified concrete areas of social relations where Afro-American women create and pass on self-definitions and self-valuations essential to coping with the simultaneity of oppression they experience. In contrast to views of culture stressing the unique, ahistorical values of a particular group, Black feminist approaches have placed greater emphasis on the role of historically specific political economies in explaining the endurance of certain cultural themes. The interest in redefining Black women's culture has directed attention to several unexplored areas of the Black female experience. One such area concerns the interpersonal relationships that Black women share with each other – the notion of sisterhood. The second is the interpersonal relationship shared by Black women with their biological children, the children in their extended families and with the Black community's children. In reassessing Afro-American motherhood, Black feminist researchers have emphasised the connections between choices available to Black mothers resulting from their placement in historically specific political economies; Black mothers' perceptions of their children's choices as compared to what mothers thought those choices should be and actual strategies employed by Black mothers both in raising their children and in dealing with institutions that affected their children's lives.

Another dimension of Black women's culture that has generated considerable interest among Black feminists is the role of creative expression in shaping and sustaining Black women's self-definitions and self-valuations. In addition to documenting Black women's achievements as writers, dancers, musicians, artists and actresses, the emerging literature also investigates why creative expression has been such an important element of Black women's culture. This third key theme in Black feminist thought – the focus on Black women's culture – is significant for three reasons. First, the data from Black women's culture suggest that the relationship between oppressed people's consciousness of oppression and the actions they take in dealing with oppressive structures may be far more complex than that suggested by existing social theory. Second, it points to the problematic nature of existing conceptualisations of the term 'activism'. While Black women's reality cannot be understood without attention to the interlocking structures of oppression that limit Black women's lives,

Afro-American women's experiences suggest that possibilities for activism exist even within such multiple structures of domination. Such activism can take several forms. Third, an analytical model exploring the relationship between oppression, consciousness, and activism is implicit in the way Black feminists have studied Black women's culture. Black lesbians portray another level of hierarchy – Black women who initially insisted that lesbianism was White women's problem insist now that Black lesbians are a threat to Black nationhood, are consorting with the enemy and are basically 'un-Black'. This has led to many Black lesbians to be in hiding – caught between the racism of White women and the homophobia of their Black counterparts. Recognition of differences not only between sexes but also within sexes is the key to the issue.

There is also a movement to relate feminism to postmodernism (Fraser and Nicholson, 1988), basically to develop a postmodern feminist positionality attuned to the cultural specificity of different societies and periods and to that of different groups within societies and periods. Hence, postmodern feminist position is inflected with temporality and with historically specific institutional categories such as the family taking precedence over functionalist categories such as reproduction and mothering. This would mean that the point of criticisms is institutions and not functions. Postmodern stance then dispenses the idea of a subject of history replacing complexly constructed conceptions of social identity, treating gender as one relevant strand among others, attending also to class, race, ethnicity, age and sexual orientation.

Third World feminist stance vehemently argues that feminism emerging from the White, middle-class heterosexual women narrowly confines itself to gender discrimination. It is called liberal, bourgeoisie, reformist feminism and has on its agenda a singularly anti-sexist struggle. The need to broaden the political terrain of feminism to incorporate the crucial categorical imperatives of race and class analysis is the core contention. This needs to be coupled with the historic struggle with aspects of imperialism and colonialism. Hence, the crucial need to politicise the women's movement – as it is not only linked to gender emancipation but also to broader struggles at the global level. The illustration of the position comes with the struggles of Black women: in their juxtaposition with the White women, they have been relegated to 'nonwoman' and 'unfeminine' categories – thereby giving space to exploit their productive and reproductive capacities to the fullest. Further, the interplay of globalisation, the neoliberal regime and the reinforcement of sexual division of labour in the process of creating a 'hospitable investment climate' for multinational corporations is discussed. The point that is made is that factors other than gender figure integrally in the oppression of Third World women and that even regarding patriarchy, many Third World women labour under indigenous inequitable gender relationships exacerbated by Western patriarchy, racism and exploitation. For Third World women resident in the West, race and class, along with gender, have been indivisible elements in their oppression. Hence, women's movement has to transcend its gender specificity, be anti-imperialist and not fall prey to the internationally orchestrated exploitation of the First World. For the same it would mean the cruciality of structural issues of poverty along with gender exploitation, taking cultural specificities into account. Further, the impact of race and class on issues of sexuality and reproduction along with the stances of the establishment needs critical deliberation is exhorted (Bartky, 1990; Johnson-Odim, 1996).

The ecofeminist movement has looked at science and technology as a patriarchal, colonial project and is geared towards reconceptualising productivity – production of life versus production for profit. Further, technocratic development, totalisation of the market and penetration and destruction of old and subsistence economies and science and technology as ideology lead to objectification and commercialisation of women's bodies and violent assaults on their physical and spiritual integrity. Hence, the themes that have in general dominated women's movement in the West are as follows: the validity of patriarchy as an organising concept in theorising the subordination of women; the centrality of the concept of the public/private division in structuring women's life and as a key to understanding women's oppression; the influence of Utopian views of liberation; the nature of subjectivity and the fusion of sexuality and gender as the central locus of women's subordination (Wilson and Weir, 1986).

In the Indian context, it can be said that the first instances of the women's movement are viewed in the Bhakti movement – particularly the Vaishnavi tradition (Meerabai, Antal, Akkamahadevi and

Bahinabai) that took refuge under theology as spaces for expressing unexpressed emotions of love, passion and desire. Nineteenth-century social reform movements and the Gandhian era visualised women in the nationalist movement albeit within the patriarchal fold and a liberal stance. Nevertheless, it provided definitions of 'womanhood', 'visibility' and 'assertions in the public sphere'. In the pre-independence era, there was women's participation in agrarian struggles and revolts – in the rural and tribal areas of different parts of the country. However, gender interests subsumed to class/caste interests – examples include Naxalbari and Tebhaga movements of West Bengal, Telangana movements, Warli tribal revolt against bondage and servitude in Maharashtra. In the 1970s, issue-based campaigns of women in arenas of livelihood, ecology and objectification (media related), predominantly spearheaded by political party affiliations, were launched. In the middle and late seventies, 'autonomous' women's organisations' adopting issue-based 'protest politics' were visualised.

Dietrich (1992) has examined the women's movement in the Indian context as interfacing with religion, ecology and development. Women have been victims of religious orthodoxy and have not been at the forefront of religious ideological production. Gandhi contributed to women's mobilisation, their participation within the political struggle; however, women remained in a domesticated role within the movement. Gandhian movement united religious reform and women's mobilisation in forceful ways, thus undermining the social rigidity of communalism and revivalism; his religious imagery remained, however, high caste. Dalit movement consciously mobilised an imagery from the below and Phule went on to establish the link between women's oppression, untouchability and caste. During the freedom struggle, social transformation was mediated by religious reform and women benefitted from this religious reform. However, since women were not involved in the ideological production of these reform movements but only participated at the level of mass mobilisation, they usually remained objects of patriarchal benevolence and could not evolve an imagery which would have helped them to express their full aspirations towards transformation of political institutions. Further, the women's movement, though facing the issue of communalism primarily in the field of personal laws, is simultaneously confronted with the issue of communal violence expressed in massive physical confrontations. Hence according to Dietrich, women's position through religion lens needs a materialist writing of history. In terms of issues of sexuality, traditional Indian values have been towards a denial of sexuality in the name of chastity – thereby creating the dichotomy between the chaste housewife and the prostitute. Using the Marxist perspective to view household labour, patriarchy and the sexual division of labour, the need for women's movement to align to class struggle is posited.

Some core positions of key writers on women's movement in the Indian content can be deliberated as follows: The adversity towards accepting Western notions of feminism was evident in the writings of Kishwar (1991) as also Desai (1995). Agnes (1994) has also argued that Indian feminists, in order to counter the attack of being Western, used Hindu iconography and Sanskrit idioms denoting women power, thus inadvertently strengthening the communal ideology. There is an exhortation to look at the question of culture in the context of women's movement in the Indian context – issues of identity and diversity (John, 1998). What has to be dealt with in the Indian context is the combined legacy of colonial encounter on the one hand and the dominance of Western theories on the other. Further, there is an important flavour of patriarchy that emerges in the Indian context – that of the Brahminical tradition or Brahminical patriarchy.

Significant differences occur between the Brahmin and the non-Brahmin traditions that symbolise the opposition between the male and female principles. The concept of marriage involving the male control over female sexuality is important for understanding how the mother goddess was incorporated into the patriarchal Brahmin religion. The features of the goddess in the non-Brahmin religion symbolise popular resistance to the control of women's power in the 'Brahmin' religious tradition. In the Brahminical form, the goddess has both aspects but is most commonly subordinate. The concept of 'femaleness' in Hinduism represents an important duality – fertile, benevolent, creator, aggressive, malevolent and destroyer. Purity-pollution rituals are also associated with female body that undergoes transitions through various life stages: the body of a child which is seen as bearing marks of a future gender identity which has not yet crystallised; the body at the onset of menstruation when it is defined as body in nature; the body in sexuality when the body of the other is discovered; the maternal body when the inner alien space is converted into a communicative space and the body at death when it finally achieves the status of the body-made-whole which is simultaneously the body without organs. Thus, gender roles are conceived, entailed and reproduced within a complex of relationships. Family and kinship structures along with the institution of caste coagulate to form the female identity. There is also a homology between the sexual asymmetry in biological reproduction as conceived by culture and sexual asymmetry in relations of production expressed in structural rules which govern ownership, control and use of productive resources (Mazumdar, 1981; Dube, 1986; Chanana, 1990).

To explicate Brahminical patriarchy, it is based on the proposition that caste hierarchy and gender hierarchy are the organising principles of the Brahminical social order and are closely interconnected. Caste and gender form the central factors for the subordination of the upper-caste women: the need for effective sexual control over such women to maintain not only patrilineal succession (a requirement of all patriarchal societies) but also caste purity, the institution unique to Hindu society. The purity of women has a centrality in Brahminical patriarchy, because the purity of caste is contingent upon it. A fundamental principle of Hindu social organisation is to construct a closed structure to preserve land, women and 'ritual quality' within it. The three are structurally linked and it is not possible to maintain all three without stringently organising female sexuality. Tracing the roots of its origins to the agrarian economy, Chakravarty (1993) posits that Brahminical patriarchy required a sharp distinction to be made between motherhood and female sexuality with the latter being channelised only into legitimate motherhood within a tightly controlled structure of reproduction which ensured caste purity (by mating only with prescribed partners) and patrilineal succession (by restricting mating only with one man). Women's general subordination was essential in this stage because it was only then that the mechanism of control upon women's sexuality could actually be effective. The mechanism of control operated through ideology, through the *stridharma*, or *pativratadharma*, internalised by women who attempted to live up to the ideal notion of womanhood constructed by the ideologues of the society. In the case of Hindu society, the design of the patriarchal caste-class structure was mapped out by the *brahmanas*; *pativrata* the specific *dharma* of the Hindu wife then became the ideology by which women accepted and even aspired to chastity and wifely fidelity as the highest expression of their selfhood.

Rege (1998) has explicated the Dalit feminist standpoint – emerging from the Black and Third World feminist work in the 1980s and 1990s. The assertion of autonomous Dalit women's organisations in the 1990s threw up several crucial theoretical and political challenges, besides underlining the Brahmanism of the feminist movement and the patriarchal practices of Dalit politics. The 1980s were marked by the newly exploding caste identity and consciousness and theoretical and political issues involved in the debate on caste and its role in social transformation came to be debated. Looking at difference as a standpoint, the attempt is to historically locate the 'difference' of Dalit women's voices in their real struggles. A historical reinscription of Dalit women's struggles into the historiography of modern India then poses challenges for the established understanding of nationalism and the women's question in nineteenth-century India. The early decades of the twentieth century saw protests against caste-based prostitution in the campaigns launched by Shivram Janba Kamble. The 1930s saw the organisation of independent meetings and conferences by Dalit women in the Ambedkarite movement. This was an obvious consequence of Ambedkar's practice of organising a women's conference along with every general meeting and Sabha that he called. In these 'parishads' of the 1930s, Dalit women delegates passed resolutions against child marriage, enforced widowhood and dowry; critiquing these practices as Brahminical. Women's participation in the Mahad Satyagraha and their support to the Independent Labour Party and the Schedule Caste Federation have been well documented. Women in large numbers supported *Dharmantar* as a need for a religion that would recognise their equal status. Women's participation in the Ambedkarite movement must be read in the context of the fact that in Ambedkar's theory of caste there is also a theory of the origins of subordination of women and that he saw the two issues as intrinsically linked. Ambedkar pointed to the inadequacy of understanding caste in terms of 'idea of pollution'. He argued that 'the absence of intermarriage or endogamy is the one characteristic that can be called the essence of castes'. Thus, it is the superimposition of endogamy on exogamy and the means used for the same that hold the key to the understanding of the caste system. Ambedkar then drew up a detailed analysis of how numerical equality between the marriageable units of the two sexes within the group is maintained. Thus, he argued that practices of sati, enforced widowhood and child marriage come to be prescribed by Brahmanism in order to regulate and control any transgression of boundaries, i.e., to say he underlines the fact that the caste system can be maintained only through the controls on women's sexuality and in this sense women are the gateways to the caste system. In his speech at the gathering of women at the Mahad *Satyagraha*, he drew linkages between caste exploitation and women's subordination by underlining this and called upon women to contest the claims of upper-caste women's progeny to purity and the damnation of that of the lower caste to impurity. He located the specificities and varying intensities of women's subordination by caste and thereby drew their attention to the specificities of their subordination, both as 'Dalit' and as 'women'. However, these contentious non-Brahmin images of identities for women came to be silenced by the Fundamental Rights Resolution of the Indian National Congress.

These counternarratives underlined the fact that the 'difference' or 'different voice' of the Dalit women was not an issue of identitarian politics or some 'authentic direct experience', but from a long lived history of lived struggles. Dalit women played a crucial role in transferring across generations, the oral repertoire of personalised yet very collective accounts of their family's interaction with Babasaheb or other leaders of the Dalit movement. Two prominent movements at that time, the Dalit Panther and the women's movement, did not look at the question of Dalit women explicitly. The Dalit Panthers made a significant contribution to the cultural revolt of the 1970s – but in both their writings and their programme – the Dalit women remained encapsulated firmly in the roles of the 'mother' and the 'victimised sexual being'. The Left party–based women's organisations made significant contribution towards economic and work-related issues as the autonomous women's groups politicised and made public the issue of violence against women. Serious debates on class versus patriarchies emerged, both parties however did not address the issues of Brahmanism. While for the former 'caste' was contained in class, for the latter the notion of sisterhood was pivotal.

The three major standpoints in the Dalit women's movement that have emerged are as follows: One of the earliest and well-defined positions is the Marxist/Phule-Ambedkarite position of the Satyashodhak Mahila Sabha and the manifesto of the Satyashodhak Communist Party. A position emerging out of the Dalit-Bahujan alliance is that of the Bahujan Mahila Mahasangh (BMM) which critiques the Vedic, Brahminical tradition and seeks to revive the Bahujan tradition of the 'Adimaya'. Even the secular position is critiqued as apolitical and individualistic and the Ambedkarite conceptualisation of Dhamma in community life is underlined. The Common Civil Code was opposed and customary law and community-based justice was upheld. Significantly the BMM sought to combine both the struggles for political power and a cultural revolution in order to revive and extend the culture of Bahujans. The third position is that of the Dalit Mahila Sanghatana which has critiqued the persistence of the 'Manuvadi Sanskriti' among the Dalit male who otherwise traces his lineage to a Phule-Ambedkarite ideology. The Sanghatana proposed to put forth its manifesto, at the centre of which would be the most Dalit of Dalit women. These non-Brahminical renderings of feminist politics have led to some self-reflexivity among the autonomous women's groups and their responses could be broadly categorised as: a *non-dialectical position* of those who grant that historically it is now important that Dalit women take the leadership but they do not revise a non-Brahminical feminist politics for themselves; the *left position* that collapses caste into class and continues to question the distinct materiality of caste and a *self-reflexive position* of those autonomous women's groups who recognise the need to reformulate and revise feminist politics for the non-Brahminical renderings (Rege, 1995).

A Dalit feminist standpoint is thus seen as emancipatory since the subject of its knowledge is embodied and visible (i.e., the thought begins from the lives of Dalit women and these lives are present and visible in the results of the thought). This position argues that it is more emancipatory than other existing positions and counters pluralism and relativism by which all knowledge based and political claims are thought to be valid in their own way. It places emphasis on individual experiences within socially constructed groups and focuses on the hierarchical, multiple, changing structural power relations of caste, class and ethnicity which construct such a group. The subject/agent of Dalit women's standpoint is multiple, heterogeneous and even contradictory, i.e., the category 'Dalit woman' is not homogenous – such a recognition underlines the fact that the subject of Dalit feminist liberatory knowledge must also be the subject of every other liberatory project and this requires a sharp focus on the processes by which gender, race, class, caste and sexuality all construct each other (Kannabiran and Kannabiran, 1991; Rege, 1998).

Discourses on Ecology

Discourses on ecology have catapulted onto movements and positionalities in the realm of environment – reinstating an ecological consciousness and a cosmocentrism of sorts vis-à-vis anthropocentrism. The key positionalities within ecological discourses are Deep ecology, social ecology, radical ecology, ecofeminism, spiritual ecology and ecotheology. All extant deliberations on ecology can be subsumed under the aforementioned perspectives. Deep ecology provides a new ontology in that humanity is regarded as inseparable from nature with emphasis on self-realisation, relational thinking and through intuitive methodology developing a personal philosophy – ecosophy (Naess, 1982). The conceptual points highlighted by Naess (1982) are an emphasis on the relational field – the protagonean 'both and' theory postulating that the basis for all that we perceive is in matter. Along with the identification, oneness wholeness and self-realisation, Deep ecology of Naess proposes the Aristotelian conception of acknowledging the existence of total perspectives other than those of human beings. In terms of further conceptual developments, Devall and Sessions (1985) postulated that Deep ecology requires a new metaphysics of humans in nature and not above it – a cosmic ecological metaphysics stressing on 'I-thou' relationships between humans and nonhuman nature – the primary focus being on developing a new version of Deep ecology linking it with Buddhism and Taoism. Tobias (1983) postulated the tenets of Deep ecology as dialectical idealism, i.e., being and non-being produce each other and a reverence for life principle. The main tenets highlighted by Watson (1997) are symbolic affirmation that all natural entities (including humans) have intrinsic worth and nature as all-inclusive (as natura naturans) infinitely diverse and alive in the broadest sense of panpsychism and also manifesting a structure in itself.

Social ecology is concerned with viewing societal relationships to nature as a form of practical reason, the radical counterpart of which accommodates political economy discourses. Social ecology accommodates the pioneering contribution of Bookchin (1966). Commencing with the discourse on dialectical naturalism, Bookchin (1966) draws and deviates from dialectical thinkers such as Heraclitus, Hegel and Aristotle. Thus, combining Hegelian logic and Aristotelian metaphysics, Bookchin evolved dialectical naturalism (phenomena in a state of becoming) employing dialectical reason (construed as ontologically ethical and dialectically logical – a guide to rational praxis) displaying the interface between the ecological and the social; the ecological viewed as a major organising principle in social development (Pojman, 1997). Social construction of nature is perceived as the basis of social ecology. Guha (1994) has conceptualised that social ecology rests on the awareness of the interdependence of the biophysical and the socioculturalist domains, juxtaposing the ecological infrastructure to the economy, polity, social structure and culture. Further, this dimension of thought considers ecological anthropological literature, documenting in great detail in a variety of regions the indigenous knowledge systems, conservation mechanisms and the adaptation to the biophysical world in tribal and peasant societies. Eder (1996) postulated a social theory of nature with a critique of the naturalistic theory of evolution, the main tenets of include the following: a natural construction of society (naturalist) or a social construction of nature (culturalist). In a naturalist theory of society, the relationship between society and nature is interpreted as one of domination (Marx and Durkheim). Social construction of nature is a necessary element in the social evolution of societies with a history of cognitive, moral and aesthetic interaction with nature. Two other domains of discussion within social ecology are socialist ecology and social ecology as rational ecology. Socialist ecology's view of the world is fundamentally that of process and change having implication for society and nature. The focus and attempt is to study the pattern that make up the natural/social community attempting to discern its history and inner logic (Merchant, 1992). Dryzek (1987) construed social ecology as rational ecology, where reason is order or negative entropy and rational norms are principles of order. Parallels were recognised between ecosystems and social systems akin to the Chicago School of Urban Sociology (whose members analysed cities and other social institutions in terms of ecological metaphors and analysis). In terms of a general critique of the perspective of social ecology, inadequate treatment of the concept of self, negation of transcendent realities and neglect of women as categorical imperatives emerge (Pojman, 1997). The indigenous version of social ecology is also found in Gandhian thought, particularly aspects of human-nature interconnectedness and the ethics of frugality.

Radical ecology focuses on mapping struggles in the relational field of nature and society as also providing a framework for emancipation. Mapping the trajectory of capitalist development, this stance focuses on a materialist realist position – the real world and its associated dynamics making a difference in human-nature relationships. The feminist component attempts to strengthen the alliance between gender perspective and the cultural critique of modernisation and the debate on power and knowledge in the new global context. Mies and Shiva (1993) highlight the important conceptual links between symbolic construction of women and nature and ways of acting upon them; gender as one of the axioms interfacing with ecology. Commenting on the discourse of ecofeminism, Apffel-Marglin (1994) states that the bond between women and earth is substantive and not symbolic in which elements of consciousness and elements of the world coalesce, thus presenting an image which allows interpretation between subjective consciousness and the world; a conception in which subject-object and nature-nurture dualism dissolves, thus providing a semiological challenge to interiorisation of Western values and domestication of concepts, and asking for insurrection of subjective knowledge. Traditional ecofeminism thus looks at the proximity and the 'first right' so to speak, of women over nature.

Ecofeminists essentially look at science and technology as a patriarchal colonial project, but in the Indian context, Dietrich (1999) proposes that the interaction of caste-class-patriarchy is more crucial. Class brings in aspects of reciprocal and redistributive exchange, and caste (along the lines of Dumont), brings in the purity-pollution element. This purity-pollution concept, which was measured by the degree of interaction with organic life, is ecofeministically significant. In an ecologically viable mode of production, interaction with organic life is of importance and thus the recapturing of the feminist principle can only be in alliance with the subalterns. Hence, traditional ecofeminism which borders on patriarchal reductionism needs to be replaced with caste-class-patriarchy analysis – catapulting the nature-culture argument towards more sophisticated realms. Continuing the critique of traditional ecofeminism, Agarwal (1999) [drawing from Ortner (1987)] argues against the stand which perceives women identified with something, every culture devalues as existentially lower. This stand has been supported by social anthropologists on several counts because nature-culture divide is not universal across cultures nor is there uniformity in the meanings attributed to nature-culture and male-female. Thus, the epistemological critique accommodates the following dimensions: critique of women as a unitary category, critique of locating women-nature domination in ideology and neglecting the material sources of domination, i.e., the socioeconomic and political structures within which domination is produced and transformed; and the connection of women and nature to biology as a form of biological essentialism which is problematic. Agarwal (1999) proposes that the new perspective on feminist environmentalism transcends the critique. In this perspective, the link between women and environment is viewed as structured by a given gender and class organisation of production, reproduction and distribution. Ideological constructs such as gender, nature and the relationship between the two are viewed (interactively) as a part of this structuring but not the whole of it. In terms of action, this perspective calls for struggles over both resources and meanings.

Spiritual ecology and ecotheology reinstate theological doctrines and metaphysical stances rejected by hegemonic rationalisation and perpetuated by the notions of the Cartesian cogito. According to these perspectives, sacralisation of nature is viewed as an ecologically viable proposition to combat the present-day ecological crisis; sacralisation as instrumental in nature preservation, also bringing in dimensions of embedded morality in human nature relationships; soul-cosmos relations revealing the individual being as the microcosm of the macrocosmic universe and the universe as a manifestation of the Ultimate Reality. Whereas spiritual ecology draws from soteriological traditions to formulate abstract epistemologies, the starting point of ecotheology is the sacredness dimensions in religious traditions pertaining to nature; picking strands from the theoretical approaches to the study of religion-phenomenology, hermeneutics and cultural analytical, drawing from the basic principles of natural theology seeking evidences for a God in the phenomena of nature.

Spiritual ecology encompasses certain transfigured perennial values, which in some transcendental mystical way pass beyond the empirical end of history into the 'transcendental great beyond' (Berdyaev, 1916). Drawing from Illingworth (1898), the underlying contention of spiritual ecology is the teleological relation between matter and spirit; spirit being the final cause of matter. Adapting Drummond's (1884) framework, it can be said that the basic proposition of spiritual ecology consists of the postulate that 'nature is a part of Revelation'. Thus, the primary concern of spiritual ecology is defining the nature of reality in terms of human-nature relationships from which two conceptual trends emerge – ideational (the ultimate true reality is supersensory and suprarational) and idealistic (the ultimate true reality is infinite, which contains all differentiations and which is infinite qualitatively and quantitatively) (Sorokin, 1952). Gaia hypothesis as a spiritual worldview commences with soteriology (the epistemological stance of transcendentalism) (Lovelock, 1983). Gaia is metaphorically equated to the ineffable universe and 'beings' are considered to be components of Gaia. Developing upon the Gaia hypothesis, Kirschner (1989) has arrived at the following variations: Influential Gaia (cosmic entities influencing each other); co-evolutionary Gaia (harmonious evolution); homeostatic Gaia (existential harmony) and teleological Gaia [which holds that the earth's atmosphere is kept in homeostasis not just by the biosphere, but by and for (in some sense) the biosphere]. Earlier conceptual contributions include Bonifazi's (1978) attempt at a discourse analysis of the 'soul of the world' by a discussion of the realm of the unknown pertaining to the phenomena of nature, drawing greatly from Locke's theory of knowledge exhorting for recognition of the horizons between what is and what is not comprehensible by us. Sjoo and Barbara (1987) have discussed the spiritual dimension in ecological discourses in accordance with the divine feminine principle. Another contribution is McDaniel's (1984) conceptualisation of spirituality in ecological discourses comprising the 'reverence for life principle'. Nollman (1990) focused on the transformation of spiritual consciousness proposing 'ecological process spirituality', that is, each stage in the evolutionary process represents a case in divine goodness. The main tenet of Nollman's spiritual reconnection is that nature is a process of fluid energy and self-organising wholes.

Ecotheology draws from a plethora of theological writings (akin to the earlier natural theology tradition) to then adapt the tenets into discourses on nature. According to Hicks (1989), ecotheology concentrates on the naturalistic definition of religion combining the phenomenological aspects dealing with dimensions of the sacred and the other cosmological arguments. Reat and Perry (1991) have proposed that ecotheology is based on certain design arguments which are moral ideals and notions of moral interconnectedness embedded in human-nature relationships; and a naturalistic worldview that includes interpretation of the phenomena of interface of religion and nature in its totality. Burghart and Cantlie (1993) have made the following propositions: acceptance of the 'resacralisation of nature' hypothesis and transformation of human consciousness and nature from self-centeredness to reality centeredness. Some conceptual developments in the Indian context on ecotheology have been by Vannucci (1992) and Chaitanya (1992). Researching into certain indigenous cultural contexts, Vannucci (1992) conceptualises ecotheology as 'being's' eagerness to participate in the cosmic drama. In the indigenous thought world, there is no distinction between the sacred and the profane – this direction set against the postulate of the Renaissance West that the measure of fulfilment is the conquest of nature. Chaitanya (1992) propounds that instead of the social contract of Hobbes that anchored in the advantage of each, ecotheology proposes a liberating contract with nature, and along the lines of Durkheim, the sacred is identified as the most fundamental religious idea or phenomenon.

Queer Theorisations and Movements of Alternative Sexuality Orientations (Lesbians-Gays-Bisexuals-Transgenders)

As contemporary manifestations, the understandings of queer theorisations have looked at the postmodern questions of identity and relationships within differential domains. Owing to the aporetic nature of the subject matter available under diverse headings and understandings, the key positions and arguments that feed into the movement have been presented here. Primarily these movements operate on the premise of gender as a social construct and more specifically the mainstream notion that there are only two sexes is refuted. At the purely biological level there is no male-female division and it is believed that in the beginning the embryo is sexually differentiated. Researchers have pointed out that there are large differences between persons of the same sex in terms of hormonal patterns. Therefore, men will have widely differing degrees of maleness from each other. Others have, depending on the balance between male-female characteristics, classified intermediate hermaphrodite sexes as ferms, herms and merms – rejecting sexual binaries and chromosomal determinism (Talwar, 1999). The other aspect that is explored is that of identity and community – against the theoretical backdrop of Appadurai and alternative-sexuality and queer theorisations. Thus, alternative sexuality theorisations have traced the genealogy of identity categories – from criminalisation, pathological conditions, legal and social condemnations and the subsequent rupture in the 1960s when the modern movement exploded as a component of the larger liberation movements. There was a demand for a new social contract and the attempt to create a clear social identity organised around sexuality. The AIDS epidemic in the 1980s accompanied by a strong societal homophobia was followed by a phase in the 1980s and 1990s comprising continued mainstreaming.

Queer theorisation possesses a liberation agenda, which attempt to be inclusive of a wide umbrella of sexual minorities and is associated with social constructionism and postmodernism inspired by French poststructuralist theory. The core proponents of queer theory are Judith Butler, Eve Kosofsky Sedgwick, David Halperin and Michael Warner – playfulness, power, indeterminacy and performance being the main contentions. Gender and sexuality are seen as social constructs to be performed, reinforced through repetition and possibly subverted. These scholars were influenced by the works of Louis Althusser, Jacques Derrida, Michel Foucault and Jacques Lacan. Opposing heterosexual hegemony, they rejected the Renaissance notion of the subject being fixed, unifying and self-determining and argued that the notion was an ideological fiction that worked to conceal and thereby perpetuate modern relations to power (Shahani, 2008).

Queer conceptualisations in the Indian context have been by Vanita (2002) who has examined texts that represent same sex relations and also many that constitute a continuity of discourse, by speaking to one another across time within particular linguistic and literary critical traditions. The proposition is that colonial and nationalist sentiments have contributed to the rewriting of multivocal sexuality traditions into univocal and unilinear ones. The modern erasure of early homocentrisms is ascribed to colonialism – heterosexualisation of the Ghazal, suppression of the Rekhti (premodern Urdu poetry narrated in a feminine voice) and the introduction of the anti-sodomy law are three markers of this transition. Further, colonial labelling of all male-male relations as inappropriate, even 'unnatural' and 'criminal', displaced precolonial readings of such relations as appropriate or inappropriate based on social status (free/slave; agent/object) rather than gender, and this displacement constitutes to be dominant even today. Assertions of equity have been defined through texts and literature that in general demonstrate a homosexual anticolonial utopianism, thereby deconstructing binaries. However modern Indian heterosexism continues to be manifested in the politics of reception, canon formation and misreading. Further, there is a structuring of homophobia by masculinities that become normative in colonial and postcolonial nationalisms. Gender-based anxieties (masculinity involving fear of the feminine in women and men; female-female desire undermining both masculinity and female homosociality) are deeply intertwined with anxieties around religious, community and national identities. Further, ambiguity in literary contents (Ghazals) on arenas of gender and identity serves to protect its content from colonial critiques – hence, transgression, reconfigurations and fictionalising become the order of the day. Homosexuality and in particular male-male friendships have been examined that constitute an identity that crosses space and time.

Rao and Sarma (2009) have, within the context of queer relationship understandings, provided a critique of heteronormativity (co-opting queers into the perpetual illusion of a heteropatriarchal family). Queer relationships and sexuality, whether genuinely submissive or transgressive, inverts the notion of sameness and difference. What is same/similar in nontransgressive sexuality is different here, for example, age and class. On the other hand, what is different in nontransgressive sexuality is same here, for example, gender. There is a redefinition of the 'other' in the self/other binary of relationships. Further, the postcolonial metaphor predominates – questioning the colonial hegemony on sexuality or rather heterosexuality as a deterministic norm.

Understandings of queer movement in the Indian context are further sharpened through a host of empirical material – social anthropological and literary in nature. In the Indian context, queer studies and studies on homosexuality have been undertaken by Vanita (2002), Ugra (2006) and Rao and Sarma (2009). Vanita (2002) has explored domains of same sex love and eroticism in Indian culture through historicity, Ugra (2006) has literary renditions on the male-male desire and Rao and Sarma (2009) have undertaken in-depth interviews to map the existential experiences of 21 queer persons. Studies have been undertaken on how the colonialists and the nationalists have re-written traditions by suppressing and misreading texts. Bhaskaran (2002) has provided the historical context for the most dramatic shift from the precolonial – the uniform criminalisation of all sexual relationships deemed unnatural. Kugle (2002), through an engaging translation of precolonial Perso-Urdu poetic texts, has shown how once widely celebrated tropes of male-male love were erased or re-written by Urdu litterateurs in the period immediately following the British suppression of the 1857 revolt as well as by the nationalists. Petievich (2002) has examined how in the same period a whole genre of Urdu poetry was labelled obscene. Chatterjee (2002) has through a historical study proposed that the colonial labelling of all male-male relations as inappropriate, even 'unnatural' and 'criminal', and displaced precolonial readings of such relations as appropriate or inappropriate based on social status (free/slave; agent/object) rather than gender, continues to be dominant even today. Sweet (2002) has undertaken a hermeneutical study looking at readings and misreading of the Kama Sutra in the nineteenth and twentieth-century India. Gandhi (2002), Dasgupta (2002), George (2002), Vanita (2002) and Cohen (2002) have examined how contesting discourses on same sex love are deployed in printed literature. Whereas Gandhi (2002) has explored the homosexual anticolonial utopianism in the works of Edward Carpenter and rewritten by novelists such as Vikram Seth, Dasgupta (2002) has discerned similar boundary crossing impulses in Suniti Namjoshi's fables and poetry. George (2002) has studied same-sex love instances in Kamala Das's fiction, and Cohen (2002) has revisited lively circulations of male-male desire in Ghazals prominent in Uttar Pradesh. In the genre of audio-visual media, Hansen's (2002) exploration of female impersonation in the late nineteenth and early twentieth-century drama which set in motion stylistic and behavioural trends that influenced both cinema actresses and 'real' women's performances of femininity. Other studies in the vein of culture studies include those by Muraleedharan (2002), who has examined male bonding in three popular Malayalam films, has argued that films ostensibly addressed to straight audiences have greater potential for encouraging a wide range of queer responses than films clearly addressed to gay and lesbian audiences – homoeroticism disrupting the apparently homosocial configurations (Waugh, 2002). Ghosh (2002) has studied how female-female eroticism earlier marginalised in cinema has appeared more centrally in films of the 1990s. Further from the media studies lens, Patel (2002) and Bachman (2002) have studied the right-wing and liberal responses and the antagonisms and contradictions in a film like 'Fire'.

LGBT assertions are primarily in the realms of sexuality, identity and attempt to pose a counterculture on the basis of perpetuating relationships as demonstrated through empirical literature. The conceptualisations on LGBT stances have revealed the following propositions: Badinter (1995) proposes that constructions of gender and hence heterosexual relationships are not a natural process, but embodied in the societal rites of passage. Lingard and Douglas (1999) have examined how there is a re-traditionalisation in gender construction when masculinity is examined from the pro-feminist standpoint. This re-traditionalisation is a deconstruction of essentialist views on role behaviours and prerogatives of men and women, asserting instead for a politics of sexuality based on a balancing of strategic essentialism and strategic pluralism – thereby making a case for lesbian and gay identities. Betcher and Pollack (1993) have, from a clinical standpoint, investigated LGBT identities through the lens of identities shaped by gender orientations which in turn are influenced a great deal by soci (onto) logies.

Some of the broad strategies adopted by the queer movements as well as LGBT assertions are combination of strategic essentialism (advocating solidarity in the interest of action) and tactical pragmatism so as to ensure unity between disparate queer activist groups; pursuing equitable changes as well as a simultaneous striving for small and big changes; media to be co-opted and used in the process of building visibility; indigenisation of the movement and recognition of the role of culture; diaspora closeted and nonqueer identified groups to be co-opted in the struggle and looking closely at the issue of HIV/AIDS. Further, these movements require methodologies that move beyond the conventional binaries where heterosexuality is un-interrogated and variations are 'deviance'. The addition of sexual orientation has only expanded gendered sexual statuses to four: heterosexual man and women, gays and lesbians. Experiences of hermaphrodites, transsexuals, transvestites, bisexuals, third gender and gender rebels can only be incorporated through designs that take into consideration critical sexual politics: struggles to move beyond the confines of the inside/outside model and look at ruptures and discontinuities. What also needs to be dealt with is perhaps the institutionalised rejection of difference.

Positions within the Disability Discourse

Literature on disability movement has demonstrated few distinctive genres of thought processes – positivist (ascribing to the medical model interpretations), constructivist (aligning to the social model drawing from social construction, hermeneutics and phenomenology), subalternist (drawing from strands of Marxism, critical theory and poststructuralism particularly Foucault) and feminist materialist (drawing from feminist domains of hegemonies and intersubjectivity). In general, the literature on theorisations of disability positions is an evolving discipline and thus what has been attempted here is to present certain highlights of the prevalent thoughts.

From the positivist standpoint, the vantage point is the understanding obtained from the philosophically dominant theories of social justice – particularly egalitarianism and consequentialist theories which tend to emphasise on questions of distributive justice. This understanding is against the backdrop of the medical model of disability theorisations which adapt to the pragmatic and empirical definitions of disability. Aristotle's notions of species essentialism predicated the understanding of the medical model which views the alignment of disability with impairment and operates within that paradigm. The ideal of emancipation in terms of functioning is Aristotelian virtue ethics – the core argument being functioning adaptability given the 'situation/condition' and the ability to overcome/surmount the disabling condition and/or cope with the same (Ralston and Ho, 2010).

The constructivist standpoint proposes that the disabled lifeworlds are influenced by the common usage of categories and concepts, understanding of the world which are historically and culturally specific. Herein labels are produced and reproduced in social interactions within institutional and cultural contexts. Further, there is a focus on the 'identity' of the disabled persons as disabled within the differential social interactionist mode. From the structuralist standpoint, aspects of positive naming and defiant self-naming as 'language games' influence disability constructions. The social model with its constructivist view propounds that the social standing of disabled persons is derived from their position in relation to the wider social conditions and relations of a given society. Hence, aspects of social construction and domains of the postmodern consumer culture determine the social position of disabled persons to a great extent – affecting disabled persons self-perceived notions of social desirability (Shakespeare, 1998; Marks, 1999).

Tremain (2005) has deliberated on the poststructuralist and the subalternist vision in examining the disability movement, referring particularly to Foucault's analytics of power and genealogies of discursive knowledge that provide critical lenses for comprehending subjectivisation and related micropolitics of hegemony. What Foucault highlights in the existential domains of the disabled subjects is the dimension of subjectivisation and ontological insecurity caused by the mutually constitutive and reinforcing relationship between power and knowledge. Within the existential repertoire is the aspect of relationships of disabled persons within themselves (identity) and with other (otherness). In terms of relationships of disabled persons with identical selves, there is a certain concordance in terms of shared realities and lifeworlds and in terms of structural linguistics a 'speaking, signifying and writing' from a similar political position, discursive field and vantage point. In terms of the disabled persons' relationship with the 'other', there are aspects of critical ontology which reveal as to how these relations are those of power which are imbricated in certain regimes of truth and lead to subjectification. Disabled subjects in these genres of relationships are in marginalised and disenfranchised social locations and can develop and deliberate on the realm of subjugated knowledge. In the Foucauldian repertoire thus, varied conceptualisations of normality, normativity and normalism are questioned, simultaneously implicating an operation of power within them. Further, within the gamut of the disability movement, are also discourses of inclusion/exclusion – inclusion implying an impulse for homogeneity – the very premise that Foucault attempts to challenge. At the same time, exclusion is coercive politics and hence undesirable. Hence, the locus classicus of movements in the context of disabled persons is to strike a balance between the telos of inclusion/exclusion – recognising simultaneously the archaeology and genealogy of the same.

The feminist materialist stance looks at previously taken for granted hegemonic categories as a means of challenging oppression. Feminist arguments within the disability set up have taken resort to questioning hegemonies akin to those observed under gender dimorphism (Morgan, 2005). Gender dimorphism as explained by Morgan (2005) refers to societies governed by a Gender Dimorph Utopia (GDU) – wherein practices that constitute gender dimorphism govern all manner of social and personal life. In GDU and other secular heteronormative societies, an 'apparatus of gender' operates. Foucault has defined the elements of the apparatus as a thoroughly heterogeneous ensemble consisting of discourses, institutions and regulatory forms. In GDU and other heteronormative cultures, this apparatus of gender naturalises gender dimorphism – any divergence from this naturalised gender dimorphism calls for an array of socio-discursive forms of gender policing. To that extent, it is a structuralist questioning of gender hierarchies on the one hand and the need for a self-valuation and visibility of disabled women within the mainstream women's movement on the other. The second strand within the feminist materialist stance comprehends the relationships between disabled women and nondisabled society that is composed of vantage points of the 'nondisabled patriarchal bourgeoisie'. Exposing the category of the nondisabled as an uncontested category of research and urging the nondisabled to explore the complexity and multiplicity of their own identities as a precursor to being able to understand and make connections with the disabled 'feminine other' who have complex and multiple identities is the main contention (Tregaskis, 2004).

In Summary

Subaltern voices and praxis nuances have emerged through the Dalit movements, tribal assertions, women's movements, discourses on ecology and alternative sexuality and disability discourses. These provide positionalities – each having normative and ideational components embedded within them. In a coagulation they form assertions, movements and reinstatements of erstwhile unheard voices.

In terms of the Dalit movements, commencing with the Bhakti period and social reform movements, the autonomous Dalit movements saw their origins in the caste *sabhas* and subsequently in the 1920s with the Adi movements and the autonomous movements along with the crucial Gandhi-Ambedkar debate. Subsequently, Dalit Panthers in Maharashtra drawing upon the Phule-Ambedkarite ideology along with development of Dalit literature made important assertions. The prominent positions within the Dalit movements reveal trajectories along the lines of Dalit Buddhism, Dalit Christian theology and the Dalit political perspectives as also Dalit feminism. Tribal stances have largely been anti-establishment – in the northeast the core issue has been that of ethnicity and subnationalisms along with issues of identity; in the other parts of the country it has been radical assertions within the state machinery as also visibility, justice and rights.

The women's movement in the transnational and national contexts commences with the Archimedean standpoint of patriarchy – understood as a totality of structural conditions that dominates, oppresses and exploits women. In the international context, the women's movement can be understood in terms of the three waves – the first wave focussing on issues of suffrage and equity (works of Wollstonecraft and Mill) and also Marxist feminist assertions of examining relations of productions, women's work and the domestic labour debate. The second wave focused on issues of sexuality and reproduction – existentialist feminism, psychoanalytical feminism and the radical feminist thought predominating the scene. The third wave has been around issues of multiple identities and assertions as also the writings of the Third World and Black feminists with their differential agenda. In the Indian context, instances of feminist assertions have been visualised through the Bhakti period, as also social reform and the nationalist struggle. However, postindependence assertions have been more protest oriented – interfacing with issues of religion, ecology and development. Some of the clear stances of the women's movement in the indigenous context have been an aversion towards Eurocentric notions of feminism, the discussions around Brahminical patriarchy and versions of Dalit feminism.

Discourses on ecology have unveiled various stances: Deep ecology, social ecology, radical ecology, ecofeminism, spiritual ecology and ecotheology. Queer theorisations and LGBT assertions have looked at aspects of social construction of gender and issues of identity and community. Discourses on disability have ranged from positivist alignments towards the medical model to more constructivist alignments stemming from the social model, poststructuralist notions as well as the feminist materialist stance. All the aforementioned stances contribute towards the subaltern versions and assertions, positionalities and different domains of praxis.

9

Social Work Perspectives in the Light of Theory, Positions and Movements

In the previous chapters, the various agendas for social theory and norms and forms of positions and movements have been examined. This chapter examines the positionalities in social work through historicity, the epistemic and praxis interlinkages with theory, positions and movements. Such an attempt has been previously undertaken by Howe (1987) in looking at social work theory. Using the paradigms of Burrell and Morgan (1979), Howe (1987) has developed four distinct paradigms that would help analyse social theory – radical humanism (consciousness raising), radical structuralism (revolution), interpretivism (meaning search) and functionalism (fixing). Within functionalism are located the systems theory, psychoanalysis and behavioural social work. Within interpretivism is client-centred and interactionist social work. Radical humanism as raisers of consciousness, tackle alienation from a fourfold stance: reification of society (Georg Lukacs), notion of ideological hegemony (Antonio Gramsci), idea of one dimensional man (Marcuse) and pathology of communication (Habermas). Consciousness raising is through radical practice and feminist social work. Based on a materialist view of the world, radical structuralists operate on norms of conflict and aim at redistribution of wealth and power through the method of socialist welfare work and Marxist practice.

This chapter looks at the various extant positionalities in social work through historicity: organised and scientific charity, clinical social work, ecological social work, radical social work, feminist social work and critical and anti-oppressive social work. For each of the perspectives, the linkages with theory, positions and movements are sought – thereby attempting to strengthen the understanding of the stances through their epistemological roots. The trajectory that is followed is that each of the perspectives has been explained through history and current positions and subsequently the linkages are sought.

Organised and Scientific Charity

The origins of organised and scientific charity lie at the continuum of theology and rationalism – both demonstrating endeavours to streamline philanthropy and charity as preliminary organs of social work. Some of the historical events that stand testimony to the same can be enumerated here: In 1750 BC in Babylonia, King Hammurabi issued his code of justice, which included a requirement that the 'people help one another during times of hardship'. In 1200 BC in Israel, the Jewish people were told that God expected them to help the poor and disadvantaged. Around 500 BC, philanthropy, from the Greek word for 'acts of love for mankind', was institutionalised in the Greek city-states. Citizens were encouraged to donate money, which was used for the public good. In 300 BC in China, the Analects of Confucius declared humans to be social beings bound to one another by Jen, a form of sympathy that was often expressed through helping those in need. Around 100 BC, in Rome, the annona civica tradition in which patrician families distributed free or low-cost grain to all Roman citizens in need was well established. Around 30 AD, the altruistic teachings of Christ predominated and around third century AD, Christianity was institutionalised by the Roman Emperor Constantine and the more affluent converts were to donate funds which the Church would utilise for the care of the poor. Around the fourth century AD, the hospitals developed in the Indian subcontinent which provided shelter for the poor and disabled persons and resembled almshouses. In 542 AD, similar such institutions were established in China and Middle East, and in Europe the first Hotel Dieu or the House of God was established in Lyons, France, that was staffed primarily by religious workers and volunteers. In 1084 AD, almshouses for the poor and disabled, similar to the hospitals in France, were established in Canterbury, England. In 1100 AD, the Roman Church issued the Decretum, a compilation of its canon law, which included an elaborate discussion of the theory and practice of charity. It stated that the rich have a legal and moral obligation to support the poor. Around the fourteenth century with the breakdown of feudalism, the vulnerability of the serfs and peasants surfaced. As a response to the same, in 1349, the Statute of Labourers was issued in England, wherein begging and almsgiving was outlawed except for the aged and those unable to work. Distinction was made between worthy poor (who were the destitute, widows and elderly) and the unworthy poor (comprising able-bodied unemployed men) (Hands, 1968).

In 1526, Juan Luis Vives, a Spaniard living in northern Europe, developed a plan for organised relief. It included registering the poor, raising private funds to help them and creating employment for the able-bodied poor. Many of his ideas were later used in European cities and influenced the Poor Laws in England and colonial America in the next century. In 1531, England's first statute dealing with poor relief was issued empowering local justices to license certain people (the aged and handicapped) to beg in their own neighbourhoods and to give harsh punishment to any unlicensed beggars. In 1536, the Henrician Poor Law, also known as the Act for the Punishment of Sturdy Vagabonds and Beggars, was established. In 1572, in England, a national tax called the Parish Poor Rate was levied. This was accompanied by a register of persons needing relief and funds left over from poor relief were used to create jobs for the able-bodied. In 1601, the Elizabethan Poor Law was established built on experiments of the earlier Henrician Poor Law (1536) and the Parish Poor Rate (1572). This legislation became the major codification of dealing with the poor in colonial America. In 1625 AD, Father Vincent de Paul (canonised as Saint Vincent de Paul in 1737) established seminaries, religious orders and charitable organisations to care for the poor of France and was the founder of organised charity in Europe. In many of those nations that did not become Protestant during the Reformation, the Church rather than the state retained more responsibility for the care of the poor. In 1642, Plymouth Colony enacted the first poor law in the New World, based on the Elizabethan Poor Law of 1601. In 1657, the first private welfare organisation in America, known as Scots' Charitable Society, was established in Boston. In 1662, the Law of Settlement and Removal was established in England as one of the world's first 'residency requirements' in determining eligibility to receive help. Municipal authorities were authorised to help only poor local citizens and to expel from their jurisdictions anyone else who might become dependent for assistance. This law caused authorities to evaluate people as to the likelihood of their becoming poor. Thus, though the law was basically harsh and punitive, some efforts to look at the causes of poverty were codified (Delon, 2001).

In 1697, the workhouse system was developed in Bristol and soon spread throughout England and parts of Europe. It was designed to keep down poor taxes by denying aid to anyone who refused to enter a workhouse. These institutions were usually managed by private entrepreneurs who contracted with the legal authorities to care for the residents in exchange for using their work. In 1729, Ursuline Sisters of New Orleans established America's first residential institution for orphaned children. In 1773, the colonies' first hospital for the mentally ill was established in Williamsburg, Virginia. In 1782, the Gilbert Act was passed in England, enabling humanitarians, appalled by the exploitation of workhouse residents, to institute reforms in many English jurisdictions. Many workhouses were closed, assistance to the poor in their own home was established and children under six were placed with families. Many private entrepreneurs were replaced by municipal employees as managers of the remaining workhouses. Kant in his lectures on Ethics made a link between poverty and charity (Infield, 1963). In 1790, the first publicly funded orphanage in the United States was established in Charleston, South Carolina. In 1795, the Speenhamland system was inaugurated. In the English district of Speenhamland a 'poverty line' was developed, and some workers were made eligible for subsidisation whenever their wages were below the amount. The amount was based on the price of bread and the worker's number of dependents. As prices increased or wages declined, the public treasury made up the difference. In 1798, the US Public Health Service was established. In 1819, Scottish preacher and mathematician Thomas Chalmers assumed responsibility for Glasgow's poor. He developed private philanthropies to help meet the economic needs of the poor and organised a system of volunteers to meet individually and regularly with disadvantaged people to give them encouragement and training. In 1824, the Bureau of Indian Affairs was established, which was the first federal organisation to attempt to provide direct assistance in the welfare of some Americans. In 1833, Antoine Frederic Ozanam established the Saint Vincent de Paul Society in Paris, using lay volunteers to provide emergency economic and spiritual assistance to the poor. In 1834, the new Poor Law was established in England to reform the Elizabethan Poor Law (1601). The underlying emphasis of the new law was on self-reliance. Public assistance was not considered a right, and government was not seen as responsible for the unemployed. The principle of 'less eligibility' (a recipient of aid could never receive as much as the lowest-paid worker) was enforced. In 1835, The Reverend Joseph Tuckerman, a Unitarian minister who was influenced by the reports of Thomas Chalmers's work in Scotland, organised the Boston Society for the Prevention of Pauperism. This organisation uses many of Chalmers's principles of individualised work with poor families, volunteer visitors, coordinated fundraising, and social action. Tuckerman's organisation was influential in the subsequent development of the Charity Organisation Societies (Barker, 1987).

In 1843, Robert Hartley, using the teachings of Thomas Chalmers, Joseph Tuckerman, and French philanthropist Baron de Gerando, established the New York Association for Improving the Condition of the Poor. The association stressed character building as a way to end poverty. Volunteers, usually middle-class Protestant laypersons, worked to get poor people to abstain from alcohol, become more self-disciplined and acquire the work ethic. In 1844, the first YMCA was established in London, England. In 1845, as a result of the social movement led by Dorothea Dix, the first state asylum for the mentally ill was established in Trenton, New Jersey. In 1853, the Reverend Charles Loring Brace, concerned about the plight of New York's street children and children living in almshouses, organised the Children's Aid Society. The society transported thousands of children every year to the West to live with rural families. In 1854, US Congress, pressured by Dorothea Dix's movement on behalf of the mentally ill, allocated funds and land to build mental hospitals. President Franklin Pierce voted the legislation, saying that charity was the province of the states and localities. In 1862, the Homestead Act was passed, giving 160 acres of unoccupied public land to any American citizen who agreed to live on it for five years. In 1863, Massachusetts established a state board of charities to investigate and supervise its almshouses, prisons and mental institutions. Other states soon followed suit. The Red Cross was established in Switzerland by writer Jean Henri Dunant, and soon there were Red Cross organisations in many other nations. In 1865, at the end of the Civil War, the United States established its first federal welfare agency, the Freedmen's Bureau, to provide temporary relief, education, employment and health care for the newly released slaves. In 1869 in London the first Charity Organisation Society was established – formally named the 'Society for Organising Charitable Relief and Repressing Mendicity', the society worked to coordinate efforts at fundraising and to disburse funds in a systematic fashion. Volunteers were recruited to befriend applicants for assistance, make individual assessments of the reasons for their poverty and help correct those reasons. By 1874, members of private charity organisations, religious agencies and public officials from several northeastern states in the United States began meetings to discuss their mutual concerns. These meetings lead to the establishment of the National Conference of Charities and Corrections (later named the National Conference on Social Welfare). In 1877, using the London organisation as his model, the Reverend S. Humphreys Gurteen established America's first Charity Organization Society (COS) in Buffalo, New York. Volunteer workers dispensed advice rather than money to the poor and information about them to philanthropists and private relief agencies. In 1878, the Reverend William Booth reorganised his East London Revival Society as the Salvation Army. In newly united Germany, Chancellor Otto von Bismarck established, in 1883, a national health insurance system and, shortly thereafter, accident insurance and old age and invalid insurance programmes. This system became a model for social security programmes in many other nations. In 1884, Toynbee Hall, the first settlement house, was established in London by Vicar Samuel A. Barnett. The settlement movement spread quickly, and facilities were developed in most larger British and American cities. Their philosophy was to eliminate the distance between socioeconomic classes by locating settlements in working-class neighbourhoods where ideas and information could be exchanged. In 1886, Stanton Coit, who had resided in Toynbee Hall, opened America's first settlement house, the Neighborhood Guild, in New York. Eventually more than 400 houses were established and their residents were involved in social advocacy, group work and community development. In 1889, in Chicago, Jane Addams and Ellen Gates Starr opened Hull House, which became one of the most influential social settlement houses in the United States (Bailey and Lee, 1982).

In 1890, the Consumer's League was established in England and, later, in the United States. The League, under the leadership of social worker-lawyer Florence Kelley, established local chapters in most larger communities and led successful campaigns to abolish child labour practices and to achieve minimum wages and shorter working hours as well as safe and effective consumer products. In 1894, Amos G. Warner's 'American Charities' the first US social welfare textbook was published. The first school of social work was established in 1898 – the New York School of Philanthropy (later to become the Columbia University School of Social Work) which grew out of a series of summer workshops and training programmes for volunteers and friendly visitors and offered a one-year educational programme. Faculty member and COS administrator, Mary E. Richmond, published 'Friendly Visiting Among the Poor'. By 1900, educator Simon N. Patten coined the term 'social workers' and applied it to friendly visitors and settlement house residents. He and Mary Richmond disputed whether the major role of social workers should be advocacy or delivering individualised social services. In 1902, Homer Folks, founder and head of the New York State Charities Aid Association, published 'Care of Destitute, Neglected and Delinquent Children'. His philosophy becomes influential in subsequent child welfare goals and methods. In 1903, Graham Taylor and others established the Chicago School of Civics and Philanthropy, which eventually became the University of Chicago School, of Social Service Administration. In 1905, a social service department was established in Massachusetts General Hospital in Boston to help patients deal with the social problems of their illnesses. In 1907, psychiatric social work began at Massachusetts General Hospital wherein social workers were hired to work with mentally ill patients. In 1909, the National Association for the Advancement of Colored People (NAACP) was founded in the United States. Social workers Mary White Ovington and Henry Moskowitz and others helped establish this voluntary organisation oriented towards the protection of the legal and social rights of Blacks and other minorities. At the same time, President Theodore Roosevelt convenes the first White House conference, bringing together social workers and other leaders to discuss the problems of America's children. Workmen's compensation laws were passed in 1910 to protect the wage earners as also social security programmes. In 1912, the US Children's Bureau headed by Julia Lathrop was established and in 1913, the US Department of Labour was created to promote the welfare of American workers. In 1917, Mary Richmond published *Social Diagnosis* as the first formal text in social work. Subsequently, the COS became oriented increasingly towards helping families and thus many local societies change their names to Family Welfare Agency (Barker, 1987). In the Indian context, organisation of charity and philanthropy was largely through religion and faith-based initiatives and the efforts of the royalty. Social reform brought to foreground certain issues of concern which bordered more on rights and empowerment vis-à-vis charity organisation. Faith-based initiatives as also the welfare initiatives of the state and establishment continue to be organs for systematising charity and philanthropy in the Indian context.

Organised and Scientific Charity in the Light of Theory, Positions and Movements

Figure 1 *Organised and Scientific Charity: Interface with Theory, Positions and Movements*

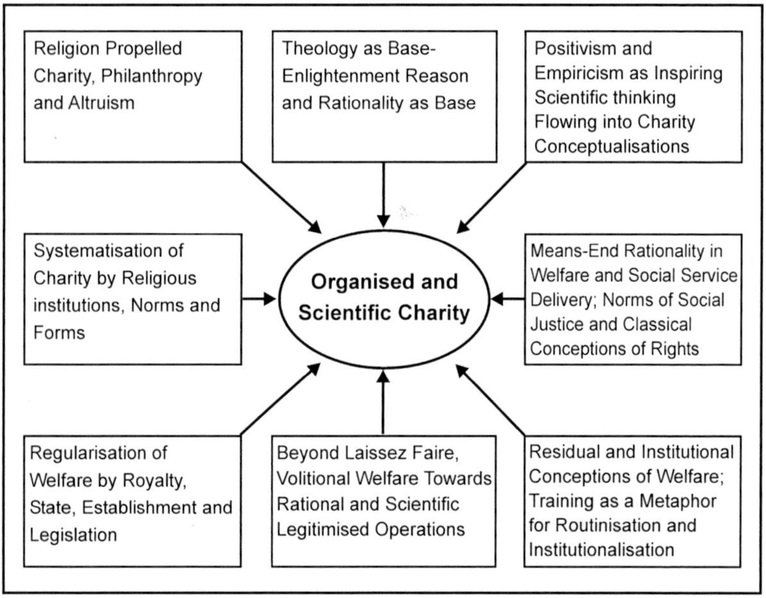

As displayed in Figure 1, the interface of organised and scientific charity with realms of theory, positions and movements can be sought as follows:

- The social dimensions of theology and religion form the base of charity with the morality embedded praxis and teleological ethics embedded within it. This led to the systematisation of charity, philanthropy through religious institutions and ensuing norms and forms of religiosity in praxis.
- The other domain of regularisation of charity emerged through the regularisation of welfare by the royalty, state, establishment and legislation which moved welfare beyond a laissez faire and volitional domain towards more rational and scientific legitimised operations.

- Hence beyond theology, enlightenment reason and rationality emerged as a base of scientific charity – propelled further by positivisms penchant for scientism and logic. Charity conceptualisations were thus influenced by reason and rationality – a conception of welfare that emerged from notion of public good and totalitarian ethics. Further, classical notions of social justice and human rights also have implications on the notions of justice and rights and subsequently welfare. These include Plato's principle of justice as governed by the ideal of equality and Aristotelian 'isotes' (geometric equality and proportionality proposing that 'equal' (just, fair) distribution of persons with unequal merit would have to be unequal). Further, there are contentions of Mill (social justice as any system of distribution and redistribution that is governed by valid moral principles) and Hobhouse (social justice as the test of operative consistency and method of synthesis of rights and duties). In terms of human rights, the classical and modern philosophers' view human rights as natural rights with differentials in terms of the role of state, is the lynchpin. Classical philosophers comprise deliberations by Plato, Aristotle, Cicero, Aquinas and Hugo Grotius as also Ockham. The modern perspectives are by Thomas Hobbes, John Locke, Spinoza, Immanuel Kant, Edmund Burke, Thomas Paine, Rousseau, Marx and Wollstonecraft. The central themes expressed within Immanuel Kant's moral philosophy such as the ideas of equality and the moral autonomy of rational human beings have important bearings on the philosophy of human rights as also welfare and organised charity.
- This effectively led to the residual (based on the trickle down approach of welfare policies to benefit the most disadvantaged) and institutional (regulated approached meant specifically for the most disadvantaged identified through a rational approach – particularly distinctions between the worthy poor and unworthy poor) conceptions of welfare impinged by poverty assessments and subsequently providing an Archimedean standpoint for 'training' for 'professional social work' – a metaphor for routinisation, legitimation, institutionalisation and regimentation.

Clinical Social Work

In 1917 with Mary Richmond's book 'Social Diagnosis', the clinical paradigm took shape. In 1926, the American Association of

Psychiatric Social Workers (AAPSW) was founded, as social work increasingly then composed of caseworkers and clinical practitioners. The US Veterans Bureau began employing social workers in its hospitals. In 1929, the Milford Conference convened to discuss whether social work is a disparate group of technical specialties or a unified profession with integrated knowledge and skills. The conclusion was that social work was one profession with more similarities than differences among its specialties. In 1929, the report of the conference was published as *Social Case Work: Generic and Specific*. In 1930, in United States, after the Great Depression, Virginia Robinson, with Jessie Taft, developed the Functional School of Social Case Work and published the first comprehensive text to integrate social and psychodynamic concepts titled 'A Changing Psychology in Social Casework'. Grace Coyle published the first comprehensive text on group work, Social Process in Organised Groups. In 1935, the US Social Security Act was signed into law. It included a workers' retirement insurance programme and coverage for dependent survivors and disabled workers. The act also establishes a federal welfare programme that helped states pay for and administer programmes in Old Age Assistance, Aid to the Blind, Aid to Dependent Children and General Assistance for needy people who did not qualify for other forms of help. Social worker Jane Hoey was appointed head of the US Bureau of Public Assistance. She influenced the state departments of public assistance so that qualified applicants for help received counselling as well as income maintenance. In 1954, in social casework, the so-called diagnostic and functional schools began to merge and lose their separate identities. The functional schools had been oriented towards a highly focused, goal-oriented approach to casework intervention. The diagnostic school had been influenced by Freudian theory, but adherents of this approach developed more of a psychosocial orientation in the 1950s. In 1962, President John F. Kennedy signed into law the social security amendments, which provided greatly increased federal support for states to employ social workers and others. The workers would provide counselling and training to help people get off the welfare rolls. In 1963, the Joint Commission on Mental Illness and Health issued its findings. President Kennedy signed into law the Community Mental Health Centers Act, which funded development of mental health centres, training programmes and outpatient treatment programmes (Barker, 1987).

Thus, clinical social work which gained further predominance after the World War II focused on solving dysfunctional behaviour patterns. The emphasis was primarily on the counselling roles of social workers, drawing from psychological sciences and psychoanalysis in particular. Hence, classical psychoanalysis and object relations school form the base for clinical practice (Yelloly, 1980; Goldstein, 1984; Preston-shoot and Agass, 1990). Classical psychoanalysis is based on Freudian understanding of unconscious sexual impulses and hedonism (pleasure/gratification seeking) – sexuality and hedonism understood as naturalistic. Further, analytical philosopher Arthur Schopenhauer has combined this understanding of human behaviour as forms of sexual desire and reduced it to the reproductive instincts of the members of the species – a 'will to live'. Hence, Freud and Schopenhauer look at human behaviour as an inevitable reflection of the biological nature with the conception of it as the free creation of the individual human will. Thus, there is continuity in behaviour patterns across periods and cultures (Gilbert, 1991). The object relations school carries forward Freudian arguments wherein the individual psychic structure is based on sexuality impulses and culture enters it relatively late in life through the ideology of the superego. This school believes that human behaviour is motivated by unconscious feelings and beliefs stemming from sexuality.

Within the clinical paradigm there is the contextual approach which focuses on techniques such as life validation, life review and interventions; assessment of individual psychology; assessment of family or systemic transactions and assessment of relational ethics. In terms of relational ethics, specifically two broad domains have been focussed upon – the quality of interpersonal relationships and their stability. Stability aspect highlights the variables that play a role in determining whether a relationship dissolves or remains intact. Two distinct positions have emerged herein – one privileging the position that relationship quality and stability are inextricably intertwined phenomena, with reduction in the quality of a relationship leading inevitably to its dissolution. The second position proposes that relationship quality and stability are not necessarily functionally interdependent attributes (Adams and Jones, 1999). The solution-focused brief therapy focuses on the problem and its immediate solution – the fact that people can resourcefully create change through meanings and experiences that are constructed between individual experiences and interactions among people. The developmental interaction model looks at the conceptualisation of all problems with a relational and developmental component. The relational component is related to the interpersonal interactions related to the problem. The developmental component refers to the changes in these interactions and in the problems over time. Bordering on the realms of social psychology, the strengths-vulnerabilities model focuses on the individual and the family life cycles (with focus on family events, themes and interpersonal processes), the developmental changes and the interactions of the individual and family life cycles to create strengths, vulnerabilities and self-enhancing factors. Hence, the clinical model has sojourned from the intensely pathological focus towards evolutionary, functional, developmental and empowerment paradigms. However, the focus remains in terms of behaviour modification, social adjustment and self-enhancement.

Clinical Social Work in the Light of Theory, Positions and Movements

Figure 2 *Clinical Social Work: Interface with Theory, Positions and Movements*

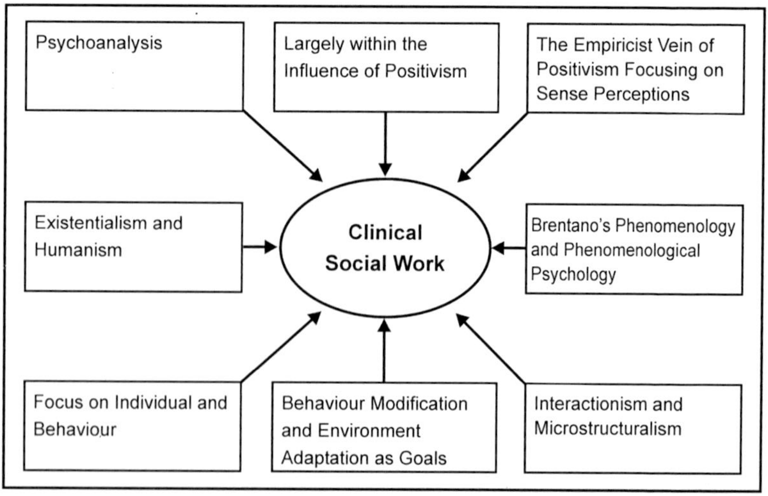

As displayed in Figure 2, the interface of clinical social work with realms of theory, positions and movements can be sought as follows:

- The chief base of clinical practice is psychoanalysis with specific reference to the works of Freud. Further, Sartrean existentialism with the focus on existential freedom also provides the underpinnings. Aesthetic existentialism proposes an existential freedom of man to say that 'there are no values external to man and no given human nature which he is obliged to fulfill' (Sartre, 1957). Humanism, drawing from existentialism, is the underlying tenet with a focus on people instead of theology, the thrust on understanding the totality of human nature and the recognition of human beings as authors of ethical, political and moral judgements. Hence, there is a focus on individual behaviours as well as behaviour modification and adaptation to the environment as concrete goals.

- Positivism with its emphasis on empiricism is also an important basis of clinical practice. The leanings are towards giving credence to the mind and sense perceptions as sources of knowledge.
- Brentano's phenomenology provides an important standpoint – from the lens of psychology he proposed the following – the empirical source of knowledge, the importance of experience and intuition. He distinguished psychological phenomena from physical phenomena and developed the doctrine of intentionality as the decisive content of psychological phenomena – acts which depict states of consciousness and transitory processes. Psychological phenomenon was divided into three basic classes – representations, judgements and emotive acts. Overall Brentano's contribution to phenomenology included widening of traditional empiricism by admitting experiences and non-inductive insights into the essential structures and relationships of empirical material; intentional reference and analogues of self-evidence in ethics.
- Phenomenological psychology with its emphasis on aspects of perceptions and experience provides understandings of the same as continual processes, each with its own autochthonous and irreducible meaning structure. It is to describe the manner in which various strata of meaning and relationships interact in our perceptions in order to determine the particular effect that they have in combination. There is a concrete description of the 'what' of experience, both in its noetic attitude and in its noematic correlate prior to and as the basis for the development of explanatory hypotheses. Thus, phenomenology is effectively a study of human expressivity. This is evident in concepts such as a pre-reflexive and apriori existence of implicit meanings of

human action and language and the 'rheoscopic' studies on human behaviour (that focus on expression in thinking and its relation to language, volition and human emotions) as having a phenomenological base. The central assumption of phenomenological psychology is that of intentionality which presents human beings as active interpreters of their experience of the world rather than passive reactors to both biophysical and environmental forces while at the same time acknowledging the role and impact of the world in shaping the means through which investigations are structured.

- Further, the phenomenological analyses of Husserl and Schutz, with aspects of lifeworld understandings, also provide a base. Lifeworld is composed of all the people perceive as their parameters of their existence and inherently is a world of natural attitude and it is the substantive content of consciousness. Interpersonal domains according to Schutz are those of intersubjectivity concerned with the 'community of attitudes' that are shared. There is a certain 'stock knowledge' which comprises a paramount reality, reciprocity of perspectives, typifications and common world presumptions.
- Interactionism and microstructuralism form another base – interactionist understanding commences with notions of the social self taken further as the analysis of self and social processes wherein self is comprehended within an interpersonal domain of relationships emerging in the context of communication with others. There are deliberations on mind, self and other aspects that aid adjustment, relationship formation and maintenance and adaptability to social environment. There are aspects of role taking, rehearsal and self-evaluation by individuals that eventually impinge on social spaces, structures and existence. Microstructuralism proposes that all macrostructures are built from certain emotional practices (rituals, forms of address) and other stereotyped presentations of self and sequences of behaviour. Denying the conception of 'structure' at the macro levels as being reifications and metaphors, the proposition rather is the 'microstructural chain of interaction rituals' that are core to human existence and relationships in the social world. Clinical practice with its intense focus on the individual holds this stance at its very core.

Ecological Social Work

Some of the historical events that preceded the development of the ecological social work paradigm can be discussed as follows: In 1936, social group workers begin regular meetings and form an association that later becomes the American Association of Group Workers (AAGW). In 1939, The Lane Report (The Field of Community Organisation, by Robert P. Lane) presented a systematic and comprehensive description of the roles, activities and methods in the field of community organisation. The work was built on previous studies by Eduard C. Lindeman in his 1921 book, *The Community*, and Jesse F. Steiner's 1930 book, *Community Organisation*. In 1940, Mary Parker Follett's posthumous book *Dynamic Administration* was published, which became an influence in the field of social welfare administration. In 1942, the Beveridge Report was issued in Great Britain, which recommended an integrated social security system that attempted to ensure cradle-to-grave economic protections for its citizens. Many of the report's recommendations went into effect after World War II. However till the 1960s, the clinical paradigm continued to dominate the profession. Alongside the focus on social justice issues that came to the forefront in the 1960s, the systems model of conceptualisation developed. This signified the coming in of the ecological and systems orientation to practice that is integrated, holistic and synthesis oriented. Society in the ecological paradigm is viewed in a systems framework which contain parts that are in an exchange relation with each other – that is, there is an interaction between systems, subsystems and related components – in the Darwinian fashion (from where essentially the classical systems framework draws its inspiration). Efforts for change are directed at the interface between systems and subsystems, the goal being enhancement of relationship between those systems. In the systems orientation, the ecological perspective has identified four components – client system, target system, action system and the change agent. Intervention is not only with the 'clients' (as in the clinical perspective) but also with the familial, social and cultural factors that impact on their social functioning (Barker, 1987; Bailey, 1989).

Traditional systems framework owes its origins to Talcott Parsons, who has proposed that as actors interact in society, they come to develop agreements and sustain patterns of interaction which become institutionalised. Such institutionalised patterns are according to Parsons called social systems. On the other hand, Niklas Luhmann proposed a general systems approach stressing the fact that human action becomes organised and structured into systems. When actions of several people become interrelated, a social system is said to exist. The basic mechanism by which actions become interrelated is communication via symbolic codes. Hence, societal systems become comprehensive systems of reciprocally accessible communication actions – which are inherently complex, the goal of the systems approach thus being to reduce complexity. Further, developments have heralded a new systems framework, the components of which are autopoiesis (self-reproduction and self-regulation), relationship between observer and observed, reduction of complexity through systems' organisation, change through the vehicle of entropy and nonequilibrium analysis, and provide a foundation for cultural and normative analysis. Kluver (2000) provides an understanding of the building blocks of complex systems – adaptation and self-organisation; self-referential dynamics (including evolution, learning and self modelling) and universal computability. Social systems are believed to consist of social actors who interact according to specific rules of interactions: the dynamics of the social systems is then the consequences of these interactions, namely, the self-organisation of social systems. According to particular demands of the environment, social systems are able to behave in an adaptive manner, that is, they can change their rules of interaction by certain meta-rules and generate this way a meta-dynamics. It is possible to model and analyse mathematically both dynamics and meta-dynamics using cellular automata and genetic algorithms – to allow the precision of natural systems. Further, there is the issue of regularities in the course of sociocultural evolution dealt with by Kluver (2002). The evolutionary process of society is defined as the generation of social roles and their relations; a role is understood as a pair of social rules and role-specific knowledge. Accordingly, evolution is the growth of cultural knowledge and the development of a network of social roles. These theoretical assumptions are clarified and tested via a mathematical model, i.e., the sociocultural algorithm (SCA). Computer simulations show that the evolutionary course of societies is determined by an evolutionary parameter, that is, the degree of differentiation or role autonomy respectively. Through an additional model of cognitive ontogenesis (aspects of mind, cognition and understanding of social beings who are a part of the society which determines their existence), it can be shown that cognitive ontogenesis and sociocultural evolution are interdependent processes that actually follow the same logic. Change in systems is through social action directed towards all components of the systems – which then lead to a higher stage in the evolution of systems.

Ecological Social Work in the Light of Theory, Positions and Movements

Figure 3 *Ecological Social Work: Interface with Theory, Positions and Movements*

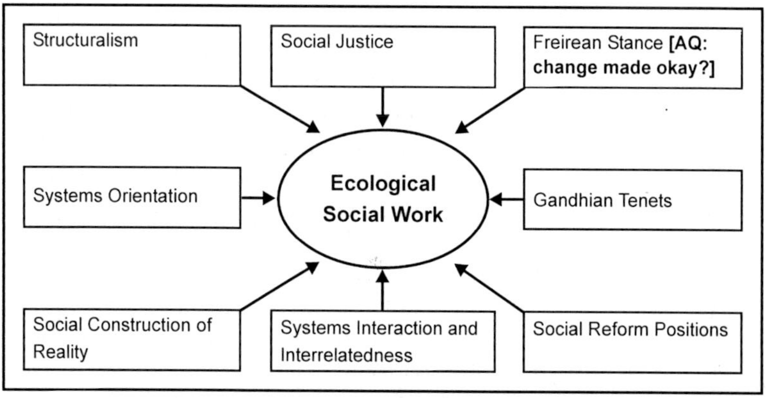

As displayed in Figure 3, the interface of ecological social work with realms of theory, positions and movements can be sought as follows:

- Structuralism and the systems framework provide the base – in the linguistic structural sense, language is the surface manifestation of fundamental mental processes which in turn are manifestations of general patterns of social and cultural organisations. Cognitive processes are viewed through the lens of ritual activities and social solidarity. Social structure as an emergent reality sui generis is understandable in terms of its own dynamics – the macrostructural norms of size, differentiation and integration as guiding points of analysis. The emphasis on systems, reality as organised in terms of binary opposites, which in turn are within the bounded rationality of language generally form the core of structuralist thought. Using Giddens' stance, social structure is viewed as utilised by active agents with mutually implicated systemic patterns – which are transformed or reproduced over time.

- Reality is construed as socially constructed – ecological social work abides by social construction of reality's notion of symbolic universes (bodies of theoretical tradition that integrate different provinces of meaning and encompassing of the institutional order in a symbolic totality) which lead to the origination social dialectics – having contentions such as the whole is a relation among parts; properties take their meanings from the whole and parts and wholes interpenetrate and change is primary.
- In terms of ideological stances – there is interlinkage with social justice, the stance of Freire, and in the indigenous context, Gandhi and tenets of social reform that emphasise on sociostructural-cultural changes. Within social justice, aspects of the ecological paradigm concur with contentions of Mill that social justice is any system of distribution and redistribution that is governed by valid moral principles and of Hobhouse that social justice as the test of operative consistency and method of synthesis of rights and duties. In the schemata of ecological perspective, embedded in the grammar of 'change' are embedded Hume's rights-based principle, Spencer's desert-based principle and Kropotkin's needs-based principles of social justice. As 'action' and 'change' are crucial to the ecological perspective, connections are alive through Freire who has discussed four keys in the struggle for social justice – literacy (the way we read the word and the world), critical consciousness, the creation of liberation and escalating economic production as people come to understand their surroundings. The key elements of Freire's construct – dialogue, discourse and critical consciousness – form the key alignment areas with the ecological stance. Critical consciousness leads to critical social justice that addresses hegemony – working against the dominant ideology and recreating reality. This further would lead to re-orientation of production through a new concept of distribution, development of critical awareness and change-oriented action. Gandhian praxis of reconstruction and action as also social reform's agenda of transitional and acculturative modes of change herald repercussions for the ecological perspective.

Feminist Social Work

Feminist social work commenced with the understanding on feminism and the women's movement. Feminist social work has at its core feminist praxis – positing an engendered subjectivity lens. The repertoire in interventions commences with the liberal stance positing realist ontologies and epistemologies and justice and equity-oriented methodologies of praxis. The Marxist/socialist stance aligning with materialist ontologies demonstrates engagements with deliberations and action that address the class hierarchies-based inequities for women in the key domains of production and reproduction. The radical stance has underlying poststructuralist epistemologies based on deconstruction of the sex class system that posits hegemonies for women in the domains of sexuality and reproduction. The postmodern stance envelops subjectivist and deconstruction-based epistemologies positing methodologies of action that examine and celebrate cultures of difference and dodges essentialisms and the micropolitics of power and violence. Embedded in the aforementioned four broad stances governing feminist praxis is an understanding of the nature of violence, power, domination, patronage and exploitation and hegemony from the Archimedean standpoint of women and their subjectivities. Feminist social work is essentially social work from an engendered lens, commencing with women centred and gender aware work towards a more political feminist stance. Feminist social work has various strands – working with women, men, families, communities, systems and structure – thus revealing the multidimensional and multisystemic framework of practice. The complexities arise due to the fact that women's realities are not universal and essential, but differential; intertwined with categories of caste, class, ethnicity and faith which create layers and intersections of power, domination and hierarchy that need to be countered.

Working with Women

Working with women encompasses the following components: understanding women within the 'structuralist' and 'conflict' societal frame; discerning the 'normal' discourses and the micropolitics of power and violence; comprehending the existential realities and the current positionalities of women (background data, duration of violence and implications in health and sexuality); linking background data to existential realities of women, thereby unearthing the intersectionalities and complexities; working with the conceptions of 'selfhood', 'womanhood' and psychological support; relooking at relationships – conjugal, consanguine and dimensions of domination; determining the range of assertions of women's rights – negotiations, support, life skills and jurisprudential; repositioning women – psychic, vital and physical (institutional and familial arrangements); and defining desirable realities with women in terms of what ought to be.

Understanding women within the conflict and societal frame implies articulation of the context, status and positionalities of women. The criticality emerges in examining the condition and position of women through critical discourses – particularly through the frame of reference of institutions precipitating inequalities. There are two broad frames that signal positionalities of women – structuralist and conflict. Multiple institutions and structures then posit that inequality. Patriarchy is an all pervasive 'norm' that mirrors structure and penetrates all institutions of the social fabric. From the 'structuralist' societal frame, interventions with women critically look at system reproduction – that is, how patterns of inequality reproduce themselves – and system contradiction – that is, from the Hegelian dialectics frame is borrowed the critical idea that material social arrangements contain patterns of social relations that are self-transforming. Further in the Durkheimian vein, there is an emphasis on social-structural differentiation and the emphasis on cognitive processes – how 'essential ideas' of space, class and substance that correspond to the most universal properties of things are like the solid frame which encloses all thought. The content of these 'essential ideas' are determined by structures of society which in turn reinforce those very structures (Acharya, 2004). The construction of 'institutional orders' through social interventions demonstrates another aspect that lays out the positionalities of women. At the level of the individual, the reproduction of societal hegemony is demonstrated in Mead's conceptualisation of 'behaviouristic structuralism' (Bryson, 1999). How existing social structures exert 'selection pressures' for the development of capacities for role taking, self and mind – which are, in turn, inherently reproductive. Social organisation is perceived to be actively sustained through the mutual reading of gestures and evaluation of selfhood/womanhood through a 'community of attitudes'. From the 'conflict' societal frame, the interventions then posit conflict as inherent in systems – facilitating a transformation of consciousness and simultaneously a polarisation precipitated by binaries. Emancipation in the conflict frame of reference, particularly through the lens of Dahrendorf's empirical categories, is an emancipation from legitimised role relationships and dichotomous authority relations – towards a redistribution. This is mirrored then onto 'realities' as perceived by feminist interventions in addressing contradictions as inherent in the social fabric (Reinharz, 1992). Hence, patriarchy is the first level of hegemony, class-caste-ethnicity being the second level. The social realities confronting women are the cultural reproduction of hegemony, un-negotiated spaces and the micropolitics of power – converted to hyperrealities of structure and structural reproduction; the utopian vision being that of structural transformation and emancipation form legitimised role relationships and dichotomous authority relations.

In terms of discerning the 'normal' discourses and the micropolitics of power and violence, feminist social work moves beyond the structuralist and conflict frame then taking a poststructuralist and postmodernist turn to address issues of 'essentialisms' and 'normalisations' (in the Foucauldian sense) towards micro categorisations, micro theory and celebrations of differences (Stanley, 1990; McCann and Kim, 2003). The following dimensions are then embedded in the analytical trajectories: women's realities are not essential and vary in accordance with differential cultural categories; historicism and culture are categorical imperatives in comprehending hegemonies; discourses that lead to 'normalisation' as macrostructural entities effecting on social realities and fabric need to be addressed (this addressing needs to move beyond real situations to hyperreal and metaphorical situations as hegemony is all pervasive); and what needs to be looked at then are 'norms' and 'forms' of gender representations, hegemony and the historical baggage that accompanies the same with intertwined dimensions of other, but crucial, categorical imperatives of class, caste and ethnicity. The conceptualisations of microdomains of power and multiple regimes of its manifestation in spheres of production and reproduction are the essence of the materialist feminist conceptions. Further, how these crucial multiple factors enliven the subalternity of women is chalked out through the analytical categories of history, culture, class and ethnicity – thereby lending credence to the poststructuralist contentions of addressing binaries and postmodernist contentions of deconstruction and difference.

The commencing point for praxis would be to understand women's vantage point. The defining criteria then translate onto comprehending the background characteristics that in effect outline the existential condition and position of women – age, socioeconomic conditions and education being primary indicators. A preliminary understanding of the nature of hegemony per se and its corresponding implications in health, sexuality and definitions of 'selfhood' is also obtained. The crucial dimension of feminist social work is to realign and reformulate the psychological self of the woman. This takes the form of first working with issues of 'selfhood' – the innate aspect of an individual woman and the notions of 'womanhood' – particularly in situations of assault on sexuality and providing then a psychological support – addressing and transforming the consciousness. This psychological support takes primarily two forms – provision of emotional support and developmental counselling. The other aspect is a reexamination of relationships within the conjugal and/or natal home. This is intricately connected to comprehending the nature of domination-subordination. This is comprehended in terms of assault on self, sexuality and rights, in the natal home, and judicial disputes emerging out of matrimonial strains and breakdowns. The range of assertions are then posited as negotiations for space – the metaphorical 'space' in the domain of conjugal/consanguine relations (as the case may be); support to enable the creation of that space through conciliation an dialogue; increase the strength of life skills through developmental counselling and the jurisprudential domain in terms of looking at property ownership and rights – matrimonial, familial and filial rights – all from the woman-centred standpoint. The assertions are then a movement towards a certain repositioning of women in the psychic, vital and physical domains. From the indicators standpoint, this is the 'empowering' move wherein the woman has greater space in all domains of her existential self. This notion of empowerment can seek alliance at two levels – one that of Sartrean freedom wherein the human (here woman) will is free to operate and choose in the domains of society and the other is that of Senian capacities and entitlements – greater diffusion, access and equity to resources, relationships and realms of power. Institutional and familial arrangements are thus geared in the direction of ensuring this emancipation for women. In the sense of utopia, the ultimate aim of feminist social work is the cartography of desirable realities. The woman's sense of comfort with her womanhood, encompassing a spate of her relationships and 'home and hearth' are primary in determining the core of all interventions and what ought to be.

Working with Men and Families

In terms of working with men and families, these are understood as composing of the meso environment of the women. It is through this that permeation into the institution of patriarchy at cognitive and vital levels takes place. Broadly the range of interventions with men and families can be categorised as follows: visualising the canvass of patriarchy and positioning feminist discourses of deconstruction; addressing the hegemony embedded in the male psyche and self; soliciting male participation in emancipation of women from oppression; understanding the 'family' in the functional sense; addressing realms of production, reproduction and sexuality of women in the household and family domains; comprehending poststructuralist deconstruction of the family; positing normative and ideational stances that move towards engendering men and families; and revisiting the social construction of gender in the family and household domains.

The commencing point herein is to comprehend the all pervasiveness of patriarchy as an institution and the fact that the roots of feminist practice lie in addressing the same. The first tryst occurs at the level of the family and the household which then escalates onto all levels of the social fabric. Unearthing the threads further, patriarchy is prevalent in linguistic and cognitive domains – determining structures of language and modes of thought, understanding and speech. In the sense of Levi-Strauss, it is these structures of language and thought governed by binaries of patriarchy that create holograms of hegemony at the microstructural level. Patriarchy then, in the words of the feminists, is a struggle concept and an omniscient institution by which men dominate, oppress and exploit women. This patriarchy is not present only in sexual binaries (men/women) but pervades all institutions of thought, cognition, structure and culture. Hence, it is a social construct based on sex class system – the 'discourse' which is addressed by the deconstructionist stance of feminist practice. This deconstruction (taking Spivak's stance of Marxist-feminist-deconstructionist position to address hierarchies) then prevails through the entire canvass of writings on patriarchy – 'erasing' popular notions of male dominance and superiority (Raheja, 2003; Rege, 2006). What emerges then is a scheme wherein patriarchy perpetuates a regime of domination and patronage which feminist deconstruction and praxis addresses. In terms of 'male psyche and self', the cognitive and subtle domains of hegemony are addressed. As patriarchy is all pervasive, this psychoanalytic approach is essential to understand structures of femininity and masculinity, psychic construction of gender identity and how gendered subjectivity is acquired based on an internalisation of certain norms and values. This dimension of intervention is thus based on addressing hegemonic masculinity through consciousness, language and meaning. What it then comprises is addressing 'anatomical determinism' and notions of 'normal' in favour of equity and justice from a feminist lens (McCann and Kim, 2003). That men need to inherently recognise the essence of equity beyond sexual binaries is the first level of assertion in the interventions. What is then addressed here are those 'unconscious mental processes' that lead to a cultural sexual imperialism. The quest then is at least towards a 'positional' identification (if not personal and diffusive identification) with women and the social construction of roles and identity. In practical terms this would translate into developing an egalitarian sense within the cognitive framework of men.

Soliciting male participation involves looking at men as a support factor – beyond the oppressive framework. Several instances in feminist practice invoke the 'supportive male figure' either in the natal or conjugal set-up. This pre-empts the engendering of men and at the same time is also a step towards moving beyond sexual binaries to seek alliance from empathetic others. Particularly, in situations wherein the best possible option for women is reconciliation and/or negotiation for greater 'spaces' – this involvement of the 'supportive male figure' plays a key role in the sense of portraying a 'liberal stance' – the Archimedean standpoint of women's emancipation. Liberal stances then become a preamble for liberatory praxis. In the general sense, the 'other' (male) is posited as one element in the regime that needs to be countered. This dimension of intervention is about looking at two things – 'sameness in the other' and the 'other as a philosophical extension of the innate self'. This philosophical essentialism also finds parallels in the liberal feminist ontology – wherein difference is disregarded as men and women are endowed with the same cognitive capacities.

Extending the earlier dimension further, the aspect of understanding the family in the functional sense takes into account the traditional anthropological 'role and functions' of the family – the accounts of Malinowski and Radcliffe-Brown wherein functional dimensions of an institution (of providing support and anchor points) play a key role in maintaining societal equilibrium (Bryson, 1999).

Feminist interventions herein take into account the fact that the 'family' and/or the household domain is the chief contact point for the individual woman's sense of ownership towards the 'meso dimensions' of the social fabric and thereby also the macro aspects of society. The fact that family in its traditionalist sense can provide a certain kind of alignment to women, particularly in situations where women choose reconciliation, arbitration and negotiation is something that cannot be negated. This also points out to an important dimension of feminist practice, that of restoring equilibrium in the woman's self and relationships with family as the key locus classicus. This integration/re-integration is not a homogeneous and cohesive enterprise. Depending on the contexts, there are philosophical and political differences in seeking the realignments – pragmatism generally prevailing in determining most appropriate/suitable options through mutual dialogue.

Even in situations of reconciliation and negotiation, the radical and socialist shades prevail. Feminist social work interventions lay emphasis on three key aspects of woman's existential realities – production, reproduction and sexuality. Against the backdrop of equity and justice, these dimensions enable the woman to reclaim 'spaces' metaphorically colonised by the hegemony of patriarchy. In the realm of production (in the sense of Boserup's seminal treatise), it is about recognising her 'role' in the work domain and thereby contribution to tangible income and addressing hierarchies embedded in sexual division, domestication and informalisation – an acculturation of thought in terms of recognising her 'work' and 'worth' (Peterson and Lewis, 1999). In the domain of reproduction and sexuality, it is about creating a cultural narrative – challenging the symbolic patriarchal capitalism on female sexuality and body, moving towards choice, freedom and ownership. This in effect creates a sense of new moods and a new sense of entitlements about the traditional sex class system. A certain positive interpretation about the woman's body/her physical self and decisions surrounding the same that then enables/catapults onto transforming social relations – of reproduction and sexuality.

The radical turn emerges wherein there is a deconstruction of dominant discourses on 'family' – recognising the same as a site of oppression, thereby reproducing dominant regimes and cultures. The normative and ideational position taken in feminist social work is that the patriarchal notions of 'family' have constructed notions of a disembodied and unlocated subject for women, thereby creating core-periphery and centre (family) and margin (outside the family) hierarchies. The recognition herein is of the dimension that 'family' in itself is a socially constructed institution – the social construction embodying within its frame a spate of discourses and hierarchies. These 'writings' or 'popular discourses' on family are then 'erased' (erasure being an essential part of writings in the Derridean sense), in favour of exploring alternatives (Bryson, 1999; D'Souza and Pereira, 2002). These alternatives outside the home/family are emblematic of new assertions. Although the options are living alone and/or institutionalisation (institutions may provide a sense of regimentation to women's lives and stories – disregarding difference), it still remains a move outside the conventional family and household domains. This is thus a crucial step which disentangles women from the web of patriarchy – family and household domains being the commencing points to the range.

Involving men and deconstructing popular discourses on masculinity/femininity in favour of more egalitarian positions is the commencing point towards developing stances that posit engendered notions. This would constitute reinstating women's visibility in household and family domains – essentially as key architects of that world. Engendering involves relooking at the very context from which mainstream discourses and notions on family emerge, which is essentially patriarchal in its norms and forms. The stance herein is to reject the Victorian model of women's essential passivity and domesticity and recognising their contribution to both male existence and family construction (D'Souza and Pereira, 2002). The fact that maintenance and acculturation roles within the family set-ups are primarily played by women which in turn shape the very notion of the family (social construction) is a case enough to argue for reinstating their crucial and primordial stake and position therein. In the quest for reconciliation, one of the key dimensions is to ensure this 'engendering of the family/household' through the women's vantage points, stories and voices. In redefining women's lives through interventions, the endeavour then is to revisit the social construction of gender in domains closest to women's lives. There is a recognition of the fact that women's lives are bound up with family concerns, emotional support and personal relationships. Relooking at the social construction aspect proposes that these personal and subjective experiences of women have as much significance for praxis as is the world of waged work and politics (Reinharz, 1992). The public-private interconnections then emerge herein where the interventions betray that the inequalities in the domestic world structure inequalities in the public sphere. That the rhythm of family lives are governed by cultural definitions of behaviour defined as appropriate to the given sexes in a given society which in turn govern power relationships and gender divisions is crucial to social construction. The radical turn to intervention with women at the level of men and families emerges at two levels – revisiting actual positions of women through reconciliations and negotiations and reexamining the discourse on family in itself by deconstructing functionalist notions in favour of more critical stances recognising the domestic domain itself as a site of oppression and subjugation of women.

Working with Communities

The positions and strategies in feminist social work in terms of working with communities can be unearthed as follows: defining notions of community – real and metaphorical; unearthing paradigms of organising (positivist, constructivist, radical and poststructuralist) and determining dimensions and parameters of 'collective', 'cooperation', 'organisation' and 'action'. An important commencing point herein is the identification of the 'real' and 'metaphorical' notions of the community – and working with them. The 'real' notions of the community constitute the spaces in the geographical proximity – outside the threshold of the home. This space then constitutes the locale for building interconnections and networks for addressing women's issues. This juncture then becomes the site (politics of location) for generating collaborative subjectivities and a sense of 'sisterhood' on varied dimensions of sexuality and experiences in the personal sphere (Berg and Acharya, 2003). Translating this, the neighbourhood community becomes the first site to build women's collectives on issues of oppression, subjugation and domination and plot endeavours to counter hegemonic forces. A place for countering discourse in the neighbourhood also then becomes a space in the larger cartography of women's emancipation by generating a sense of communitas based on sisterhood experiences. Building locality groups also aligns to the Rossian locality development approach to community organisation from an engendered lens. The dialogue and deliberation that then occurs at subtle and overt levels has crucial significance for visibility, representation, generating a Freire's conscientisation and a Foucauldian archaeology and genealogy of consciousness transcending hierarchies of private/public.

The metaphorical notions of the community traverse geographies and go beyond boundaries to promote collectivisation in the surreal sense. It is a notion of creating a sense of womanhood through building women's experiences through consciousness. This is not to deny difference – it is very integral to the resurgence discourse. The metaphorical collectivisation does take into account and institutionalises crosscultural differences. In the postcolonial sense, it also takes into account the politics of location (geographical, cultural, psychic and imaginative boundaries) which provide ground for collective definitions (albeit also taking into account the difference) (Berg and Acharya, 2003; Acharya, 2004). There is a certain alignment with the decolonisation stances with focus on questions of subjectivity and identity (Reinharz, 1992). The quest here is to examine historical interconnections and transform discrete histories into sense of collective identities and politics of identity – difference being embedded in the experience. Simultaneously, there is a certain reinstatement of universality of gender oppression, the essential ground for collectivisation. But this universalism is not essentialist, in the sense that there is a codification of difference through the naturalisation of analytic categories – race, caste, class, ethnicity and faith – those which have crosscultural validity. What is then constructed is a politics of collectivisation embedded at the crossroads of universalism and difference. The universalism is on account of gender subordination and difference along cultural categorical imperatives.

Positionalities are derived from paradigms and hence alliance with them produces certain ways of seeing and action. Although 'organising' is essentially feminist/antiracist/Third wordlist/ postcolonial in its essence, the real encounters and the politics of experience unearth the following standpoints of organising. In the positivist frame of reference, there is a certain logic embedded in coming together, a sense of being parts of whole and dimensions of the universal. Alignment herein happens by virtue of being a woman, which endows dimensions of shared experiences and togetherness. Sisterhood is pronounced on grounds of a logical similarity (stemming from real empirical experiences and in the sense of the Cartesian cogito – the corollary being 'she thinks therefore she is'). In the constructivist sense, organising is around notions of subjectivity – a construed sense of togetherness that emerges from domains and contexts that are socially governed. Constructivist organising has materialist overtones, in the sense that it is to counter those notions that are determined by social contexts (overtones of hegemony embedded in the same). The radical turn of organising takes the form of 'protest', countering the regimes of patronage and exploitation and dealing with the micropolitics of power. Power then becomes the central concern in the radical consciousness, addressing its micro and subtle as well as macro and conspicuous modes as being primary. The methodologies of tracing the archaeology and genealogy of power (in the typical Foucauldian sense) fall within this domain. Protest and countering is then positioned against modes of 'power' perpetuated by patriarchy. The poststructuralist modicum of organising signifies broadly two things – a shift from the structural analysis to that of cultural hegemony and deconstruction. This questions the text in favour of the contexts (thereby celebrating the emic perspective) and reinstates the subalternity of women, thereby to recreate historiographies.

Beyond outlining paradigms, it is crucial to determine parameters of 'collective', 'cooperation', 'organisation' and 'action' to situate interventions accordingly. Collective represents a sense of togetherness – a dimension of aligning on logical grounds based on empirical evidences. This is also possibly the first step in conscientisation. Moving beyond the senses of togetherness is the aspect of 'cooperation', having in it a built-in ethos of shared realities, subjectivities and aspirations. Cooperation also proposes the desire towards a common utopia, determining a micro level political economy of what ought to be? The sense of transcendence from collective and cooperation emerges in 'organisation'. It posits stances where differences are neatly coagulated to create feminist encounters and locate the politics of experience. In the traditional Rossian sense, there are two arms in the process of organising – locality development and social planning. When the conditionalities and positionalities of organising are ironed out, 'action' gets concretised. Action has elements of addressing and redressal – beyond public/private binaries to reinstating positions and countering dominant discourses. It is postcolonial in its very essence and embodiment – encompassing within its fold discursive fields (to address innate irrationalities) and politics of desires, experiences and subjectivities (Raheja, 2003).

The principles of forming collectives are reinstating a sense of togetherness and unification on account of similarities on grounds of sexual unification. The whole idea of exchange (stemming from the interactionist perspective) lending credence to women's assertions and identities is the governing framework. Further, a unification that does not deny difference and does not support essentialisms is the point of view forwarded. The modicum of forming collectives in the intervention process is aligning with activities that contain a normative and ideational similarity to the on-going processes of interventions. This kind of aligning stems from the 'sisterhood' framework – albeit recognising crosscultural differences and heterogeneity. The 'sameness' is of interests, perspectives, experiences and goals of emancipation from patriarchal subjugation and oppression. The outcome of collectives is to portray dimensions of 'women's experiences' and history, thereby leading to a particular self-presentation of women (Rege, 2006). This is then a specific codification that gives a rationale to the alignment and eventually suggestions for political strategy. What then occurs is a discursive production and dissemination of notions of universal sisterhood based on shared aspirations.

Cooperation is then to further the dialogue on solidarity and notions of shared goodwill. The principles of cooperation have postcolonial overtones which attempt to erase patriarchal imperialism. It is the first step to action, having embedded within it analytic categories and strategic decisions that have material effects. It also signifies a certain construction of forces that are anti-hegemonic and countering patriarchy. The parameters that then emerge are 'woman as victim' and 'woman's version of truth about her experiences' that then form common conditions to facilitate cooperation. The modicum of constituting cooperation is tapping this very idea of 'commonness', which signifies shared perspectives, shared goals and shared experiences of women (drawing from Robin Morgan's discussions on Planetary Feminism). This cooperation is not based on biological essentials (a biological materialism of sorts), but through the psychologisation of complex and contradictory historical and cultural realities. The outcome of this unification based on 'secondary sociological universals' is a bonding of women based on the 'sameness of their oppression' and the 'sameness of their struggles' at multiple levels (McCann and Kim, 2003). Hence, cooperation is predicated on the definition of 'experiences of oppression' where the difference is only that of the overarching binary of male/female.

The second level of cooperation is then organisation which moves beyond cooperation based on the experiences of oppression, towards relating that experience to history and accounting for difference. Organising has twin goals – feminising history which then catapults onto contemporary discursive practices and celebrating differences of positionalities (emerging from ethnicity, caste, class and faith) and sexualities. The key principle of organisation is the engendered experience of victimisation and oppression which is 'real' – unsullied by rhetoric or diplomatic abstractions (McCann and Kim, 2003). The modicum or organising is creating subaltern alignments that posit new historiographies. This comprises a coalition of violated women's voices from the below, capturing oral histories and personal testimonies, thereby creating different versions and different cultures of social networks (D'Souza and Pereira, 2002). The outcome of this interconnection/organisation is to address the social reproduction of inequalities (also cultural and economic) which manifests as sexual division in different spheres. The goal is then to reinstate a certain freedom of choice – structuring the world in Manichaean terms, where, women are visualised in opposition to male domination (Bryson, 1999). The logical strategy then emerges as political transcendence – from imperial forces.

The political transcendence as expressed in the ultimate strategy of organisation then takes the form of action (in working with communities) – for assertions, negations and erasures. The ideational frame at this juncture is essentially poststructuralist – deconstruction of norms, forms and totality as being the prime focus. An interesting dimension that emerges herein is that behind the concrete realities of action and transcendence also lie the abstract realities and desires of reconciliation and peace (seen in cases wherein family and household still remain key domains of the woman's lifeworld and motherhood as a crucial discursive range). The key principle of deconstruction is then coloured with shades of unification of desires and aspirations stemming from womanhood and motherhood. The modicum of action is erasure of difference as inequality and political location. There is a certain assertion of the 'woman's agency' which is based on the logic of appropriation and incorporation – facets of assertion (Raheja, 2003). The negations and erasures are of diachronic and dominant narratives of thought form, action and existence which violate women. Interestingly the rewriting does not attempt to create isolated and autonomous narratives, but narratives that co-exist at least in essence by dominant figurations. That is to say that women's liberation and emancipation that stems out of action is not always meant to achieve 'full freedom', but an equity. This equity envisages a co-existence of women with men in the social world as crucial and important actors.

Working with Systems

The fourth pillar or dimension of feminist social work is working with systems – a certain element of collaboration with the administrative (government and police) and judicial (law and courts) systems so as to strengthen the purport of interventions. Hence, the approach is largely positivist in its intent and content, where the prime endeavour is to unearth strategic solutions and postulates to 'tackle' existing systemic domains (structures in the existing contexts). The key objective is then obtaining engendered versions of solutions/judgements primarily in favour of/in the larger interest of the woman. The other domain is aligning with and utilising, as well as promoting, certain aspects inherent in the systems (which are engendered) and partnering for promotion and visibility of the same. Some of the key strategies of working with systems that emerge are building a discourse on the key paradigm governing working with systems; discerning the nature of reality embedded in the systems (police and judiciary/legal); studying the system in its interaction and exchange modes – the agency, actors and malleability/ductility; devising differential strategies and modes of working with systems and aligning/collaborating to reinforce engendered visions and versions of action.

The key commencing point herein is to comprehend and develop discourses on the key paradigms of working with systems. The very essence of working with systems posits a positivist stance with reality overtones. There is a certain 'abiding by' to the normal and conventional modalities of working with existing systems. The key outlook is then structural-functional in its intent and content. The proposition is that systems exist apriori (are a given) and all the modicum and modalities need to be developed around the same is the abiding principle. However, that existence need not purport and enforce an essentialism which is hierarchical and hegemonic. Transformation of those very systems is possible and inevitable. But this change needs to occur in certain formulations – to follow a path which is prescribed – addressing organs and micro systems that already exist (rather than deconstructing existing ones and reconstructing new ones). Hence, positivism, constructivism and realism are the key governing paradigms. Accompanying the same are certain elements (discourses) embedded in the paradigms that go feminist overtones largely underlie this dimension of praxis in subtle forms – overlapping with the dominant structural-functional approach.

With paradigms construed, the next dimension of working with systems is to discern the nature of reality – what systems are, what they depict and how things are construed due to the systems. In epistemological terms, this actually depicts the soci (onto) logy of systems which needs to be understood in its sociological, political, economic and enmeshed forms such as political economy, social history and social geographies. From the social history point of view, it is the historical genesis – the historiography, archaeology and genealogy of these systems (police and legal) that needs to be understood. Particularly the presence, focus and visibility of women and an engendered perspective is what needs to be discerned. This also leads to positing a certain nature of the subaltern lens towards systems to view the woman's perspective therein. The basic formulation that systems in themselves are a projection of the patriarchal schema that needs an engendered focus (as historical baggage has to be unburdened) is created for intervention. Social geographies are about spatial location of social categories – and social geographies of systems are about the physical access and availability of systems to different sections of the population – particularly women (Berg and Acharya, 2003; Acharya, 2004). When criterion of physical accessibility of systems is met, then the social geographies of the same can be said to be engendered. This indicates a vision and lens which is metaphorical in its intent but practical in its content and approach. Engendering social geographies of systems is about making systems available/accessible to women in their physical domains. Discerning actualities and endeavouring to achieve the desirable realities is an important aspect of intervention. The sociology of systems would basically comprise an understanding of the structure, norms and forms of systems in all their conflict, exchange and interaction modes. The understanding of the structure gives (in the Weberian frame of reference) a comprehension and view of the various dimensions of bureaucracy and leadership to aid functioning. Norms and forms of systems provide a critical hermeneutic view into the same so as to aid the planning of strategies and interventions (Peterson and Lewis, 1999). The puritan political understanding of systems gives an insight into the governing ideational frame (the larger political ideology reflecting onto systems and organs of its functioning machinery) and the dynamics embedded therein. Economics of systems is about their positions in the monetary allocation schemata, which contributes to their soundness/permeability (Peterson and Lewis, 1999). But from the practice point of view, it is the political economy dynamics – grasping the overt and covert antagonisms and contradictions embedded in the systems and working a way through them is the key dimension. This would involve identifying the 'tension areas' within the police and the judiciary/legal systems and of the systems with other components of society. Further, the difference between the actual and rhetorical positions and condition of the systems and working towards turning rhetoric towards actualities, in both the positional as well as the conditional domain is the key dimension of practice.

Systems then need to be comprehended in their interaction and exchange modes – conflict being an underlying dimension to the same. From the interaction mode, it is the systems' permeability that is examined – to what extent the systems are influenced by other systems and superstructures. In the exchange mode, the dependency element is examined – that is, to what extent systems 'obtain and give' other systems and structures. Putting interaction and exchange together, it is the composite of what can be called 'system hermeneutics' that is taken into account. How the agency (comprising structures and essences) and the actors (the human agency) employ and enact within the system framework to give an interpretation of reality of systems (which is complex and at times possibly unequal) is the key element of examination. Through exchange and interaction, the malleability/ductility test of systems is undertaken. That is, whether systems are mouldable and what dimension of the same can be altered/engendered is the main argument. Practice is then driven by the overarching position on systems and change endeavours are geared in that direction. Post comprehension is the laying of the ground for action – action with systems as a derivative of understanding the systems. There are levels, strategies and modes of working with the varied systems. In terms of levels of working, two key levels emerge – the social structural and the psychological. At the social structural level, there is an examination of the institutionalised pattern of functioning, particularly the regionalised and routinised contexts. In feminist, functioning with systems at the social structural levels reveals the following: interaction with other (social systems) in contexts; continued reflexive monitoring of actions; rationalisation through discursive consciousness and interpretation through practical consciousness; revisiting unconscious pressures and motives that inhibit the engendering of discourses and moving towards a level of 'ontological security' with (police and legal) systems based on elements of trust and positive/progressive exchange. The above practiced positions emerge through a continued engagement with systems in actualities. However, the psychological level is innate – in terms of certain cognitive level changes which are aimed at. These cognitive changes/engendering preclude social structural changes at one level and at another, both processes move simultaneously. The strategies then emerge as pathways to tackle the subversive tactics and align with mechanisms and machinery (police and legal) that are supportive. Hence, the approaches that emerge are protectionist; equity promotion and countering of the embedded patriarchy in the systems. The protectionist strategy is conservative and unproblematically asserts the roles of the systems as protecting violated women. Hence, differential legislations and women as subjects and recipients of protectionist policies are universalised and naturalised norms. The equity promotion strategy posits 'systems' as key organs in advancing gender equality – a certain 'colonial' frame of operations where systems are posited as instruments of social reconstruction and ensuring equality. There is a certain emphasis on the role of systems as promoting engendered social engineering and drawing from the liberal feminist stance. The third strategy in intervention as that of countering of the embedded patriarchy in the systems is based on a semantic, semiological and syntactic analysis of oppressive meanings and hidden agendas embedded in the systems. Operating within the overarching poststructuralist frame, this approach attempts to counter the notions of 'normal' and 'regulated' within the operation of systems (viewing them largely as outcomes of the male-dominated framework), towards shaking the roots of this sustained oppression which is at times subtle and hidden. Sensitisation programmes play a key role in the same.

In the spirit of Habermasian communicative rationality, feminist social work interventions then move towards creating a lifeworld of action which counters dominant regimes and moves towards equity. In working with systems, although aligning/collaborating is the key modicum, it certainly does not always capture the ambivalence that characterises the nature of women's oppression and attempts to counter the same. Hence, interventions whose overarching focus is engendering action, tries to collate two different positions – one, the dominant and liberal feminist view of allied systems as permitting a social engineering through reform endeavours, and the other, more radical view of systems themselves as instruments of patriarchal oppression. However, within the collaborative regime, two key modes emerge as paradigms – engendered rationalism and engendered structuralism. The engendered rationalist mode approaches women's issues with systems from a logical, real and scientific angle – positing equality as the sole and inevitable outcome of deliberations and actions – systems naturally being made to gear towards the same. The engendered structuralist mode approaches women's issues with systems with an application for 'agency modifications' to ensure gender justice – a sensitisation in the cognitive domain of human agency in the systems and the same translating onto action.

Addressing the Structure

The mature stage of feminist social work interventions is purely in its critical, radical and deconstructionist forms wherein hegemonies of thought, form, structures and action are addressed. Operating on the philosophical premise of poststructuralism and postmodernism, the entire regime of colonial domination as manifested through systems which perpetuates the subalternity of women is addressed. Erasures and re-writings are the norms that predominate and the modus operandi is continued engagements with existential realities of structures and systems (with a radical deconstructionist lens) so as to change notions of 'normalisation', 'power', 'binary oppositions' and 'difference' in favour of Rawlsian justice, Habermasian decolonisation of the lifeworld and possibly Kantian perpetual peace (combining deontological and teleological ethics of justice and fairness with feminist overtones). Studying existing interventions, some dimensions that emerge, of addressing the structure can be discussed through the following conceptual groupings: comprehending the poststructuralist frame of reference; the postcolonial couch of embedding difference; understanding the subalternity of violated women; understanding positions of postmodern feminism; assimilating the history and notions of structure; determining the normative and ideational frames as also the strategies of action and determining the utopian visions.

Addressing the structure is essentially poststructuralist in its formulations and feminist interventions lend the feminist lens to the same in its renditions with structures (societal and legal), systems (police, governance and law) and institutions (family, marriage and kinship). Hence, it is an imperative to comprehend the complexities of poststructuralist positions – which are proposing a subjectivity that is constantly being reconstituted in discourse. The way the woman subject is constituted in and through multiple and contradictory discourses, that, creates space for agency. Hence, there is a continuous process of 'negotiation' through a multiplicity of discourses exercising reflection, choice and action (to address the subordination of women). This means to recognise the multiple and shifting dimensions of women's oppression and that structures, systems and institutions have in them embedded dimensions of inequalities that subjugate women. This allows for creation of spaces to deconstruct debates and discourses such as the sameness/difference debate (which is at the heart of feminist interventions and intersectionalities) (D'Souza and Pereira, 2002). The insights obtained on the discursive knowledge and subjectivities for/-of women and the fact that situations of violence are not either/or but require a more complex understanding of the woman subject is the core understanding.

In the vein of comprehending approaches of addressing the structure, the postcolonial position attempts to provide justifications for further embedding the difference. It is a transgression from the colonial subject and mentality, towards temperaments that reinstate freedom (of the nature of Sartrean existentialism) albeit recognising some bounds. The very essence of poststructuralist discourses – recognising disjunctures and differences/discontinuities in 'dominant colonial discourses' which have defined state, structure, systems and institutions to a great extent – also forms the heart of feminist social work interventions. History and time become important reference frames, wherein the historical baggage of violence (inspired by colonial patriarchy) and the ontological insecurity of women (propelled by colonial forces in domains of structures and institutions) move simultaneously. Hence, the 'woman's being' (in and for herself) needs to traverse through the histories of colonial constructions (which shape structures and systems) to a time where these structures and systems are deconstructed (from their historical baggage) to take into account women's current positions and realities (Acharya, 2004). Hence, the 'woman's being' and the 'time of postcolonial epistemologies' are intertwined as they signify a movement towards engendering erstwhile 'colonial structures' and build spaces to understand new structures.

Comprehending the nature of subalternity of violated women through domains of historicism and culture (Gramscian legacy) forms a crucial step in praxis. The entire subaltern position of reconstructing historiographies through views from below translates herein to 'reconstructing historiographies through the voices of women' – women who are subjects of continued patriarchal oppression. Subalternity can be understood through an interplay of culture, space and power in the neo-colonial postmodern regime (of transcending binaries and asserting micropolitics) (Reinharz, 1992). Although complex in its inherent constitution, the subalternity can be outlined through the following trajectory of culture, space and power. Addressing existential realities requires a typical 'beyond the modernity' lens as it is about movements from objectivity to subjectivity; rationalism and scientism to a move towards phenomenological and emic perspectives and from grand theorising towards celebrating differences and micronarratives. Particularly in domains of violence, it is about comprehending the multidimensionality and complexities and the fact that 'realities' of women determine the nature and character of subjugation – domination/patriarchy does not thus have essentialist norms and forms. Putting together the 'postpositivist' notions of action, the next step in addressing the structure in feminist social work interventions is determining the nature of structure itself and what needs to be addressed. The reality of structures in feminist interventions interface with the key pillars of governance – (particularly in the democratic regime they are the executive, legislature and judiciary) – the police, executive machinery and judiciary/legal systems. Understanding the colonial temperaments of the structures and determining spaces and visibility for women is the key component herein. The modicum lies in presenting 'what needs to be addressed' in the existing structures. The answers that emerge pertain to the colonial histories that carry with them the inherent baggage of domination; the social fabric of democracy which although posits equity for women does not portray it in actuality and the nature of jurisprudence itself, all of which are not always equitable for women. The colonial histories of structures paint the global linkages which systems have in their norms and forms and the way they precipitate a practice which is inherently unequal. There is an unequal cultural and social reproduction of forms of governance (from the materialist feminist lens) that have few spaces for voices of violated women. Democracy proposes gender equality on paper, but whether it translates to micro practice is what needs to be addressed. Further, whether jurisprudence really asserts gender equality moving beyond protectionist and equitarian domains, towards radical changes in worldviews favouring women, is what needs to be addressed.

Addressal of structures needs ethical pathways (teleological ethics in particular) which actually bring in a method to the madness of post (structuralism, colonialism, modernism) and the deconstruction brouhaha. Ethical pathways are governed by moral laws determining action and the desirable (the results). For feminist social work interventions, the ethical pathways address the structure of working within the norms and forms of the existing structure. Changes in the police system, law and governance are sought through the mechanisms and machinery embedded in those very systems. Addressing structure has to thus occur at multiple levels – as engendering is a deep-rooted exercise. Deconstruction is the soul of addressing structures which occurs at the levels of cognition, structure, functions, interaction, exchange, consciousness and narratives. Systematic addressal occurs while positioning levels of deconstruction and differential strategies of action. They could be discussed as follows: The climax is to determine the utopia – the vision of what ought to be? Radical notions of addressing structures, systems and institutions eventually lead to a deconstruction or a realignment of sorts (of familial structures, system structures and functions) which is a marked departure from earlier arrangements, norms and forms. Herein the dilemmas of feminist social work interventions arise in terms of whether the desirable outcome is a 'radical deconstruction' or a 'cultivated reconstruction'. What accounts for is the woman's voice, vision and worldview – her ideas about reconciliation, arbitration and adjudication at the micro level and in the context of family/household at the meso leve. Deconstructing patriarchal notions and cultivating an engendered vision is the desirable goal. At the macro level, particularly in the context of 'systems and structures', it is a tightrope walk between dismantling existing notions and structures (which are essentially patriarchal) in favour of newer ones and working within existing institutions to inject a more egalitarian and engendered consciousness. (Somewhere this also signifies a move beyond deconstruction and postmodernity towards a structuration of sorts – where agency and actors together determine comfort zones in regionalised contexts so as to retain ontological security – as some structures are essential to ensure the same). Hence, effectively, a balanced vision – albeit an engendered one – is largely the core.

The amalgamated version of praxis then matures into an integrated vision of feminist social work. This amalgamation combines episteme, praxis, strategies and the very 'worker self' which is crucial to the feminist social work process. Hence, there is a two way movement – an outward one which is towards ideational positions, praxis coalitions and strategic interventions and the inward one which tackles the cognitive domains of first: the worker self, and then, catapulting onto the social frame. This tackling of the thought processes and discourses is essentially at the subtle levels – which are aimed at an engendering and inculcating of a lens that is directed towards deconstructing hegemonic notions.

Feminist Social Work in the Light of Theory, Positions and Movements

Figure 4 *Feminist Social Work: Interface with Theory, Positions and Movements*

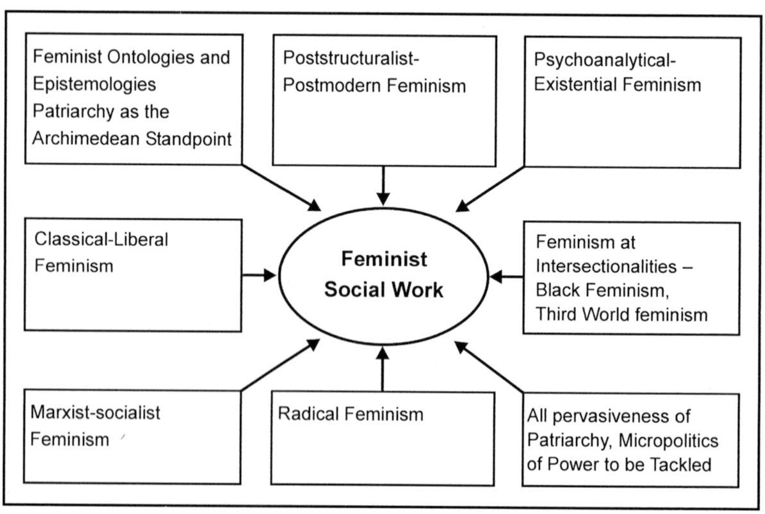

As displayed in Figure 4, the interface of feminist social work with realms of theory, positions and movements can be sought as follows:

- The critical juncture in the repertoire of feminist social work is composed of determining the epistemic intent that governs praxis and strategies. Drawing from feminist epistemologies and enmeshing the same with the domain and range of informed practice, the intent in feminist social work interventions strategically takes the following forms: radical, poststructuralist, postmodern and liberal/socialist. The tenets are not puritan but essentially hybridised in their manifestations with combinations figuring in strategies and outcomes. The radical face is a staunch exponent of the sex class system and discourses on sexuality – that being an important domain by which men dominate, oppress and exploit women.
- Sexuality is thus the core of all deliberations, and examining the micropolitics of power and domination in that domain is the key arena of discourse (Bryson, 1999; McCann and Kim, 2003). The quest is towards attaining a Foucauldian politics of discourse and Sartrean freedom in the realm of sexuality – where women's choices predominate. Any departure from 'choice' (which in itself may be governed by politics of discourse) would invite conceiving of hegemony in those microdomains and subsequent action.
- The poststructuralist lens is a repertoire on subjectivity of women's cultures and spaces that move beyond structures created by social imagery and language – towards deconstructing those structures in favour of more egalitarian ones (Bryson, 1999). Poststructuralist feminism as an epistemic intent operates on two key propositions – deconstruction and discerning language games. Deconstruction comprises revisiting of hijacked realities of violated women which are socially constructed in favour of newer compositions in personal and structural domains (determined by women). Discerning language games is about examining deeper structures of inequity embedded in the mind (structures of patriarchal operation) and manifesting through language and dialogue (all language constructions being 'essential' within a male favouring and male-dominated framework).

- Postmodern feminist lens is essentially about decentring the woman subject, difference and transcending binaries (of varied nature) to then work through the 'aporia' of sorts to attain the utopia of equity (Bryson, 1999). This lens essentially also demonstrates the gap between episteme and praxis as norms of episteme are too abstract to translate onto tangible practice. Hence, these remain guiding forces for steering practice in a more radical domain. At the critical juncture of this radicalism is the liberal socialist view, which allows for spaces of reconciliation – as institutions of family (and the household domain) are sanctified as the basis of deliberations on production/reproduction for women.
- The praxis content then reveals the gamut of domains of operation that qualify feminist social work interventions. In the conventional systems terminology, they actually reveal the levels of working – from micro to macro. The qualifying aspect of practice in feminist social work interventions is its imperativeness to be epistemologically informed – due to the nature of political positions that need to be taken both in the domains of production and reproduction. Hence, this graduates the practice towards praxis and this praxis is 'dialectical materialism' with feminist overtones. The quality of dialectics is because it goes through a series of antagonisms and contradictions to then arrive at answers to situations (which in themselves may be conflicting). The very nature of teleological ethics of practice in feminist social work interventions is writ with dilemmas that are of a transcendental nature – as interests of women and extant institutions (of marriage and family) at times need to be balanced. Hence, the woman centric viewpoint is not absolute, but relative – the relativeness emerges from women's self-determination on one hand, to the nature of negotiations and jurisprudential forms on the other. The materialist nature arises from understanding of realities that social conditions determine the woman subject's sense of identity and nature of existence (the very origin of colonisation and patriarchy). The feminist overtones qualify the feminist subjectivity which repositions the dialectical materialism as feminist dialectical materialism (Stanley, 1990). It signifies that through a series of contradicting propositions and antagonisms, newer assertions are made and positions achieved, for violated women.

- Further the praxis involves work in multiple domains and at multisystemic levels – micro level signifies work with women, the meso level is about work with men and families, the exo domains is about work with communities and the macrodomain is working with systems and addressing the structure. This creates an entire web of interventions across domains that impact the existential realities of women. The multiple arenas of functioning then invite an amalgamated approach – intervening with proximate and remote determinants that affect and effect women's realities.
- Working with women is thus about tackling notions of selfhood, sexuality and identity – oscillating between deconstruction of dominant cultures and reassertions of subdomains and subcultures. Men and families are composed of the near and tangible realities of women – which affect the very notion of production, reproduction and sexuality, determining to a great extent on women's lives and stories (and also experiences of violence and abuse). Working with communities is a move towards collectivisation of sorts (the Marxian and the subaltern notions of a unity of the feminine proletariat). To attain utopia, the final dimensions are negotiations, arbitration, reconciliation and reassertions – all to be derived from (at one level) and addressing (at another) systems and structures.
- Thus, the praxis domains envelop 'strategies' that actually determine the modus operandi – action that then manifests as change. Through the feminist social work interventions, four key strategies (engendered and feminist overtones) emerge distinctly – negotiation, reconciliation, realignment and deconstruction. They also signify levels of action and desired results (desiderate), serving as 'conceptual epilogues' that leave further spaces to be discerned and visions to be attained.

Radical Social Work

Radical social work posits a clear anti-establishment stance with a focus on revisiting and altering structures, institutions and inequalities (Brake and Bailey, 1980). Particularly in the neoliberal scenario the profession has taken differential shapes – faced with various structural and institutional challenges coupled cumulatively with Western ideas, philosophies and practices. There is also the risk of commodification and domination of managerial imperatives and budgetary considerations – the market forces that have led to the transformation of the profession. In the wake of these extraneous factors, radicalisation has been propelled by new social movements around issues of war, poverty, genetically modified foods and the destruction of the environment. Systemically thus, this poses a strong case for reconceptualisation of praxis – taking into account the structural inequities and the need for indigenisation – particularly in this postmodern scenario. Further, this also consolidates the need to deconstruct the historiographical notion of social justice and reconstruct it accommodating the antagonisms and contradictions writ within the very concept and sociopolitical realities that surround the same. Radicalisation further advocates a strong 'emic' view – with a people centrism that dissolves the distance between the objective worker and the subjective situation. This dissolution would concretise the protest waves that are an inevitable feature of a world divided by vast inequalities, lack of political accountability, economic competition and the incessant drive to war. Further, it is celebrated in a customary neo-Marxist fashion, the power of the 'third titan' drawing from John Rees' seminal account of the modern world. The first two being the power of the nation-states and the international economy and the third is the power of the 'working people' on whom all states, armies and corporations ultimately depend. This third titan, in the nature of pontificating of the subaltern genre, is concerned with reconstructing historiographies – of people and eventually of social work – beyond profession, to the world of social protest and contestation. The engagement and thought processes within this radical kernel are largely to challenge the deterministic logic of neoliberalism and imperialism both at the local and global levels. In envisioning this radicalisation of the profession, social justice is identified as its core value, a justice which attempts to link structural factors and personal experiences, which relates 'public issues' and 'private troubles', which emphasises the value of collective approaches and a connectivity between social work practice and wider social movements. The radical notions further draw from the Gramscian deliberation of addressing social reproduction of economic inequalities through a concretisation of a concerned collective consciousness (Lavalette and Ferguson, 2007). Literature per se on radical practice is minimum, shades being visualised in feminist and critical and anti-oppressive practice. In feminist practice, aspects are visualised in the components of addressing the structure. In critical and anti-oppressive practice, dimensions are visualised in the anti-establishment and the subaltern stance. In view of the paradox of the emergence of social work in countries where it previously did not exist through the spread of neoliberal globalisation on the one hand and the crisis of social work in the Western context due to the dominance of market-based approaches, the need for a reassessment of that radical partisan kernel in social work, which has celebrated the injunction of linking public issues and private troubles – thereby making a marriage of social work practice and wider social movements, has come to foray.

Radical Social Work in the Light of Theory, Positions and Movements

Figure 5 *Radical Social Work: Interface with Theory, Positions and Movements*

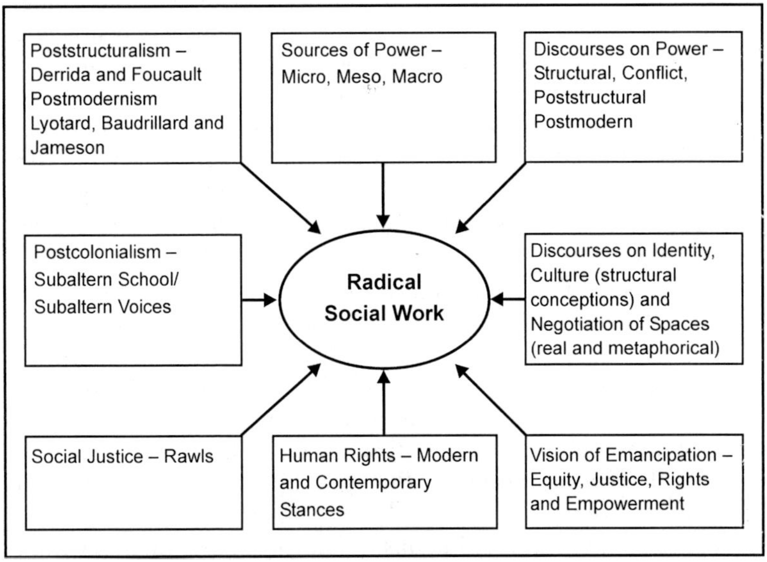

As displayed in Figure 5, the interface of radical social work with realms of theory, positions and movements can be sought as follows:

- The influences of the post-genres predominate as also the subaltern voices. Rawlsian conceptions of social justice along with contemporary stances of human rights are dominant. The contention is that of micropolitics of power – multiple sources and discourses on power which need to be countered. The counter discourses then take the form of discourses on identity, culture and spaces (real and metaphorical) that need to be negotiated. Eventually the visions of emancipation include aspects of equity, justice, rights and empowerment.

- The poststructuralists contest domains of language, logic and binary oppositions guided by notions of Sartrean freedom. Foucault's poststructuralist discourses feature prominently herein particularly the argument that individual freedom is limited or constrained by social conditioning which surrounds the individual – the micropolitics of power. Foucault's epistemology revolves around the central argument of 'knowledge is power', truth tied to the operations of power and domination and that power, knowledge and truth are interconnected through discourses and texts. Derrida's poststructuralist contentions commence with the Archimedean standpoint that things do not have a single basic meaning and there is essentially a fragmentation, conflict and discontinuity in matters of history, identity and culture. The core to his epistemology is 'deconstruction' stemming from an understanding as to how meanings of texts can be 'plural' and 'unstable' instead of fixing them to a rigid structure. Deconstruction is a method of inquiry with difference as the basic guiding principle stratifying the 'hidden' meanings of texts that carry baggage of discourse.
- Postmodern theorising brings in a stress on subjectivity and derivativeness of meaning replacing philosophical conceptions of the subject, representation, causality, truth and value with a perspectivist orientation. As discourses on plurality and difference, there is a celebration of difference and a critique of representation and reason. Conceptions of Lyotard, Jameson and Baudrillard heavily influenced by Nietzsche's work on fragmentation of the inexplicable, focused on rejection of metanarratives and limitations of knowledge production within hegemonic norms and micropolitics of society. In Jameson's analysis of culture in terms of late capitalism, postmodern culture is integrated into commodity production – culture which subordinates class analysis. Thus, postmodernism signifies the cultural logic of late capitalism – characterised by post-industrial

regimen wherein the globalised market economy as the repository of power. Focusing on a post-Marxian analysis of consumption, Baudrillard conceptualisation of postmodern society is a social stratification based on 'consumption of signs and images' that in turn reproduce social categories. Hence, signs and images represent an ontology which is metaphorical and hyperreal governing the palpable and real.

- The postcolonial discourse focuses on questioning imperial structures and has 'resistance', 'retrieval', 'transgression', 'confrontation' and 'opposition' as its key concepts. Attributed to scholars such as Ranajit Guha, Spivak, David Hardiman and others, the subaltern thoughts' key preoccupation is reconstructing historiographies – endowing a view from the below, employing Gramsci's ideas of 'cultural hegemony' as a standpoint of analysis.
- In terms of social justice, Rawls' principles of 'equal basic liberty' and 'difference' principle form the core. Further, the discussion is centred on the latter works of Rawls reaffirming the Kantian interest in developing and exercising individual moral powers of rational autonomy and fair dealing. Hence, it signifies not a search for universal principles of justice albeit a recognition of ideals of relativity.
- In terms of human rights, some of the core contentions of the contemporary perspectives are as follows: sole natural right as that of freedom which accrued to humans on grounds of morality guaranteeing them choice and autonomy; exchange relationship between rights and duties – both jointly building into the 'real' nature of human rights; social rights according to him are construed rights – the moral and political responsibility of guaranteeing which is on legal and political institutions of society; focus on equality and non-discrimination and focus on equity, freedom and liberty as also freedom from oppression. Contemporary discourses on human rights have looked at several issues: the need for alternative reading of histories to reexamine the origin of human rights (the real originators being people in struggle and communities of resistance rather than the conventional authorship endowed to the west) and the politics of human rights (which treats human rights languages and logics as an ensemble of means for the legitimation for governance and domination).Contemporary epistemology of human rights is

writ by plurality and multiplicity of expressions of human rights as ethical imperatives, as grammar of governance, as languages of global governance, as insurrectionary praxis, as juridical production and as culture.

- Broadly thus, the ways that have shaped the radical stance are as follows: fragmented universality (particularly in the neo-colonial context, newer ways to contain the sovereignty of the Third World have been discovered; creationist logic of self-determination that give language to the aspiration of politics of identity and difference of new nations is curtailed under global political economy dynamics), the Marxian critique and the Foucauldian episteme – recognising the multiple matrices of violence within which the contemporary paradigm of violence emerges. There is an interpenetration of ideological positions, politics of existence and spaces and the worlds of power which then signifies the global institutionalisation of the anti-establishment embedded in the postmodern politics of identity and difference.

Critical and Anti-Oppressive Social Work

Critical and anti-oppressive practice primarily is identified from the radical stance through its clear subaltern stance – a view from the below. Basically, this pertains the voices of the marginalised – at the margins on grounds and intersectionalities of race, caste, class, gender and Third World existence. However, the base is drawn from critical theory as also the subaltern school tenets. The tenets of the Frankfurt School are predominated by Horkheimer's philosophical premises of a critical soci (onto) logy aligning to Kantian tenets of a critique of pure reason, Adornian negative dialectics, Marcuse's treatise on the alienation thesis through the lens of one dimensionality or Habermasian renditions of a reconstructed lifeworld, thus positing an array of discourses on power, identity and difference. Whereas the operational premise of critical theory is discourse, identity and difference, the poststructuralists dwell on language games and grammatology to cultivate new ways of knowing, seeing and believing. Critical and anti-oppressive social work draws on the epistemes of both the traditions to highlight the critical potential of the social work profession (Fook, 2002). Departing from the one-dimensional belief of linking social work to 'helping' and 'change' alone, critical and anti-oppressive practice posits the profession at a crucial juncture of translating critical ideals into practice – an informed envisioning of the lifeworlds. The historiography of the critical tradition incorporates the critique of logocentrism and dichotomous thinking and arguments in favour of the idea of difference, deconstruction, multiple discourses and situated subjectivity. The critical approach to social work is thus outlined as projecting the premises that domination is structural, the recognition of the process of operation of 'false consciousness' within essentially capitalist societies and a critique of positivism as a major ideology. The postcolonial discourse in the globalisation era is suitably inserted in the form of a critique of neo-colonialism precipitated through the neoliberal regime. That social work as a profession needs to justifiably be sensitive to the contemporary debates, and the Foucauldian stance of micropolitics of power is reiterated.

There is a focus on 'new ways of knowing' drawing from Foucault's premises of knowledge as power and that power, knowledge and truth are interconnected through discourses and texts; and Derrida's contentions that knowledge reflects particular constructions of reality and these constructions are always tied up in history, society and politics. This critical perspective is woven through reflective exercises on knowledge and power and how the interplay is comprehended particularly for social work practice. In terms of power tenets from Foucault and Baudrillard are combined with emphasis on explicating the complex construct of 'empowerment'. From Foucault is derived the multidimensionality and the micropolitics – articulated through the twin methodologies of archaeology and genealogy. The Baudrillardian leanings are visualised in terms of viewing stratification in the postmodern society on the basis of what signs and images are consumed. From Frederic Jameson is derived the understanding of the commodification of the postmodern culture which when integrated into commodity production leads to emergence of micropolitics. From thereon is articulated the process of what the empowerment practice might look like in the context of critical and anti-oppressive practice. Thus, the emphasis is on deconstruction, redefinition and reconceptualisation of situations and power relations. Further, the focus is on the understanding of discourses and their operations, thus providing an opening into how power operates; and narratives are posited as specific frameworks of understanding a particular phenomenon. Ideology is critiqued as false consciousness leading to a dualism of action and consciousness through its directionality, overarching structures and polarisations. Discourse provides the answer to comprehending contesting realities by celebrating interpretative approaches – deconstructing and revisioning the construct of 'social work' itself, thereby laying fertile grounds for critical practice. Ideas of the professional self are reformulated in the conundrums of identity politics and the dilemma of difference. Hence, through the renditions on ways of knowing, power, discourse and identity/difference, the twofold context is established – critical examination of social processes through the poststructuralist and postmodernist frames and a critical examination of the social work profession, the key constructs of empowerment and social change and the professional self (Fook, 2002).

Hence, practice is redeveloped and there are newer ways in which an analysis of discourse can be translated onto practice. There is a focus on deconstructive methods in practice – the process involving critical deconstruction, resistance, challenge and critical reconstruction. In terms of empowerment, the need to reformulate the concepts of power in the light of the contextual and changing nature of power is emphasised. The need is to visualise a shift from a structural comprehension of power and discourse to the cultural cognition – the paradigm shift from structure to culture conceived by Gramsci and further developed by social theorists such as Bourdieu. There is a focus on deconstruction of professional assessment and the multifacetedness of problematising, accommodating simultaneously the politics and the context. Those professional narratives are by themselves hegemonic and need to be deconstructed, and then to empathetically reconstruct these narratives accommodating the emic perspective and subaltern historiographies is the essence. Multiperspectival visions in practice are celebrated as also strategies for working in and with contexts are carved out – involving continuous reconstruction, reconceptualisation and revisioning, the summum bonum of critical practice.

Critical and Anti-Oppressive Social Work in the Light of Theory, Positions and Movements

Figure 6 *Critical and anti-oppressive social work: Interface with theory, positions and movements*

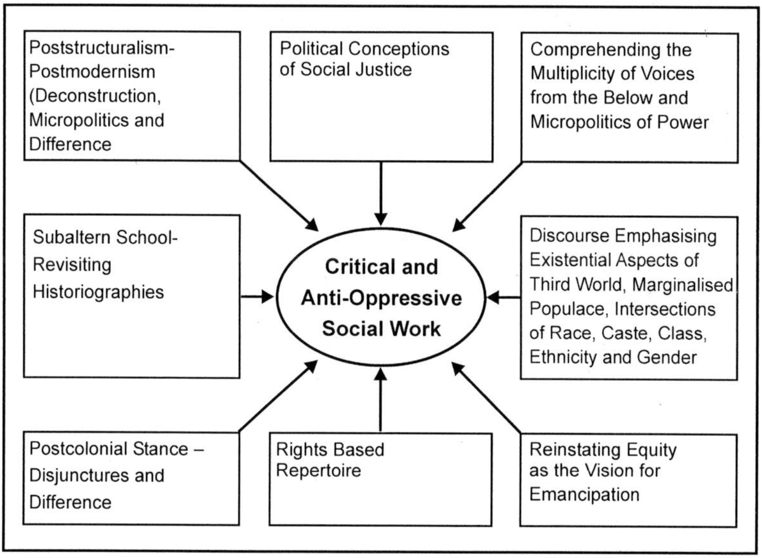

As displayed in Figure 6, the interface of critical and anti-oppressive social work with realms of theory, positions and movements can be sought as follows:

- From poststructuralism is drawn from the aesthetics of difference and the fact that social texts are indeterminate and unstable as also dualistic – the binary oppositions embedded within them need to be countered. Postmodernism signifies a moving away from bourgeoisie nationalisms and overarching cultures and recognising a different cultural politics of sorts. There is a challenging of a broad array of discourses and institutionalised forms of power, thus bringing about a visibility to important ideological and structural forces such as race, gender and class by acknowledging the question of power and value in the construction of knowledge and subjectivities.
- From the subaltern school is drawn the key preoccupation of reconstructing historiographies – endowing a view from the below, employing Gramsci's ideas of 'cultural hegemony' as a standpoint of analysis. There is a concern with 'nationality', role

of culture in nationalism and relationship between states and popular politics gave rise to thoughts pertaining to reimagining and transgressing boundaries of the 'nation-state'. In the efforts to reimagine history itself – post–Cold War, epistemologies are brought under critical scrutiny – engulfing under its frame cultural politics – discursively deconstructing cultural power and recuperating everyday resistance, thus moving beyond modernity, positivism and enlightenment. Thus, the key dimension herein is the politics of language, media and representation. Ontologically, there is a reinvention of 'subalternity' by going beyond Gramscian formulations and positing it vis-à-vis colonial elitism and bourgeoisie nationalist elitism. Politics and representation are two aspects of subalternity that are looked at in records of action and discourse – both evoking anti-hegemonic possibilities. Epistemologically, there is an addressal of the question of subaltern consciousness as a composite culture of resistance to and acceptance of domination and hierarchy – explored through the 'colonial subject'. There is an emphasis on subversive cultural politics because it exposes forms of power/knowledge that oppresses subaltern people. This evokes a new cultural history which is nonlinear, capturing indigenous dissent, symbolic and vernacular.

- From postcolonialism are derived aspects of 'resistance', 'retrieval', 'transgression', 'confrontation' and 'opposition' as its key concepts. What is visualised is the subject's conflict with self, imperial structures, occidental histories and a revisiting of the past, history and reality from this position. Deconstruction rules with citation, reinscription and re-rerouting the historical being core to the discourse which celebrates the margins and the periphery.
- There are also drawings from the rights-based repertoire, the political conceptions of justice comprehending the multiplicity of voices from the below and micropolitics of power; discourse emphasising existential aspect of Third World, marginalised populace – intersections of race, caste, class, ethnicity, gender and re-instating of equity as the vision for emancipation.

In Summary

Thus, theoretical underpinnings engulf in their fold paradigms display shifts in epistemology – towards a finer comprehension of the brouhaha, that is, social reality. Writ with inherent antagonisms and contradictions, the encapsulation of this social reality contains the propensity for social change, a utopia or emancipation. There is a certain liaison with praxis and consciousness which is developed, that then display the allegiance to ideologies and perspectives. Practice positions derive their episteme from these very ideologies and perspectives. It becomes imperative then that these paradigm dialogues of social theory be internalised along with embarking the ideological sojourn. Then practice will be more adequately positioned and informed.

Some of the core interlinkages which have emerged can be discussed as follows: There is a certain allegiance towards the positivism and theology discourses in domains of welfare and organised and scientific charity approaches – particularly positivism's penchant for scientism and logic. The realist propositions of causality and nonessentialism (particularly the relative truth contentions), phenomenological flavours of subjectivity and differential consciousness and the hermeneutics of social construction feed into an informed comprehension of the systems and ecological perspectives of practice characterised by a fetish for interdependency and multi-causalities stemming from social consciousness. The Marxian and the critical theory veins with propositions of materialism, dialectics, critique, reason and justice feed into flavours of radical practice with inclinations for social action and the rights-based leanings. The renditions of 'decolonisation of the lifeworld' find meanings in this approach. Poststructuralism and postmodernism, with propositions of deconstruction, micropolitics, power/ knowledge/ discourse deliberations and a celebration of plurality, difference and multinarratives, provide testimonies to that flavour of radical praxis which has structuralist/poststructuralist overtones – viewing oppression, hierarchy, hegemony and anti-establishment stances as the core of interventions. The clear leanings towards indigenous voices and narratives are the locus classicus of social work interventions, and people-centred dialogues of emancipation and empowerment find its epistemic locale in postcolonial and subaltern renditions. Aspects of centre-periphery discourses, the repertoire of truth, order and reality, politics of identity and reconstructing historiographies by countering bourgeoisie nationalisms and signifying a paradigm shift from structure to culture as the fulcrum of the lever of interventions are the key arenas. When put together, they form the base of critical and anti-oppressive practice. The engendered view of reality lent by feminist ontologies and epistemologies feed into discourses on feminist social work as also domains of gender and sexuality.

References

Acharya, J. (2004). *Gendered Spaces: Craftswomen's Stories of Self Employment in Orissa, India*. Doctoral Thesis at Norwegian Institute of Science and Technology.

Adams, J.M. and Jones, W.H. (1999). *Handbook of Interpersonal Commitment and Relationship Stability*. New York: Kluwer Academic/Plenum Publishers

Agarwal, B. (1999). The Gender and Environment Debate. In Menon, N. (Ed.). *Gender and Politics in India* (pp. 32–54). Delhi: Oxford University Press.

Agnes, F. (1994). Women's Movement in a Secular Framework: Redefining the Agenda, *Economic and Political Weekly*, 29 (19), 1123–1128.

Ali, T. (2003). *The Clash of Fundamentalisms: Crusades, Jihads and Modernity*. Delhi: Rupa and Co.

Aloysius, G. (1997). *Nationalism without a Nation in India*. Delhi: Oxford University Press.

Anderson, B. (1983). *Imagined Communities: Reflections on the Origin and Spread of Nationalism*. London: Verso.

Anhelm, F.E. (1999). Religion and Civil Society: What is the Relationship Between Them? In Akuhata-Brown, M. and Civicus-Staff (Ed.). *The Promise of Civil Society* (pp. 43–67). West Hartford: Kumarian Press.

Apffel-Marglin, S. (1994). *Women and Nature*. New York: Oxford University Press.

Appadurai, A. and Breckenridge, C.A. (2004). The South Indian Temple: Authority, Honour and Redistribution. In T.N. Madan (Ed.). *India's Religions* (pp. 161–175). Oxford: Oxford University Press.

Armstrong, A.H. (1976). Classical Mediterranean Spirituality. In Armstrong, A.H. (Ed.) *Classical Mediterranean Spirituality: Egyptian, Greek and Roman* (pp 1–45). London: Routledge and Kegan Paul.

Armstrong, K. (2001). *The Battle for God*. New York: Ballantine Books.

Arnold, D. (1982). Rebellious Hillman: Gudem-Rampa Rising 1839–1924. In Ranajit Guha (Ed.). *Subaltern Studies 1* (pp. 53–67). Delhi: OUP.

Ashenden, S. and Owen, D. (1999). *Foucault contra Habermas: Recasting the Dialogue between Genealogy and Critical Theory*. London: Sage Publications.

Bachmann, M. (2002) 'After the Fire'. In Vanita, R. (Ed) *Queering India: Same Sex Love and Eroticism in Indian Culture and Society*. London: Routledge. pp. 243 –243.

Badinter, E. (1995). *XY: On Masculine Identity*. New York: Columbia University Press.

Bailey, K.D. (1989). *Sociology and the New Systems Theory: Towards a Theoretical Synthesis*. London: Oxford University Press.

Bailey, R. and Lee, P. (Ed.). (1982). *Theory and Practice in Social Work*. Oxford: Blackwell.

Balcerowicz, P. (2003). *Essays in Jaina Philosophy and Religion*. Delhi: Motilal Banarasidass.

Bannet, E.T. (1993). *Postcultural Theory: Critical Theory After the Marxist Paradigm*. London: Macmillan.

Barker, R.L. (1987). *The Social Work Dictionary*. Silver Spring, MD: National Association of Social Workers.

Barlas, A. (1995). *Democracy, Nationalism and Communalism: The Colonial Legacy of South Asia*. Boulder, CO: Westview Press.

Barlingay, S.S. (1992). *Buddhist and Jaina views in Indian Philosophy*. Pune: Datta Lakshmi Trust.

Barnes, B. (1982). *T S Kuhn and Social Sciences*. London: MacMillan Press.

Barnes, N.S. (1987). Buddhism. In Sharma, A. (Ed.). *Women in World Religions* (pp. 43–54). Delhi: India Books Centre.

Bartky, S.L. (1990). *Femininity and Domination: Studies in the Phenomenology of Oppression*. New York: Routledge.

Basu, S. (2002). *Religious Revivalism as Nationalist Discourse: Swami Vivekananda and New Hinduism in Nineteenth Century Bengal*. Delhi: Oxford University Press.

Bataille, G. (1992). *Theory of Religion*. New York: Zone Books.

Bawa, N. (1993). *Development and the Social Science Method*. New Delhi: Utpal Publishing House.

Baxi, U. (2006) The Future of Human Rights. Delhi: Oxford University Press.

Baxi, U. (2006) The Future of Human Rights. Delhi: Oxford University Press.

Bayly, S. (2007). *Asian Voices in a Postcolonial Age: Vietnam, India and Beyond*. Cambridge: Cambridge University Press.

Beckerlegge, G. (2003). Saffron and Seva: The Rashtriya Swayamsevak Sangh's Appropriation of Swami Vivekananda. In Copley, A. (Ed.). *Hinduism in Public and Private* (pp. 31–65). Delhi: Oxford University Press.

Beckford, J.A. (1986). New Religious Movements. In Beckford, J.A. (Ed.). *New Religious Movements and Rapid Social Change* (pp. 23–48). London: Sage Publications.

Bell, C. (1836). *Natural Theology*. London: Charles Knight.

Berdyaev, P. (1916). *Investigating the Transcendental Great Beyond*. London: George Allen and Unwin.

Berg, N. and Acharya, J. (2003). *The Place of Feminist Geography Methodologies and Personal Narrative Analysis in research on Self-employment: The Case of Field Work in Orissa, India*. Trondheim, Norway: Norwegian University of Science and Technology.

Berger, P. (1961). *The Noise of Solemn Assemblies*. New York: Anchor Books.

Berger, P. and Luckmann, T. (1966). *The Social Construction of Reality*. Garden City, New York: Doubleday.

Berger, P.L. and Luckmann, T. (1967). *Social Construction of Reality*. London: Allen Lane.

Bertocci, P.A. (1985). The Logic of Creationism Advaita and Vishishtadvaita. In Mahadevan, T.M.P. (Ed.). *Essays in Philosophy* (pp. 37–69). Bombay: Popular Publishing.

Best, S. and Kellner, D. (1998). *Understanding Postmodernism*. London: Routledge and Kegan Paul.

Betcher, R.W. and Pollack, W.S. (1993). *In a Time of Fallen Heroes: The Recreation of Masculinity*. New York: Atheneum.

Bhagavan, M. and Feldhaus, A. (2008). Introduction. In Bhagavan, M. and Feldhaus, A. (Ed.). *Claiming Power from the Below: Dalits and the Subaltern Question in India* (pp. 3–32). Delhi: Oxford University Press.

Bhagwan, M. and Feldhaus, A. (2008). Introductory. In Bhagwan, M. and Feldhaus, A. (Ed.). *Speaking Truth to Power: Religion, Caste and the Subaltern Question in India* (pp. 1–27). Delhi: OUP.

Bhaskaran, S. (2002). The Politics of Penetration: Sec 377 of the IPC. In Vanita, R. (Ed.). *Queering India: Same Sex Love and Eroticism in Indian Culture and Society* (pp. 15–29). London: Routledge.

Biedelman, T. (1982). *Colonial Evangelism: A Socio-Historical Study of an East African Mission at the Grassroots*. Bloomington: Indiana University Press.

Billimoria, P., Prabhu, J. and Sharma, R. (2007). *Indian Ethics: Classical Traditions and Comparative Challenges*. Delhi: Oxford University Press.

Biswas, D. (2000). Emergence of the Aranyaka, In Roy, B.I. (Ed.). *Facets of Vedic Studies* (pp. 42–58). Delhi: Kaveri Books.

Boehmer, E. (2005). *Colonial and Postcolonial Literature: Migrant Metaphors*. New York: Oxford University Press.

Bonifazi, C. (1978). *The Soul of the World*. US, North Carolina: University of North Carolina Press

Bookchin, M. (1966). *The Philosophy of Social Ecology*. Jaipur: Rawat Publications.

Boone, J. A. (1990). Of Me (n) and Feminism: Who (se) is the Sex That Writes? In Boone, J.A. and Cadden, M. (Ed.). *Engendering Men: The Question of Male Feminist Criticism* (pp. 11–25) New York: Routledge.

Bottomore, T. (1978). Marxism and Sociology. In Bottomore, T. and Nisbet, R. (Ed.). *Masters of Sociological Thought* (pp. 118–148). Jaipur: Rawat Publications.

Bottomore, T. and Nisbet, R. (2004). Structuralism. In Bottomore, T. and Nisbet, R. (Ed.). *A History of Sociological Analysis* (pp. 132–153). Delhi: Rawat Publishers.

Boulding, K.E. (1962). Social Justice in Social Dynamics. In Brandt, R.B. (Ed.). *Social Justice* (pp. 43–62). Englewood Cliffs, NJ: Spectrum.

Brake, M. and Bailey, R. (Ed.). (1980). *Radical Social Work and Practice*. London: Edward Arnold.

Brandon, S.G.F. (1965). *History, Time and Deity: A Historical and Comparative Study of the Conception of Time in Religious Thought and Practice*. New York: Manchester University Press.

Brandt, R.B. (Ed.). (1962). *Social Justice*. Englewood Cliffs, NJ: Spectrum.

Broadbeck, M. (1968). *Readings in the Philosophy of Science*. New York: MacMillan.

Bronner, S.E. and Kellner, D.M. (1989). *Critical Theory and Society*. New York: Routledge.

Brooks, C.K. (1989). *The Hare Krishnas in India*. Princeton, NJ: Princeton University Press.

Brun, C. and Jazeel, T. (2009). Spatializing Politics. In Brun, C. and Jazeel, T. (Ed.). *Spatializing Politics: Culture and Geography in Postcolonial Sri Lanka*. Delhi: Sage Publications.

Bryson, V. (1999). *Feminist Debates*. Washington Square: New York University Press.

Bryson, V. (1999). *Feminist Debates*. Washington Square: New York University Press.

Bucke, R.M. (1901). *Cosmic Consciousness: A Study of the Evolution of Humankind*. Philadelphia: University Press.

Bucke, R.M. (1960). *Cosmic Consciousness: A Study of the Evolution of Humankind*. Philadelphia, PA: University Press.

Burghart, R. and Cantlie, L. (1993). *Indian Religion*. London: Curzon Press.

Burghart, R. and Cantlie, L. (1995) *Indian Religion*. London: Curzon Press.

Burrell, G. and Morgan, G. (1979). *Sociological Paradigms and Organisational Analysis*. London: Heinemann.

Butler, J. (1990). *Gender Trouble: Feminism and the Subversion of Identity*. New York/London: Routledge.

Butler, J. (1993). *Bodies that Matter: On the Discursive Limits of Sex*. New York/London: Routledge.

Butler, J. (1997). *Excitable Speech: A Politics of the Performative*. New York: Routledge.

Butler, J. (1999). *Gender Trouble: Feminism and the Subversion of Identity*. New York/London: Routledge.

Caldicott, A. and Mackintosh, H.R. (1904). *Selections from the Literature of Theism*. Edinburgh: T&T Clark.

Callinicos, A. (1983). *Marxism and Philosophy*. Oxford: Clarendon Press.

Callinicos, A. (1985). Post Structuralism, Post Modernism and Post Marxism, Theory, *Culture and Society*, 2 (3), 85–102.

Callinicos, A. (Ed.). (1989). *Marxist Theory*. Oxford: Oxford University Press.

Campbell, J. (1988). *The Inner Reaches of Outer Space: Metaphor as Myth and Religion*. New York: Harper and Row Publishers.

Carlson-Thies, S. (1999). Faith-Based Institutions Co-operating with Public Welfare: The Prominence of Charitable Choice Provision. In Davis, D. and Hankins, B. (Ed.). *Welfare Reforms and Faith-Based Organisations* (pp. 137–158). Waco, TX: JM Dawson Institute of Church-State Studies.

Carmody, D.L. (1987). Judaism. In Sharma, A. (Ed). *Women in World Religions* (pp. 27–42). Delhi: India Books Centre.

Chaitanya, K. (1992). The Earth as Sacred Environs. In Sen, G. (Ed.). *Indigenous Vision: Peoples of India: Attitudes to the Environment* (pp. 21–33). Delhi: Sage Publications.

Chakrabarti, M. (1989). *Gandhian Mysticism*. Delhi: Atlantic Publishers and Distributors.

Chakrabarty, D., Majumdar, R. and Sartori, A. (2007). *From the Colonial to the Postcolonial: India and Pakistan in Transition*. Delhi: Oxford University Press.

Chakravarty, U. (1993). Conceptualising Brahmanical Patriarchy in Early India: Gender, Caste, Class and State, *Economic and Political Weekly*, 28 (14), 579–585.

Chanana, K. (1990). The Dialectics of Tradition and Modernity and Women's Education in India, *Sociological Bulletin*, 39 (1/2), 75–91.

Chandra, B. (1979). *Nationalism and Colonialism in Modern India*. Delhi: Orient Longman.

Chatterjee, A. (2010). Objective Helping, Hegel and Three Indian Reformers in the Colonial Civil Society: Prefacing the Personalytical History of Social Work, *Indian Journal of Social Work*, 71 (2), 145–166.

Chatterjee, I. (2002). Alienation, Intimacy and Gender: Problems for a History of Love in South Asia. In Vanita, R. (Ed.). *Queering India: Same Sex Love and Eroticism in Indian Culture and Society* (pp. 61–76). London: Routledge.

Chatterjee, M. (2009). *Inter-religious communication: A Gandhian Perspective*. New Delhi: Promilla and Co.

Chatterjee, P. (1993). *The Nation and Its Fragments: Colonial and Postcolonial Histories*. Princeton, NJ: Princeton University Press.

Chatterjee, P. (2009). The Small Voice of History. In Chatterjee, P. (Ed.). *Ranajit Guha: The Small Voice of History: Collected Essays* (pp. 1–56). Delhi: Permanent Black.

Chattopadhyay, D.B. (Ed.). (1978). *Studies in the History of Indian Philosophy*, Vols. 1–3. Calcutta: K.P. Bagchi & Co.

Chattopadhyaya, D.P., Basu, S., Mitra, M.N. and Mukhopadhyay, R. (2000). Realism. In Chattopadhyaya, D.P., Basu, S., Mitra, M.N. and Mukhopadhyay, R. (Ed.). *Realism: Responses and Reactions* (pp. 3–35). Delhi: Indian Council of Philosophical Research.

Chodorow, N. (1978). *The Reproduction of Mothering*. Berkeley, CA: University of California Press.

Chodorow, N. (1994). *Femininities, Masculinities, Sexualities: Freud and Beyond*. Lexington: University Press of Kentucky.

Choudhary, K. (2002) *Materialist View of Social Science*. IRMA Working Paper 169. Anand: IRMA.

Choudhary, K. (2002). *Materialist View of Social Science*. Working Paper 169. Institute of Rural Management, Anand.

Clarke, S. (1998). *Dalits and Christianity: Subaltern Religion and Liberation Theology in India*. Delhi: Oxford University Press.

Coakley, S. (1997). Religion and the Body. In Coakley, S. (Ed.). *Religion and the Body* (pp. 1–28). Cambridge: Cambridge University Press.

Cochrane, C.N. (1972). *Christianity and Classical Culture: A Study of Thought and Action from Augustus to Augustine*. London: Oxford University Press.

Cohen, L. (2002). What Mrs. Besahara Saw: Reflections on the Gay Goonda. In Vanita, R. (Ed.). *Queering India: Same Sex Love and Eroticism in Indian Culture and Society* (pp. 149–162). London: Routledge.

Cohen, M., Nagel, T. and Scanlon, T. (Ed.). (1997). *Equality and Social Justice*. Princeton, NJ: Princeton University Press.

Cohn-Sherbok, D. (1999). *Judaism*. London: Routledge.

Colebrooke, H.T. (1977). *Essays on History Literature and Religion of Ancient India*, Vols. 1 & 2. Delhi: Cosmo Publications.

Collins, P. (1986). Learning from the Outsider Within: The Sociological Significance of Black Feminist Thought, *Social Problems*, 33 (6), S14–S32

Collins, P. (1990). *Black Feminist Thought: Knowledge, Consciousness and the Politics of Empowerment*. Boston: Unwin Hyman.

Comaer, M. (2000). *The Method of Early Advaita Vedanta*. Delhi: Motilal Banarasidass (MLBD).

Copleston, F. (1993). *A History of Philosophy*, Volumes 1–3. New York: Image Books.

Copleston, F. (1993). *A History of Western Philosophy*. New York: Anchor Books.

Copleston, F. (1994). *A History of Philosophy*, Volumes 4–6. New York: Image Books.

Copleston, F. (1995). *A History of Philosophy*, Volumes 7–9. New York: Image Books.

Copleston. J. (1956). *Contemporary Philosophy: Studies in Logical Positivism and Existentialism*. London: Burns and Oates.

Copley, A. (1997). *Religion in Conflict: Ideology, Cultural Contact and Conversion in Late Colonial India*. Delhi: Oxford University Press.

Copley, A. (2000). *Gurus and their Followers*. Delhi: Oxford University Press.

Corbin, H. (1960). *Avicenna and the Visionary Recital*. Princeton, NJ: Princeton University Press.

Coward, R. and Ellis, J. (1977). *Language and Materialism*. London: RKP.

Craig, E. (1998). *Encyclopaedia of Philosophy*, Volume 3. Routledge: London.

Craig, E. (1998). *Encyclopaedia of Philosophy*. Volume 8. Routledge: London.

Critchley, S. (2007). *The Ethics of Deconstruction*. Delhi: Motilal Banarasidass.

Crombie, A. (1827). *Natural Theology: Or Essays on the Existence of the Deity and of Providence on the Immateriality of the Soul and the Future State*, Vols. 1 and 2. London: Macmillan.

Crombie, A. (1829). *Natural Theology: Or Essays on the Existence of the Deity and of Providence on the Immateriality of the Soul and the Future State*, Volumes 1 and 2. London: Macmillan.

Crossley, N. (2005). *Key Concepts in Critical Social Theory*. London: Sage Publications.

Crouter, R. (1997). *On Religion: Speeches to Its Cultural Despisers. Schleiermacher*. Cambridge: Cambridge University Press.

Culler, J. (1999). Derrida. In Sturrock, J. (Ed.). *Structuralism and Since: From Levi Strauss to Derrida* (pp. 142–158). Oxford: OUP.

Cumming, R.D. (2003). *The Philosophy of Jean Paul Sartre*. New York: Vintage Books.

Cupitt, D. (1998). *Mysticism after Modernity*. London: Basil Blackwell.

D'Souza, D. (1982). *The Growth and Activity of Catholic Church in North India, 1757–1858*. Lucknow: University of Lucknow.

D'Souza, E. and Pereira, L. (2002). *Women's Voices: Selections from Nineteenth and Early Twentieth Century Indian Writing in English*. Delhi: Oxford University Press.

Dahlerup, D. (1986). Introduction. In Dahlerup, D. (Ed.). *The New Women's Movement: Feminism and Political Power in Europe and USA* (pp. 3–34). London: Sage Publications.

Dalton, D. (1998). *Gandhi's Power: Nonviolence in Action*. Delhi: Oxford University Press.

Damle, Y.B. (1993). *Theory, Rhetoric and Social Reality*. I.P. Desai Memorial Lecture–7. Surat: Centre for Social Studies.

Damodaran, V. and Unnithan-Kumar, M. (2000). Postcolonial India: An Introduction. In Damodaran, V. and Unnithan-Kumar, M. (Ed.). *Postcolonial India: History, Politics and Culture* (pp. 1–43). Delhi: Manohar Publications.

Das, N.K. (2003). Culture, Religion and Philosophy. In Das, N.K. (Ed.). *Culture Religion and Philosophy: Critical Studies in Syncretism and Inter-Faith Harmony* (pp. 1–37). Jaipur: Rawat Publications.

Dasgupta, A. (2002). Do I remove my skin? Interrogating Identity in Suniti Namjoshi's Fables. In Vanita, R. (Ed.). *Queering India: Same Sex Love and Eroticism in Indian Culture and Society* (pp. 100–110). London: Routledge.

Date, V.H. (1973). *Vedanta Explained*, Vols. 1 and 2. Delhi: Munshiram Manoharlal Publishers Ltd.

Datta, B.N. (1954). *Swami Vivekananda: Patriot-Prophet*. Calcutta: Navbharat Publishers.

Datta, D.M. (1953). *The Philosophy of Mahatma Gandhi*. Madison: The University of Wisconsin Press.

Davids, T.W.R. (1997). *Buddhist India*. Delhi: Motilal Banarasidass.

Davis, H.B. (1978). *Towards a Marxist Theory of Nationalism*. New York: Monthly Review Press.

De Beauvoir, S. (1949, 1953). *The Second Sex*. New York: Routledge and Kegan Paul.

Dean, T. (1997) (Ed.). *Religious Pluralism and Truth: Essays on Cross-Cultural Philosophy of Religion*. Delhi: Sri Satguru Publications.

Dean, T. (1997). Religious Pluralism and Truth. In Dean, T. (Ed.). *Religious Pluralism and Truth: Essays on Cross-Cultural Philosophy of Religion* (pp. 1–29). Delhi: Sri Satguru Publications.

Delanty, G. (1997). *Social Science Beyond Constructivism and Realism*. Buckingham: Open University Press.

Delon, M. (2001). Charity. In Delon, M. (Ed.). *Encyclopaedia of Enlightenment*, Vol. 1 (pp. 67–88). Chicago: Fitzroy Dearborn Publishers.

Delphy, C. (1970). The Main Enemy, *Partisans*, 54 (3), 21–33.

Delphy, C. (1990). *Rethinking Sex and Gender*. London: University Press.

Desai M. (2002). *Ideologies and Social Work*. Jaipur: Rawat Publications.

Desai, M.R. (1972). *Yoga Sutras of Patanjali*. Kolhapur: Desai Publications Trust.

Desai, N. (1995) The Making of a Feminist, *Indian Journal of Gender Studies*, 2 (2), 78–92.

Devall, B. and Sessions, G. (1985). *Deep ecology*. Salt Lake City: Peregrine Smith.

Dews, P. (1987). *Logic of Disintegration: Poststructuralist Thought and the Claims of Critical Theory*. London: Verso.

Dietrich, G. (1992). *Reflections on the Women's Movement in India: Religion, Ecology, Development*. Delhi: Horizon India Books.

Dietrich, G. (1999). Women, Ecology and Culture. In Menon, N. (Ed.). *Gender and Politics in India* (pp. 55–72). Delhi: Oxford University Press.

Doshi, S.L. (2003). *Modernity, Postmodernity and Neo-Sociological Theories*. Jaipur: Rawat Publications.

Drummond, H. (1884). *Natural Law in the Spiritual World*. London: Oxford University Press.

Dryzek, J.S. (1987). *Rational Ecology: Environment and Political Economy*. Oxford: Basil Blackwell.

Dube, L. (1986). Seeds and Earth: Symbolism of Biological Reproduction and Sexual Relations of Production. In Dube, L., Leacock, E. and Adrener, S. (Ed.). *Visibility and Power: Essays on Women in Society and Development* (pp. 45–61). New Delhi: Oxford University Press.

Dube, S. (1997). *Postcolonial Passages: Contemporary History-writing on India*. Delhi: Oxford University Press.

Dube, S. and Banerjee-Dube, I. (2006). *Unbecoming Modern: Colonialism, Modernity, Colonial Modernities*. New Delhi: Social Science Press.

Dupre, L. (1966). *The Philosophical Foundations of Marxism*. New York: Harcourt, Brace and World Inc.

Durant, W. (1961). *The Story of Philosophy*. New York: Simon and Schuster.

Dwight, T. (1822). *Theology Explained*, Volume 1–5. London: William Baynes and Sons.

Eagleton, T. (1991). *Ideology: An Introduction*. London: Verso.

Eatwell, R. and Wright, A. (Ed.). (1999). *Contemporary Political Ideologies*. Delhi: Rawat Publications.

Eco, U. (1973). Social Life as a Sign System. In Robey, D. (Ed.). *Structuralism: An Introduction* (pp. 31–56). Oxford: Clarendon Press.

Eder, I. (1996). *The Social Construction of Nature*. London: Sage Publications.

Edie, J.M. (Ed.). (1965). *An Invitation to Phenomenology: Studies in the Philosophy of Experience*. Chicago: Quadrangle Books.

Emad, P. and Maly, K. (1980). *Hegel's Phenomenology of Spirit: Martin Heidegger*. Bloomington: Indiana University Press.

England, P. (1993). *Theory on Gender/Feminism on Theory*. New York: Aldine De Gruyter.

Fakhry, M. (1958). *Islamic Occasionalism and Its Critique by Averroes and Avicenna*. London: George Allen and Unwin.

Farber, M. (1943). *The Foundation of Phenomenology: Edmund Husserl and the Quest for a Rigorous Science of Philosophy*. Cambridge: Harvard University Press.

Feenberg, A. (1983). *Lukacs, Marx and the sources of Critical Theory*. New York: Oxford University Press.

Feyerabend, P.K. (1981). *Realism, Rationalism and the Scientific Method*. Cambridge: Cambridge University Press.

Flint, T.P. and Rea, M.C. (2009). Philosophical Theology. In Flint, T.P. and Rea, M.C. (Ed.). *The Oxford Handbook of Philosophical Theology* (pp. 9–36). Oxford: Oxford University Press.

Folkert, K.W. (1993). *Scripture and Community – Collected Essays on the Jains*. Atlanta, GA: Scholars Press.

Fonow, M. and Cook, J. (1989). Introduction. In Fonow, M. and Cook, J., *Beyond Methodology – Feminist Scholarship as Lived Research* (pp. 1–47). Bloomington/Indianapolis: Indiana University Press.

Fook J. (2002). *Social Work: Critical Theory and Practice*. London: Sage Publications.

Forgie, J.W. (1997). Hyper Kantianism in Recent Discussions of Mystical Experience, *Religion Studies*, 21 (2), 12–29.

Forrester, D.B. (1980). *Caste and Christianity: Attitudes and Policies on Caste of Angle Saxon Protest Missions in India*. Delhi: Oxford University Press.

Frankena, W.J. (1962). The Concept of Social Justice. In Brandt, R.B. (Ed.). *Social Justice* (pp. 1–27). Englewood Cliffs, NJ: Spectrum.

Fraser, A.C. (1895). *Philosophy of Theism*. Edinburgh: William Blackwood and Sons.

Fraser, N. and Nicholson, L.J. (1988). Social Criticism without Philosophy: An Encounter Between Feminism and Postmodernism, *Communication*, 10 (3/4), 345–366.

Freund, P.A. (1962). Social Justice and the Law. In Brandt, R.B. (Ed.). *Social Justice* (pp. 63–87). Englewood Cliffs, NJ: Spectrum.

Fromm, E. (1950). *Psychoanalysis and Religion*. New Haven: Yale University Press.

Galloway, G. (1948). *The Philosophy of Religion*. Edinburgh: Edinburgh University Press.

Ganachari, A. (2004). *Nationalism and Social Reform in a Colonial Situation*. Delhi: Kalpaz Publication.

Gandhi, L. (2002). Loving Well: Homosexuality and Utopian Thought in Postcolonial India. In Vanita, R. (Ed.). *Queering India: Same Sex Love and Eroticism in Indian Culture and Society* (pp. 87–99). London: Routledge.

Gandhi, L. (2009). Ahimsa and Other Animals: The Genealogy of an Immature Politics. In Ganguly, D. and Docker, J. (Ed.). *Rethinking Gandhi and Nonviolent Relationality: Global Perspectives* (pp. 21–46). Delhi: Orient Blackswan.

Gandhi, V.R. (1970). *The Systems of Indian Philosophy*. Mumbai: Shri Mahavira Jaina Vidyalaya.

Ganguly, D. (2009). Vernacular Cosmopolitanism: World Historical Readings of Gandhi and Ambedkar. In Ganguly, D. and Docker, J. (Ed.). *Rethinking Gandhi and Nonviolent Relationality: Global Perspectives* (pp. 309–333). Delhi: Orient Blackswan.

Ganguly, D. and Docker, J. (Ed.). (2009). *Rethinking Gandhi and Nonviolent Relationality: Global Perspectives*. Delhi: Orient Blackswan.

Garfinkel, H. (1967). *Studies in Ethnomethodology*. Englewood Cliffs, NJ: Prentice Hall.

George, R.M. (2002). Queerness All Mine: Same-Sex Desire in Kamala Das's Fiction and Poetry. In Vanita, R. (Ed.). *Queering India: Same Sex Love and Eroticism in Indian Culture and Society* (pp. 111–126). London: Routledge.

Gewirth, A. (1962). Political Justice. In Brandt, R.B. (Ed.). *Social Justice* (pp. 88–103). Englewood Cliffs, NJ: Spectrum.

Ghosh, S. (2002). Queer Pleasures for Queer People: Film, Television and Queer Sexuality in India. In Vanita, R. (Ed.). *Queering India: Same Sex Love and Eroticism in Indian Culture and Society* (pp. 207–221). London: Routledge.

Giddens, A. (1974). *Positivism and Sociology*. London: Heinemann.

Giddens, A. (1978). Positivism and its Critics. In Bottomore, T. and Nisbet, R. (Ed.). *A History of Sociological Analysis* (pp. 54–78). Jaipur: Rawat Publications.

Giddens, A. (1985). *The Nation State and Violence*. Cambridge: Polity Press.

Giddens, A. (1987). *Social Theory Today*. Oxford: Clarendon Press.

Giddens, A. and Held, D. (1982). *Classes, Power and Conflict: Classical and Contemporary Debates*. London: Macmillan.

Gilbert, P. (1991). *Human Relationships: A Philosophical Introduction*. Oxford: Basil Blackwell.

Giri, A.K. (2008). *Self-development and Social Transformations: The Vision and Practice of the Self-study Mobilisation of Swadhyaya*. Jaipur: Rawat Publishers.

Glustrom, S. (1966). *The Language of Judaism*. New York: Jonathan David.

Goldstein, E. (1984). *Ego Psychoanalysis and Social Work Practice*. New York: The Free Press.

Gorowitz, S. (1975). John Rawls: A Theory of Justice. In de Crespingy, A. and Minougue, K. (Ed.). *Contemporary Political Philosophers* (pp. 172–189). London: Methuen.

Gough, K. (1979). Modes of Production in Southern India, *Economic and Political Weekly*, 25 (5–7), 337–364.

Greene, T. and Hudson, H.H. (Trans.). (1960). *Religion within the Limits of Reason Alone By Immanuel Kant*. New York: Harper Torchbooks.

Grenberg, J. (1999) Poststructuralism: Derrida and Foucault in Popkin, R.H. (ed) *History of Western Philosophy* (pp 167–88). London: Pilmico.

Gross, R.M. (1987). Tribal Religions: Aboriginal Australia. In Sharma, A. (Ed.). *Women in World Religions* (pp. 55–71). Delhi: India Books Centre.

Grossberg, L. and Nelson, C. (Ed.). (1990). *Marxist Interpretation of Literature and Culture*. Urbana: University of Illinois Press.

Grossman, R. (1984). *Phenomenology and Existentialism: An Introduction*. London: Routledge and Kegan Paul.

Guba, E. (2002). *The Paradigm Dialogue*. London: Routledge.

Guha, R. (1982). Introductory. In Guha, R. (Ed.). *Subaltern Studies*, Vol. 1 (pp. 1–38). Delhi: OUP.

Guha, R. (1983). *Elementary Aspects of Peasant Insurgency in Colonial India*. Delhi: Oxford University Press.

Guha, R. (1989). *The Unquiet Wood: Ecological Change and Peasant Resistance in Himalaya*. Delhi: Oxford University Press.

Guha, R. (1994). *Social Ecology*. Delhi: Oxford University Press.

Gupta, D. (2000). *Culture, Space and the Nation State*. Delhi: Sage Publications.

Gupta, K.P. (1973). Religious Evolution and Social Change in India: A Study of the Ramakrishna Movement, *Contributions to Indian Sociology*, 8 (1), 26–50.

Gupta, S.R. (1996). *The World Speaks to the Faustian Man Vols. 1–3*. Delhi: MLBD.

Gupta, V.K. (1996). *Perspectives on Human Rights*. Delhi: Vikas Publishing.

Gurwitsch, A. (1965). The Phenomenology of Perception: Perceptual Implications. In Edie, J.M. (Ed.). *An Invitation to Phenomenology: Studies in the Philosophy of Experience* (pp. 76–99). Chicago: Quadrangle Books.

Habib, I. (2007). *Religion in Indian History*. Delhi: Tulika Books and Aligarh Historians Society.

Haley, W. (1836). *Natural Theology*. London: Charles Knight.

Halfpenny, P. (1982). *Positivism and Sociology: Explaining Social Life*. London: George Allen and Unwin.

Hands, A.R. (1968). *Charities and Social Aid in Greece and Rome*. Great Britain: Thames and Hudson.

Hansen, F.R. (1985). *The Breakdown of Capitalism: A History of the Idea in Western Marxism, 1883–1983*. London: Routledge and Kegan Paul.

Hansen, K. (2002) 'A Different Desire, a Different Feminity: Theatrical Transvestism in the Parsi, Gujarati and Marathi Theatres, 1850–1940'. In Vanita, R. (Ed) (2002) *Queering India: Same Sex Love and Eroticism in Indian Culture and Society*. London: Routledge. pp. 163–180.

Hansen, T.B. (1999). *The Saffron Wave: Democracy and Hindu Nationalism in Modern India*. Delhi: OUP.

Hardiman, D. (2003). *Gandhi: In His Times and Ours*. Delhi: Permanent Black.

Hardin, S. (1991). *Whose Science, Whose Knowledge: Thinking from Women's Lives*. Ithaca: Cornell University Press.

Hardtman, E. (2009). *The Dalit Movement in India: Local Practices, Global Connections*. Delhi: Oxford University Press.

Hartshorne, C. (1948). *The Divine relativity: A Social Conception of God*. New Haven: Yale University Press.

Harvey, G. (2000). Indigenous Religions. In Harvey, G. (Ed). *Indigenous Religions* (pp. 1–28). London: Cassell.

Harvey, R. and Roberts, M. (1993). Lyotard and Postmodern. In Harvey, R. and Roberts, M. (Ed.). *Lyotard: Towards the Postmodern* (pp. 1–42). Atlantic Highlands, NJ: Humanities Press.

Hawkes, T. (1997). *Structuralism and Semiotics*. London: Methuen.

Hawley, J.S. (1994). Fundamentalism and Gender. In Hawley, J.S. (Ed.). *Fundamentalism and Gender* (pp. 1–16). New York: Oxford University Press.

Hawley, J.S. and Juergensmeyer, M. (2004). *Songs of the Saints of India*. Delhi: Oxford University Press.

Hayes, C.J. (1931). *The Historical Evolution of Modern Nationalism*. New York: The Macmillan Company.

Hayes, M.A. and Gearon, L. (1998). Contemporary Catholic Theology. In Hayes, M.A. and Gearon, L. (Ed.). *Contemporary Catholic Theology: A Reader* (pp. 8–42). New York: Continuum.

Heath, S. (1984). Male Feminism, *Dalhousie Review*, 64 (2), 70–101.

Heehs, P. (1998). *Nationalism, Terrorism and Communalism*. Delhi: OUP.

Heim, M. (1998). *Virtual Realism*. New York: Oxford University Press.

Heimsath, C. (1964). *Indian Nationalism and Hindu Social Reform*. Princeton, NJ: Princeton University Press.

Held, D. (1980). *Introduction to Critical Theory: Horkheimer to Habermas*. London: Hutchinson and Co.

Held, D. (1990). Critical Theory: Introduction. In Held, D. (Ed.). *Introduction to Critical Theory* (pp. 1–56). London: Hutchinson.

Henry, J. (2002). *Knowledge is Power*. London: Icon Books.

Hick, J. (1963). *The Philosophy of Religion*. Engelwood Cliffs: Prentice Hall.

Hicks, G.D. (1937). *The Philosophical Bases of Theism*. London: George Allen and Unwin.

Hicks, G.D. (1938). *Critical Realism: Studies in the Philosophy of Mind and Nature*. London: Macmillan and Co.

Hicks, J. (1984). *An Interpretation of Religion*. London: Macmillan.

Hicks, J. (1989). *An Interpretation of Religion*. London: Macmillan.

Hobsbawm, E.J. (1990). *Nations and Nationalism Since 1780: Programme: Myth and Reality*. Cambridge: Cambridge University Press.

Holloway, J. and Picciotto, S. (1978). *State and Capital: A Marxist Debate*. London: Edward Arnold.

Holscher, L. (1986). *The Reality of the Mind: St Augustine's Philosophical Arguments for the Human Soul as a Spiritual Substance*. London: Routledge.

Holub, R. (1992). *Antonio Gramsci: Beyond Marxism and Postmodernism*. London: Routledge.

hooks, b. (1981). *Ain't I a Woman: Black Women and Feminism*. Boston: South End Press.

Horkheimer, M. (1972). *Critical Theory: Selected Essays*. New York: Herder and Herder.

Houtart, F. and Lemerciner, G. (1984). The Great Asiatic Religions and Their Social Functions. Delhi: D.K. Agencies.

Howe, D. (1987). An Introduction to Social Work Theory: Making Sense of Practice. Michigan, Ann Arbor: Wildwood Press.

Humes, C.A. and McDermott, R.F. (2009). Introductory. In Humes, C.A. and McDermott, R.F. (Ed.). *Breaking Boundaries with the Goddess: New Directions in the Study of Saktism* (pp. 7–49). Delhi: Manohar Publications.

Ichimura, S. (2001). *Buddhist Critical Spirituality: Prajna and Sunyata*. Delhi: Motilal Banarasidass.

Illingworth, J.R. (1898). *Divine Immanence: An Essay on the Spiritual Significance of Matter*. London: Macmillan and Co.

Immanuel, D. (1984). *God's Messengers: A Reformed Church of American Missionaries in South India*. Chicago: Lutheran School of Theology.

Infield, L. (Trans.). (1963). *Poverty and Charity, in Kant's Lectures on Ethics*. New York: Harper and Row.

Iraqi, S. (2009). *Bhakti Movement in Medieval India: Social and Political Perspectives*. Delhi: Manohar Publications.

Irigaray, L. (1981). This Sex Which Is Not One. In Marks, E. and De Courtivron, I. (Ed.). *New French Feminisms* (pp. 56–79). Claudia Reeder (Trans.). New York: Routledge.

Isherwood, M. (1954). *The Root of the Matter: A Study in the Connections Between Religion, Psychology and Education*. London: Victor Gollancz Ltd.

Iyer, R. (1973). *The Moral and Political Thought of Mahatma Gandhi*. Delhi: Oxford University Press.

Jaffrelot, C. (1993). *The Hindu Nationalist Movement and Indian Politics: 1925–1990s*. London: Sage Publications.

Jaffrelot, C. (Ed.). (2007). *Hindu Nationalism: A Reader*. Delhi: Permanent Black.

Jaffrelot, C. and Hansen T.B. (1998). BJP and Indian Politics. In Jaffrelot, C. and Hansen, T.B. (Ed.). *The BJP and the Compulsions of Politics in India* (pp. 12–57). Delhi: OUP.

Jaini, P.S. (2000). *Collected Papers on Jaina Studies*. Delhi: Motilal Banarasidass.

James, W. (1941). *The Varieties of Religious Experience*. London: Longman and Co.

Jameson, F. (1991). *Postmodernism or the Cultural Logic of Late Capitalism*. London: Verso.

Jameson, F. (1998). Foreword to Lyotard's 'The Postmodern Condition'. In Taylor, V.C. and Winquist, C. (Ed.). *Postmodernism: Critical Concepts* (pp. 281–294). London: Routledge.

Jay, M. (1984a). *Adorno*. Glasgow: Fontana Paperbacks.

Jay, M. (1984b). *Marxism and Totality: The Adventures of a Concept from Lukacs to Habermas*. Cambridge: Polity Press.

Jay, M. (1998). Habermas and Postmodernism. In Taylor, V.C. and Winquist, C. (Ed.). *Postmodernism: Critical Concepts* (pp. 382–398). London: Routledge.

Jenkins, A. (1979). *The Social Theory of Claude Levi-Strauss*. London: Macmillan.

Jennings, T.W. (1985). *Beyond Theism: A Grammar Of God Language*. New York: Oxford University Press.

Joad, C.E.M. (1950). *A Critique of Logical Positivism*. London: Victor Gollancz Ltd.

John, M.E. (1996). *Discrepant Dislocations: Feminism, Theory and Postcolonial Histories*. Delhi: Oxford University Press.

John, M.E. (1998). Feminism in India and the West: Recasting a Relationship, *Cultural Dynamics*, 10 (2), 52–68.

Johnson-Odim, C. (1996). *Common Themes, Different Contexts: Third World Women and Feminism*. New York: W.W. Norton.

Johnston, D. (1994). The Churches and the Apartheid in South Africa. In Johnston, D. and Sampson, C. (Ed.). *Religion, the Missing Dimension of Statecraft* (pp. 139–165). New York: Oxford University Press.

Johnston, D. and Sampson, C. (Ed.) (1994). *Religion: The Missing Dimension of Statecraft*. New York: Oxford University Press.

Joll, J. (1977). *Gramsci*. Glasgow: Fontana Paperbacks.

Jones, K.W. (1989). *Socio-Religious Reform Movements in British India*. Cambridge: Cambridge University Press.

Joseph, S. (1988). Political Theory and Power. Joseph, S. (Ed.). *Political Theory and Power* (pp. 1–45). Leiden, The Netherlands: E.J. Brill.

Juergensmeyer, M. (1991). *Radhasaomi Reality: The Logic of Modern Faith*. Princeton, NJ: Princeton Press.

Juschka, D.M. (Ed) (2001). *Feminism in the study of Religion*. London: Continuum.

Kachapally. J. (2005). *Gandhi and Truth: An Approach to the Theology of Religions*. Delhi: Akansha Publishing House.

Kachuck, B. (2003). Feminist Social Theories: Themes and Variations. In Rege, S. (Ed.). *Sociology of Gender: The Challenge of Feminist Sociological Knowledge* (pp. 29–48). Delhi: Sage Publications.

Kaelin, E. (1965). The Visibility of Things Seen: A Phenomenological View of Painting. In Edie, J.M. (Ed.). *An Invitation to Phenomenology: Studies in the Philosophy of Experience* (pp. 187–202). Chicago: Quadrangle Books.

Kamitsuka, D.G. (1999). *Theology and Contemporary Culture: Liberation, Postliberal and Revisionary Perspectives*. Cambridge: Cambridge University Press.

Kandyil, A. (2009). *Writing Indian History: A View from the Below*. Kolkata: Samya.

Kane, P.V. (1970). *History of Dharmashastra (abridged)*. Mumbai: Maharashtra Rajya Sahitya and Sanskriti Mandal.

Kannabiran, V and Kannabiran, K. (1991). Caste and Gender: Understanding Dynamics of Power and Violence, *Economic and Political Weekly*, 26 (37), 798–806.

Kaufman, W. (1958). *Critique of Religion and Philosophy*. Princeton, NJ: Princeton University Press.

Kelleher, T. (1987) Confucianism. In Sharma, A. (Ed.). *Women in World Religions* (pp. 72–84). Delhi: India Books Centre.

Kellner, D. (1989). *Critical Theory, Marxism and Modernity*. Oxford: Basil Blackwell.

Kelly, J. (1982). Early Feminist Theory and the Querrelle des Femmes: 1400–1789, *Signs* 8 (1), 4–28.

Kennedy, M.T. (1925). *The Chaitanya Movement*. Calcutta: Associates Press.

Kenny, A. (1980). *Aquinas*. Oxford: Oxford University Press.

Khan, D. (2004). *Crossing the Threshold: Understanding Religious Identities in South Asia*. London: I.B. Tauris Publishers.

Khan, H.I. (1995). *The Sufi Message Vols. 3*. Delhi: Motilal Banarasidass.

Khan, M.I. (2004). Religious Devotion and Politics at Hazratbal in Kashmir. In T.N. Madan (Ed.). *India's Religions* (pp. 113–145). Oxford: Oxford University Press.

Kim, S.K. (1996). *The Philosophical Thought of Mahatma Gandhi*. Delhi: Vikas Publishing House.

King, H. (1928). *Theology for the Third Millennium: An Ecumenical View*. New York: Anchor Books.

King, R. (1999). *Orientalism and Religion: Postcolonial Theory, India and the Mystic East*. Delhi: OUP.

Kinsley, D. (1998). *Tantric Visions of the Divine Feminine*. Delhi: MLBD.

Kirschner, J.W. (1989). The Gaia Hypothesis: Can It Be Tested? *Review of Geophysics*, 27 (3), 223–235.

Kishwar, M. (1991). Why I Do Not Call Myself a Feminist? *Manushi*, 61 (1), 2–8.

Klee, R. (1999). Scientific Inquiry. In Klee, R. (Ed.). *Scientific Inquiry: Readings in the Philosophy of Science* (pp. 2–35). Oxford: Oxford University Press.

Kluver, J. (2000) *The Dynamics and Evolution of social systems: New Foundations of a mathematical sociology*. Dordrecht: Kluwer Publishers.

Kluver, J. (2002) *An Essay Concerning Socio-cultural evolution: Theoretical principles and mathematical models*. Dordrecht: Kluwer Publishers.

Kolakowski, L. (1978). *Main Currents of Marxism*, Vols. 1–3. Oxford: Clarendon Press.

Kopf, D. (1979). *The Brahmo Samaj and the Shaping of the Modern Indian Mind*. Princeton, NJ: Princeton University Press.

Korsch, K. (1970). *Marxism and Philosophy*. London: NLB.

Kraybill, R. (1994). Transition from Rhodesia to Zimbabwe: The Role of Religious Actors. In Johnston, D. and Sampson, C. (Ed.). *Religion: the Missing Dimension of Statecraft* (pp. 110–138). New York: Oxford University Press.

Krishna, D. (1997). *Indian Philosophy: A New Approach*. Delhi: Sri Satguru Publications.

Krishnaraj, M. (1992). Theoretical Perspectives for Women's Studies, *Indian Journal of Social Work*, 53 (3), 281–294.

Kugle, S. (2002). Sultan Mahmud's Makeover: Colonial Homophobia and the Persian-Urdu Literary Tradition. In Vanita, R. (Ed.). *Queering India: Same Sex Love and Eroticism in Indian Culture and Society* (pp. 83–93). London: Routledge.

Kumar, S. (Ed.). (2008). *Demolishing Myths or Mosques and Temples: Readings on History and Temple Desecration in Medieval India*. Delhi: Three Essays Collective.

Kunin, S. and Miles-Watson, S. (2006). *Theories of Religion*. Edinburgh: Edinburgh University Press.

Kurzweil, E. (1980). *Age of Structuralism: Levi Strauss to Foucault*. New York: Columbia University Press.

Laird, J. (1940). *Theism and Cosmology*. London: George Allen and Unwin.

Lakatos, T. and Musgrave, A. (1970). Criticism and Growth of Knowledge. In Lakatos, T. and Musgrave, A. (Ed.). *Criticism and Growth of Knowledge* (pp. 1–36). Cambridge: Cambridge University Press.

Lalye, P.G. (1995). The Panca Mahabhutas: Origin and Myth in Vedic Literature. In Vatsyayan, K. (Ed.). *Prakriti: The Integral Vision*, Vol. 4 (pp. 445–448). Delhi: IGNCA.

Lane, M. (1970). Structuralism. In Lane, M. (Ed.). *Structuralism: A Reader* (pp. 12–29). London: Jonathan Cape.

Langan, T. (1959). *The Meaning of Heidegger: A Critical Study of an Existentialist Phenomenology*. London: Routledge and Kegan Paul.

Lapp, J.A. (1972). *The Mennonite Church in India 1897–1962*. Scottdale, PA: Herald Press.

Larrain, J. (1983). *Marxism and Ideology*. London: Macmillan Press.

Lash, S. (1990). *Sociology of Postmodernism*. London: Routledge.

Lavalette, M. and Ferguson, I (2007). International Social Work and the Radical Tradition. In Lavalette M. and Ferguson, I. (Ed.).

. *International Social Work and the Radical Tradition* (pp. 2–40). Great Britain: Venture Press.

Lavalette, M. and Ferguson, I. (2007). Introduction. In Lavalette, M. and Ferguson, I. (Ed.). *International Social Work and the Radical Tradition* (pp. 2–40). Great Britain: Venture Press.

Leeuw, G. Van Der (1937). *Religion in Essence and Manifestation: A Study in Phenomenology*. London: George Allen and Unwin.

Lefebvre, H. (1968). *The Sociology of Marx*. London: Allen Lane.

Leuba, J.H. (1972). *The Psychology of Religious Mysticism*. London: Routledge and Kegan Paul.

Lieuw, G. Van Der (1933). *Religion in Essence and Manifestation: A Study in Phenomenology*. London: George Allen and Unwin.

Limbale, S. (2004). *Towards an Aesthetic of Dalit Literature: History, Controversies and Considerations*. Hyderabad: Orient Longman.

Lindenfeld, D.F. (1980). *The Transformation of Positivism*. Berkeley: University of California Press.

Lindsay, S. (1897). *Recent Advances in the Theistic Philosophy of Religion*. London: William Blackwood and Sons.

Lingard, B. and Douglas, P. (1999). *Men Engaging Feminisms: Pro-Feminism, Backlashes and Schooling*. Buckingham: Open University Press.

Livingstone, R. (Trans.). (1968) *Georg Lukacs: History and Class Consciousness*. London: Merlin Press.

Long, R.D. (2003). Charisma and Commitment in South Asian History. In Long, R.D. (Ed.). *Charisma and Commitment in South Asian History: Essays* (pp. 5–29). Presented to Stanley Wolpert. Hyderabad: Orient Longman.

Lorenzen, D. (1995). Bhakti Religion in North India. In Lorenzen, D. (Ed). *Bhakti Religion in North India* (pp. 2–56). Albany: State University of New York Press.

Louis, P. (2003). *Political Sociology of Dalit Assertion*. Delhi: Gyan Publishing.

Lovelock, J.E. (1983). Daisy World: A Cybernetic Proof of the Gaia Hypothesis, *Coevolution Quarterly*, 38 (1), 66–72.

Ludden, D. (2002). A Brief History of Subalternity. In Ludden, D. (Ed.). *Reading Subaltern Studies: Critical History, Contested Meanings and the Globalization of South Asia* (pp. 1–49). Delhi: Permanent Black.

Luttwak, E. (1994). Franco-German Reconciliation: The Overlooked Role of the Moral Re-armament Movement. In Johnston, D. and Sampson, C. (Ed.). *Religion, the Missing Dimension of Statecraft* (pp. 5–18). New York: Oxford University Press.

MacDonnell, A.A. (1960). *Vedic Reader*. London: OUP.

MacGregor, G. (1964). *Introduction to Religious Philosophy*. London: MacMillan.

Madan, T.N. (1991). *Religion in India*. Delhi: Oxford University Press.

Madan, T.N. (2004). India's Religions. In Madan, T.N. (Ed.). *India's Religions* (pp. 1–35). Delhi: Oxford University Press.

Mahadevan, T.M.P. (1998). *Selections from 108 Upanishads*. Delhi: Motilal Banarasidass.

Mahajan, G. (1998). *Democracy, Difference and Social Justice*. Delhi: Oxford University Press.

Majumdar, R.C. (1965). *Swami Vivekananda: A historical review*. Calcutta: General Printers Publishers.

Malik, J. and Reifeld, H. (Ed.). (2005). *Religious Pluralism in South Asia and Europe*. Delhi: Oxford University Press.

Malkani, K.R. (1989). Vasudhaiva Kutumbakam: A Socio-Historical Perspective in Bharatiya Swayamsevak Sangh, 1989. *Amar Bharati Souvenir, 1989, Nairobi, Bharatiya Swayamsevak Sangh, East Africa*, pp. 109–117.

Mannheim, K. (1954). *Ideology and Utopia: An Introduction to the Sociology of Knowledge*. New York: Harcourt, Brace and Co.

Marcuse, H. (1968). *Negations: Essays in Critical Theory*. London: Allen Lane/The Penguin Press.

Marks, D. (1999). *Disability: Controversial Debates and Psychosocial Perspectives*. New York: Routledge.

Marulasiddaiah, H.M. (1996). Bhakti Movement in India. In Marulasiddaiah, H.M. (Ed.). *Dimensions of the Bhakti Movement in India* (pp. 1–24). Mysore: Akhil Bharatiya Sahitya Parishad.

Marwaha, S.B. (2006). *Colours of Truth: Religion, Self and Emotions*. Delhi: Concept Publishing.

Marx, K. and Engels, F. (1848). *The German Ideology*. London: Routledge and Kegan Paul.

Masih, Y. (2002). *A Critical History of Western Philosophy*. Delhi: Motilal Banarasidass.

MaxMueller, F. (1889). *Essays on language, mythology and religion. Volumes 1 and 2*. London: Spottswoode and Co.

MaxMueller, F. (1972). *Introduction to the Science of Religion*. Varanasi: Bharata Manisha.

MaxMueller, F. (1973). *The Six Systems of Indian Philosophy*. Delhi: Associate Publishing House.

Mazumdar, S. (1981). The Socialisation of Hindu, Middle Class-Bengali Women, *South Asia Bulletin*, 1 (1), 29–41.

McCann, C.R. and Kim, S.K. (Ed.). (2003). *Feminist Reader*. New York: Routledge.

McCarthy, T. (1978). *The Critical Theory of Jurgen Habermas*. Cambridge: Polity Press.

McDaniel, J. (1984) *Of Gods and Pelicans: A theology of reverence for Life*. Louisville: Westminister Press.

McDaniel, J. (1989). *The Madness of the Saints*. Chicago: University of Chicago Press.

McGregor, R.S. (1992). Devotional Research in South Asia. In McGregor, R.S. (Ed.). *Devotional Research in South Asia: Current Research 1985–1988* (pp. 1–39). Cambridge: Cambridge University Press.

McLellan, D. (1986). *Ideology*. Milton Keynes: Open University Press.

Mclennan, G. (1989). *Marxism, Pluralism and Beyond*. Cambridge: Polity Press.

Mensching, G. (1976). *Studies and Patterns of Religion*. Delhi: Motilal Banarasidass.

Merchant, C. (1992). *Radical Ecology*. London: Routledge.

Miall-Edwards, D. (1963). *Philosophy of Religion*. Calcutta: Progressive Publishers.

Michael, S.M. (1999). *Dalits in Modern India: Visions and Values*. Delhi: Vistaar Publications.

Mies, M. (1981). *Social Origins of the Sexual Division of Labour*. Occasional Paper. The Hague: Institute of Social Studies.

Mies, M. and Shiva, V. (1993). *Ecofeminism*. London: Oxford University Press.

Mill, J.S. (1874). *Nature, the Utility of Religions and Theism*. London: Longman.

Miller, D. (1976). *Social Justice*. Oxford: Clarendon Press.

Mills, C.W. (1959). *The Sociological Imagination*. Harmondsworth, England: Penguin.

Minakshi Sundaram, T.P. (1985). Advaita Tattva. In Mahadevan, T.M.P. (Ed.). *Essays in Philosophy* (pp. 48–67). Bombay: Popular Publishing.

Misra, R.S. (1971) *Studies in Philosophy and Religion*. Varanasi: Bharatiya Vidya Prakashan.

Mitchell, J. and Oakley, A. (1976) Introduction. Mitchell, J. and Oakley, A. (Ed.). *The Rights and Wrongs of Women* (pp. 2–34). Harmondsworth, Middlesex: Penguin Books.

Mohanty, J.N. (2000). *Classical Indian Philosophy*. Delhi: Oxford University Press.

Mohanty, J.N. (2009). *Lectures on Consciousness and Interpretation*. Delhi: Oxford University Press.

Moi, T. (1989). Men Against Patriarchy. In Kauffman, L. (Ed.). *Gender and Theory: Dialogues on Feminist Criticism* (pp. 181–188) Oxford: Basil Blackwell.

Moore-Gilbert, B. (1997). *Postcolonial Theory: Contexts, Practices, Politics*. London: Verso.

Moraga, C. and Anzaldua, G. (1981). Writings. Moraga, C. and Anzaldua, G. (Ed.). *This Bridge Called My Back: Writings of Radical Women of Colour* (pp. 3–37) Watertown, Massachusetts: Persephone Press.

Moraga, C. and Anzaldua, G. (Eds) (1981) *This Bridge called my Back: Writings of Radical Women of Colour*. Watertown, Massachussetts: Persephone Press.

Morearty, J. (1975). *The Two Edged Word: The Treacherousness of Symbolic Transformation: Rammohan Roy, Debendranath, Vivekananda and 'The Indian Golden Age'*. Studies in Bengal, Papers Presented at the 7th Annual Bengal Studies Conference, University of Minnesota, Minneapolis. Michigan: Asian Studies Centre.

Morewedge, P. (1973). *The Metaphysics of Avicenna*. London: Routledge and Kegan Paul.

Morgan, P.K. (2005) Gender Police in Tremain, S. (Ed.) (2005) Foucault and the Government of Disability. Ann Arbor: University of Michigan Press. Pp 298–328.

Morgan, P.K. (2005) Gender Police in Tremain, S. (Ed.) (2005) Foucault and the Government of Disability. Ann Arbor: University of Michigan Press. Pp 298–328.

Morgan, R. (1970). Sisterhood. Morgan, R. (Ed.). *Sisterhood is Powerful: An Anthology of Writings from the Women's Liberation Movement* (pp. 1–27). New York: Vintage Books.

Mukhopadhyay, K.K. (1995). Volunteerism and Volunteers in Welfare and Development: Some Observations, *Indian Journal of Social Work*, 56 (1), 73–92.

Mukhopadhyay, P.K. (1995). Bhutas: Some Inter-related Themes in Indian Cosmology. In K. Vatsyayan (Ed.), *Prakriti: The Integral Vision*, Vol.4 (pp. 509–520). Delhi: IGNCA.

Muraleedharan, T. (2002). Queer Bonds: Male Friendships in Contemporary Malayalam Cinema. In Vanita, R. (Ed.). *Queering India: Same Sex*

Love and Eroticism in Indian Culture and Society (181–192). London: Routledge.

Murray, M. (1980). *Seeking the Master: A Guide to the Ashrams of India*. Jersey: Neville Spearman.

Nadel, S.F. (1954). *New Religion*. London: Routledge.

Naess, A. (1982). Deep Ecology, *Environmental Ethics*, 10 (3), 231–243.

Nandy, A. (1983). *The Intimate Enemy*. New Delhi: Oxford University Press.

Nariman, F.S. (1999). *Zoroastrianism: The Faith of the Parsis in India*. Delhi: India International Centre.

Natarajan, L. (1979). The Santhal Insurrection: 1855–56. In Desai, A.R. (Ed.). *Peasant Struggles in India* (pp. 91–101). Bombay: Popular Prakashan.

Nelson, L. (2000) The Dualism of Non-dualism: Advaita Vedanta and the Irrelevance of Nature. In L. Nelson (Ed.). *Purifying the Earthly Body of God: Religion and Ecology in Hindu India* (pp. 163–194). Delhi: D.K. Printworld.

Neville, R.C. (Ed.). (2001). *The Human Condition*. Albany: State University of New York Press.

Nichols, B. (1994). Religious Conciliation between the Sandinistas and the East Coast Indians of Nicaragua, In Johnston, D. and Sampson, C. (Ed.). *Religion: The Missing Dimension of Statecraft* (pp. 15–29). New York: Oxford University Press.

Nollman, J. (1990). *Spiritual Ecology: A guide to reconnection with nature*. New York: Bantam Press.

Norris, C. (1997). *Resources of Realism: Prospects for 'Post Analytic' Philosophy*. London: Macmillan.

Nussbaum, M. (2006). *Frontiers of Justice: Disability, Nationality, Species Membership*. Delhi: Oxford University Press.

O'Connell, J. (1999). New Religious Movements. In O'Connell, J. (Ed.). *Organisational and Institutional Aspects of New Religious Movements* (pp. 5–45). Shimla: IIAS.

O'Hear, A. (1980). *Karl Popper*. London; Routledge and Kegan Paul.

Olson. W. (1965). On Avoiding the Void: Ideals and Principles. In Edie, J.M. (Ed.). *An Invitation to Phenomenology: Studies in the Philosophy of Experience* (pp. 46–75). Chicago: Quadrangle Books.

Omvedt, G (1995). *Dalit Visions: The Anti-caste Movement and the Construction of an Indian Identity*. Hyderabad: Orient Longman.

Oomen, T.K. (2004). *Nation, Civil Society and Social Movements*. Delhi: Sage Publications.

Ortner, S. (1974). Is Female to Male as Nature to Culture? In Rosaldo, M.Z and Lamphere, L. (Ed.). *Women, Culture and Society* (pp. 231–245). Stanford, CA: Stanford University Press.

Ortner, S. (1987). *Ecology and Culture*. London: Oxford University Press.

Pai, S. (2002). *Dalit Assertion and the Unfinished Democratic Revolution: The Bahujan Samaj Party in UP*. Delhi: Sage Publications.

Palmquist, S.R. (2000). *Kant's Critical Religion*. Aldershot: Ashgate.

Pandey, V. (1995). *Divergences within Poststructuralism: Foucault-Derrida and Lyotard*, IRMA Working Paper Series 99.

Pandya, S. (2006). *A Study of Volunteerism in Indic Faith-Based Voluntary Organisations*. Unpublished Ph.D. Thesis, TISS.

Pandya, S. (2008). Teaching History and Ideologies of Social Work: Some Reflections, *Indian Journal of Social Work*, 69 (4), 485–506.

Pandya, S. (2009). Understanding Social Theory for Social Work, *Indian Journal of Social Work*, 70 (3), 353–374.

Panikkar, K.N. (2007). *Colonialism, Culture and Resistance*. Delhi: Oxford University Press.

Parthasarathy, A. (1983) *The symbolism of Hindu Gods and Rituals*. Bombay: Popular Prakashan.

Parthasarathy, A. (1983) *The symbolism of Hindu Gods and Rituals*. Bombay: Popular Prakashan.

Patel, G. (2002) 'On Fire: Sexuality and its Incitements'. In Vanita, R. (Ed) *Queering India: Same Sex Love and Eroticism in Indian Culture and Society*. London: Routledge. pp. 222 –233.

Patel, G. (2002) 'On Fire: Sexuality and its Incitements'. In Vanita, R. (Ed) *Queering India: Same Sex Love and Eroticism in Indian Culture and Society*. London: Routledge. pp. 222 –233.

Paul, M.C. (1989). *Dimensions of Tribal Movement in India: A Study of Udayachal in Assam Valley*. New Delhi: Inter India Publications.

Pereira, L. (1976). *Hindu Theology*. Delhi: Motilal Banarasidass.

Peterson, J. and Lewis, M. (1999). Feminist Economics. In Peterson, J. and Lewis, M. (Ed.). *The Elgar Companion to Feminist Economics* (pp. 1–56). Cheltenham, UK: Edward Elgar.

Peterson, J. and Lewis, M. (Ed.). (1999). *The Elgar Companion to Feminist Economics*. Cheltenham, UK: Edward Elgar.

Petievich, C. (2002). Doganas and Zanakhis: The Invention and Subsequent Erasure of Urdu Poetry's Lesbian Voice. In Vanita, R. (Ed.). *Queering*

India: Same Sex Love and Eroticism in Indian Culture and Society (pp. 47–60). London: Routledge.

Physicus (1878). *Theism*. London: Tribune and Co.

Piet, J.H. and Prasad, A. (2000). *Comparative Religious Ethics*. Delhi: Cosmo Publications.

Pilling, G. (1980). *Marx's Capital*. London: Routledge.

Pimpley, P.N. and Sharma, S.K. (1983). Arya Samaj and the Untouchables of Punjab, *Punjab Journal of Politics*, 7 (2), 83–99.

Pivcevic, E. (1970). *Husserl and Phenomenology*. London: Hutchinson University Library.

Plant, R. (2001). *Politics, Theology and History*. Cambridge: Cambridge University Press.

Plott, G.C. (1987). *Global History of Philosophy*, Vols. 1–5. Delhi: Motilal Banarasidass.

Plott, J.C. (1974). *A Philosophy of Devotion*. Delhi: Motilal Banarasidass.

Pojman, L. (1997). *Environmental Ethics*. Belmont: Wadsworth.

Popkin, R.H. (1999). Introduction. In Popkin, R.H. (Ed.). *History of Western Philosophy* (pp. 1–23). London: Pilmico.

Popkin, R.H. (Ed.). (1999). *History of Western Philosophy*. London: Pilmico.

Popper, K. (1963). *Conjectures and Refutations*. London: Routledge and Kegan Paul.

Popper, K. (1972). *Objective Knowledge: An Evolutionary Approach*. Oxford: Clarendon Press.

Popper, K. (1983). *Realism and the Aim of Science*. London: Hutchinson.

Popper, K.R. (1959). *The Logic of Scientific Discovery*. London: Hutchinson of London.

Potter, K. (Ed.). (2001–2008). *Encyclopedia of Indian Philosophies*. Volumes 1–14. Delhi: Motilal Banarasidass.

Praharaj, D.M. (1988). *Tribal Movement and Political History in India: A Case Study from Orissa. 1803–1949*. New Delhi: Inter India Publications.

Preston-Shoot, M. and Agass, D. (1990). *Making Sense of Social Work*. London: The Macmillan Press.

Pruthi, R. and Devi, R. (1999). *Social and Cultural History of Modern India*. Jaipur: Pointer Publishers.

Puri, H.K. and Judge, P.S. (2000). *Social and Political Movements: Readings on Punjab*. Delhi: Rawat Publishers.

Quinn, P.L. and Maker, K. (2000). Philosophical Challenge of Religious Diversity. In Quinn, P.L. and Maker, K. (Ed.). *The Philosophical*

Challenge of Religious Diversity (pp. 1–49). New York: Oxford University Press.

Radhakrishnan, S. (1923). *The Vedanta according to Shankara and Ramanuja*. London: George Allen and Unwin.

Radhakrishnan, S. (1940). *Indian Philosophy,* Volumes 1 and 2. London: George Allen and Unwin.

Radhakrishnan, S. (1957). *A Source Book on Indian Philosophy*. Princeton, NJ: Princeton University Press.

Raheja, G. (2003). *Songs, Stories, Lives: Gendered Dialogues and Cultural Critiques*. Delhi: Kali for Women.

Ralston, D.C. and Ho, J. (2010). Philosophical Reflections on Disability. In Ralston, D.C. and Ho, J. (Ed.). *Philosophical Reflections on Disability* (pp. 1–43). London: Springer.

Ramos, M.B. (Trans.). (1996). *Paulo Freire: Pedagogy of the Oppressed*. London: Penguin.

Randle, H.N. (1976). *Essays on History Literature and Religion of ancient India,* Vols. 1 and 2. Delhi: Cosmo Publications.

Rangacharya, M. and B.V. Aiyangar (1961). *Vedanta Sutras with Shri Bhasya of Ramanujacharya,* Vols. 1 and 2. Madras: Educational Publishing Co.

Rao, R.R. and Sarma, D. (2009). *Whistling in the Dark*. Delhi: Sage Publications.

Rasmussen, D. (1996). Critical Theory. In Rasmussen, D. (Ed.). *Critical Theory* (pp. 26–39). London: Routledge.

Rasmussen, D. (1998). Critical Theory. In Rasmussen, D. (Ed.). *Critical Theory: A Reader* (pp 1–45). Routldege: London.

Ray, B.N. (1998). *Critical Theory: The Marx Marcuse Encounter*. Delhi: Ajanta.

Ray, B.N. (2000). Introduction. In Ray, B.N. (Ed.). *John Rawls and the Agenda of Social Justice* (pp. 1–37). Delhi: Anamika.

Reat, R. and F. Perry (1991). *A World Theology: The Central Spiritual Reality of Humankind*. Cambridge: Cambridge University Press.

Reed, B. (1987). Taoism. In Sharma, A. (Ed.). *Women in World Religions* (pp. 85–102). Delhi: India Books Centre.

Rege, M.P. (1995). Samkhya Theory of Matter. In Vatsyayan, K. (Ed.). *Prakriti: The Integral Vision – Vol. 4* (pp. 531–546). Delhi: IGNCA.

Rege, S. (1995). Hegemonic Appropriation of Sexuality: The Case of the Erotic Lavani of Maharashtra, *Contributions to Indian Sociology*, 29 (I/2), 32–53.

Rege, S. (1998). Dalit Women Talk Differently: A Critique of 'Difference' and Towards a Dalit Feminist Standpoint Position, *Economic and Political Weekly*, 33 (44), WS39–WS46.

Rege, S. (2003). Sociology of Gender. In Rege, S. (Ed.). *Sociology of Gender: The Challenge of Feminist Sociological Knowledge* (pp. 1–38). Delhi: Sage Publications.

Rege, S. (2006). *Writing Caste/Writing Gender: Narrating Dalit Women's Testimonios*. Delhi: Zubaan an Imprint of Kali for Women.

Reinharz, S. (1992). *Feminist Methods in Social Research*. New York: Oxford University Press.

Rennie, B. (Ed.) (2001). *Changing Religious Worlds: The Meaning and End of Mircea Eliade*. Albany: State University of New York Press.

Rennie, B.S. (1996). *Reconstructing Eliade: Making Sense of Religion*. Albany: State University of New York Press.

Rich, A. (1976). *Of Woman Born: Motherhood as Experience and Institution*. New York: W.W. Norton.

Robertson, S. (2006). *Bhakti Tradition of the Vaisnava Alvars and Theology of Religions*. Kolkata: Punthi Pustak.

Robey, D. (Ed.). (1973) *Structuralism: An Introduction*. Oxford: Clarendon Press.

Robinson, R. (2004a). Church and Community in Goa. In Madan, T.N. (Ed.). *India's Religions* (pp. 56–72). Oxford: Oxford University Press.

Robinson, R. (2004b). Introduction. In Robinson, R. (Ed.). *Sociology of Religion in India* (pp. 5–28). New Delhi: Sage Publications.

Robinson, R. and Clarke, S. (2003). Religious Conversion in India. In Robinson, R. and Clarke, S. (Ed.). *Religious Conversion in India: Modes, Motivations and Meaning* (pp. 2–34). Delhi: Oxford University Press.

Rocher, L. (1985). Introduction. In Rocher, L. (Ed). *Studies in Indian Literature and Philosophy* (pp 1 –23). Delhi: MLBD.

Rodrigues, V. (1989). Religion as an Ideological Apparatus: The Role of the Catholic Church in Dakshina Kannada. In Shakir, M. (Ed). *Religion, State and Politics in India* (pp. 249–270). Delhi: Ajanta.

Rosen, S.J. (1996). Vaishnavi: Women and the Worship of Krishna. In Rosen, S.J. (Ed.). *Vaishnavi: Women and the Worship of Krishna* (pp. 1–23). Delhi: Motilal Banarasidass.

Roy, Bhaskar (1975). *A Realist Theory of Science*. Leeds: Basic Books.

Roy, Bhaskar (2002). *Meta Reality*. London: Sage Publications.

Roy, B.K. (1970). *Socio-political View of Vedanta*. New Delhi: People's Publishing House.

Roy, P. (1998). *Indian Traffic: Identities in Question in Colonial and Postcolonial India*. Delhi: Vistaar.

Royle, N. (2007). *Jacques Derrida*. London: Routledge.

Ruether, R.R. (1987). Christianity. In Sharma, A. (Ed). *Women in World Religions* (pp. 103–131). Delhi: India Books Centre.

Sampson, C. (1994). To Make Real the Bond Between Us All: Quaker Conciliation during the Nigerian Civil War. In Johnston, D. and Sampson, C. (Ed.). *Religion, the Missing Dimension of Statecraft* (pp. 30–52). New York: Oxford University Press.

Santideva, S. (1999). *Encyclopaedia of Tantra*. Delhi: Cosmo Publications.

Saran, A.K. (1969). Hinduism in Contemporary India, *Convergence*, 3 (1), 3–10.

Saraswati, B. (2000). Sociology of Religions. In Gore M.S. (Ed.). *Third Survey of Research in Sociology and Anthropology* (pp. 160–207). Delhi: ICSSR.

Sartre, J.P. (1957). Existentialism and Human Emotions. New York: Philosophical Library.

Satyamurthy, T.V. (1994). *State and Nation in the Context of Social Change*. Delhi: Oxford University Press.

Satyashrava, S. (1955). *History of Vedic Literature Vol.3, Brahamana and Aranyaka Works*. Delhi: Pranava Prakasham.

Satyashrava, S. (1955). *History of Vedic Literature Vol.3, Brahamana and Aranyaka Works*. Delhi: Pranava Prakasham.

Saxena, A. and Mishra. M. (1987). Christian Missionaries in Chhattisgarh. In Sharma, S. (Ed.). *Reform Protest and Social Transformation* (pp. 145–168). New Delhi: Ashish Publishing House.

Sayer, A. (1984). *Method in Social Sciences: A Realist Approach*. London: Hutchinson.

Sayers, A. (1979). Freud and Feminism, *Women's Studies International Quarterly*, 4 (1), 21–45.

Schutz, A. (1952). *Collected Papers*. Vol. 1. The Hague: Martinus Nijhoff.

Schutz, A. (1970) *On Phenomenology and Social Relations*. Chicago: University of Chicago Press.

Seeley, O.R. (1882). *Natural Religion*. London: Macmillan and Co.

Seidman, S. (1994). The Postmodern Turn. In Seidman, S. (Ed.). *The Postmodern Turn: New Perspectives on Social Theory* (pp. 1–57). Cambridge: Cambridge University Press.

Seybold, T. (1971). *God's Guiding Hand: A History of Central Indian Mission, 1868–1967*. Philadelphia, PA: The United Church Board for World Ministries of the United Church of Christ.

Shah, G. (1998). Social Justice. In Shah, G. (Ed.). *Social Justice: A Dialogue* (pp. 1–28). Jaipur: Rawat Publications.

Shah, G. (2004). *Social Movements in India: A Review of Literature*. Delhi: Sage Publications.

Shahani, P. (2008). *Gay Bombay: Globalisation, Love and (Be) longing in Contemporary India*. Delhi: Sage Publications.

Shakespeare, T. (1998). Social Science Perspectives on Disability. In Shakespeare, T. (Ed.). *The Disability Reader: Social Science Perspectives* (pp. 2–45). London: Continuum.

Sharma, A. (1987). Women in World's Religions. In Sharma, A. (Ed.). *Women in World Religions* (pp. 1–12). Delhi: India Books Centre.

Sharma, G. (1997). *Human Rights and Social Justice*. Delhi: Deep and Deep Publications.

Sharma, M. (2003). *Postcolonial Indian Writing: Between Co-option and Resistance*. Jaipur: Rawat Publications.

Sharma, P.K. (2006). *Dalit Politics and Literature*. Delhi: Shipra Publications.

Shetty, S. (2009) The Quack Whom We Know: Illness and Nursing in Gandhi. In Ganguly, D. and Docker, J. (Ed.). Rethinking Gandhi and Nonviolent Relationality: Global Perspectives (pp. 47–83). Delhi: Orient Blackswan.

Shorter, A. (1988). *Toward a Theology of Inculturation*. New York: Orbis Books.

Singh, Y. (1973). *Modernisation of Indian Tradition: A Systematic Study of Social Change*. Delhi: Thompson Press.

Sinha, S.P. (1984). *Life and Times of Birsa Bhagavan*. Patna: Secretarial Press.

Sjoo, M. and Barbara, B.M. (1987). *The Cosmic Mother: Rediscovering the Religion of the World*. San Francisco: Harper and Row.

Skolimowski, H. (1991). Reverence for Life. In R. Engel and Y. Engel (Ed.). *Ethics of Environment and Development* (pp. 39–56). London: OUP.

Smart, C. (1989). *Feminism and the Power of Law*. London: Routledge

Smart, N. (1969). *The Religious Experience of Mankind*. New York: Charles Scribner's Sons.

Smart, N. and Murthy, B. S. (Ed.). (1996). *East-West Encounters in Philosophy and Religion*. Mumbai: Popular Prakashan.

Smith, C. (Trans.). (1962). *Phenomenology of Perception: Maurice Merleau Ponty*. London: Routledge and Kegan Paul.

Smith, J.I. (1987). Islam. In Sharma, A. (Ed.). *Women in World Religions* (pp. 132–152). Delhi: India Books Centre.

Soja, E.W. (1997). *Postmodern Geographies: The Reassertion of Space in Critical Social Theory*. Jaipur: Rawat Publications.

Sorokin, P.A. (1952). *Social Philosophies of an Age of Crisis*. London: Adam and Charles Black.

Spiegelberg, H. (1982). *The Phenomenological Movement: A Historical Introduction*. The Hague: Martinus Nijhoff Publishers.

Spinelli, E. (2005). *The Interpreted World: An Introduction to Phenomenological Psychology*. London: Sage Publications.

Spivak, G.C. (1999). *A Critique of Postcolonial Reason: Towards a History of the Vanishing Present*. Calcutta: Seagull.

Srinivas, M.N. (1966). *Social Change in Modern India*. Berkeley, University of California Press.

Stanley, L. (1990). Feminist Praxis. In Stanley, L. (Ed.). *Feminist Praxis* (pp. 1–33). London: Routledge.

Stanley, L. (Ed.). (1990). *Feminist Praxis*. London: Routledge.

Stanley, L. and Wise, S. (1992). Feminist Epistemology and Ontology: Recent Debates in Feminist Social Theory, *Indian Journal of Social Work*, 53 (3), 147–163.

Steele, D. (1994). At the Front Lines of the Revolution: East Germany's Churches Give Sanctuary and Succor to the Purveyors of Change. In Johnston, D. and Sampson, C. (Ed.). *Religion, the Missing Dimension of Statecraft* (pp. 53–75). New York: Oxford University Press.

Steenberghen, C.F. Van (1952). *Ontology*. New York: Joseph Wagner.

Stewart, J.A. (2000). *Reconstructing Science and Theology in Postmodernity*. Aldershot: Ashgate.

Strathern, P. (1998). *The Essential Sartre*. London: Virgin Books.

Stroll, A. (1967). *Epistemology: New Essays in the Theory of Knowledge*. New York: Harper and Row Publishers.

Sturrock, J. (1999) Structuralism and Since. In Sturrock, J. (Ed.). *Structuralism and Since: From Levi Strauss to Derrida* (pp. 1–48). Oxford: OUP.

Sturrock, J. (Ed.). (1979). *Structuralism and Since: From Levi-Strauss to Derrida*. London: Oxford University Press.

Suhrud, T. (2009). Emptied of All but Love: Gandhi's First Public Fast. In Ganguly, D. and Docker, J. (Ed.). *Rethinking Gandhi and Nonviolent*

Relationality: Global Perspectives (pp. 84–102). Delhi: Orient Blackswan.

Sullivan, B.M. (1985). *The Place of the Spiritual Master: A study of the International society of Krishna Consciousness*, Trinity University, MA Thesis.

Sullivan, B.M. (2000). Theology and Ecology at the Birthplace of Krishna. In Nelson, L. (Ed.). *Purifying the Earthly Body of God: Religion and Ecology in Hindu India* (pp. 32–67). Delhi: D.K. Printworld.

Sundararajan, K.R. and Mukerji, B. (2003). *Hindu Spirituality: Postclassical and Modern*. Delhi: Motilal Banarasidass.

Sushila, R. (1990). *Liberty, Equality and Social Justice: Rawls' Political Theory*. Delhi: Ajanta.

Sutherland, S., Clark, P. and Leslie, J. (Ed.). (1988). *The World's Religions*. London: Routledge.

Sweet, M.J. (2002). Eunuchs, Lesbians and Other Mythical Beasts: Queering and Dequeering the Kama Sutra. In Vanita, R. (Ed.). *Queering India: Same Sex Love and Eroticism in Indian Culture and Society* (pp. 77–86). London: Routledge.

Talwar, R. (1999). *The Third Sex and Human Rights*. Delhi: Gyan Publishing.

Tambiah, S.J. (1989). Purity and Auspiciousness at the Edge of the Hindu Context – In Theravada Buddhist Societies. In Carmen, A. and Marglin, F. (Ed.). *Purity and Auspiciousness in Indian Society* (pp. 87–103). Brill: Leiden.

Taylor, D. (1987). Charismatic Authority in the Sathya Sai Baba Movement. In Burghart, R. (Ed.). *Hinduism in Great Britain: The Perpetuation of Religion in an Alien Cultural Milieu* (pp. 182–199). London/New York: Tavistock Publications.

Taylor, V.C. and Winquist, C. (1998). Postmodernism: Critical Concepts. In Taylor, V.C. and Winquist, C. (Ed.). *Postmodernism: Critical Concepts* (pp. 1–23). London: Routledge.

Tennant, F.R. (1930). *Philosophical Theology*. Cambridge: Cambridge University Press.

Thibaut, G. (Trans.). (1962). *The Vedanta Sutras of Badarayana with the Commentary of Shankara*, Vols. 1 and 2. Delhi: MLBD.

Tigunaut, R. (1983). *Seven Systems of Indian Philosophy*. Honesdale, PA: Himalayan International Institute of Yoga Science and Philosophy.

Tobias, M. (1983). *Deep Ecology*. Santa Monica: IMT.

Toot, M.H. (1957). *Practical Metaphysics of Zoroastrianism*. Mumbai: Popular Prakashan.

Toynbee, A. (1956). *A Historian's approach to Religion*. London: OUP.

Tregaskis, C. (2004). *Constructions of Disability: Researching the Interface between Disabled and Non-Disabled People*. London: Routledge.

Tremain, S. (2005). Foucault and Disability. In Tremain, S. (Ed.). *Foucault and the Government of Disability* (pp. 1–54). Ann Arbor: University of Michigan Press.

Turner, J.H. (1987). *The Structure of Sociological Theory*. Jaipur: Rawat Publications.

Uberoi, P. (Ed.). (1996). *Social Reform, Sexuality and the State*. Delhi: Sage Publications.

Ugra, P.B. (2006). *Chocolate and Other Writings on Male-Male Desire*. Delhi: Oxford University Press.

Van Buitenen, J.A.B. (1971). *Studies in the history of Indian Literature and Philosophy Vols. 1–3*. Delhi: MLBD.

Vanita, R. (2002). Homophobic Fiction/Homoerotic Advertising: The Pleasures and Perils of Twentieth Century Indianness. In Vanita, R. (Ed.). *Queering India: Same Sex Love and Eroticism in Indian Culture and Society* (pp. 127–148). London: Routledge.

Vannucci, M. (1992). Tradition and Change. In Sen, G. (Ed.). *Indigenous vision: People of India: Attitudes to the environment* (pp. 78–90). Delhi: Sage Publications.

Veer, P. Van Der (1994). *Religious Nationalism: Hindus and Muslims in India*. Delhi: Oxford University Press.

Vlastos, G. (1962). Justice and Equality. In Brandt, R.B. (Ed.). *Social Justice* (pp. 28–42). Englewood Cliffs, NJ: Spectrum.

Vries, Hent de and Sullivan, E. (2007). *Political Theologies: Public Religions in a Post-secular World*. Delhi: Social Science Press and Orient Longman Private Ltd.

Wagle, N.K. (Ed.). (1999). *Writers, Editors and Reformers: Social and Political Transformations of Maharashtra 1830–1930*. Delhi: Manohar Publications.

Wainwright, W.J. (1918). *Philosophy of Religion*. Milwankee: University of Wisconsin.

Walker, R.C.S. (1978). *Kant: The Argument of Philosophers*. London: Routledge and Kegan Paul.

Ward, G. (1997). *The Postmodern God: A Theological Reader*.: London: Wiley-Blackwell.

Ward, J. (1889). *Supernatural Religion: An inquiry into the Reality of Divine Revelation Vols1–3*. London: Longman.

Warder, A.K. (2000). *Indian Buddhism*. Delhi: Motilal Banarasidass.

Watson, M. (1997). *Man's Responsibility for Nature*. London: Duckworth Press.

Waugh, T. (2002). I Sleep Behind You: Male Homosociality and Homoeroticism in Indian parallel cinema. In Vanita, R. (Ed.). *Queering India: Same Sex Love and Eroticism in Indian Culture and Society* (pp. 193–207). London: Routledge.

Webb, C.C.J. (1926). *Kant's Philosophy of Religion*. Oxford: Clarendon Press.

Webster, J.C.B. (1999). *Religion and Dalit Liberation*. Delhi: Manohar Publications.

Weiner, P. (Trans.). (1964). *Ways of Thinking of the Eastern Peoples: India, China, Tibet, Japan – Hajime Nakamura*. Delhi: Motilal Banarasidass.

White, H. (1999). Michel Foucault. In Sturrock, J. (Ed.). *Structuralism and Since: From Levi Strauss to Derrida* (pp. 24–43). Oxford: OUP.

White, L.J. (1972). The Sai Baba Movement: Approaches in the Study if Indian Saints, *The Journal of Asian Studies*, 31 (3), 863–878.

White, L.J. (1992). The SaiBaba Movement: Approaches in the Study if Indian Saints, *The Journal of Asian Studies*, 31 (4), 863–878.

White, S.K. (1991). Rethinking Justice. In *Political Theory and Postmodernism*. Cambridge: Cambridge University Press.

Wiebe, P. and Peter, S.J. (1977). *The Catholic Church and Caste in Rural Tamil Nadu*. In H. Singh (Ed.). *Caste among Non-Hindus in India* (pp. 37–47). New Delhi: National Press.

Wieland, C. (2006). *Nation State by Accident: The Politicisation of Ethnic Groups and the Ethnicisation of Politics: Bosnia, India, Pakistan*. Delhi: Manohar Publications.

Wild, J. (1965). Authentic Existence: A New Approach to Value Theory. In Edie, J.M. (Ed.). *An Invitation to Phenomenology: Studies in the Philosophy of Experience* (pp. 203–234). Chicago: Quadrangle Books.

Williams, R.B. (1984). *A New Face of Hinduism: the Swaminarayan Religion*. Cambridge: Cambridge University Press.

Wilson, E. And Weir, A. (1986). *Hidden Agendas: Theory, Politics and Experience in the Women's Movement*. London and New York: Tavistock Publications.

Wooster, H. (1994). Faith at the Ramparts: The Philippine Catholic Church and the 1986 Revolution. In Johnston, D. and Sampson, C. (Ed.). *Religion, the Missing Dimension of Statecraft* (pp. 76–109). New York: Oxford University Press.

Wuthnow, R. (1998). *Loose Connections: Joining together America's Fragmented Communities*. Cambridge: Harvard University Press.

Yelloly, M. (1980). *Social Work Theory and Psychoanalysis*. London: Van Nostrand Reinhold.

Yoshinori, T. (1995). *Buddhist Spirituality*. Delhi: Motilal Banarasidass.

Young, K.K. (1987). Hinduism. In Sharma, A. (Ed.). *Women in World Religions* (pp. 11–26). Delhi: India Books Centre.

Zavos, J. (2000). *The Emergence of Hindu Nationalism in India*. Delhi: Oxford University Press.

Zelliot, E (1992). *From Untouchable to Dalit: Essays on the Ambedkar Movement*. Delhi: Manohar Publications.

Zilboorg, G. (1967). *Psychoanalysis and Religion*. London: George Allen and Unwin.

Index